To Kay Blacker,

good friend and colleague,
on the occasion of the Morton Levitt
Memorial Lectures;
with admiration and respect, and
appreciation of your ideas and
your openness to the ideas of others,
out of your belief in psychoanalysis
as a science.

Cal Settlage
November 14, 1985

NEW IDEAS IN PSYCHOANALYSIS

THE PROCESS OF CHANGE IN A HUMANISTIC SCIENCE

NEW IDEAS IN PSYCHOANALYSIS

The Process of Change
in a
Humanistic Science

Edited by

Calvin F. Settlage, M.D.
and
Reed Brockbank, M.D.

 THE ANALYTIC PRESS
1985

Distributed by
LAWRENCE ERLBAUM ASSOCIATES, PUBLISHERS
Hillsdale, New Jersey   London

Distributed solely by

Lawrence Erlbaum Associates, Inc., Publishers
365 Broadway
Hillsdale, New Jersey 07642

Library of Congress Cataloging in Publication Data
Main entry under title:

New ideas in psychoanalysis.

    Based on the meetings of Western Regional
Psychoanalytic Societies held in Mar. 1983 in San
Francisco.
    Includes bibliographies and index.
    1. Psychoanalysis — Congresses. 2. Psychoanalysis —
Philosophy — Congresses. I. Settlage, Calvin F., 1921-
II. Brockbank, Reed. III. Western Regional Psycho-
analytic Societies. [DNLM: 1. Psychoanalysis —
congresses. 2. Psychoanalytic Theory — congresses.
WM 460 N5315 1983]
BF173.N397 1985   150.19′5   85-9104
ISBN 0-88163-040-3

Printed in the United States of America
10 9 8 7 6 5 4 3 2 1

Contents

PART IV. AN APPLICATION OF NEW IDEAS IN PSYCHOANALYTIC RESEARCH: CONSENSUAL ANALYSIS

Contributors

JACOB A. ARLOW, M.D.
> Past President, American Psychoanalytic Association;
> Former Editor-in-Chief, *Psychoanalytic Quarterly.*

GERALD ARONSON, M.D.
> Training and Supervising Analyst, Los Angeles Psychoanalytic
> Society and Institute.

DONALD P. CLIGGETT, Ph.D.
> Faculty member, Department of Psychiatry, University of California, San Francisco.

RUDOLF EKSTEIN, Ph.D.
> Training and Supervising Analyst, Los Angeles Psychoanalytic
> Society and Institute and Southern California Psychoanalytic
> Institute;
> Clinical Professor, Neuropsychiatric Institute, University of California, Los Angeles.

JOHN E. GEDO, M.D.
> Training and Supervising Analyst, Chicago Institute for Psychoanalysis;
> Clinical Professor of Psychiatry, Abraham Lincoln School of
> Medicine, University of Illinois.

MAXWELL GITELSON, M.D. (1902–1965)
> Dr. Gitelson was president of the American Psychoanalytic Association (1955) and president of the International Psychoanalytic
> Association (1961–1965). He was a Training Analyst at the
> Chicago Institute for Psychoanalysis.

RALPH R. GREENSON, M.D. (1911–1979)

Dr. Greenson was a Training and Supervising Analyst at the Los Angeles Psychoanalytic Society and Institute. He was also a Clinical Professor of Psychiatry at the University of California, Los Angeles.

HEINZ HARTMANN, M.D. (1894–1970)

Dr. Hartmann was president of the International Psychoanalytic Association (1951–1959). He was a Training and Supervising Analyst at the New York Psychoanalytic Institute.

MARDI J. HOROWITZ, M.D.

Professor of Psychiatry, University of California, San Francisco; President, San Francisco Psychoanalytic Institute and Society.

SANDOR LORAND, M.D.

Professor Emeritus of Psychiatry, Downstate Medical Center, State University of New York;
Honorary President, The Psychoanalytic Association of New York.

NORMAN L. MAGES, M.D.

Faculty, San Francisco Psychoanalytic Institute;
Associate Clinical Professor of Psychiatry, University of California, San Francisco.

ROBERT R. NUNN, M.D.

Training and Supervising Analyst, Seattle Psychoanalytic Institute;
Clinical Associate Professor, University of Washington, Seattle.

JOSEPH SANDLER, M.D.

Sigmund Freud Professor of Psychoanalysis and Director of the Sigmund Freud Center at the Hebrew University of Jerusalem.

CALVIN F. SETTLAGE, M.D.

Training and Supervising Analyst in Adult and Child Psychoanalysis, San Francisco Psychoanalytic Institute;
Clinical Professor of Psychiatry, University of California, San Francisco.

ESTELLE SHANE, Ph.D.

President, Center for Early Education, Los Angeles;
Research Psychologist in Adult and Child Analysis and Faculty Member, Los Angeles Psychoanalytic Society and Institute.

MORTON SHANE, M.D.
> Training and Supervising Analyst in Adult and Child Analysis, Los Angeles Psychoanalytic Society and Institute;
> Associate Clinical Professor in Child Psychiatry, University of California, Los Angeles.

ALAN Z. SKOLNIKOFF, M.D.
> Training and Supervising Analyst, San Francisco Psychoanalytic Institute;
> Associate Clinical Professor of Psychiatry, University of California, San Francisco.

LEO STONE, M.D.
> Faculty member, New York Psychoanalytic Institute;
> Faculty member, Columbia University Center for Psychoanalytic Training and Research.

ROBERT L. TYSON, M.D.
> Training and Supervising Analyst in Adult and Child Psychoanalysis, San Diego Psychoanalytic Institute;
> Clinical Professor, Department of Psychiatry and Human Behavior, University of California College of Medicine, Irvine.

ROBERT S. WALLERSTEIN, M.D.
> Professor and Chairman, Department of Psychiatry, University of California, San Francisco;
> Training and Supervising Analyst, San Francisco Psychoanalytic Institute.

EMANUEL WINDHOLZ, M.D.
> Training and Supervising Analyst, San Francisco Psychoanalytic Institute;
> Clinical Professor of Psychiatry, University of California, San Francisco.

SHERWYN M. WOODS, M.D., Ph.D.
> Professor of Psychiatry and the Behavioral Sciences, University of Southern California School of Medicine, Los Angeles;
> Supervising and Training Analyst, Southern California Psychoanalytic Institute, Los Angeles.

Acknowledgments

This volume is based upon the Meetings of the Western Regional Psychoanalytic Societies held in March 1983 in San Francisco and hosted by the San Francisco Psychoanalytic Society and Institute. The meeting addressed the theme "Historical and Current Perspectives on New Ideas in Psychoanalysis: Issues and Integrations." Included are the invited papers, prepared discussions, and clinical case material from the panel presentations. The Western Regional Psychoanalytic Societies include: The Los Angeles Psychoanalytic Society; The Mexican Psychoanalytic Association; The San Diego Psychoanalytic Society; The San Francisco Psychoanalytic Society; The Seattle Psychoanalytic Society; and The Southern California Psychoanalytic Society.

The 1983 Regional Meetings were conceived, planned, and implemented by the following representatives of their respective societies:

The Planning Council

Arthur Malin, M.D. and Richard P. Fox, M.D. (Los Angeles); Manuel Isaías López, M.D. (Mexico); Harry B. Woods, M.D. and Leroy Jaret, M.D. (San Diego); Maxine K. Anderson, M.D. and Austin Case, M.D. (Seattle); Marvin P. Osman, M.D. and David Markel, M.D. (Southern California); and the members of the San Francisco Steering Committee.

The Steering Committee (San Francisco)

Reed Brockbank, M.D., Chair; Fariborz Amini, M.D.; George C. Kaplan, M.D.; Norman L. Mages, M.D.; Owen Renik, M.D.; Calvin F. Settlage, M.D.; Sheldon Wolfe, M.D.

Arrangements Committee (San Francisco)

Morris L. Peltz, M.D. and Elaine Brockbank, Co-Chairs; Hannah Green-berg; Patricia Kaplan; and Carol Peltz; Melvyn B. Schupack, M.D.

This volume also includes papers not presented at the Western Regional So-cieties' Meeting. The editors are grateful to the following authors for making their papers available: Donald P. Cliggett, Ph.D.; John E. Gedo, M.D.; Sandor Lorand, M.D.; Norman Mages, M.D.; Joseph Sandler, M.D.; and Leo Stone, M.D. We are also grateful to the families of the deceased authors for permission to publish the papers by Maxwell Gitelson, M.D.; Ralph R. Greenson, M.D.; and Heinz Hartmann, M.D. The following journals and publishers kindly granted permission to republish papers: *The International Journal of Psycho-Analysis; The Psychoanalytic Quarterly;* International Universities Press; New York University Press; Jason Aronson; Basic Books.

The editors also express appreciation to Elaine Brockbank for her most able assistance in the preparation of this volume for publication.

The Editors

Preface

The major objective of this volume is to examine the process of change in psychoanalysis and to delineate the criteria for acceptance of new ideas. Our pursuit of this objective rests on the premise that psychoanalysis is a science. As is true of all sciences, psychoanalytic theory and its practical application are subject to change as new discoveries are made and new ideas are advanced, assessed, and accepted. A second objective is to examine and attempt to further the scientific dialogue among psychoanalysts.

The approach to these objectives provides both historical and current perspectives. It stems from the twofold observation that psychoanalytic theory and its application have, in fact, undergone and continue to undergo change from the beginnings of psychoanalysis to the present, and that conflict and controversy have characterized the field, sometimes as part of a healthy dialogue and sometimes not.

The development of science — whether physical, natural, or social science — regularly involves conflict between tradition and innovation. It is not that these forces are exclusive of each other, but rather that it is necessary to decide what to retain from traditional theory and practice and what to add from new theory and practice. All science, including psychoanalysis, is thus characterized by what historian of science J. D. Bernal (1971) terms "the cumulative tradition of science." This same struggle over the old and the new is commented upon by Sandor Lorand (1948): "Rather than substitution of the old theory, there should be reconstruction of the old on the basis of the new clinical and therapeutic experiences."

Scientific advance involves the integration of new ideas with the insights of the past. Both tradition and creative innovation are essential. Even the scientific revolution or breakthrough, delineated by Kuhn (1962), is built upon and does not totally discard the past. Whatever new psychoanalytic theory is proposed or new therapeutic technique is attempted, they must be fully understood and carefully tested over time in relation to traditional theory.

The current need for dialogue about psychoanalysis as a science and about psychoanalytic theory and practice is abundantly evident. There is, for example, the continuing dissatisfaction with psychoanalytic metapsychology as epitomized by George Klein's proposal that it be abandoned in favor of clinical theory (Klein, 1976), and as challenged by Roy Schafer's proposed delimitation of psychoanalytic process to his action language (Schafer, 1976). There is the issue in psychoanalytic treatment as to whether the patient's reports of life experiences are to be regarded as narrative truth or actual truth, as addressed by Spence (1982). Related to this is the broader question of whether psychoanalysis is a science or a more narrowly defined hermeneutic discipline concerned with meaning (Ricouer, 1979, 1977; Steele, 1979). (In these same regards, see Horowitz, this volume.)

On the clinical level, there is the much-debated issue of the importance of pathogenic preverbal and preoedipal experience in the etiology and psychoanalytic treatment of the various mental disorders, including the neuroses. As another example, there is the controversy over the theoretical and clinical validity of Kohut's self-psychology (Kohut, 1971, 1977).

The 1975 London Congress of the International Psycho-Analytical Association had the objective of viewing and discussing change in psychoanalysis. Its theme was "Changes in Psychoanalytic Practice and Experience: Theoretical, Technical, and Social Implications." The criteria for acceptance of new ideas and the nature and problems of the scientific dialogue were in some measure addressed by the Congress, but these were not major subjects of discussion. The keynote papers by Andre Green (1975) and Leo Rangell (1975) and the plenary session discussion by the authors, as reported by Shengold and McLaughlin (1975), presented two widely divergent views of how psychoanalysis and psychoanalysts should respond to changes in the field. (See also Tyson, this volume.) Green argued for more open-mindedness to innovation and more acceptance of newer theories and techniques within the widening scope of psychoanalytic practice. Rangell took the more conservative position that we should hold on to our hard-won concepts and basic theories and add new concepts or incorporate new techniques only when they fit comfortably into our standards of practice. Green sees the necessity for exploring and defining the role of preverbal and preoedipal experience in pathogenesis and therapeutic process, and for the derivation of new constructs and treatment techniques, especially in order to work with the more serious disorders. Rangell feels that it is not yet time for a new model of neurosis and sees no need to change current theory and practice because of the more serious disorders.

During the preparation of this volume, it became evident that its objectives would be well served by the inclusion of noteworthy historical papers in each of the volume's four parts. Under the constraint of space limitations and with awareness that papers other than those chosen could provide such perspectives, the editors selected what they felt to be representative papers written by Max-

well Gitelson (1964), Ralph Greenson (1969), Heinz Hartmann (1959), Sandor Lorand (1948), and Leo Stone (1954). These papers round out the picture
of the process of change and the scientific dialogue in psychoanalysis, providing perspectives on the evolution of psychoanalysis that offer interesting comparisons with those of today's authors. They also assist in the culling of criteria
for change in this almost century-old science.

In amplification of the current views expressed by the analysts participating
in the 1983 Western Regional Psychoanalytic Societies' Meeting, the editors
invited the paper by John Gedo and arranged for the republication of the paper
by Joseph Sandler (1983).

With regard to psychoanalysis as a science, the term "humanistic science" in
the title of this volume bears definition. In a scholarly historical review, Gedo
and Wolf (1976) note than an early form of introspective psychology was
linked to the humanists, a particular type of renaissance intellectuals who, in
addition to their classical learning, focused their professional activities within
the areas of poetry, history, and moral philosophy (p. 12). At the beginning of
the 16th century, as exemplified by the work of Montaigne, there began to
emerge a humanistic, introspective psychology focused on the study of the individual self (pp. 16, 17). Subsequently, science was born as the successor to
humanism. But the influence on 17th-century science of Cartesian dualism,
sharply dividing mind from matter and denying the capacity of reason to
arrive at universal and necessary truths, moved psychology away from introspection and toward empiricism (pp. 40, 41). Still later, in the 18th century,
Kant's work provided the philosophical underpinnings for a future scientific
psychology that would reintegrate the humanistic introspective mode into the
study of man, thus paving the way for psychoanalysis (p. 43).

In keeping with this historical evolution, the term "humanistic science" de-
fines psychoanalysis as an introspective psychology and a science. Psychoanalysis is unique in its introspective mode of study and its field of study. Its mode
includes the introspection of the patient and of the analyst, and its field includes both the conscious and unconscious human affective and mental processes. As a nomothetic science, psychoanalysis is committed to the derivation of
laws and theories of human development and behavior that can be generalized
beyond the clinical therapeutic situation (Holzman, in press).

Collectively, the papers in this volume take a considered and sometimes
broadly philosophic look at the evolution of psychoanalytic thought and practice. This look includes attention to the determinants of change and the criteria
for the acceptance and integration of new ideas. The papers also comment on
the nature and vicissitudes of the scientific dialogue within psychoanalysis and
compare it with the dialogue in other fields.

In thus reminding psychoanalysts of their scientific heritage and demonstrating kinship of the psychoanalytic dialogue and other dialogues, the intent
of the volume is to provide an orientation to psychoanalysis as a science and to

offer a helpful, reassuring perspective on the necessity and inevitability of controversy.

The volume provides an overview of the evolution of psychoanalytic ideas in Part I, followed by Parts II and III covering the major topic areas within psychoanalysis, and Part IV presenting an application of new ideas in psychoanalytic research. The Introduction to each of the four parts provides orientation to their content. The editors' Epilogue presents some observations and reflections pertaining to the volume's objectives.

The Editors

REFERENCES

Bernal, J. D., (1971), *Science in History,* Vol. 1. Cambridge, Mass.: MIT Press.

Gedo, J. E., & Wolf, E. S. (1976), From the history of introspective psychology: The humanist strain. In: *Freud: The Fusion of Science and Humanism: The Intellectual History of Psychoanalysis.* New York: International Universities Press.

Green, A. (1975), The analyst, symbolization and absence in the analytic setting (on changes in analytic practice and analytic experience). *Internat. J. Psycho-Anal.,* 56: 1–23.

Holzman, P. S. (in press), Is the therapy destroying the science? *J. Amer. Psychoanal. Assn.*

Klein, G. S. (1976), *Psychoanalytic Theory: An Explanation of Essentials.* New York: International Universities Press.

Kohut, H. (1971), *The Analysis of the Self.* New York: International Universities Press.

_____ (1977), *The Restoration of the Self.* New York: International Universities Press.

Kuhn, T. S. (1962), The structure of scientific revolutions. In: *International Encyclopedia of the Unified Sciences: Foundations of the Unity of Science,* Volume 2, Number 2, ed. O. Neurath, R. Carnap, & C. Morris. Chicago: University of Chicago Press, 1970.

Rangell, L. (1975), Psychoanalysis and the process of change: An essay on the past, present and future. *Internat. J. Psycho-Anal.,* 56: 87–89.

Ricouer, P. (1970), *Freud and Philosophy: An Essay on Interpretation.* New Haven: Yale University Press.

_____ (1977), The question of proof in Freud's writings. *J. Amer. Psychoanal. Assn.,* 25: 835–871.

Sandler, J. (1983), Reflections on some relations between psychoanalytic concepts and psychoanalytic practice. *Internat. J. Psycho-Anal.,* 64: 35–45.

Schafer, R. (1976), *A New Language for Psychoanalysis.* New Haven: Yale University Press.

Shengold, L., & McLaughlin, J. T. (1976), Plenary session on "Changes in Psychoanalytic Practice and Experience: Theoretical, Technical, and Social Implications." *Internat. J. Psycho-Anal.,* 57: 261–274.

Spence, D. P. (1982), *Narrative Truth and Historic Truth: Meaning and Interpretation in Psychoanalysis.* New York: Norton.

Steele, R. S. (1979), Psychoanalysis and hermeneutics. *Internat. Rev. Psycho-Anal.,* 6: 389–411.

NEW IDEAS IN PSYCHOANALYSIS

The Process of Change in a Humanistic Science

I THE EVOLUTION OF PSYCHOANALYSIS: OVERVIEW

Introduction

To provide an overview of the evolution of psychoanalysis from several perspectives, Jacob Arlow's keynote address to the Western Regional Psychoanalytic Societies' Meeting is complemented here by a new (not previously published) paper by John Gedo and a historical paper by Maxwell Gitelson, written in 1964.

Arlow traces the introduction of new ideas into psychoanalysis with a historical perspective and with attention to the criteria for change. He compares and contrasts the current ferment in psychoanalytic theory and practice with Freud's own introduction of new ideas. Arlow outlines change along an evolutionary pathway from the beginning of Freud's work with Breuer to innovations by other analysts before and after Freud's death.

Gedo's writings during the past ten years have focused attention on the incongruities of current theory and practice, as well as the inadequacies of our metapsychological theory, our clinical theory, and our techniques for dealing with the more archaic personalities seen in his and other psychoanalysts' offices. Despite these difficulties, Gedo's contribution to this volume is guardedly optimistic about the future evolution of psychoanalysis.

Speaking twenty years ago on the identity crisis in American psychoanalysis, Gitelson stated: "I think the time has come for psychoanalysis to accept its identity as a separate scientific discipline. . . . We suffer not only from confusion about what psychoanalysis is, but also from irresolution about what its position should be. We are caught in an identity conflict between psychiatry, which is a therapeutic speciality of medicine, and psychoanalysis, which is a basic science." In this address to the American Psychoanalytic Association, Gitelson placed psychoanalysis, with all of its schisms, orthodoxies and heresies, within the framework of a "normal science" (Kuhn, 1963) and observed that psychoanalysis "as an aspect of biology, occupies a middle ground between the extreme scientific positions of physics and historical learning."

The Editors

3

1

Issues in the Evolution of Psychoanalysis: Criteria for Change

JACOB A. ARLOW, M.D.

The theme for this conference, "Historical and Current Perspectives on New Ideas in Psychoanalysis," could not have been chosen at a more appropriate time. The recent death of Anna Freud only serves to dramatize the need for such discussion. I believe we are entering upon a new phase in the history of psychoanalysis. Within a few years, there will be no survivors of "the golden age of psychoanalysis." No longer will there be any individuals who were direct pupils of Freud or who had continuing contact with him. We are on the threshold of the post-apostolic period of psychoanalysis, in which no one will be able to substantiate a claim of being the confirmed representative of the fountainhead of psychoanalytic authority.

Despite charges from critics of our slavish admiration for Freud and his work, the fact is that, historically speaking, psychoanalysts have been an unruly lot, given to polemics and schisms, and just as likely as not to go off on their own. In the process, they have introduced new concepts, given fresh meaning to old terminologies, and altered radically the technical procedures they inherited from their teachers. It is a fact that Hartmann, K. is, and Loewenstein (1946) undertook their historic collaboration in an effort to clar-

Presented as the keynote address at the Western Regional Psychoanalytic Societies Meeting, San Francisco, California, March, 1983.

ify and, hopefully, to standardize the manner in which technical terms are employed in psychoanalytic discourse. They said:

> Psychoanalysis has developed under social conditions rare in science. Small teams of private practitioners everywhere formed the nuclei of larger professional groups. During the early stages of team work, writen communication was supplemented to such an extent by personal contact on an international scale—mainly by training analyses with the few instructors—that mutual understanding was not endangered by uncertainties of terminology. With the increase of the number of psychoanalysts, that condition was bound to change. The situation of the 1940's is hardly reminiscent of the period of early team work; large groups of psychoanalysts work in ever looser contact with each other and the diffusion of psychoanalytic concepts in psychiatry, their extension into psychosomatic medicine, social work, and various educational and psychological techniques opens up new vistas of development. Every step of this development, every new context in which psychoanalytic propositions are being tested or used raises anew the problems of adequate communication. Since scientific communication is impaired by ambiguity of meaning, the need for clarification has become urgent. (pp. 11–12)

Looking back some 40 years after these words were written, I think we can agree that the efforts of the authors were only partially successful. Today, new ideas abound, new developments are afoot in almost every quarter. We are met in this conference to get some perspective on these ideas and to discuss how they may be assimilated and integrated into the developing body of psychoanalytic knowledge.

To anticipate the central theme of this presentation, historically viewed, the significance accorded new ideas in psychoanalysis has been determined, for the most part, by the degree to which such ideas hold out the promise of enhancing the therapeutic effectiveness of psychoanalysis. Freud himself was perhaps the best exemplar of this principle. In this regard, his own development demonstrates some striking contradictions. Although fundamentally oriented towards a career in scientific, biologic research, Freud was intrigued by Breuer's description of a patient who had initiated her own "cure" by talking, by "sweeping out the chimney," while under hypnosis. Despite his frequent disclaimers of any compelling interest in therapeutic successes, it can be demonstrated that, once the problem of how to make psychoanalysis work as a therapy took hold of Freud, he was never able to free himself of its grasp. Psychoanalysis was born in an atmosphere of healing the sick, and it has retained that essence down to the present time. In spirit, as Stone (1961) pointed out, all analysts are doctors, whether they have a medical degree or not.

Indeed, Freud's first model of the dynamics of hysterical symptoms was eminently a medical model, and the terminology appropriate to the concepts he used borrowed heavily from ideas current at the time in pathology and neurophysiology (Arlow, 1956). Hysterical phenomena originated in a trauma. A repressed memory acted like a foreign body in the mind. It became the core of a secondary organization, drawing into its structure contiguous memories, events, and impulses, until it began to sound like the pathology of a tubercle or, if acute, took on a form resembling a purulent abscess. Relief was possible only when the accumulated toxic substances could be drained off through a process called catharsis.

There were several obstacles that barred Freud's way to therapeutic success. After improving, following satisfactory abreaction, some patients relapsed into their former symptomatology. What he had considered to be the pathogenic trauma, he now reasoned, was only a derivative expression of an even earlier traumatic experience. He kept pushing back the period of significant traumatization to the age of three or four and, in the case of the Wolf Man (1918), to an even earlier time. The origin of the genetic principle of psychoanalysis, it seems clear, was definitely related to the quest for a stable therapeutic result.

The second obstacle was patently clear. Many patients could not be hypnotized. Freud expanded his therapeutic armamentarium. He used suggestion; he pressed on the patient's forehead; he insisted upon recollection; all to no avail. It was at this point, Freud tells us in *An Autobiographical Study* (1925), that he recalled an experiment that he witnessed while he was with Bernheim.

> When the subject awoke from the state of somnambulism, he seemed to have lost all memory of what had happened while he was in that state, but Bernheim maintained that the memory was present all the same, and if he insisted on the subject remembering, if he asseverated that the subject knew it all and had only to say it, and if, at the same time, he laid his hand on the subject's forehead, then the forgotten memories used, in fact, to return, hesitatingly at first, but eventually in a flood and with complete clarity. (p. 27)

Reflecting on these observations, Freud changed his method of investigation. He devised the psychoanalytic situation and the principle of free association. A repressed wish rather than a repressed memory had a dynamism of its own. It stimulated the mind to produce derivatives; disguised, distorted or sometimes allusive representations of that wish. In fact, the recovery of the forgotten name Signorelli, which Freud included in *The Psychopathology of Everyday Life* (1902), is a clear example of the associative method of interpretation put into practice. Thus, not only the organization of the psychoanalytic situation, but the principles underlying the theory of drives in large measure originated out of Freud's need to overcome a specific obstacle to his therapeutic efforts.

So also, once having made the momentous discoveries of infantile sexuality, Freud directed the libido theory towards clarifying and facilitating the goals of therapy. The main point to be established in the case of Little Hans (1909) was to demonstrate that every attack of anxiety was the direct consequence of an upsurge of undischarged libido. The technical principle that grew out of this concept was the need to arrange for the discharge of the repressed libidinal cathexes of the System Ucs by bringing them into connection with the verbal representatives of the System Pcs. The analyst's interpretations constituted the bridge between the two. The principles involved may be said to resemble the process of catharsis, but the integration of the new ideas was clearly at a higher and more sophisticated level.

It would be possible, but by no means practical, at least in this presentation, to apply the same considerations to how Freud integrated so many of his other observations and ideas into the body of psychoanalysis. A few examples will have to suffice.

That remarkable finding, the existence of transference, Freud first viewed as a resistance, in the sense that it constituted an obstacle to recollection, the very process on which cure depended. However, he soon was able to bend the transference to serve the purpose of therapy in two ways. Realizing that transference was a form of repetition of what could not be remembered, he used it as a substitute, as an alternative to recall. Second, he enlisted transference as an ally in the analyst's case. Through the libidinal tie to the therapist, the resistance that ordinarily prevented the patient from accepting the analyst's interpretations could be circumvented or overcome. The practical consequence of these ideas was expressed in the technical maxim to defer interpretations until the patient was in a phase of so-called "positive transference."

The most significant examples, however, of the integration of new ideas into the psychoanalytic system — namely, the dual instinct theory, the structural hypothesis, and the concept of anxiety as a signal — can be traced directly to Freud's efforts to overcome impediments to progress during psychoanalytic treatment. In a number of papers published in the years immediately preceding this major revision, Freud, either directly or indirectly, dealt with patients who, though given accurate interpretations, nonetheless did not seem to improve. Some patients, because they felt they were exceptions (1916b), would not abide by the rules of the analysis. Others, harboring deep feelings of guilt, were wrecked by the success of gaining insight or making progress (1916b). These patients, like many others, exhibited a negative therapeutic reaction. They had to suffer, either in gratification of some hidden neurotic impulse, or out of a compulsion to punish themselves for crimes (1916b), they knew not what.

Furthermore, in almost all patients, Freud noted that the therapeutic effectiveness of correct interpretations was often frustrated by various mental maneuvers that fended off the significance of the new insights. It was clear to him that he had to come to terms technically with the phenomenon of aggression directed against the self, as well as with a new concept of mental conflict, one that would encompass the phenomenon of one agency of the mind passing judgment and exacting punishment on the other, and a further agency that seemed to inhibit or facilitate the demands originating in the rest of the mind.

As we well know, he set down his new perspectives in three major works, *Beyond the Pleasure Principle* (1920), *The Ego and the Id* (1923), and *Inhibitions, Symptom and Anxiety* (1926). To this list we must add Anna Freud's *The Ego and the Mechanisms of Defense* (1936), written under her father's supervision, if not in direct collaboration with him.

Pursuing the theme of this conference, "Historical and Current Perspectives on New Ideas in Psychoanalysis," we will do well to consider the fate of these literary milestones in our science. There is no doubt that *Beyond the Pleasure Principle* was a radical book in its time. It broke sharply with traditional psychoanalytic thought. The concept of an impulse toward self-destruction, of a drive towards death, went beyond the fundamental faith in the pleasure principle. The approach is primarily theoretical; the ideas are abstract and rooted in biological speculation and philosophical analysis. It should not be too difficult to make a fairly safe assessment of the fate of this volume and of the ideas it advances. To be sure, *Beyond the Pleasure Principle* appears in the syllabus of every psychoanalytic institute, and it is generally read and taught, but hardly, one would say, with any great enthusiasm. Except for the concept of the repetition compulsion, which in most cases is applied in a mechanical fashion, most of the ideas contained in this book have been only feebly integrated into the corpus of psychoanalytic thought.

By way of contrast, at the other end of the spectrum, Anna Freud's *The Ego and the Mechanisms of Defense* glows brilliantly. It is probably the most popular text in psychoanalysis. For years it served as a handbook for psychoanalytic technique. It is read and studied, discussed and referred to regularly. The insights contained in this book were quickly assimilated and promptly put to practical use in the psychoanalytic situation.

Wherein lies the reason for the difference in the reception that psychoanalysts gave the ideas of these two volumes — both volumes, it should be noted, being essentially the product of the same mind? The answer, I believe, is simple and fundamental. It can be summed up by referring to two related criteria — clinical relevance and the promise of improved therapeutic efficacy. Psychoanalysis has both the advantages and drawbacks of being at one and the same time a method of investigation as well as a form of therapy. The psychoanalytic community is essentially a community of practitioners, dedicated to the relief of suffering. The psychoanalytic situation is the ultimate testing ground for new ideas and concepts in psychoanalysis. The fate of such new ideas will depend on how well they make sense of the data of observation and/or on what promise they hold for improving therapeutic effectiveness. The two are not necessarily the same.

In psychoanalysis, the nature of treatment is intimately linked to the theory of pathogenesis. To use another metaphor, theories of therapy and theories of pathogenesis are obverse sides of the same coin. How we treat our patients derives from how we understand the nature of the pathogenic process. We have seen how, with each challenge to his therapeutic efforts, Freud reexamined his views concerning pathogenesis. In fact, most of the new ideas put forward in the development of psychoanalysis seem to have begun with some elaboration or change in the prevailing theory of pathogenesis. In this respect, the same problems that Freud faced have been faced by successive generations of analysts.

For purposes of discussion, it may be convenient to consider the problem of pathogenesis from three interrelated points of view. In practice, of course, they cannot be separated, but some approaches accentuate one aspect of the problem more than another. The headings I propose are the following: (1) The Nature of the Trauma or the Pathogenic Process; (2) The Timing of the Trauma or the Period of Pathogenic Vulnerability; and (3) The Specificity of the Trauma or the Pathogenic Element. Historically, most of the controversies over competing concepts and new ideas in psychoanalysis have raised issues relating to these three central questions.

Broadly speaking, the issues involved in theories of pathogenesis may be categorized as active or passive, i.e., what was done or what was not done to the individual during his early development. In his early theories, Freud (1916a) emphasized the harmful psychological effects of certain kinds of experiences, such as seduction at an early age, threats to one's physical integrity, and loss of an important object. After he defined the evolution of the libidinal drive, he paid more attention to constitutional factors, to elements connected with the intensity of drive endowment. Individuals who develop perversions, he said, have an unusually powerful endowment of a particular component drive, a fact which makes it difficult for their libidinal organization to progress beyond a certain level of fixation. Some years later (1919), he modified this point of view. Nonetheless, it is clear that the classic conflict between nature and nurture appeared early in the history of psychoanalysis, and persists today.

Some years back, Hartmann and Kris (1945) tried to resolve this polarity by indicating the intimate interplay of maturation and development. Their main emphasis, however, fell on how these processes influence the form and functions of the ego, since for them the factor that tips the balance towards health or illness is the capacity of the ego to master the insistent pressure of the drives and to resolve conflicts so engendered in a constructive, that is, adaptive way. Thus, Hartmann concentrated on the transformations of drive energy, on discharge, neutralization and deneutralization, and he applied these ideas to such areas of interest as sublimation (1955), the psychopathology of schizophrenia (1953), and the patient's response to interpretations during psychoanalytic treatment (1950). Whatever original enthusiasm greeted these ideas, they seem since to have lost their appeal, and, in practice, even the associated terminology has been fading gradually from our psychoanalytic lexicon.

It is in the work of Melanie Klein (1932), however, that one finds the most consistent utilization of a theory of pathogenesis that centers on abnormal endowment of drive energy — in this case, the energy of the aggressive instinct.

The normal, appropriate balance between Eros and Thanatos has not taken place, so that, primarily by the processes of projection and introjection, the psychic apparatus struggles to redress the imbalance. The timing of the disturbance perforce has to be very early in life, and symptomatology tends to be conceptualized as expressions of concrete fantasy formations — formations envisioned at a level of complexity unacceptable to the more developmentally minded psychoanalysts. This issue has remained a subject of continuing controversy, and while the critics of the Kleinian school have nonetheless borrowed many of their concepts, the debate seems no closer to resolution. The followers of Klein, on the other hand, claim that they have found rich clinical application of her ideas, particularly regarding transference phenomena and cases with severe psychopathology, and the number of proponents of Klein's theories has continued to grow.

Factors that could determine a constitutional predisposition to psychic illness were considered by Greenacre (1950). Drawing on her years of experience as a pediatrician, she outlined the vicissitudes of the individual's earliest somatic experiences, including intrauterine events, and she suggested how these elements, in conjunction with other experiential circumstances, could foster a constitutional intolerance of anxiety. She offered suggestive speculations on the possible psychic sequelae to early somatic distress. Plausible though these ideas may be, confirmation is difficult, either through reconstruction of development during psychoanalytic treatment or from direct infant observation by psychoanalysts. Some analysts offered possible clinical illustrations of Greenacre's thesis, but convincing, validating evidence remains hard to come by. Thus, a potentially important contribution withers away, awaiting an appropriate method of investigation. I can recall only one paper, by Alpert, Neubauer, and Weil (1956), that offered observational data and some methodology for assessing the constitutional factors — in this case, drive endowment.

This, too, is a continuing issue in present-day psychoanalysis. Without abandoning the idea of a fundamental psychobiological unity, some analysts seem more comfortable laying the foundations for their new ideas on a ground base of data accumulated within the psychoanalytic situation. In connection with the theory of aggression, Anna Freud (1972), Brenner (1971) and others pointed to the futility of trying to establish a parallelism between the libidinal drive, so clearly based in biology, and the drive of aggression. Data sustaining the need for the concept of an aggressive drive, they say, derive from the clinical situation, and the need for such a theory stems from the practical necessities of the treatment setting. Brenner (1975) even suggests that it would be more parsimonious to apply the same principles to the libidinal drive.

Of the events that shape character and determine vulnerability to neurosogenesis, psychoanalysts traditionally have concentrated on what takes place during the phallic phase, on that concatenation of relationships known as the Oedipus complex. The awesome image of the frightening father dominates the

scene; but also, by the time of the phallic phase, the individual has not only acquired language and fantasy function, but psychic structure has advanced to
the stage that makes some form of persistent balance between impulse and defense possible. However, as Fenichel (1931) and others pointed out, there are
many varieties of the Oedipus complex, their form and resolution being influenced by what happened to the individual during the preoedipal period.

At first, the accent fell on the side of the drives, on the experiences leading to
fixation of the drive to some early object. In this process, experiences of overindulgence and frustration were most significant. With the introduction of the
structural hypothesis, however, interest shifted to the side of the ego, to the examination of how the vicissitudes of the drives and the quality of object relations determine identifications, ego structure, and the choice of preferred
mechanisms of defense or modes of adaptation. At first, it was thought that the
insight into the nature of the preferred mechanisms of defense would resolve
the problem of the choice of neurosis (Wangh, 1959), but this did not turn out
to be the case. Today, the question of choice of neurosis continues to be a vital
issue.

The ideas connected with the new structural view were quickly integrated
into the technique of psychoanalysis. There were two approaches: to correct
what had gone wrong, or to supply what had been missing. Those who followed the structural model consistently sought, by interpretation and insight,
to bring about a restructuring of psychic functioning, so that the ego would
master the previously uncontrolled and automatic responses to danger. For
many, perhaps most, analysts, this remains the standard paradigm for psychoanalytic therapy. This point of view, as we shall see, has been challenged from
many quarters in recent years.

Two examples of correcting the effects of poor object relations and of sup-
plying, in the course of therapy, what had been missed during development,
may be cited from the contributions of Alexander (1950) and Zetzel (1956). Although these contributions represent conceptualizations of very different degrees of sophistication, the ideas nevertheless belong together. Alexander proposed that, during therapy, the analyst should aim to bring about a "corrective
emotional experience," one that would dramatize the difference between the
noxious relationship to the original object and the realistic, adaptive relationship with the analyst. Zetzel suggested that a working therapeutic alliance
could not be effected in some patients, unless a certain amount of preliminary
work, interpreting and clarifying the distorted early relationship to the
mother, was first accomplished. And Strachey (1934) maintained that such a
process takes place willy-nilly in every analysis. In fact, he felt that the therapeutic effectiveness of psychoanalysis depended on a process of piecemeal introjection of the image of the benign superego of the analyst into the superego
of the patient, a process which results in a concomitant ousting of the bad superego introject.

All of these approaches imply, however subtly, some departure from the neutral, technical stance of the analyst and, I believe, link up with more recent ideas concerning the need of the analyst to be "humane," according to one school, and/or "empathic," according to another. These issues reappear in an even more significant context as psychoanalysts engage new psychopathological entities, beyond those of the classic transference neuroses.

To what extent analysts knowingly widened the scope of conditions to which to apply psychoanalytic therapy (Stone, 1954), as opposed to how much the scope, shall we say, widened on its own account, is hard to say. Analysts either took up the challenge of trying to treat conditions ordinarily considered beyond the scope of psychoanalytic intervention (perhaps because they felt there was little else that offered promise of help), or, having begun with patients who seemed in the beginning to have appropriate indications for psychoanalytic therapy, they soon found themselves confronted with types of psychopathology they had not quite dealt with in the past.

At this juncture, certain issues took on fresh significance. The new trends re-emphasized findings dealing with preoedipal psychology, with the quality of object relationships and a new appreciation of the sense of identity and the self. The latter led inevitably to considerations of narcissism and the vicissitudes of self-esteem. If the image of the omnipotent father had been dominant in the past, the role of the nurturing mother now became paramount. When her efforts are judged to be flawed or insufficient, she is identified as the villain of psychopathology, the initiator of deformed character, low self-esteem and mental illness (Arlow, 1981). Paralleling, and perhaps even displacing, the prototypical developmental dangers of the past, such as loss of the object, loss of the object's love, bodily injury and superego approach, in this new context we find a new set of dangers — danger of merger, of dissolution, of a loss of boundaries of the self and a loss of self-cohesion.

To sustain these concepts, through validating observations from the therapeutic situation or by means of inferences from long-term developmental studies, presents very difficult, perhaps almost insuperable, problems. Since psychopathology in these instances is traced to the very early stages of the individual's existence, to a period beyond the reach of memory and before the development of language, the data offered to support such theses must be tenuous indeed. Sometimes a self-fulfilling prediction is used as evidence, e.g., because a mother's efforts were insufficient, the child became ill, and the child's illness is proof that the mother was less than adequate in her caring.

Several different approaches are being used in an attempt to resolve this issue. One is a time-honored approach, but still the subject of considerable controversy. It consists of interpreting the events of the transference during psychoanalytic therapy as a base from which to reconstruct, i.e., infer, what happened during the first two years of a person's life. The issue involved concerns the limits of reconstruction beyond memory, beyond recall. This is an issue which still divides our colleagues today, and many of them have taken a stand on one side or another of the controversy. Greenacre (1971) feels confident in the possibilities of such reconstruction, while Anna Freud (1969) was more dubious and urged caution in this regard.

Another approach is to be found in the use of carefully documented, long-range studies of child development, carried out by psychoanalytic observers. Work done by investigators like Mahler (1968, 1975), Emde, Kligman, Reich, and Wade (1978), Stern (1977), Call, Galenson and Tyson (1983), Kestenberg (1975) and Weil (1970) provides a data base from which inferences may be drawn. These workers, especially Mahler, continue with the tradition of examining the events that influence the formation of psychic structure, of the nature of one's identity, and of the sense of the self. In addition, her work also has a clinical base, inasmuch as it originated from her investigation into the possibility of treating autistic and psychotic children.

Nonetheless, developmental studies represent observation from the outside, and ultimately must depend upon a high degree of empathic interpretation of manifest behavior. The danger of adultomorphic projection is considerable. However, Mahler still operates within the structural model of drives and object relations, conflict and defense. The most precise application of the structural approach to the pathology of narcissism and self-esteem regulation, in my mind, is to be found in the contributions of Annie Reich (1953, 1960). In many quarters, these works are regarded as classics on the subject. She has suggested a new definition of the term "narcissistic neuroses," and her interpretation of the pathology and treatment of these conditions is clinically based, with the data organized according to the principles just outlined. Because of this last fact, it has been relatively easy for practitioners to apply her ideas in the clinical setting.

Kohut (1971) has resolved these issues to his satisfaction in a relatively simple way, and, in doing so, he has actually founded a new school of thought within psychoanalysis. For him the process of narcissistic pathology, and a good deal of other pathology, begins with inadequate parenting, with a failure of empathic caring and responsiveness. Almost everything that happens afterwards is secondary or derivative. For him, evidence to support his thesis abounds and is ready at hand. This is so because he depends upon empathy as a direct form of observation. The empathic therapist *perceives* immediately and directly the nature of the patient's experience. He regards indirect introspection as a universal form of scientific observation and, in contrast to other observers (such as Beres and Arlow, 1974), he dispenses with the need for cognitive disciplining of insights made possible through empathy and available through introspection.

According to Kohut, the treatment situation becomes the setting where the untoward effects of thwarted narcissism are overcome, and the patient may grow and develop according to his "true" core self, as a result of the benign, empathic attitude of the therapist. It is the therapist who supplies what was lacking in the past and who thus places the patient back on the course of correct development. In this body of theory, pathogenesis and therapy are very specific. They center on the principle of empathy. The rigors of tracing out patterns in the patient's communications and of determining the unconscious drives that present derivatives to consciousness play a lesser role. One wonders why the proponents of self-psychology still use the psychoanalytic situation as their method of investigation, inasmuch as the psychoanalytic situation is structured in terms of drive, defense, and compromise formation. To be sure, when the therapist can rely upon direct empathic perception, technique becomes simpler, interpreting the patterns of the associations less important, making interpretations easier.

The issues raised by Kohut's psychology of the self have been vigorously debated and, I believe, will continue to be debated for quite a while. I have several reasons for saying this. To begin with, Kohut has directed our attention to forms of psychopathology and to clinical manifestations of narcissistic disturbances that classic psychoanalysis has long overlooked. The specificity of pathogenesis, its relation to a standard model, i.e., unempathic parenting, simplifies concepts of psychopathology, as well as the approach to therapy. More than that, self-psychology offers the promise of therapeutic effectiveness for certain conditions that have not responded favorably to standard psychoanalytic procedures. Historically, the promise of therapeutic efficacy presents an appeal to analysts that is practically irresistible. If I were to guess, I would say that the issue will be decided, not on the basis of logical consistency of theory, or on the correlation of clinical observation with hypotheses, but rather on the basis of how effective a therapeutic instrument self-psychology proves to be.

The emphasis of self-psychology on the importance of the nurturing mother is only one manifestation of a very powerful current in present-day psychoanalytic thought. From England, France, and the United States have come many contributions, all of which make the point that the essential feature in psychoanalytic psychotherapy is the diatrophic, nurturing role of the therapist. To some authors (Nacht, 1962), the therapist is expected to demonstrate unconditional kindness and perfect empathy.

Friedman (1978) characterizes the techniques of the object-relations school as a replacement form of therapy, that is, an attempt to recreate and improve during the analytic treatment the mother-child relationship of the first years of life. Treatment represents a recapitulation of development under more favorable conditions, with an appropriate mother surrogate. In this process, there is a restructuring of the psychic apparatus, a developmental advance under the aegis of an appropriate, empathic, affective relationship with the therapist. One of the ideas implicit in this approach is the notion that growth is a nonstructured phenomenon that happens automatically, if not interfered with by the noxious intrusions of the less-than-adequate, unempathic mother.

Theories of pathogenesis based on the malignant effects of experiences during the earliest months of life hark back to the time when the individual had only needs and no responsibilities. The least culpable, the completely innocent victim is, of course, the very young infant. . . . (Arlow, 1981, p. 503)

I will only mention here some of the issues involved in questions of timing and specificity. Pushing the significant pathogenic factors farther and farther back in time raises the question of the precise way in which such events influence subsequent development. Is there, perhaps, some form of somatic memory devoid of object concept and, if so, what is the evidence? Some object-relations theories treat the earliest interpersonal relationships as if they were a fixed structure in the mind with a persistent dynamic thrust, independent of the vicissitudes of drive development.

I will not review the history of the concept of specificity in psychoanalysis. It is a long and detailed one, having been applied to such issues as psychosomatic disorders, the origin of perversions, and the genesis of specific character traits. Much as the principles of overdetermination and multiple function are honored in psychoanalytic essays, it is hard to overcome the appeal of a concept like specificity of pathogenesis, a concept that simplifies questions of theory and, at the same time, seems to point to new promises of therapy. Current emphasis on the malignant effects of unempathic parenting in the earliest months of life, a concept very popular and fundamental in many different schools of psychoanalytic thought, is only the latest example of the appeal of specificity.

Psychoanalysts are particularly open and receptive to new concepts. Correlating theory with the clinical data obtained in the psychoanalytic situation is quite another matter. It is not unusual for a new idea to be accepted with enthusiasm and, instead of being used as an instrument for research, to become a shibboleth in treatment. One of the by-products of Mahler's meticulously conducted studies of separation-individuation has been a change in terminology. Formerly, we hoped that a patient would become independent and self-reliant. What we hear now is that he or she must learn how to separate and how to individuate. Self-reliance and individuation are, of course, concepts of an entirely different order. Clearly, what is required in both psychoanalytic practice and teaching is greater attention to problems of method and validation. Therapeutic zeal is commendable, but it can become an obstacle to conceptual clarity and scientific progress.

REFERENCES

Alexander, F. (1950), Analysis of the therapeutic factors in psychoanalytic treatment. *Psychoanal. Quart.,* 19:482–500.

Alpert, A., Neubauer, P. B., & Weil, A. P. (1956), Unusual variations in drive endowment. *The Psychoanalytic Study of the Child,* 11:125–163.

Arlow, J. A. (1956), *The Legacy of Sigmund Freud.* New York: International Universities Press.

———— (1981), Theories of pathogenesis. *Psychoanal. Quart.,* 50:488–514.

Beres, D., & Arlow, J. A. (1974), Fantasy and identification in empathy. *Psychoanal. Quart.,* 43:26–50.

Brenner, C. (1971), The psychoanalytic concept of aggression. *Internat. J. Psycho-Anal.,* 52: 137–144.

———— (1975), Affects in psychic conflict. *Psychoanal. Quart.,* 44:5–28.

Call, J. D., Galenson, E., & Tyson, R. L. (1983), *Frontiers of Infant Psychiatry.* New York: Basic Books.

Emde, R. N., Kligman, D. H., Reich, J. H., & Wade, T. D. (1978), Emotional expression in infancy. In: *The Development of Affect,* ed. M. Lewis & L. Rosenblum. New York: Plenum.

Fenichel, O. (1931), Specific forms of the oedipus complex. *International Zeitschrift fur Psychoanalyse,* 17:37–54. Also in: *Collected Papers,* Vol. 1, pp. 204–220.

Freud, A. (1936), *The Ego and the Mechanisms of Defense.* New York: International Universities Press.

———— (1969), *Difficulties in the Path of Psychoanalysis.* New York: International Universities Press.

———— (1972), Comments on aggression. *Internat. J. of Psycho-Anal.,* 53:163–171.

Freud, S. (1902), The forgetting of proper names. In: The Psychopathology of Everyday Life. *Standard Edition,* 6:1–7.

———— (1909), Analysis of a Phobia in a Five-Year-Old Boy. *Standard Edition,* 10:3–149.

———— (1916a), Introductory Lectures on Psychoanalysis. *Standard Edition,* 15 & 16.

———— (1916b), Some Character Types Met with in Psychoanalytic Work. *Standard Edition,* 14:311–333.

———— (1918), From the History of an Infantile Neurosis. *Standard Edition,* 17:7–124.

———— (1919), A Child Is Being Beaten. *Standard Edition,* 17:175–204.

———— (1920), Beyond the Pleasure Principle. *Standard Edition,* 18:3–64.

———— (1923), The Ego and the Id. *Standard Edition,* 19:3–66.

———— (1925), An Autobiographical Study. *Standard Edition,* 20:3–74.

———— (1926), Inhibition, Symptom and Anxiety. *Standard Edition,* 20:77–175.

Friedman, L. (1978), Trends in the psychoanalytic theory of treatment, *Psychoanal. Quart.,* 47:524–567.

Greenacre, P. (1950), *Trauma, Growth and Personality.* New York: W. W. Norton.

———— (1971), Notes on the influence and contribution of ego psychology to the practice of psychoanalysis. In: *Separation-Individuation,* ed. J. McDevitt & C. Settlage. New York: International Universities Press, pp. 171–200.

Hartmann, H. (1950), Comments on the psychoanalytic theory of the ego. *The Psychoanalytic Study of the Child,* 5:7–17.

———— (1953), Contribution to the metapsychology of schizophrenia. *The Psychoanalytic Study of the Child,* 8:177–198.

———— (1955), Notes on the theory of sublimation. *The Psychoanalytic Study of the Child,* 10:9–29.

———— & Kris, E. (1945), The genetic approach in psychoanalysis. *The Psychoanalytic Study of the Child,* 1:11–29.

———— ———— & Loewenstein, R. M. (1946), Formation of psychic structure. *The Psychoanalytic Study of the Child,* 2:11–38.

Kestenberg, J. (1975), *Children and Parents: Psychoanalytic Studies of Development.* New York: Jason Aronson.

Klein, M. (1932), *The Psychoanalysis of Children.* London: Hogarth Press.

Kohut, H. (1971), *The Analysis of the Self.* New York: International Universities Press.

Mahler, M., & Furer, M. (1968), *On Human Symbiosis and the Vicissitudes of Individuation.* New York: International Universities Press.

———— Pine, F., & Bergman, A. (1975), *The Psychological Birth of the Human Infant.* New York: Basic Books.

Nacht, S. (1962), The curative factor in psychoanalysis. *Internat. J. Psycho-Anal.*, 43:206–211.

Reich, A. (1953), Narcissistic object choice in women. *J. Amer. Psychoanal. Assn.*, 1:22–44.

—— (1960), Pathologic forms of self-esteem regulation. *The Psychoanalytic Study of the Child*, 15:215–232.

Stern, D. N. (1977), *The First Relationship: Infant and Mother.* Cambridge: Harvard University Press.

Stone, L. (1954), The widening scope of indications for psychoanalysis. *J. Amer. Psychoanal. Assn.*, 2:567–594.

—— (1961), *The Psychoanalytic Situation.* New York: International Universities Press.

Strachey, J. (1934), The nature of the therapeutic action of psychoanalysis. *Internat. J. Psycho-Anal.*, 15:127–159.

Wangh, M. (1959), Structural determinants of phobia. *J. Amer. Psychoanal. Assn.*, 7:675–695.

Weil, A. (1970), The basic core. *The Psychoanalytic Study of the Child*, 25:442–460.

Zetzel, E. R. (1956), Current concepts of transference. *Internat. J. Psycho-Anal.*, 37:369–376.

2

Fluctuat Nec Mergitur*

JOHN E. GEDO, M.D.

I

The twenty years since publication of Maxwell Gitelson's essay (Chapter 3, this volume) on the state of psychoanalysis have produced astonishing changes in every aspect of the field. This internal evolution has, undoubtedly, been hastened by the markedly unfavorable shift of the societal matrix of the profession: loss of public favor and insurance coverage, competition from a host of aggressively promoted therapies promising easier results, slippage in the economic status of parts of our clientele, and the general turn of American intellectual life away from introspection and humanism (Gedo, 1983, 1984). Faced once again with an inhospitable reception, reminiscent in many ways of its difficult origins, psychoanalysis has met the challenge through salutary scientific ferment — or, if you will, a bewildering loss of the consensus Gitelson always strove to embody.

In 1964, as president of the International Psycho-Analytic Association and spokesman of our establishment, Gitelson's chief concern was the potential absorption of psychoanalysis by an eclectic "dynamic psychiatry," in which our hard-won insights would be misused in arbitrary ways as apotropaic formulae — the sophisticated tools of a contemporary suggestive technique. In this regard, his fears have proved to be groundless; far from incorporating psychoanalysis, American psychiatry has all but abandoned psychological methods

---

*Motto quoted by Freud to predict the survival of psychoanalysis despite dissension; from the seal of the city of Paris, it means: It may waver, but will not sink.

involving introspection and empathy. Psychoanalysts are, therefore, no longer threatened with the loss of their specific identity as explorers of the human depths. By the same token, however, they are no longer in command of the privileges — or subject to the temptations — of being ordained ministers of 20th-century mass culture.

Of course, most of us did not share Gitelson's preference for emulating Diogenes; we coveted the rewards of public favor and have reacted to its loss with a decided sense of defeat. I believe this to be true of my generation of analysts, at any rate — those of us trained during the 1950's and currently serving as senior faculty in psychoanalytic institutes. Our natural reactions have run the full gamut, from the impulse to compel the attention of our colleagues (and a wider audience, if possible) through creative iconoclasm to the opposite extreme, the tendency to enshrine existing theories and procedures as if they were sacred texts and liturgies. It cannot be coincidental that the resultant loss of cohesion within the psychoanalytic community has occurred at one of those junctures in the history of psychoanalysis — times of great ferment and change that seem to recur about once in every generation — when the scientific consensus that has long prevailed would tend to break down in any case. In other words, our loss of public favor probably reflects, at the same time, our diminishing clinical and scientific self-confidence.

Of course, it is something of a paradox to believe that the clinical psychoanalyst has lost faith in his effectiveness while the profession has been proclaiming that the scope of its therapeutic tools has steadily widened (Panel, 1954). Yet the dwindling proportion of analytic work (in the strict definition of the term) within the professional activities of members of the American Psychoanalytic Association attests to this disenchantment. Whatever the claims of optimistic expansionists about their favorable results with the analytic method (Gedo, 1981a, 1984), the routine technique practiced throughout the country has led to disappointing outcomes. These setbacks have ranged from the relatively low proportion of analyses found to have culminated in mutually agreed-upon termination (Erle, 1979), through the unsatisfactory results obtained with patients treated at the Menninger Clinic via psychoanalysis (when compared with matched groups of patients who received analytically informed psychotherapy there [Wallerstein, 1983]), to the sobering yield of a variety of follow-up investigations (Firestein, 1979; Schlessinger and Robbins, 1983). It would seem that, collectively, we have failed to teach the graduates of our training programs to carry out our difficult therapeutic prescriptions with the requisite skill. Little wonder that, as a group, they shy away from attempting what is beyond their reach and prefer to offer their patients psychotherapeutic alternatives.

At the same time, there is good reason to believe that our contemporary technical armamentarium is capable of achieving more than analysis could aim for when our teachers began their careers (Freud, 1937). I can certainly assert this on the basis of personal experience, as I have extensively reported elsewhere (Gedo, 1979, 1981b, 1984). It is self-evident that our better clinicians have always obtained results superior to the prevailing standards; but as our clinical understanding has expanded, so have our expectations. Analysts can always apply the clinical theories they have learned to the therapeutic contingencies they encounter in practice, often with striking therapeutic benefit; but these results do not demonstrate the validity and relevance of the interpretations offered. Good results may flow from the use of appropriate analytic methods, or they may reflect the charisma of the therapist. In order to benefit from the suggestive effects of such a pseudo-analytic encounter, however, the analysand needs to experience the magic of an omniscient healer. In other words, we tend to profit from these unintended non-analytic transactions to the greatest extent whenever we have full confidence in our theories and technical methods.

When American psychoanalysis reached the peak of its popular success, in the years following World War II, our collective approach had scarcely departed from the positions of the aged Freud. The cutting edge of progress was the ego psychology promulgated by Heinz Hartmann and his co-workers (or, for the devil's advocates among us, the id mythologies emanating from the British Psycho-Analytic Society). We had a virtual monopoly on psychological medicine and could fill our analytic schedules while selecting patients in accord with the most stringent criteria of analyzability. More recently, in extensive travels around the Continent as lecturer, site visitor for the Association, or as a private person, I have found no colleague able to pursue such a policy; individuals seeking analysis for neurotic problems confined to oedipal issues are scarcely to be found.

Most observers seem to agree with Kohut (1977), who held the view that new forms of psychopathology have become prevalent among our clientele, albeit few would concur with Kohut's nosological suggestion that the typical sickness of our time is the incapacity to fulfill one's destiny. Although we lack the evidence to resolve this question definitively, I am convinced that our diagnostic impressions have changed, not because the people who consult us are significantly different from their precedessors twenty-five or fifty years ago, but because the preconscious schemata we use to process our observations have gradually evolved in startling ways. Thus, the apparent changes in potential analysands merely reflect the general progress of psychoanalysis in the past generation.

Perhaps the clearest example of one step in this evolution was the initial impact of Kohut's own work (1966, 1971). Although he was, at first, careful to point out that he was focusing on a set of observations widely reported for some time by many colleagues—he subtitled his 1971 book on these matters "a systematizing attempt"—the very fact that Kohut brought these observations into the central position they occupied in his mature work, and thereby captured the attention of a wide segment of the analytic community, soon led him and a set of followers "more Catholic than the Pope" to assume that a novel group of nosological entities had been "discovered." A subjective report of the great impact of this "discovery" on an analytic novice, troubled by her ineffectiveness, exemplifies the problems in our training that I have already outlined (Goldberg, 1978, p. 203).

It did not take long for those whose analytic perplexities were relieved by replacing the schemata they had employed by the new ones proferred in Kohut's writings to stop using the old conceptual categories altogether. Their observations, sometimes valid, were no longer thought of as examples of the universally expectable emergence of one or another "narcissistic" transference constellation. In the first stage of their shift to a new clinical theory, they would diagnose the particular analysand under observation as a sufferer from a "narcissistic personality disturbance." A new illness had appeared on the social scene! Around 1970, in our extensive personal discussions, Kohut estimated that about four patients out of ten in his practice properly belonged to this new nosological category.

Expanding public interest in his exciting innovations soon led Kohut and a growing band of students continually to revise this estimate upward. At the present time, the Kohutians I most respect continue to believe, on reflection, that the concepts of traditional Freudian psychoanalysis are fully adequate in a small handful of cases. In other words, they adhere to the distinction between *Guilty Man* and *Tragic Man* that Kohut proposed in 1977, but they feel that *Guilty Man* is a dying breed, no longer produced in late 20th-century industrial societies. Hence, they use Kohut's clinical concepts as the (all-but-) universal explanatory framework for their analytic activities; they have become "self-psychologists." It is entirely predictable that those who accept this framework will never again encounter a live patient of the kind who populated our consulting rooms before we read Kohut's revolutionary message, and the observations of those analysts who continue to do so will be explained by the adherents of "self psychology" as iatrogenic artifacts.

I have summarized the historical evolution of Kohut's impact on our community not because its progression has been exceptional; on the contrary, I regard it as entirely typical. Let me review the steps I have outlined in terms of generalizations applicable across a broad range of examples. First, a set of clinical observations is highlighted as a previously neglected aspect of clinical theory. Next, those instances in which the novel observations seem to be significant are defined as a nosological entity that was hitherto overlooked. Third, the mode of functioning characteristic of the new class of pathology is detected in ever wider circles of patients in analysis. As a logical consequence of this realization, the patterns in question lose their relevance for differential diagnosis and are elevated into the cardinal feature of a new theoretical framework, intended to replace a previous psychoanalytic paradigm. Skeptics will then collect clinical observations poorly explained within this latest clinical theory, and the process of revisions begins anew.

II

Our difficulties as a scientific community stem from the fact that our consensus inevitably breaks down at each stage of this normal progression. To return to the illustrative case of Kohut's impact on American psychoanalysis: even the preliminary announcement of his basic clinical findings (Kohut, 1968), initially delivered under the impeccable auspices of the New York Psychoanalytic Society as a Brill Lecture and published in that most traditional forum, *The Psychoanalytic Study of the Child,* failed to carry universal conviction. Every clinician had, of course, encountered the phenomena of idealization and subject-centered grandiosity that Kohut was calling to our attention with such emphasis; but only a minority was prepared to accept his main conclusion — the assertion that the appearance of certain varieties of these behaviors within the analytic transference constitutes the repetition of essentially expectable childhood attitudes of cardinal developmental significance.

In his 1971 book, Kohut clarified his position: he stated that the transference patterns in question are evoked in a more definite manner if the analyst conducts himself in certain ways than if other technical procedures are followed. Depending on individual inclinations, based either on emotional preference or on preexisting theoretical commitments, clinicians either tried to promote or to discourage the emergence of those transference patterns that Kohut then believed to be pathognomonic of "narcissistic personality disturbance." It should be kept in mind that both choices could, in the hands of skillful analysts, lead to useful therapeutic results; but, as fascinating follow-up studies (Schlessinger and Robbins, 1983) have begun to document, the improvements achieved by following these alternative treatment programs — not to speak of the difficulties left in their wake — are distinct enough to be difficult to compare (see Firestein, 1978; Goldberg, 1978; and the discussion of the results they report in Gedo, 1980).

Some observers, myself included, predicted that the assumption of polemical positions about Kohut's hypotheses would inevitably lead to a split in the analytic community. Partly in an effort to forestall such polarization into extremist factions, in *Models of the Mind* (Gedo and Goldberg, 1973) I tried to map out a framework for clinical theory potentially broad enough to accommodate the findings of analysts of every persuasion. Despite the favorable reception of that hierarchical schema, it had little effect on the evolution of psychoanalytic opinion about Kohut's work. Commentaries rejecting his proposals in toto (Stein, 1974) began to appear in tandem with early announcements (Terman, 1976) about the possibility of developing "self psychology" — as Kohut's ideas were now called by his adherents — into a system of purportedly universal applicability. Ecumenicism was now repudiated by both camps, a tendency that gained momentum when Kohut (1977) endorsed the most radical claims for his views: the transferences he had originally seen as characteristic of narcissistic pathology were now regarded as ubiquitous; renamed "self-object transferences," for Kohut *these* patterns of human relationship now assumed decisive significance in health and disease.

The majority of those who had welcomed Kohut's delineation of so-called idealizing and mirror transferences as promising first approximations in an unfamiliar observational field could not accept his new position, which was widely regarded as reductionistic and, therefore, scientifically regressive. At the same time, this group of skeptical clinicians continued to disagree with hard-line conservatives who insisted that neurosogenesis is more or less exclusively determined by oedipal issues. Unlike the conservatives or the "self psychologists," the middle group—vide the earlier controversies within the British Society—consisting of analysts of heterogeneous views, lacked consensus, and only agreed to adopt a "plague on both their houses" attitude toward the warring camps.

Despite its heterogeneity, it is possible to discern two dominant trends within the uncommitted faction. A large segment of this group, perhaps the majority, is resigned to the theoretical disarray implicit in espousing bits of clinical theory, derived from a variety of uncoordinated viewpoints. Sometimes, this attitude might better be described as complacent, rather than resigned: many colleagues seem to feel no discomfort about choosing, in an ad hoc manner, among Freudian, Mahlerian, Winnicottian, Kohutian, and even Kleinian propositions, if these possess some degree of clinical heuristic usefulness. Others try to paper over the underlying incoherence of this procedure by stressing that the work of each author they cite is centered on a developmental perspective, as if alternating, without apology, between incompatible schemata of development were scientifically justified. (Needless to say, I am unwilling to accept such thinking—even if apologies were offered!) This thinking is not to be confused with genuine attempts at assessment, correlation, and integration of old and emerging new theory, as guided by accumulating developmental knowledge. Some contributors are keenly aware of the epistemological problems posed by the lack of integration of their clinical concepts; Modell (1983), for one, regards this state of affairs as inevitable and invokes the example of modern physics to justify the need to use complementary theoretical fragments for psychoanalysis.

If the authors I have been discussing follow the epistemological example of Niels Bohr, there are others within psychoanalysis—George Klein (1976), Roy Schafer (1976), and Hans Loewald (1980) might be cited as the most prominent—who have opted to emulate that of Albert Einstein in seeking to create a single theory for psychoanalysis, based on consistent premises. Thus far, none of these proposals has captured the imagination of any large segment of the analytic community. On the one hand, theories that profess to dispense altogether with any metapsychological framework, like those of Klein and Schafer (see also Gill and Holzman, 1976), seem to take little account of the behavioral phenomena formerly included within the Freudian rubric of the repetition compulsion. Stated differently, psychoanalytic theories that focus exclusively on matters that can be deciphered in terms of their significance within a hermeneutic system can scarcely hope to encompass the legacy of the earliest phases of childhood, those preceding the acquisition of symbolic thought.

On the other hand, theorists who attempt to ascribe the fundamental patterning of personality to the vicissitudes of early object relations, like Loewald (or Kohut, for that matter) do not seem to give sufficient emphasis to the importance of inborn capacities in molding the individual's personal destiny. In both cases, I have stressed the *apparent* crux of the authors' theorizing, without necessarily making a judgment about their actual intentions, because I am, at this time, only trying to indicate why these various proposals are not likely to win the allegiance of a majority of analysts.

From the point of view of theoretical inclusiveness and coherence, in other words, none of the revisionist systems can rival the structure erected by Freud around the armature of drive theory. The latter has continued to serve as the organizing framework used by most analysts, despite repeated demonstrations of its epistemological failings (Basch, 1976, 1977; Swanson, 1977), because of the shortcomings of alternative proposals. Those of us who insist on building psychoanalytic theory on epistemologically sound foundations are, for the moment, forced to make do with developmental concepts, derived from the greatest variety of observable phenomena—a veritable mosaic of evolving capacities in transaction with the infant's milieu (A. Freud, 1965; Gedo and Goldberg, 1973). Although such conceptual schemata can be built on the basis of internally consistent criteria—in other words, they could potentially avoid the use of seemingly complementary but mutually inconsistent assumptions—the resulting outline of the progressive acquisition of functional capacities will only be useful in direct proportion to its complexity.

The particular version of such a schema of personality organization that I have advocated (Gedo, 1978, 1981b, 1981c) was intended only to serve as a skeletal suggestion of how the self-organization should be mapped out. Apparently, however, even this simplified hierarchical model has impressed many analysts as too unwieldy for practical purposes. Those who have applied my concepts clinically have rightly pointed out that the schema actually needs further elaboration (Gustafson, 1984; Robbins, 1983; Whitehead, 1983).

III

If efforts to integrate the varied clinical experiences of a heterogeneous psychoanalytic community are, for the moment, unlikely to result in consensus, this disquieting state of affairs actually reflects the stunning expansion of our psychology in the past decade into hitherto unplumbed depths of the human condition. Controversy may continue to rage over the extent to which psycho-analytic technique may legitimately be stretched to accommodate patients whose archaic transferences require various measures "beyond interpretation," to echo the title of my 1979 book. Whatever we may decide to call the analytic therapies through which we succeed in modifying profound disturbances in character that originate within the vicissitudes of the first two or three years of life (Gedo, 1984), the clinical observations made in the course of such treatments have profoundly altered our data base. These new findings from the analyses of children and adults are also congruent with the results of psychoanalytically informed observational studies of infants — a field recently surveyed by Lichtenberg (1983).

In view of the volume of new information that must be incorporated into our clinical theory, there is no reason to feel discouraged about the relative disarray in our ranks concerning theoretical matters. Probably every generation of analysts will abide by one of the conceptual alternatives available while that cohort finds its professional identity; it is not reasonable to expect practitioners with decades of experience to adopt radically novel theories. The dominant psychoanalytic paradigm of the decades to come will turn out to be one that appeals to the intellectual elite of the current group of analysts-in-formation. These are the individuals who commit themselves wholeheartedly to the exercise of their demanding analytic craft and gain sufficient technical mastery to obtain better results than those reported in the disheartening follow-up studies I have cited.

For in every generation, there have been analysts who do better treatment than the best we can expect if the model technique of contemporary psycho-analysis is optimally performed. Without conscious intent, they operate in accord with necessary technical precepts that have not as yet been codified in the literature. As Bergin and Lambert (1978) have shown, such covert aspects of the clinical transaction must account for the effectiveness of a whole variety of therapies poorly grounded in theory. Progress in the theory of psychoanalytic technique takes place when we succeed in formulating explicit therapeutic principles on the basis of consistently successful ad hoc interventions. One illustration from my own work is the recommendation (Gedo, 1984) to communicate with certain patients suffering from developmental deficits in language skills through affectively charged messages. This is one measure "beyond interpretation" that may be necessitated by the presence of psychopathology referable to the vicissitudes of very early developmental phases — in this instance, that of language acquisition.

Before the introduction of such measures into the analyst's regular armamentarium by providing them with an explicit rationale, they are employed, more or less preconsciously, as part of the analyst's therapeutic art. It is very likely that superior therapists will espouse those clinical theories that offer them convincing rationales for the greatest number of successful technical innovations. By the same token, I suspect that theories will fall into disuse when they can no longer generate successful corollaries in terms of technique. I have the impression that this is the current fate of "ego psychology," the school of thought almost universally accepted in this country in Gitelson's day. Its propositions have never been repudiated, as such, but one hears less and less of them, as the focus of psychoanalytic interest shifts away from the realm of intersystemic conflicts in the direction of behaviors under the sway of the compulsion to repeat.

Some sixty-five years ago, Freud encouraged the adherence of the maverick therapist, Georg Groddeck, to psychoanalysis by insisting that anyone who took proper account of the phenomena of transference and resistance in psychological treatment qualified as an analyst (Groddeck, 1977). In the current atmosphere of sectarian rancor, we can only feel nostalgia for the tolerance of diversity implicit in Freud's attitude. It is true that the integration of important new ideas into the fabric of psychoanalysis was to take place almost entirely within Freud's mind for another thirty years, so that the founding father could well afford to be generous toward his professional progeny. By comparison, contemporary psychoanalysis resembles the electorate of a democratic society; those who would gain popular favor must woo the voters by promising them bread and circuses. This social situation may encourage the acceptance of ideas characterized by simplicity rather than rigor, and the creation of analytic superstars, distinguished by charisma instead of rationality. No doubt, Freud's marked distaste for the New World was based on his understanding that its ethos would subject psychoanalysis to such populist pressures. Let us hope that the voice of the intellect will prevail nonetheless, as he predicted.

REFERENCES

Basch, M. (1976), Theory formation in Chapter VII: A critique. *J. Amer. Psychoanal. Assn.,* 24:61–100.

———— (1977), Developmental psychology and explanatory theory in psychoanalysis. *The Annual of Psychoanalysis,* 5:229–263. New York: International Universities Press.

Bergin, A., & Lambert, M. (1978), The evaluation of therapeutic outcomes. In: *Handbook of Psychotherapy and Behavior Change* (2nd. ed.), ed. S. Garfield & A. Bergin. New York: Wiley, pp. 139–189.

Erle, J. (1979), An approach to the study of analyzability and analyses: The course of forty consecutive cases selected for supervised analysis. *Psychoanal. Quart.,* 48:198–228.

Firestein, S. (1978), *Termination in Psychoanalysis.* New York: International Universities Press.

Freud, A. (1965), *Normality and Pathology in Childhood.* New York: International Universities Press.

Freud, S. (1937), Analysis Terminable and Interminable. *Standard Edition,* 23:216–253. London: Hogarth Press, 1964.

Gedo, J. (1979), *Beyond Interpretation.* New York: International Universities Press.

———— (1980), Reflections on some current controversies in psychoanalysis. *J. Amer. Psychoanal. Assn.,* 28:363–383.

_____ (1981a), A psychoanalyst reports at mid-career. *Amer. J. Psychiat.*, 136:646–649.

_____ (1981b), *Advances in Clinical Psychoanalysis*. New York: International Universities Press.

_____ (1981c), Measure for measure: A response. *Psychoanal. Inq.*, 1:289–316.

_____ (1983), *Portraits of the Artist*. New York: Guilford.

_____ (1984), *Psychoanalysis and Its Discontents*. New York: Guilford.

_____ & Goldberg, A. (1973), *Models of the Mind*. Chicago: University of Chicago Press.

Gill, M., & Holzman, P., ed. (1976), *Psychology Versus Metapsychology: Psychoanalytic Essays in Honor of George S. Klein. Psychological Issues,* Monogr. 36. New York: International Universities Press.

Goldberg, A., ed. (1978), *The Psychology of the Self: A Casebook*. New York: International Universities Press.

Groddeck, G. (1977), *The Meaning of Illness: Selected Psychoanalytic Writings*. New York: International Universities Press.

Gustafson, J. (1984), An integration of brief dynamic psychotherapy. *Amer. J. Psychiat.*, 141:935–944.

Klein, G. (1976), *Psychoanalytic Theory: An Exploration of Essentials*. New York: International Universities Press.

Kohut, H. (1966), Forms and transformations of narcissism. *J. Amer. Psychoanal. Assn.*, 14:243–272.

_____ (1968), The psychoanalytic treatment of narcissistic personality disorders. *The Psychoanalytic Study of the Child*, 23:86–113. New York: International Universities Press.

_____ (1971), *The Analysis of the Self*. New York: International Universities Press.

_____ (1977), *The Restoration of the Self*. New York: International Universities Press.

Lichtenberg, J. (1983), *Psychoanalysis and Infant Research*. Hillsdale, NJ: The Analytic Press.

Loewald, H. (1980), *Papers on Psychoanalysis*. New Haven: Yale University Press.

Modell, A. (1983, October), The two contexts of the self. Paper presented to the 50th Anniversary Symposium, Boston Psychoanalytic Society and Institute.

Panel (1954), The widening scope of indications for psychoanalysis. *J. Amer. Psychoanal. Assn.*, 2:565–620.

Robbins, M. (1983), Toward a new mind model for the primitive personalities. *Internat. J. Psycho-Anal.*, 64:127–148.

Schafer, R. (1976), *A New Language for Psychoanalysis*. New Haven: Yale University Press.

Schlessinger, N., & Robbins, F. (1983), *A Developmental View of the Psychoanalytic Process*. New York: International Universities Press.

Stein, M. (1974), In: Panel on "Advances in psychoanalytic technique," A. Freedman, reporter. *J. Phila. Assn. for Psychoanal.*, 1:44–54.

Swanson, D. (1977), A critique of psychic energy as an explanatory concept. *J. Amer. Psychoanal. Assn.*, 25:603–633.

Terman, D. (1976, December), Distortions of the Oedipus complex in severe pathology: Some vicissitudes of self development and their relationship to the Oedipus complex. Paper presented to the American Psychoanalytic Association.

Wallerstein, R. (1983, October), Psychoanalysis and psychotherapy: Relative roles reconsidered. Paper presented to the 50th Anniversary Symposium, Boston Psychoanalytic Society and Institute.

Whitehead, C. (1983, December), On the Ascelpian spirit and the future of psychoanalysis. Paper presented to the American Psychoanalytic Association.

On the Identity Crisis in American Psychoanalysis

MAXWELL GITELSON, M.D.

It is thirty years since I have been committed to psychoanalysis. These years span nearly its entire modern period, most of which has been centered in the United States. The events which changed the world after Hitler came to power halted the development of psychoanalysis in Europe and moved it to the western hemisphere with a surviving foothold only in Britain. By far the larger number of European psychoanalysts found a haven and an opportunity for many scientifically productive years in this country. But these years have also seen the gradual appearance of social issues and problems like those which confronted Freud and his early collaborators. I have been in close touch with and to a considerable extent involved in these revived issues and problems and I propose to review and discuss them.

I

Speaking before the A.A.A.S. at its Atlanta meeting in 1955, Harold K. Schilling (1958) referred to science as having the qualities of a "social enter-

Presented under the title, "Psychoanalytic Introspections, Retrospects and Prospects," at the Sunday Morning Plenary Session of the Annual Meeting of the American Psychoanalytic Association, May 3, 1964, Los Angeles.

Reprinted by permission from the *Journal of the American Psychoanalytic Association,* 12: 451–476. New York: International Universities Press, 1964.

prise" which involved interaction, cooperation and sharing. He pointed out that "intersubjective testability" (Sullivan's "consensual validation") is a synonym for "objectivity" and that the word "empirical" refers primarily to social rather than solitary experience. "Science," he said, "is [of necessity] communal." The scientific community is characterized by having its typical way of life; its own ideals, standards, mores, conventions, signs and symbols, language and jargon; its ethics, sanctions, authority and control, its institutions and organizations; "*its own creeds and beliefs, orthodoxies and heresies* [italics added] — and effective ways of dealing with the latter." This way of life is very hard to describe: "nearly ineffable — though nevertheless real. There is something intimate about it, something shared and deeply felt, though unspoken [and] it can be understood only from within the community."

How easy it would be to conclude that the statement I have just cited was made by a devoutly orthodox analyst touting the "psychoanalytic movement." But this is a professor of physics speaking! If we turn to our own "language and jargon" for a moment, who will fail to note that Professor Schilling is paraphrasing the psychoanalytic view that reality testing is not simply a solipsistic ego function but is also a manifestation of social validations internalized in the superego? Does it not seem that "hard science" also has its credo and its "establishment"? And if we think of this, is it so surprising that it was necessary for the pioneers of psychoanalysis to have to struggle for toleration if not acceptance by those whose orthodoxy was nineteenth-century science?

Furthermore, the sciences which preceded psychoanalysis had faced a similar necessity and had been motivated by the same kind of extrascientific dedication. There is nothing inherent in the nature of science which would have insured without effort the continuity of the points of view, ideas, techniques, and findings of those who had become convinced of the validity of empiricism. It took "faith" in the substance of science to provide the energy for engineering the social conditions for its operation. The so-called "basic sciences" also had to struggle for a beachhead in their time, and to work for its consolidation into a viable social organization which could provide the stimulation, collaboration, and mutual criticism which they needed for their survival and development.

In the seventeenth century the Royal Society began as a small group of men who met together to inform and animate each other, and to provide a publication and other means of communication for the spread of scientific knowledge. The French Academy had a similar beginning, as did the American Philosophical Society. Such organizations tend to grow. They are "social movements" out of which a scientific community develops. Their growth is a measure of their success in stimulating scientific creativity. "Scientists look upon social stimulation as a natural resource, and they join up" (Boring, 1963). In the same way those who took up Freud's discoveries and organized the ways and means for their preservation and propagation began what has continued to be called the "psychoanalytic movement." Despite the stigmatic connotation of the word "movement" we see that it is applicable with equal appropriateness to the history of all the sciences.

II

But there is another way of looking at the problem of scientific movements. Recently, Thomas Kuhn's (1963) analysis of "The Structure of Scientific Revolutions" has provided evidence that what *we* refer to as a "movement" is the social reflection of an intellectual crisis in science. Such crises occur when existing basic assumptions in the understanding of natural phenomena no longer work; when new experiences produce paradoxes which do not fit into existing hypotheses. The consequence is an attempt at a new synthesis. In the naturalistic phase of science all phenomena have equal relevance and attention ranges over the whole gamut of facts at hand. The practical crafts were a rich source of such facts and the creative curiosity these evoked was of necessity attended by rationalization. But it is not such primordial beginnings of knowledge that concern us. For it was not until there were theories which attempted to introduce system and method into observations and their rationalization that we had science. Science is as dependent on a point of view as it is on its procedures and observations. Generalizations which are inclusive of these have been called "paradigms" by Kuhn.

A scientific paradigm has the following characteristics: It is a generalization which is "sufficiently unprecedented [and intellectually challenging] to attract an enduring group of adherents away from competing modes of scientific activity"; simultaneously a paradigm "is sufficiently open-ended to leave all sorts of problems for the redefined group of [scientific] practitioners to resolve." A successful paradigm is one that has solved some of the problems that have been outstanding; but its chief importance rests on the fact that at the same time it has redefined the "legitimate problems and methods of a research field" and points to possible directions for its "future articulation and expansion." Thus a paradigm is largely a *promise of success* which must be actualized in the practice of what Kuhn calls "normal science."

Normal science is the long course of follow-up work that succeeds on the appearance and acceptance of a paradigm which has revolutionized a previous outlook on nature; it is the "mopping up operation" which engages most scientists throughout their careers. "Normal science" is what we see in the present state of psychoanalysis as contrasted with the scientific revolution produced by its paradigms. Normal science may be defined as a point of view and mode of research concerned with the solution of puzzles that have been generated by a paradigm. The consensus and commitment produced by a successful paradigm initiate and sustain "normal science."

Physics, astronomy, chemistry, and biology had already experienced a number of intellectual revolutions when psychoanalysis emerged from medicine. Before this audience there is no necessity for even an adumbration of the history of Freud's encounter with paradoxical phenomena which could not be understood in terms of existing biological and medical postulates and which required a new departure. However, it was not the discovery of previously unrecognized phenomena, for example, transference, or the puzzlement produced by old phenomena, such as hypnosis, that produced a scientific crisis. As Kuhn states it: "the act of judgment that leads scientists to reject a previously accepted theory is always based upon more than a comparison of that theory with the world. The decision to reject [an existing paradigm] is always simultaneously a decision to accept another, and the judgment leading to that decision involves the comparison of both paradigms not only with nature *but also with each other*" (italics added).

It is such a fundamental intellectual clash between old and new views which produces scientific revolution. It is the enlistment of followers in the cause of a new paradigm which generates the social mobilization which can be recognized as a "movement" in all the sciences, not only in psychoanalysis to which the term has been applied as a pejorative. Scientific revolutions lead to the restructuring of a given area of knowledge and research; scientific movements provide the necessary social organizations in support of the new idea. While these are at first quite informal, and may in some instances remain so, more often formalization occurs in the organization of new societies, with their meetings, journals, conferences, and committees. These are necessary and useful in carrying on the normal work of a science during its quiet phase when elaboration of the factual details and the solution of new problems projected by a generally accepted paradigm are in process. The question is: what is the optimal degree of such social organization of science?

The scientist needs both privacy and communication. Descartes isolated himself in various hiding places in Holland to ensure the former. But he maintained contacts through an intermediary with selected colleagues with whom he found it possible to exchange both collaborative and controversial views. "It is almost impossible to imagine a scientist's contributing to knowledge without any stimulus at all." The minds of many creative individuals "work best with constant stimulation from small groups of others" — whether these be disciples or peers (Boring, 1963).

However, the continued growth of a society deprives it of its original advantage for its science. This growth results from the fertility of the original idea which it was established to promulgate. A scientific society provides a necessary clearing house for the relevance of the accumulating facts in its field, their fit with its theory, and the possible articulations of ambiguous facts with the theory. It is the latter function which encounters difficulties as the field enlarges and the number of its practitioners increases. For it is in this area that fractures of a paradigm tend to occur. And it is where this danger is present that intimacy, informality, and friendship among small groups of workers in the field make possible the kind of rigorous and collaborative scrutiny which can lead to the identification of articulations or the birth of a new paradigm.

As matters stand, while the social activation of creativity continues to be the professed purpose of scientific societies, professional advantage increases in importance; recognition begins to loom larger as a goal than does scientific achievement; "new little societies [with special interests] are formed in an attempt to recapture the advantages of the lost [social] stimulation" (Boring, 1963). These develop either as splits from the parent body, or by the introduction of organizational structure into small, originally informal groups which feel "starved for social activation." This is what Boring called the "paradoxical growth" by which a healthy scientific society loses its original usefulness and is followed by the appearance of new generations of smaller groups which in turn become too large. "[This] has been the pattern of the proliferation of the sciences" (Boring, 1963). It has occurred along lines of cleavage provided by the evolution of established theory, and in the gaps left by the appearance of insoluble anomalies. As the findings in each field of investigation increase, and as these begin to include paradoxical new findings, the effort to articulate new facts with old theory and new theory with new and old facts produces branchings, divagations, and new departures. In each instance a new supporting "movement" may appear. Movements are an intrinsic aspect of the social nature of the scientific community and of scientific history. Psychoanalysis is of that history and community.

Such "movements" have often been subliminal. The transition from Newtonian physics to relativity theory — not yet fully complete — and the theory of quantum mechanics which in its turn produced doubts and qualms in Einstein are examples of the emergence of new paradigms which have attracted followers — both incidentally and as specialists — followers whose quiet work of application and validation has remained contained within the parent science. Comparably there have been several quietly accepted revisions of theory in psychoanalysis. I refer to such changes as have occurred in the theory of anxiety, in the model of psychic structure, and in the place of ego psychology in genetics and psychic functioning. Such developments in psychoanalysis are of the same order as the theoretical revisions which Kuhn has described for the other sciences. Some of them have been revolutionary. Certainly there have been and there are those who have not gone along with them. But no more than in the case of physics has this sundered the scientific body of psychoanalysis.

However, there are certain peculiar aspects of the process of scientific revolution in psychoanalysis. Some of these stem from intrinsic factors, and others from surrounding historical conditions. I refer to the fact that in psychoanalysis there have been numbers of divergences which have taken schismatic forms. Sometimes these have been lethal theoretical mutations of the parent stock, such as Jungian and Adlerian psychology, in which the theory simply did not fit the body of the relevant facts. I do not intend to dwell on these splits and others like them in the earlier history of psychoanalysis. But there are more recent viable adaptations to new conditions which stem from the psychoanalytic corpus — for example, the so-called "basic science" of psychodynamics and its offspring, dynamic psychiatry and psychotherapy (Gitelson, 1942, 1951, 1956, 1962). Though currently there has appeared an inclination to invalidate even these (Grinker, 1964, p. 230), nevertheless they require our attention since they are the basis for the view — though not stated in these terms — that a scientific revolution is in process in psychoanalysis (Rado, Grinker, and Alexander, 1963). There is an inclination to declare the existing psychoanalytic paradigm defunct or rapidly expiring (Grinker, 1964, p. 228); psychoanalysis, though actually operating as "normal science" (Kuhn, 1963) has been declared bankrupt; a new synthesis which will clarify everything is thought to be already here or visible on the horizon (Grinker, 1964, p. 234).

It is questionable if this is indeed the case. It takes more than the fact that there is something less than a perfect fit between a prevailing theory and its data to vitiate such a theory. For it is one of the functions of a hypothesis to define the existence and nature of unsolved problems for which the hypothesis provides a principle of solution; the normal work of the sciences consists of the application of such principles to the solution of such puzzles; until such puzzles become anomalies which current theory and method can no longer resolve there is no stimulus to new paradigm formation; when such a stimulus is generated by the actual state of affairs in a given science, then a new paradigm may be born; and when that happens and it seems to be more fruitful by comparison with the existing paradigm, in application to the relevant data, then we may speak of the resulting debate on the substantive issues as a state of scientific revolution. Such a debate will inevitably be characterized by the human qualities of the scientifically qualified participants in it, but it will in the end be resolved by the logic of the relevant facts. However, *without a clearly defined alternative paradigm for explicit comparison with an existing paradigm,* and with the facts which are relevant to the problems and anomalies projected by the existing paradigm, *we do not have the conditions for a scientific revolution* (Kuhn, 1963). This I believe to be the situation in psychoanalysis today. Nevertheless, the conditions do obtain for rebellion without a cause. It will be my attempt now to discuss these conditions.

III

By the time the forced emigration of psychoanalysis was at its height it had become more or less stabilized in Europe as a valid branch of knowledge. The criteria for this statement rest on the fact that its basic theories had been formulated and were being examined and extended; that psychoanalytic practitioners and investigators were to be found in most of the countries of Europe and in America; that there was an established literature of journals and books with a relatively wide circulation, and that standards of training and education had been worked out and were being applied. These developments are all concordant with the establishment of "normal science," as Kuhn has described it, after a scientific revolution has been successful. The "psychoanalytic movement," as the inevitable supporting and propagandistic arm of a new development in science, had thus served its purpose and was on the wane.

The paradoxical fact is that in the United States, at the same time, a "movement" was being born. But it was not a psychoanalytic movement. Specifically, it was a two-pronged development: one broadly social — the mental hygiene movement; the other, comparable to the movements we see in underdeveloped areas seeking to eke out their deficits — the efforts of psychiatry to escape from its neurological sterility and institutional thralldom, and to establish for itself a scientific foundation as an effective therapeutic specialty. Thus, even before the political situation in Europe forced the massive transfer of psychoanalysis to the United States, the social situation in the United States had stimulated its importation from Europe. These factors operating together resulted in what has been called a "psychoanalytic movement" in the United States. But as I have indicated, psychoanalysis was already a "normal science" by the time it became established here. It was the hope drawn from it by social idealists and idealistic neurologists and psychiatrists that generated what was really an extra-analytic movement in support of Freud's already accomplished scientific revolution.

As you will remember, until the twenties it was customary for American doctors to complete their educations in the medical centers of Europe. American neuropsychiatrists followed this course toward the new science of psychoanalysis. Returning, they sought out their like-minded fellows and gathered into small psychoanalytic parlor groups, "to inform and animate each other." Like the European pioneers of whom we have been recently reminded by the publication of the *Minutes of the Vienna Psychoanalytic Society* (Nunberg and Federn, 1962), they too made their experiments in the psychoanalytic method; they too debated and discussed its data and concepts. But there was this difference in the early phase of American psychoanalysis: it was welcomed to a landing on the shores of the American scientific community by a significant group of its respected members; it received a serious intellectual hearing — even a band wagon and a honeymoon. For the scientific beach-head had been gained in Europe; in the United States it was carried far inland on an indigenous "wave of the future." Its cogency made psychoanalysis a basic element of human sciences in America — an element which may be denied or disowned but of which there can be no riddance.

Thus, while we can see that the "psychoanalytic movement" was a socio-historical necessity which had its day in Europe, we must also recognize that such a need never really existed here. The over-optimistic burgeoning of the mental hygiene movement in the twenties, and the subsequent expansion of psychiatry as a profession in the thirties were more than enough to foster the social acceptance and scientific prestige of psychoanalysis. In the end this fact has received a curious but not unfamiliar twist. For it was the wishful humanism of the mental hygiene movement and the need for a scientific foundation by a psychiatry whose barrenness diminished its professional stature which, together, projected on psychoanalysis their own extravagant social hopes and ambitions, and fell in love with the image.

The American penchant for getting things done, in so many ways an admirable quality with great social usefulness, provided the conditions for this. There were so many mentally ill people; so many pleas and demands for help. Those of us who came to psychoanalysis from psychiatry were drawn to it intellectually certainly, but we were also driven by social guilt, or something that passed for it. At any rate, dynamic psychiatry and dynamic psychotherapy, the American offspring of psychoanalysis and psychiatry, were generated by this drive (Gitelson, 1951). In different terms such a development was long ago envisioned and welcomed by Freud (1919); it is without question a rational and valid social application of psychoanalysis—one in which analysts may take some pride. Unhappily, however, this has not been the sole outcome.

I began my career in psychiatry and psychoanalysis near the beginning of this unhappy affair. I was, in fact, one of those who was a partner to it (Gitelson, 1942). Under the influence, as I then thought, of the brave campaign to empty the mental hospitals into the child guidance clinics, and the pious hope that ultimately even the need for these would disappear through the instrumentality of psychoanalysis, I participated in these wishes and ambitions. I recognize some here, and there are others in this audience and elsewhere who were my companions in this venture into a brave new world. None of us can say that we were not disillusioned. Unfortunately many have also been bitterly disappointed. The difference is as between insight and transference reaction. The consequences have been several.

It was Freud and his more sophisticated collaborators and successors who first became aware of the existential boundaries of the therapeutic efficacy of the new technique; it was Freud who stated that only neurotic unhappiness and its manifestations could be affected by psychoanalysis, that there were certain limitations even here, and that the most important function of psychoanalysis belonged to its potentialities as an investigative method. The original repudiation of psychoanalysis in Europe which gave the psychoanalytic "movement" its extraordinary intensity was putatively directed against its theory. In the United States the theory not only found a place in the cognate sciences, and among intellectuals generally, but from the beginning and until this day it has had its central place in psychiatry, no matter how misunderstood, disguised, or denied. Nevertheless the stronger appeal of psychoanalysis for American medicine derived from its psychotherapeutic and social hygienic promise. Too much was read into that promise. It is understandable, therefore, that it was the *presumed* universal and exclusive therapeutic efficacy of psychoanalysis that first drew criticism. Only secondary to this has psychoanalytic theory also come into question.

IV

Paradoxically, but not incomprehensible to psychoanalysts, the child has turned against the father while accepting its birthright. Some of the more obvious and prevailing manifestations of this are seen in the terminology. The most well-established is the word "psychodynamic" as a replacement for "psychoanalytic." Another word used similarly though far less extensively is "biodynamics." The phrase "psychoanalytically oriented" is tending to disappear. Increasingly present in current discourse are such terms as "interpersonal" and "transactional"; these sometimes appear in the context of the term "psychoanalysis" or stand by themselves and represent a more exclusive and inclusive generalization. In recent years we have been hearing also the term "adaptational psychodynamics" spoken of as the "introspectional branch of human biology" and said to be derived from Freud's "introduction of the tool of introspection" (*sic!*).[1] The curious fact is that insofar as such terms and propositions have substance, it is to be found in the survival in them of the pale shadow of existing psychoanalytic concepts.[2]

Moving beyond such ambivalent attachment to psychoanalysis, and thus altogether beyond its horizon, are such developments as research that assumes the parity of animal and human psychology, and of the psychoanalytic situation and the psychotherapies derived from psychoanalysis. One is a degradation of the problem presented by the configuration which is the human mind; the other represents insufficient sensitiveness to the meaning of unconscious processes, of resistance, and of transference, all of which are affected by the artifacts that are introduced in psychotherapy.

Lustman (1963) in a recent discussion of current issues in psychoanalytic research comments on the regressive revival of a "nineteenth-century [antitheoretical] criterion of science which is [being] brought to bear on psychoanalytic theory." This is leading "some research analysts to abandon the analytic method for the comparative methodological safety of laboratory research . . .

---

[1]See "International Psychoanalytic Forum Meets in Amsterdam," N.Y. State District Branch (A.P.A.), *Bulletin,* December 1962, p. 11.

[2]Zetzel's (1963) critique of the adaptive hypothesis shows this clearly.

and others to not so creative borrowing." He says further, and I agree with him, that: "The hue and cry for fastidious methods and meticulous theory seem not to recognize that method and theory cannot be superimposed, regardless of fit, but must be precisely geared to the phenomenon under study—if it is to be meaningful even though not neat." Thus, while "lack of experimental sophistication" is one of the "sophisticated" criticisms of psychoanalysis, this attitude overlooks the fact that "experimental sophistication and scientific sophistication are not synonymous" (Lustman, 1963). It is precisely the fact of scientific sophistication "which prevents [or should prevent] analysts from distorting and diluting their area of study through the use of *available* experimental techniques developed by neighboring disciplines" (Lustman, 1963). Nevertheless, we are in the midst of increasing amounts of this sort of thing. The rationalization for it is that psychoanalysis has reached a dead end and is in need of a revolution.

V

There is in the psychiatric literature evidence that psychiatry is once again on the march in search of a scientific foundation (Grinker, 1964). It is held, for example, that psychoanalysis, together with hypnosis, the introspection of the phenomenologists, and the psychotherapy of Janet "swung the emphasis in psychiatry away from description toward deeper phenomena whose 'meanings were interpreted as causes and whose metaphors were considered as reality' "; it is said (regretfully) that the " 'dynamic' approaches within a dyad have superseded and even resulted in a depreciation of the basic psychiatric technique through which so much progress was made in the 19th century"; it is said that "observation of behavior rather than inference about feelings [*sic!*] is the keystone of psychiatric research"; it is said that "the acquisition and validity-testing of behavioral data are the core operations of psychiatry as a science"; and that "careful clinical observations and descriptions *as contrasted with inferences based on stereotypes* [italics added] yield information which can be handled statistically and reported in form suitable for replication and for correlation with other measurable systems." Such expressions in the community of "big science" are significant for psychoanalysis because they represent a return of the repressed in the form of the wish to reverse history by expunging the effects that psychoanalysis has had and still exerts on psychiatry—even if this be only in the form of "psychodynamics." I think they represent repudiations of psychoanalysis.

This is the sort of thing which I have referred to previously as rebellion without a cause. This is a return to a naturalistic pre-paradigmatic state of science in which human phenomenology is dehydrated into existence in "a total field of multiple transactions *without connotations of significance, hierarchical importance or conceptual devices called levels*" (Grinker, 1964; italics added). In effect, we are being advised to go fishing with whatever bait we have and see what we come up with. There is nothing wrong with this excepting for its scientific atavism. It is rather late in the day for us to disregard the fact that we know the differential ecology of trout and shark and that to catch one or the other we have to know where we are and what we are looking for. It is too late for us to expunge the experience which sixty years of psychoanalysis has brought to us. Nevertheless, scientism in the accoutrements of science seems to have large attractions.

VI

Paul Weiss (1962) has discussed a comparable problem in biology. "Experience prompts and guides experiment," he says, and "experiments confirm or amplify or modify the content of experience. . . . Experience, experiment and logic play back and forth upon each other in mutual enhancement; it takes this triple interplay to promote knowledge." But (in biology) experiment is a "junior partner in this partnership." Its targets must be the products of experience which should shape expectation and expectation should dictate experiment. "The historic successes of our predecessors still argue for the virtue of taking off for the exploration of the unknown from clear-cut questions born from expectations, not from vague expectancy . . ." (Weiss, 1962), and expectations arise from experience.

We can see the cogency of this to our own field if we are reminded of the fact that it was Freud's preliminary experience with hypnosis and with forced verbalization which produced the "expectations" which resulted in that most long-sustained and most often repeated of all experiments — the use of free association in the analytic situation. In the years that have passed it has become clear that the very knowledge we have gained from that experiment has, within the context of psychoanalysis, precluded its modification. For it happens to have shown itself to be exquisitely suited for both confronting nature "with conditions unprecedented in her standard repertory" (Weiss, 1962) *and at the same time* preserving full respect for the human prerogatives of the subject. An alternative experiment capable of demonstrating endopsychic and interpsychic processes without violating our human responsibility has not yet been devised. Thus we are confronted by a paradox for scientific method: the psychoanalytic experiment has itself become an extended life experience which, as such, provides a foundation for possible conventional experiments based on expectations logically derived from that experience.

What I am trying to demonstrate is that psychoanalysis, an aspect of biology, occupies middle ground between the extreme scientific positions of physics and historical learning. The one concentrates on general principles expressible in a minimal number of formulae. The other is concerned with "the particular, specific and often unique shape of events." The life sciences have moved along this axis from the descriptive-normative toward the analytical-formulative (Weiss, 1962). But psychoanalysis, like biology, will never attain as such the putatively complete reductionism of physics. Like biology, it is destined to retain its autonomy — its mechanisms will have to be studied in their own right and in their full diversity; its generalizations, which are bound to stop short of the inclusiveness of the laws of physics, may each be subject to experimentation. But no such studies of the human personality will have their necessary scientific sophistication, no matter how refined their "design," unless they are governed by the psychoanalytic experience.

As a matter of fact, a number of psychoanalytic generalizations have been examined by nonanalytic methods, but so far as I am aware no such study has been other than confirmative. Nothing has been found that did not fit psychoanalytic theory when it was psychoanalytic theory that was being tested. Hartmann (1964) has said of such efforts that on the whole they have "not so far decisively contributed toward a clarification or systematization of psychoanalytic theory." Despite all claims to the contrary there are lacking the prime requirements for a scientific revolution: apparent counterinstances which do not articulate with existing theory, and new theory which bears more heavily on known facts. When these considerations are kept in mind assertions such as: "psychoanalysis . . . has not become the therapeutic answer" and psychoanalysis "seems to have mired in a theoretical rut vigilantly guarded by the orthodox and, except for relatively few examples, prevented from commingling with science" (Grinker, 1964) — such assertions, I repeat, remain simply that. The one is irrelevant; the other is incorrect.

This is only a sampling of the situation out of which there has developed a new "movement" — though none of its protagonists would like to consider it that. It is a movement without scientific grounds: it has not invalidated any of the data of psychoanalysis; it ignores the articulations which psychoanalysis has effected between its data and its theory; it has not exposed new data which cannot be articulated with psychoanalytic theory; it appears to be unaware of the developments in psychoanalytic ego psychology which in fact meet the criticisms which have been directed against the putative solipsism of psychoanalytic theory; and most important, it has not produced the shadow of a comprehensive theory which can be weighed against psychoanalytic theory and the data on which it is based. We are presented with a point of view which has no thesis — only an antithesis in the form of a shibboleth: "dogmatic orthodoxy."

VII

Let me refer again to Kuhn's (1963) monograph beginning on its page 77. I shall quote from it while making running insertions to clarify points specifically relevant to psychoanalysis:

"Let us then assume" Kuhn says, "that crises [in science] are a necessary pre-condition for the emergence of novel theories and ask how scientists respond to their existence. Part of the answer, as obvious as it is important, can be discovered *by noting first what scientists never do* when confronted by even prolonged and severe anomalies; *they do not renounce the paradigm which has led them into crisis.* They do not, that is, treat anomalies as counterinstances . . . this generalization is simply a statement from historic fact . . . once it has achieved the status of a paradigm, *a scientific theory is declared invalid only if an alternative candidate is available to take its place*" (all italics added). It is not enough to dream wishfully for the coming into being of an alternative candidate for paradigm status. Nor, as I have said before, does an apparently new fact without an adequate theory to account for it upset a previous theory; it simply becomes one of the puzzles which the existing theory may not be able to solve, though it may indeed one day be solved by the actual birth of a new paradigm.

This is the state of affairs in psychoanalysis. No more than other scientists can psychoanalysts reject their paradigms when faced with anomalies or counterinstances. "They could not do so and still remain scientists. Though history is unlikely to record their names some men have undoubtedly been driven to desert science because of their inability to tolerate crisis. Like artists, creative scientists [and psychoanalysts] must occasionally be able to live in a world out of joint . . . [and to endure] the 'essential tension' implicit in scientific research. . . . Once a paradigm through which to view nature has been found, there is no research in the absence of the paradigm. To reject one paradigm without simultaneously substituting another is to reject science itself. That act reflects not on the paradigm but on the man. Inevitably it will be seen by his colleagues as 'the carpenter who blames his tools.' . . . [For] there is no such thing as research without counterinstances . . . the puzzles that constitute normal science exist only because no paradigm that provides a basis for scientific research [in any field] ever completely resolves all these problems . . . every problem that normal science sees as a puzzle can be seen, from another viewpoint, as a counterinstance and thus as a source of crisis" (Kuhn, 1963).

Restating the issue in my own terms, it is not enough to declare that there are seeming divergences from theory, as is the case with those who turn away from psychoanalysis. Such divergences must in fact be proven to be unassimilable into the existing theory whose validity, as I have shown, must in the meanwhile be assumed. If this cannot be accomplished, then indeed a new theory must be attempted. But the evidence for its cogency must be convincing if it is to generate a scientific revolution. We do not have such evidence.

VIII

This brings me again to the history of American psychoanalysis. We have seen that, like the other sciences, psychoanalysis has had its paradoxical social growth: its arduous and small beginnings, its heyday of enthusiastic and rapid development, and, in the United States, its attainment of at least relatively large organizational stature with its inevitable offshoots. What is interesting and important for us today is the particular nature of the paradox which has characterized the growth of psychoanalysis here.

It can be said that in the United States psychoanalysis and psychiatry grew up together. At the same time that the Nazi storm was scattering psychoanalysis in Europe, psychiatry was at last becoming a profession in the United States. The American Board of Psychiatry and Neurology was organized in 1934; its examinations paid more than a little attention to "psychodynamics." As early as 1932 psychiatrists were receiving foundation support for higher level training in psychiatry—that is, in psychoanalysis.[3] In my own psychiatric beginnings case conferences were already "psychoanalytically oriented"; out of a group of ten interns (there were no "residents"), three about whom I knew were being formally analyzed, while the rest of us were, of course, "analyzing" each other. When I was being examined for the Board by one of the great psychiatrists of the day I did not find it surprising, or unfair, or offensive that he asked me to account psychoanalytically for the disappearance of a life-long stammer in the acutely ill schizophrenic patient who had been assigned to me. The point is that psychoanalysis in the United States grew simultaneously from two directions. Its pioneers and its students arrived on the scene together.

These happenings did not stem from a psychoanalytic movement. As we have seen, that had had its necessary day in Europe. In the United States the psychoanalytic idea no longer needed such fosterage. Psychiatrists were not turning to the new psychoanalytic institutes because these were conducting a campaign for converts. The students of the institutes were the progeny of the mental hygiene movement and of the reborn psychiatry of the thirties. They were turning toward what seemed a promise for the future to many of their leaders as well as to themselves. The Second World War affirmed this (Gitelson, 1955). Psychoanalysis, deployed as dynamic psychiatry, was able to meet the demands of a brutal reality. Psychiatry discovered that even with only the rudiments of psychoanalytic theory it was possible for medical officers to qualify for the kind of psychotherapeutic improvisation that Freud had looked forward to (Freud, 1919). The military experience confirmed for psychiatry its own hopes of the thirties that psychoanalysis could indeed provide it with a psychotherapeutic rationale. The postwar consequence was a tremendous surge toward psychiary and psychoanalysis as *a profession*. I state this in the singular because the choice was unitary; psychiatry without psychoanalysis had become unthinkable (Brosin, 1952; Gitelson, 1951, 1956, 1962).

It seems necessary to repeat, *for this is the crux of the matter:* the rapid growth of American psychoanalysis in the last twenty years has been the consequence of

---

[3]For example, at the Chicago Institute for Psychoanalysis.

its being caught in the current of a new social movement — now the mental *health* movement. Psychiatry carried psychoanalysis along for its own purposes in this movement and is disappointed to discover that the real thing is rather more of a burden than the idea of it.[4] On the other hand, *psychoanalysis has become involved in a crisis which is not its own.* The nature of its beginnings in America, and the perpetuation of that in its statutory requirements for affiliation with psychiatry, have placed psychoanalysis in an impossible position for the untrammeled development of its intrinsic scientific possibilities. Psychoanalysts having had social responsibility thrust upon them by the exigencies of the World War crisis have found themselves committed to it in peace.

Reacting to this pressure, the American Psychoanalytic Association at one point considered the possibility of drastically modifying basic principles of training (Gitelson, 1948). A number of institutes for a time actually experimented with modifications. While all this proved fruitless, there *was* a considerable postwar expansion of existing institutes, an increase in their number, and a corresponding increase in admissions to training. The impelling motives were first, the feeling that it was necessary to match the expansion of a psychiatry in which "dynamic psychology" had become an established fact of life; and second, the wish to take advantage of government money which had become available for that purpose. Not only was there a great increase in the number of candidates but in the opposite direction there was an unprecedented demand, to which analysts responded, to undertake the teaching of the "dynamic psychiatry" which the best residencies required. This was not a bad idea. Psychiatry and psychoanalysis can supplement each other. But neither has been content with that and each has suffered consequences (Gitelson, 1962).

On the one hand, those engaged in the training of psychiatrists have attempted an outright transplantation of psychoanalysis into the wards and clinics (Gitelson, 1962). Alternatively, those trained in these wards and clinics have tended to bring with them into analysis often ineradicable eclectic attitudes which are incompatible with the postulates and methods of a special field (Gitelson, 1954). I am in agreement with Rado's position[5] that "psychiatry is a heterogeneous collection of basic sciences without unified structure." In this respect it is like medicine whose therapeutic eclecticism is necessarily dictated by the variety of the fields of knowledge which are concerned with the phenomenon in which it is interested. It need be no derogation to speak of psychiatry as riding "in all directions" (Grinker, 1964). Psychiatry as such is not a science: it

---

[4]The "Associated Psychiatric Faculties" of Chicago, which attempted for some years to operate a unified training program in collaboration with the Chicago Institute for Psychoanalysis, in the end suspended the effort.

[5]As reported in (Grinker, 1964, p. 229), referring to "5: Rado, S., in Hoch, P. and Zubin, J., editors: *The Future of Psychiatry,* New York: Grune and Stratton Inc., 1962."

would indeed be derelict if it did not search out everything the natural and social sciences can offer to support its great and necessary labor. But psychoanalysis *is* a basic science: despite the fact of its unavoidable embedment in a
special therapeutic procedure it is first and foremost human individual psychology. Out of the necessity of its subject matter *it cannot be other* than that its
postulates, theories, and methods must be special and separate. Psychoanalysis is not psychiatry; it is only selectively applicable in psychiatry even as mechanics, or chemistry, or molecular biology are applicable in medicine. Psychiatry can enrich the life experience of the psychoanalyst. It cannot determine
the scientific course of psychoanalysis. Thus, only in the light of the history of
psychoanalysis in the United States can one accept as reasonable a recent editorial in the *Journal of the American Medical Association* (March, 21, 1964) which
begins with the statement: "Psychiatry *and* [italics added] psychoanalysis today
have not lived up to their well-advertised and hoped-for promise." I would consider this a fitting obituary for a marriage of convenience.

IX

I have been discussing the historical basis of the crisis which psychoanalysis
has borrowed from psychiatry. However, this is not its only problem. In another place (Gitelson, 1964), I have referred at some length to other factors that
need to be considered and in the present context I shall again mention one of
them. I refer to our own discontent with the apparent stasis in the scientific development of psychoanalysis. Many are puzzled and troubled that there seems
to be no sign of impending "break-throughs" — even though some of the pessi-
mists have themselves been brilliant participants in the achievements of the
past. We tend to overlook or to discount the continuing and able spadework
which goes on and which is, as I have noted, the task of any science during its
"normal" period of testing and working through (Kuhn, 1963). More than we
like to contemplate we are reacting to the conditions of which I have been
speaking, and to the existential anxiety of our times (Gitelson, 1964). There
may be among ourselves a return of the repressed. Such factors, I think, may be
having their reflected as well as direct effects on younger colleagues particularly. Add to this the social conditions created by the present inflation of scientific currency (Lustman, 1963; Gitelson, 1964), and we receive some hint of
the motives for the excessive ardor attached to the hope for and the pursuit of a
revolution in psychoanalysis. In some instances the latter has burst through
the boundaries of our field (Lustman, 1963).

   This is not to say that there is not a quiet ferment going on within the body of
psychoanalysis today. There have always been the individuals, the unique
ones among us — some of them so-called controversial figures — who have been

continuously stirring the brew which we have elected to cook.[6] There are also informal and more or less formal small groups pursuing the solution of puzzles generated by and relevant to the psychoanalytic paradigm.[7] And there are now larger organized trends toward the stimulation of thought and work in psychoanalysis — I refer to the projected postgraduate program of the American Psychoanalytic Association. All this is characteristic of a living science during its longer or shorter "normal" state after one paradigmatic revolution and before the *bona fide* appearance of another one. Revolutions arise from such internal ferment. They do not, like tumorous growths "unrestrained by differentiation and functional adjustment" (Weiss, 1962) burst through their organismal boundaries. Revolutions in science are born, not made. Unfortunately, in American psychoanalysis this is obscured by the fact that schism has had the putative direction of "liberalization." Whatever implications it may have for the therapeutic applications of psychoanalysis, this appealing political term applied to the work of a science serves only to obscure the definition of that science rather than to report a revolutionary development in it.

It may be that this view will seem oriented toward a policy of isolation. On the contrary, I am proposing a policy of "differentiation and functional adjustment" within the context of the human sciences as a whole. This is not a new proposal. It is the position arrived at nearly forty years ago by Freud (1926, 1927). I, myself, have moved through most of my career to come to it.

To sustain this position it is necessary to define clearly the differences between psychoanalysis as a profession and psychoanalysis as a scientific activity. In the first aspect we have gone a great way in the United States. Much of what I have said is concerned with the history of that course and its consequences. These consequences include much that is good. I think it is correct that the therapeutic application of psychoanalysis and its derivatives have found a wider scope here than anywhere else in the relevant Western world; and this is not to be decried. But the problems of psychoanalysis in the United States have arisen because the course of this achievement has obscured the boundaries of psychoanalysis as an investigative science. Therapeutic versatility and scientific rigor are incompatible. Those who impugn psychoanalysis as "rigid" overlook this. They do not recognize, or they refuse to accept, the necessity for the integrity of the classical model of the psychoanalytic situation as the only available condition for the controlled study of human individual psychology in its deepest sense.

Perhaps this is too much to ask of doctors of medicine whose calling stems from the healing impulse. Perhaps it is necessary to revise the exclusive

---

[6]Erikson's and Rapaport's work may be considered examples of this.

[7]The collaboration of Hartmann, Kris, and Loewenstein, and of the Yale group are examples of this.

operational relationship between psychoanalysis and psychiatry. Perhaps we must realize that we need to redefine our place in the family of sciences and to redesign our format accordingly.

X

Freud's (1927) view was that "psychoanalysis is not a specialized branch of medicine" and that "a scheme of training for psychoanalysts . . . must include elements from the mental sciences, from psychology, the history of civilization and sociology, as well as from anatomy, biology and the study of evolution." Kubie (1954, 1957) not so long ago gave considerable thought to these problems and proposed a specialized modern curriculum and a distinctive degree for students primarily interested in psychotherapy (and psychoanalysis?). More recently Shakow (1962) proposed that if psychoanalytic institutes are to be attached to universities, then they ought to have independent academic status and be available to all relevant departments, including the medical school. I do not discount such ideas. They may perhaps one day materialize. But I think it is necessary to start from where we are today.

Therapeutic emphasis in psychoanalytic training is eventuating in psychoanalytic careers which are increasingly eclectic, increasingly indistinguishable from the skilled practice of intensive psychotherapy, increasingly validating the position of those who a few years back favored the establishment of a psychoanalytic subspecialty board of the American Board of Psychiatry and Neurology. No one can object to this in so far as it provides a higher grade of professional care for those who can benefit from it. For I think the primary function of psychiatry is *mental healing*. Therapeutic psychoanalysis may be considered a part of it — if you wish. Therapeutic psychoanalysis, and its modifications and derivatives — whether they carry the name or not — is therefore here to stay. However, the danger foreseen by Freud (1927) and now materializing, is that therapeutic investment may submerge scientific development. None more than psychoanalysts understand and value the importance of the ramifications of *affect, feeling,* and *emotion;* and none are more subject to the essentially *anti-intellectual trends* which, in recent years, have been expressing themselves "intellectually" toward the psychoanalytic method of scientific investigation. The problems for psychoanalytic training today arise from these facts.

In the same context as the one from which I have previously quoted him, Freud (1927) said: "I am bound to admit that, so long as schools such as we desire for the training of analysts are not yet in existence, people who have had a preliminary education in medicine are the best material for future analysts." This situation has not changed. The history of psychoanalysis in this country commits it to training medically qualified therapeutic specialists. Does this mean that we may not reconsider the qualifications which are important for those who can be psychoanalysts with scientific grounding and outlook as well as with the rudiments of technical skill?

Perhaps it is necessary to cast a wider net for students of psychoanalysis. The emotional qualities that ensure the fulfillment of the human obligation to patients are basic to the practice of medicine. But in the psychoanalytic field the practitioner must also have the intellectual qualities and scope which will bring to it the necessary scientific sophistication. The present timorous and tentative approach to the training of specialists from other disciplines, *for research in their own fields,* conceivably might be bolder and broadened into a program of unhedged training which would fully qualify them for a research career in psychoanalysis itself. The prevailing tendency to place exclusive value on antecedent psychiatric training as such may need to be revised in respect to the barrier it erects against scientists with other qualifications who might advance the conceptual horizon of psychoanalysis (Shakow, 1962). While there may have been valid reasons in the late thirties for American psychoanalysis to declare its exclusive adhesion to medicine as its parent discipline, the question must be raised whether these reasons retain their cogency today. In respect to this it may be comforting to recall that psychiatry itself has gone a long way since then and is looking with favor on the practice of psychotherapy by psychologists, the clergy, and other persons of good will.

It is clear that I have returned to the "question of lay analysis" (Freud, 1927). I have been turned in this direction by my consideration of the history of psychoanalysis in America and of the upshot of that in its present situation. *I think the time has come for psychoanalysis to accept its identity as a separate scientific discipline* whose practitioners can be various kinds of intellectually qualified persons who are humanly qualified for the human experiment which is the psychoanalytic situation.

XI

It could be argued that the debate in which I have been engaged this morning is itself evidence of a scientific crisis *in* psychoanalysis and of a pending scientific revolution in the field. However, this debate is not concerned with the scientific substance of psychoanalysis but with the social and psychological issues surrounding that substance. It is a debate peculiar to our field in which matrix cannot with ease be separated from substance. It is a debate which is compelled by what is clearly a "countermovement" to psychoanalysis which itself had long ago ceased to be a "movement" and had become concerned only with its substance.

I suppose I should feel apologetic to this audience for belaboring it with such argumentation as I have. I feel no such need. I think it is necessary for all of us to be reminded of what we know. The point is that analysis does not end all conflict; it provides us only with a tool for dealing with it under future unforeseen conditions of life which may evoke old conflicts and stimulate new ones. As it happens Freud predicted such future conditions in the United States and we are now in their midst. The repressed has returned. In a new social situation which attaches rich secondary gains to conventional scientific compliance, the effort at re-repression is taking the form of dilution or denial of what we know. We suffer not only from confusion about what psychoanalysis is, but also from irresolution about what its position should be. We are caught in an identity conflict between psychiatry which is a therapeutic speciality of medicine and psychoanalysis which is a basic science. In such a situation, confrontation, I hope, may free us to analyze rather than to "act," and to behave in accordance with our understanding.

REFERENCES

Boring, E. G. (1963), The social stimulus to creativity. *Science,* 142:622–623.

Brosin, H. W. (1952), Psychoanalytic training for psychiatric residents and others. *Amer. J. Psychiat.,* 109:188–195.

Freud, S. (1919), Turnings in the ways of psycho-analytic therapy. *Collected Papers,* 2:392–402. London: Hogarth Press, 1959.

_____ (1926), The question of lay analysis. *Standard Edition,* 20:183–250. London: Hogarth Press, 1959.

_____ (1927), Postscript. *Standard Edition,* 20:251–258. London: Hogarth Press, 1959.

Gitelson, M. (1942), Evaluation of therapeutic results in psychotherapy. In: *Proceedings of the Brief Psychotherapy Council.* Chicago: Institute for Psychoanalysis.

_____ (1948), Problems of psychoanalytic training. *Psychoanal. Quart.,* 17:198–211.

_____ (1951), Psychoanalysis and dynamic psychiatry. *A.M.A. Arch. Neurol. & Psychiat.,* 16:280–288.

_____ (1954), Therapeutic problems in the analysis of the "normal" candidate. *Internat. J. Psycho-Anal.,* 35:174–187.

_____ (1956), Psychoanalysis, U.S.A., 1955. *Amer. J. Psychiat.,* 112:700–705.

_____ (1962), The place of psychoanalysis in psychiatric training. *Bull. Menn. Clin.,* 26:57–72.

_____ (1964), On the present scientific and social position of psychoanalysis. *123d Bull. I.P.A.,* in *Internat. J. Psycho-Anal.,* 44:521–527.

Grinker, R. R., Sr. (1964), Psychiatry rides madly in all directions. *A.M.A. Arch. Gen. Psychiat.,* 10:228–237.

Hartmann, H. (1959), Psychoanalysis as a scientific theory. In: *Essays on Ego Psychology.* New York: International Universities Press, 1964.

Kubie, L. S. (1954), The pros and cons of a new profession: A doctorate in medical psychology. *Texas Reports on Biol. & Med.,* 12:125–170.

_____ (1957), Need for a new subdiscipline in the medical profession. *A.M.A. Arch. Neurol. & Psychiat.,* 78:283–293.

Kuhn, T. S. (1963), *The Structure of Scientific Revolutions.* Chicago: University of Chicago Press.

Lustman, S. L. (1963), Some issues in contemporary psychoanalytic research. *The Psychoanalytic Study of the Child,* 18:51–74. New York: International Universities Press.

Nunberg, H., & Federn, E., eds. (1962), *Minutes of the Vienna Psychoanalytic Society,* Vol. 1. New York: International Universities Press.

Rado, S., Grinker, R. R., Sr., & Alexander, F. (1963), Editorial. *A.M.A. Arch. Gen. Psychiat.,* 8:527-529.

Schilling, H. K. (1958), A human enterprise. *Science,* 127:1324-1327.

Shakow, D. (1962), Psychoanalytic education of behavioral and social scientists for research. *Science and Psychoanalysis,* 5:146-161. New York: Grune and Stratton.

Weiss, P. (1962), Experience and experiment in biology. *Science,* 136:468-471.

Zetzel, E. R. (1963), The significance of the adaptive hypothesis for psychoanalytic theory and practice. *J. Amer. Psychoanal. Assn.,* 11:652-660.

II THEORETICAL CONCEPTS

Introduction

Part II includes four papers from one section of the Western Regional Psychoanalytic Societies' Meeting on "Change and Integration in Theoretical Concepts." These papers address fundamental concepts, developmental theory, and psychopathology, all from a historical and current perspective. Complementing these presentations is a historical paper by Heinz Hartmann, written in 1959.

In the first paper, Rudolf Ekstein looks at the changes that have occurred in the fundamental concepts of psychoanalysis from the vantage point of his own introduction to psychoanalytic theory in Vienna, as well as changes in his own thinking from those early years to the present. His focus is on the process of change in psychoanalysis and psychotherapy and on the languages used in the interpretive process with patients and in discussion among analysts.

In the second paper, Morton and Estelle Shane present a careful reassessment of preoedipal developmental theory. They discuss the challenges to conventional theory posed by experimental studies on infants and children. Arguing the need for efforts to integrate various theories, they offer an integration of the developmental postulates of Mahler and Kohut with each other and with psychosexual theory.

The third paper of this section, by Robert Nunn, offers a comprehensive review of developments and change in the theories of psychopathology—from Freud and Breuer's *Studies on Hysteria* to what Nunn terms the "contemporary period." He proposes an integration of historical and contemporary theories of psychopathology and suggests a conceptualization designed to eliminate current contradictions between so called "deficit" and "conflict" pathologies.

In his discussion, Sherwyn Woods challenges the three previous presentations. Using a clinical vignette, he raises a number of questions that underline the reasons for the complexity of current theorizing. At the same time, he too argues for integration and criticizes the main body of psychoanalysis for its resistance to innovation and a tendency to exclude, rather than integrate, new knowledge and concepts.

The historical paper by Heinz Hartmann was chosen because it offers the reader an opportunity to review the theoretical position and scientific status of psychoanalysis, as perceived in 1959 by one of the most influential contributors to psychoanalytic theory.

The Editors

4

Fundamental Concepts: Prolegomena to the Study of the Languages of Psychoanalysis and Psychotherapy

RUDOLF EKSTEIN, Ph.D.

The title that I have chosen for my work makes plain which of the traditional approaches to the problem of dreams I am inclined to follow. The aim which I have set before myself is to show that dreams are capable of being interpreted.... For "interpreting" a dream implies assigning a "meaning" to it....
— Sigmund Freud (1900)

A philosopher has temptations which an ordinary person does not have. We could say he knows better what the word means than the others do. But actually philosophers generally know less *because ordinary people have no temptations to misunderstand language.*
— Ludwig Wittgenstein (1936)

These quotations indicate the basic thrust of this paper, which is in the nature of a *prolegomenon* or introduction to the hermeneutic aspects of psychoanalysis. The theory of meaning underlying communication systems within psychoanalysis as applied to psychotherapy has long been an interest of mine.

I would like to clothe my considerations of changes that have taken place in psychoanalysis in an autobiographical garb (see also Ekstein, 1972). As I re-

member my beginning in the field — the first sessions and seminars in Vienna
and the study of the literature — I imagine that time as unburdened by theoretical scruples. It seemed a time of comparative simplicity when psychoanalytic
theory seemed clear and simple, beyond dispute, almost inviting naive faith,
in spite of the fact that I came to psychoanalysis from the usual university
struggles with philosophical and sociological disputes of the time. That was a
time of searching for clarity; and the *Wiener Kreis* (the philosophy group of the
foremost students of Wittgenstein, Schlick, Carnap, Neurath, Zilsel, and
others) seemed to place my search for and love of truth into a convincing frame.
My view of the philosophical world divided language into meaningful and
meaningless propositions: a statement that could be verified or falsified was
meaningful; and that which could not be verified and could not be falsified in
principle had no meaning. The simplicity of that philosophy was tempting and
reassuring for a short time, since the problem of my search for meaning could
be solved on the surface of everday grammar. But it applied to only a small
area of the concern in our field with language — with communication of meaning in a wider and deeper sense of the word.

After that small university island, I discovered another island, the Vienna
Psychoanalytic Institute. As long as one remained on an island of communication, things seemed to be very easy. It all depended on the capacity of a young
student to identify with the way the teacher spoke, and to ignore all other ways
of speaking or communicating. Those simple transferences and identifications
with my teachers would not last long, however. Even at that time we struggled
in seminars with differences of opinion and differences of language that needed
to be resolved — with the Adlerians and the Jungians, whose theories were simply considered deviations from the basic positions of the master. While dealing
with various academic schools of thought — with those who had left Freud by
then (Jung, Adler, Rank) — I created a safe island of learning for myself in
preparation for a career. My first analytic publications reflected that naive
early view.

Soon after my training at the Institute I had to escape my native country because of the Nazi invasion and occupation, and found myself in America as a
refugee. Before long, I felt some beginning uneasiness, probably due to my
early philosophical training, which taught me to look at communication with
an eye that requires (to use a phrase of the Wittgensteinians) that one "see
through the surface grammar of a word to its depth grammar" (McGuinness,
1982). That was true for me, not only for the communication of the patients,
but also for the language of the therapist or psychoanalyst; and not only for the
language of the therapeutic process, but also for communication systems between analysts and in groups of analysts.

It was no wonder that I experienced the American world, removed as I was
from the comparatively unified language in the Institute in Vienna, as
strange. I now found myself in a new world of struggle on the East Coast,

which reminded me of God's punishment of a confusion of tongues inflicted on the people who had dared to build the Tower of Babel. At that time I published a paper (Ekstein, 1950) called *The Tower of Babel in Psychology and Psychiatry: Towards a Theory of Determinants in Psychology,* written several years earlier in an attempt to clarify for myself the struggle among the different schools of psychology, psychoanalysis, and psychiatry — a struggle that has not ended, and still competes in the marketplace. I often yearned then for the simplicity of the early days at Berggasse, although I have since discovered that it only seemed simple to me as a young student — a willing follower in need of an intellectual home that offered faith and a safe language. It is now not the mother tongue, but rather the father tongue, the language not simply of early desire, but of later capacity to compete and to function on a higher level. Where Id was, there must now be ego.

The urgent need for the safe home — that powerful Tower of Babel with only one language within the unity of the family — can surely be recognized in the ongoing need of students to belong to a special school of thought, to master the chosen language of the master teacher with whom one identifies. The search for that unifying father, the commitment to him and his chosen group, can be found in every university department and certainly also in our psychoanalytic institutes. The early *idealization,* that Tower of Babel complex, must give way to *realization* and its transition period: the confusion of the tongues. How easy it was to speak the mother tongue, and how difficult it will be with the different tongues of the fathers. A process has to be lived through, which leads from the Oedipal struggle to its heir — the scientific conscience and the task of the examination of language, its surface as well as its depth grammar.

The paper (1950) cited above was one of my early steps in that direction. Just as in the psychoanalytic process, in this task of philosophical clarification there is no real end; there is only an ongoing process. There is no final thought, only continued thinking. At that time, I suggested that we should look at theories in psychoanalysis and psychotherapy in terms of ideological components, which can only be fully understood if we keep in mind that every theory is really a secret, a covert description of the therapeutic instruments that the therapist is using. The different schools of psychotherapy offer theories of personality that are simply reflections of a way we deal with patients and communicate with them. Therefore, they are incomplete and constantly open to change. The dogmatic or ideological aspect of each theory and its form should be considered as stimulus for research along such lines, with less stress on the explanatory value of the theories and more on their value as indirect prescriptions for psychotherapeutic techniques or ways of communicating with patients for the purpose of therapeutic change.

Each theory, if we are willing to view it as a commitment to a special therapeutic language, is aimed at change; and it is primarily in this realm that the theory is also to have predictive power, requiring rules of verification and falsification, a task for scientific research in the field of psychotherapeutic activity. Of course, each theory also lends itself to studies in the field of emotional and mental development, and to applications in other fields of human endeavor. But the discussion in this presentation is limited to *psychoanalysis as a technical instrument of change.*

Nearly a decade later, my concern (Ekstein, 1959) moved away from reflections about the nature of theory to reflections about the nature of interpretation; but my general thinking was still aimed toward developing a theory of determinants in psychology. Instead of one comparatively simple family of psychoanalysis, that I recalled nostalgically from the institute in Vienna, there were now many psychoanalytic training centers, which were united in one large organization, but spoke different languages.

The following quotation from Scriptures suggests in more poetic form the new state of affairs in psychoanalysis that I tried to deal with at that time:

> And Jehova said, "Behold, they are one people, and they have all one language; and this is what they begin to do: And now nothing will be withholden from them, which they purpose to do. Come, let us go down, and there confound their language, that they may not understand one another's speech." So Jehovah scattered them abroad from thence upon the face of all the Earth: And they left off building the city. Therefore was the name of it called Babel; because Jehovah did there confound the language of all the Earth: And from thence did Jehovah scatter them abroad upon the face of all the Earth.

When psychoanalysis was driven out of central Europe, those of us forced to emigrate suffered from the confusion of the tongues in more than one sense. Not only did we lose our old home and the old certainty, but we were confronted with a broader — perhaps a richer — but often a diluted application of the work of Freud and the first and second generation of his students and colleagues. In more than one way, I wanted to sharpen my ear and hear better what was being said and what was meant in the psychotherapeutic dialogue that takes place within the analytic, therapeutic situation.

My major interest was in the nature of interpretation. What is meant by "interpretation"? Frequently, the patient experiences the analyst's words as an explanation. Is "interpretation" an explanation? Many descriptions of clinical events give the impression that the therapist often uses language which seems to explain to the patient what he or she is doing and how the patient came to be this way. The dialogue seems to describe a psychological situation in which the patient expects an answer from the authority, hoping for a final explanation that will make his life clear, perhaps even listening for a secret order that will force him to change. The analyst, then, has to work constantly with the transference distortion, and we are reminded of Freud's (1914) phrasing, when he spoke of his procedure as the analysis of transference and resistance.

At times, Fenichel (1935) spoke about interpretation as a method of translation — the translation of the unconscious to the conscious. He suggests that:

> When there is a minimum of distance between allusion and what is alluded to, the analyst gives the patient words to express feelings just rising to the surface and thereby facilitates their becoming conscious....This procedure of deducing what the patient actually means and telling it to him is called interpretation.

Here the stress is not on explanatory power, but rather on the search for meaning. But even here, Fenichel speaks about interpretation as if it were a pronouncement and as if there is a final meaning — *the* meaning. It reminds us of the revelations that God gives or withholds from us. I am also reminded of Freud's (1900) comment in a letter to Fliess, when he spoke about the secret of the dream having revealed itself to him. Such language overawes the listener or reader by indirectly forcing one to overvalue the noun — the interpretation or the revelation. The use of the noun, perhaps, characterizes the position of the therapist in the patient's mind and the transference situation, and it does not allow us to move toward a concept of interpretation that includes empathy, affect, subtle interpersonal meaning, and above all, the notion of process and change.

At this time (Ekstein, 1959), I suggested another difficulty which stands in the way of fully appreciating the nature of the psychoanalyst's work. Freud (1900) actually spoke about *Deutung,* telling us in the second chapter of *The Interpretation of Dreams* that he deliberately chose the word *Deutung* in order to return to a view that was given up by the scientists of his day. He chose the word used by pre-scientific dream interpreters, and he spoke of "the art of *Deutung,*" noting that its origin is pre-scientific, religious or superstitious, and subjective in nature. I think of the notion of interpretation, as I stated then, as a poor translation. Bettelheim (1983) later pointed out many other examples that show how difficult it is to appreciate fully the meanings of some of Freud's concepts. He speaks about the "loss of the soul," and the "loss of psyche," in translating *Psychischer Apparat* as "mental apparatus."

As I suggested almost 25 years ago (Ekstein, 1959), we should speak about *the interpretative process* rather than about interpretation. That process has been described in many different ways. Freud (1900), speaking about the art of interpretation, called attention to the intuitive aspects. Waelder (1939) quoted Freud's teacher, Charcot, who defined the intuitive way of working in psychoanalysis when he urged the therapist to "look at the phenomena so long until they seem to tell the story by themselves." Reik's *Surprise and the Analyst* (1937) and *Listening with the Third Ear* (1949) stressed the role of empathy, as did Kohut (1971, 1977) in *The Analysis of the Self* and *The Restoration of the Self.*

In order to indicate my way of looking at the interpretive process in the interchange between therapist and patient, I will touch on some problems in the relationship between technique and theory. It is difficult to show whether new technical methods used in therapy have changed theory, or whether theoretical changes have invited technical innovations. The topographic model of the psychic apparatus could invite an analytic dialogue characterized by Freud (1904) as aiming "to make the unconscious conscious," while the structural model suggested a concept of cure in terms of Freud's (1923) phrasing: "Where the Id was there shall ego be." Sigfried Bernfeld (1932) understood the interpretive process as one where the patient is shown a pattern of *Gestalten* or structures in his productions, while Waelder (1939) suggested that the interpretive process can be understood as similar to the task of the detective, who slowly sees the hidden tracks of the crime or the sin. Each of these ways of looking at the psychotherapeutic dialogue produces a different system of give and take between patient and therapist.

It is the communication system between analyst and patient that I consider to be the primary clue to understanding the therapeutic or interpretive process. A brief review of the history of language development can be instructive: The infant moves from hunger cries and sounds of satisfaction, to the primary language — at first consisting of signals and signs, and slowly developing to the symbolic representation of thoughts, bewilderment, themes; then we go on to secondary language, including the languages of fantasy and play, of acting out and acting in, of dreams, daydreams, and hypnagogic reveries. In therapy, patients may switch from one to another kind of language when talking to the analyst — in revealing their secrets, or holding them back and in defending themselves even against certain relevations, constantly switching in levels of understanding or ways of listening to the therapist. This is the nature of free association or freely suspended attention — the language of the patient. The therapist's language is the language of interpretation.

In an essay published in 1978, "Further Thoughts Concerning the Nature of the Interpretive Process," and another published in 1980 concerned with Waelder's paper (1939) on the *Criteria of Interpretation,* I have continued to support the view that sees in theory a condensed summary of the technical language utilized in the interpretive process, as well as my belief that we should speak not about the interpretation, but rather about the interpretive process: the kind of dialogue between patient and doctor which promotes the process of cure.

I see language of such a dialogue as not merely a private, autistic production, but rather as a system of communication, following special rules. It moves beyond the ordinary, everday dialogue where it seems that both people speak the same language (more or less); and I suggest that the purpose of the dialogue will define the rules of the game, the rules of the conversation, and will, therefore, require a different grammar. When I speak about grammar, I do not mean the surface rules of language, but examination of the deeper meaning of language. Let us think, for example, about the kind of communication system two people build up who are in a situation of courtship—of pursuit and delay; or between the District Attorney and the accused; or the parishioner and the priest in confession. The purpose of each of these interchanges creates a completely different process—different ends and different means. The old proverb, that the end justifies the means, could be turned around, and I would suggest that the means determine the end. In other words, the linguistic means are the rules of language that each participant in any of these situations uses to achieve a defined purpose.

While I do not believe that the analytic process is a combat—although frequently experienced as such within the context of transference—the following analogy from antiquity may be useful. The Roman Caesars of old entertained the masses through *panem et circenses*—bread and games, such as the deadly battles fought by the gladiators. One special consideration was granted to gladiators who had to fight each other with uneven arms. (One of them would fight with shield and a short sword, while the other was to fight with net and trident.) Each had to understand the other man's means of attack and defense; although they fought with different arms, each gladiator had to learn about the other man's use of his arms. The purpose was to defeat the opponent.

Granting that the analogy does not fit perfectly, we could think of interpretation and free association—the languages of the therapist and of the patient—as different languages (or arms), each specializing in methods of revealing, and at the same time, defending against revelation of the secret on both conscious and unconscious levels. While they may fight each other, they actually work toward the same purpose, but with completely different means which sometimes overlap. Each has to know the rules of the total game, including the rules of the other's language. Although they may both be speaking English or German, each is speaking a different language; the words are the same, but the deeper rules of the words and sentences—the thoughts that each expresses or withholds—are different.

I want to note at this point that Ludwig Wittgenstein, in later years, gave up his earlier philosophical position—the search for rules of verification and falsification that intrigued me in my student days, and studied the aspects of language that go beyond meeting the criteria of verification or falsification. He realized that the realms of fantasy and of jokes, the dream, the poem, the allusion to literature, the fairy tale, the myth may not contain truth in the customary sense of empirical science, but do contain psychological truths. In order to understand the deeper layers of language, one must learn the underlying rules within these realms.

This process is carried out through a kind of language game (Ekstein, 1978, 1980; Wright, 1982) or *Sprachspiel,* in which each participant follows different rules. In psychoanalysis, the patient says whatever comes to mind, expressing freely all thoughts, on whatever level they may occur. The analyst speaks an entirely different language, based on different rules, which avoids giving orders, criticizing, and moralizing—addressing only the meaning of what the patient really intended to convey. Ideally, the analyst can throw some light in this way on things that the patient says, in order to help the patient see the meaning of his or her own communications. The analyst must, of course, be careful to select moments when the light will not be too blinding for the patient, in other words, waiting until the patient is ready to have innermost thoughts and communications elucidated. Recalling Freud's remark that he did not want the patient constantly staring at him, and therefore he sat behind the couch, it occurs to me that by sitting in this position, I make it more possible to throw light on the patient's material, since it is more feasible for the patient to become his or her own observer, to see the material revealed in the new light I throw on it, rather than worrying about my facial expressions.

The analyst will, of course, have many ways to use such a flashlight in the interpretation process, for example, by selecting targets (aimed at with the light) that are important for the task of change. This takes us back to theories about the process of analytic interpretation, and the different schools, different models of mental apparatus, and different approaches to developing a therapeutic language.

Before resuming this discussion, I would like to digress to draw a comparison between psychoanalytic and philosophical thinking by comparing Freud and Wittgenstein, two outstanding contributors to the intellectual life of Vienna during the first twenty-five years of this century. Freud thought that the interpretive process would help the patient bring to light what is repressed, symptom-producing, and stands in the way of maturity, of choosing new options, and of developing fully the capacity to love and work. He (Freud, 1909; Bernfeld, 1951) suggested that what is buried in a human being, like the ruins of Pompeii covered by the ashes of a volcano, may be unearthed and see the light of day again. Now that Pompeii is unearthed, Freud suggested, what was preserved under the ashes will be destroyed. He also drew an analogy with the mummy excavated from Egyptian graves that starts to vanish when exposed to air. The psychological problem made conscious, the conflict exposed to the light of day and the light of the interpretive process, will vanish to make way for normal activity not dominated by repressed conflicts.

The philosopher (Wittgenstein, 1922) sees his task differently: as the clarification of concepts, statements, theories, and hypotheses, which may be vague and create the kinds of problems referred to as metaphysical or *Scheinprobleme* that are seen as ideological—the basis of ideological warfare among different psychological schools (Ekstein, 1949). Clarification of the meaning of these concepts, which are actually not yet true, well defined scientific concepts, will end our discontent and cause the philosophical problem to vanish, says the philosopher.

However, although the philosophical problem or the symptomatic problem of the patient may vanish, real-life problems are not solved by means of philosophy or psychoanalysis. The task accomplished is to make the symptom or the philosophical confusion vanish, so that there will be greater energy and capacity for problem-solving on a new and higher plane.

It is obvious that in recent years psychoanalysts everywhere have renewed the struggle about their different theories, their specific metapsychological views, and their technical innovations. The Tower of Babel complex has not left us. A new and strong tendency has developed seeking to devaluate metapsychology and to stress the use of clinical language. This is seen in contributions by Merton Gill (1978), George Klein (1973), Robert Holt (1972), Roy Schafer (1976), and others. Some of the clinical languages developed and discussed in recent literature of course hide the implied theoretical preferences, as all such languages do. Some start from theory and move to technique; others start with clinical data and develop theory; but the dialectic struggle cannot be averted.

The struggle is not merely an intellectual struggle or a scientific discussion, but also mirrors deep emotional commitments. Students are committed to the language of their teachers: the father tongue. And the teachers— perhaps as a countertransference phenomenon—tend toward a special language of their own. It is an interesting question whether schools of thought are founded by leaders, or whether the students and followers force the leaders into that defined position. Evidently, there is a struggle between identification and counteridentification.

Thinking of my own experience and my development as an analyst, I realize that with one eye I look to my old teachers, my supervisors, and the books I studied; but with the other eye I look at the patients. There is, after all, not only the mother tongue and the father tongue, but also the language of the child—the language of the learning child who is the patient. During my career I have dealt with children, adolescents, adults, and now, frequently, with very old patients. In each case, I had to develop a somewhat new language in order to understand what was being said by and about the patient and about me as analyst. I listened to the language of free association, the language of play, and the language of acting out; and though I always try to mantain the language of interpretation, I needed to adjust that language.

In recent works, I have often discussed metaphoric language—the language of allusion, the use of jokes, the distant comparisons; the problem of tact, including the problem of timing; and the language that is determined by the culture of the patient, his literary knowledge, that moves, at times, on esoteric or primitive levels. As I move through a day's activity, I find myself speaking differently with each patient; this experience might suggest that I have become multilingual. Since I am not a gladiator or a lawyer who believes in an adversary procedure, I do not insist on my special language, my special theoretical or ideological underpinning. Rather, I try to identify with the language of the patient—the idioms and allusions, the shifting language as the rhythm of the therapeutic process brings out the regressed language of the night along with the more reality-oriented language of the day and the language in between, the language of suffering, of despair, and the language of hope. But I do not move completely into the patient's mind, so to speak. I also remain myself, knowing that I must convey ideas to throw light on the material offered, which is clothed in a somewhat different language. The task is not only to understand the material, but to create a situation in which identification and counteridentification can take place within the framework of psychotherapy, maintaining appropriate distance so that transference and countertransference responses further the therapeutic process, rather than stymie the process and become merely agents of pathology.

Am I, then, embracing every school of thought? Not quite, but I would play with every school of thought, and I would borrow from the languages and the concepts of my colleagues. I find these most valuable, though, if I put less emphasis on theories and try to learn mainly from their clinical examples, demonstrations, process notes, or verbatim material. I discover then, as I follow their responses, the rules of language, ideas of change, and also the difficulties they encounter in their approaches. And I try to use what I consider effective with my own material.

Working at the University of Vienna in recent years, I ran into an interesting experience in the Departments of Child Psychiatry and Adult Psychiatry, which are eclectic — not much different from those in the United States. Assigned to supervise many of the staff members, I found myself engaged in an interesting experiment involving my response to the current facts of psychiatry in Vienna. As I proceeded through the days of supervisory work, I was seeing colleagues who each belonged to another school of thought. I might start in the morning with a behavior modifier, go on to an Adlerian, see an analytic candidate, and then deal with a student trained in non-directive Rogerian psychotherapy.

At first I was puzzled, wondering why these people would want to be supervised by an analyst. But apparently I was something special for them, being a Viennese and an American analyst at the same time, and they were curious. I was also curious as I noticed the usual student transferences to their supervisors, and I began to listen to their language, trying my best to answer with the language of the theoretical or clinical school to which they belonged. After a while, realizing that I was trying to understand and speak their professional language, they wanted to know how I would have handled certain problems, or how I would have put them in my language as a psychoanalyst of Freudian persuasion. Identification and counteridentification took place, and both teacher and students learned. A good teacher can always learn from students, and such teachers usually have conscientious students. I wish it were possible to add a chapter about this Vienna experience to the volume on *The Teaching and Learn-*

ing of Psychotherapy (Ekstein and Wallerstein, 1972) first published some 25 years ago.

I have tried to convey in this paper what I have put together from my studies in philosophy and linguistics with what I have learned about the human mind and the therapeutic process. It is the difference of experience, of language, of thought, I am convinced, that people need to bring out in building a creative, productive partnership. Looking back, I recall that this was actually happening at my first, my early Camelot, the Institute in Vienna. In my fantasy, at the beginning of this paper, I pictured it as a simple place, with one language, one clear theory, in a united family. Was it that simple?

At that time, Anna Freud developed child analysis — a new technique and a new way of speaking with children and encouraging them to speak their own language of play, rather than using free association. There was also August Aichhorn, who taught us how to listen to delinquents and how to speak a language with them that could be termed "outdeceiving the deceiver." And there was Paul Federn, who taught us languages and actions to be used with schizophrenic patients. Hartmann enlarged on the beginnings of ego psychology and enriched our language and our tools with the notion of adaptation. Freud moved us through different models of the psychic apparatus — different ways of moving beyond hypnosis, guiding interpretation toward the model of classical analysis. I could go on and on, describing that first creative group in my experience. In other words, upon reflection, I realize that it was really not a simple group. But, as a naive young man identifying with teachers, and with an institution, I had experienced it as a family. That institution was, of course, not without its quarrels; neither was Camelot. But it offered a basis for discussion and for working together that left its imprint on all of us.

As I set down my thoughts, remembering the different positions I have taken through the years, as expressed in my writings, I realized that during the life cycle of a productive professional such changes, reflecting growth, increased tolerance, and increased capacity to live with the ideas of other people, are to be expected.

When I decided to offer this audience a kind of professional autobiographical sketch, I thought of the playwright, Lillian Hellman, and her autobiographical *Pentimento.* The playwright sets the stage as if a play is to take place. This is not unlike analysis, where the patient replays the drama of his life as both *tragedia* and *comedia,* and we try to throw some light on that drama. During this process we might change the outcome. Almost like directors who change the play by influencing the actors in their work on the play's theme, we can change the autobiography of the patient. In the end there might be a completely different outcome, since the patient has given up the myth of childhood and introduces a new myth — the myth of adulthood. I suggest that each stage of life, each new task, each new conflict creates another myth. Perhaps the later myth is closer to reality, since there is actually more reality in the experience of the adult who now functions better. The capacity to love and to work prevails; however, since the child is the father of the man, the myths of the past — neurotic, psychotic or borderline — never completely vanish.

Lillian Hellman (1973) writes:

> Old paint on canvas, as it ages, sometimes becomes transparent. When that happens it is possible, in some pictures, to see the original lines: a tree will show through a woman's dress, a child makes way for a dog, a large boat is no longer on an open sea. That is called Pentimento because the painter "repented," changed his mind. Perhaps it would be as well to say that the old conception, replaced by a later choice, is a way of seeing then seeing again.

We are come together in conferences in order to see, and then to see again, to learn and to see better, even though we also notice that a basic theme remains, whatever the changes. Freud (1925), in his autobiography, spoke about "the patchwork of my labor." He was able to see and to see again, and to see differently. He was willing to change his theories and his way of working. And that is the school of thought that I feel a part of; a way of working that Freud and Wittgenstein followed. There is no final view. There is only process and endless search: psychoanalysis and philosophical clarification interminable.

REFERENCES

Bernfeld, S. (1932), Der Begriff der Deutung. *Zeitschrift fur Angewaudte Psychologie,* 42:448–497.

Bernfeld, S. C. (1951), Freud and archeology. *American Imago,* 8:107–128.

Bettelheim, B. (1983), *Freud and Man's Soul.* New York: Alfred A. Knopf.

Ekstein, R. (1949), Ideological warfare in the psychological sciences. *Psychoanal. Rev.,* 36: 144–153.

———— (1950), The tower of Babel in psychology and psychiatry: Towards a theory of determinants. *American Imago,* 2:77–141.

———— (1959), Thoughts concerning the nature of the interpretive process. In: *Readings in Psychoanalytic Psychology,* ed. M. Levitt. New York: Appleton Century Crofts, pp. 221–247.

———— (1972), In quest of the professional self. In: *Twelve Therapists,* ed. A. Burton. San Francisco: Jossey-Bass.

———— (1975), From the language of play to play with language. In: *Adolescent Psychiatry,* Vol. IV, pp. 142–162.

———— (1978), Further thoughts concerning the nature of the interpretive process. In: *The Human Mind Revisited: Essays in Honor of Karl A. Menninger,* ed. S. Smith. New York: International Universities Press.

———— (1980), Robert Waelder's criteria of interpretation revisited. *Bull. Phila. Assn. Psychoanal.,* Vol. VII, Nos. 3 & 4, 113–128.

———— (unpublished), *Metapsychology and the Languages of Psychoanalysis and Psychotherapy.*

———— & Wallerstein, R. (1972), *The Teaching and Learning of Psychotherapy.* Second Edition. New York: International Universities Press.

Fenichel, O. (1935), Concerning the theory of psychoanalytic technique. *International Zeitschrift fur Psychoanalyse,* 21:78.

Freud, S. (1900), The interpretation of dreams. *Standard Edition,* 4 & 5. London: Hogarth Press, 1953.

———— (1900), The origins of psychoanalysis. In: *Letters to Wilhelm Fliess, Drafts and Notes: 1887-1902.* New York: Basic Books, 1954.

———— (1904), Freud's psychoanalytic procedure. *Standard Edition,* 7. London: Hogarth Press, 1953.

———— (1909), Notes upon a case of obsessional neurosis. *Standard Edition,* 10:155-318. London: Hogarth Press, 1959.

———— (1914), The history of the psychoanalytic movement. *Standard Edition,* 14. London: Hogarth Press, 1957.

———— (1925), An autobiographical study. *Standard Edition.* London: Hogarth Press, 1959.

Gill, M. (1978), Metapsychology is irrelevant to psychoanalysis. In: *The Human Mind Revisited: Essays in Honor of Karl A. Menninger,* ed. S. Smith. New York: International Universities Press.

Hellman, L. (1973), *Pentimento.* Boston: Little, Brown.

Holt, R. (1972), Freud's mechanistic and humanistic images of man. In: *Psychoanalysis and Contemporary Science,* Vol. I, eds. R. Holt & E. Peterfreund. New York: Macmillan.

Klein, G. (1973), Two theories or one. *Bull. Menn. Clinic,* 37:102-132.

Kohut, H. (1971), *Psychoanalysis of the Self.* New York: International Universities Press.

———— (1977), *The Restoration of the Self.* New York: International Universities Press.

McGuinness, B. ed. (1982), *Wittgenstein and His Times.* Chicago: University of Chicago Press.

———— (1982), Freud and Wittgenstein. In: *Wittgenstein and His Times,* ed. B. McGuinness. Chicago: University of Chicago Press.

Reik, T. (1937), *Surprise and the Psychoanalyst.* New York: E. P. Dutton.

———— (1949), *Listening With the Third Ear: The Inner Experience of a Psychoanalyst.* New York: Farrar, Straus.

Schafer, R. (1976), *A New Language for Psychoanalysis.* New Haven: Yale University Press.

The Holy Bible (1901), American Standard Version. New York: Thomas Nelson & Sons.

Waelder, R. (1939), Criteria of interpretation. In: *Psychoanalysis — Theory, Application: Selected Papers by Robert Waelder,* ed. S. Guttman. New York: International Universities Press, 1976.

Wittgenstein, L. (1982), *Tractatus Logico Philosophicus.* London: Kegan Paul, Trench Trubner.

Wright, G. H. (1982), Wittgenstein in relation to his times. In: *Wittgenstein and His Times,* ed. B. McGuinness. Chicago: University of Chicago Press.

5

Change and Integration in Psychoanalytic Developmental Theory

MORTON SHANE, M.D.
ESTELLE SHANE, Ph.D.

THE PLACE OF DEVELOPMENT IN THE HISTORY OF PSYCHOANALYSIS

Historically, development has been so integral to psychoanalysis that when Gill and Rapaport (1959) attempted to formulate the definitive points of view in metapsychology, they seriously considered not delineating a developmental point of view separately — it seemed so pervasive. From one perspective, psychoanalytic development *is* psychoanalysis. For example, psychoanalysis was seen for a long time inseparable from formulations concerning libidinal stages of development.

Settlage (1980) proposed a historical division of psychoanalysis into three eras, and Friedman (1982) has proposed a fourth. We can use these rough divisions to demonstrate how our conceptions of development have changed over time. In the first era, that of id psychology, concepts of development were organized around drive development, perceived in Freud's (1905) "Three Essays" as the oral, anal, phallic oedipal, latency, and adolescent drive organizations, culminating in genital primacy. In the succeeding period of ego psychology, which spans the 20's, 30's, 40's and 50's, and encompasses the developmental theories of Sigmund Freud, Anna Freud, Hartmann, Rapaport, and Kris, the focus was on ego development and its primary and secondary autonomous functions.

With the later work of Hartmann, and the writings of Erikson, Fairburn, Jacobson, Sandler and Rosenblatt, and Kernberg, a third era of psychoanalysis was ushered in, with a new emphasis on the development of object relations. Thus, with Hartmann's distinction between self and ego, the way was open for distinctive delineations of self-representations, object representations, and the internalized representational world as contents of the ego. Theories of development in this third period focused upon the gradual attainment of libidinal object constancy, self-constancy, dyadic and triadic relationships, and — with the original, inventive formulations and elaborations of Mahler and her coworkers — on the separation-individuation process.

At present, with the more recent work of Schafer, Kohut, Gill, and Gedo, we may, following Friedman's lead, see ourselves in a new era of psychoanalysis, grounded in holistic humanism. In this view, development is conceptualized in terms of the person — in Schafer's sense of a progressive and interactive search for and invention of meanings — with a less structurally segmented, more integrated approach incorporating a developmental hierarchy of motives.

Our point is that views about development have changed along with psychoanalysis. It is important to note, however, that new is not necessarily better or more comprehensive, and that, for the most part, the ideas of earlier periods have been retained and integrated with later formulations. For example, while the era of id psychology is over, drive development is still honored, one way or another, in every new theory of psychoanalysis, although the drives themselves may be defined differently, or relegated to a secondary role. Since we have an interest in the integration of developmental theories, we would like to call attention to the way in which the history of the psychoanalytic paradigm itself conserves psychoanalytic constructs, thus inevitably integrating old with new — whether innovators choose to acknowledge it or not, and whether or not this legacy enhances or impedes their efforts. Such integration of old constructs with new modifications remains inevitable until a new paradigm is invented; and despite vigorous efforts and fruitful additions, such a new paradigm remains elusive, in our opinion.

DEVELOPMENTAL ORIENTATION AND APPROACH

Before turning to a discussion of specific developmental theories, and congruences that can be noted among them, we would like to point up an important contribution to the conceptualization of development within psychoanalysis: The 1974 report of the Committee on Psychoanalytic Education and Research

(COPER; see Goodman, 1977), which assumed as its task a prediction of the state of psychoanalysis ten years later. That committee predicted that development would be prominent in psychoanalytic theory, practice, research, and education. Following Loewald (1960), the Committee's report conceptualized analysis itself as a developmental process; following Erikson (1950), it conceptualized the life cycle as an ongoing developmental process that does not terminate with adolescence; following Mahler (1968), it stressed the importance of early development (the preoedipal experience) in the later structuring of the ego and the superego; and following Spitz (1965) and Anna Freud (1965), it focused on the value of applying observations of infant and child development to clinical understanding of the adult. The totality of assumptions embodied in this report is the foundation of the developmental orientation and approach.

We refer to the work of this Committee and its assumptions, not only because of its focus on development in psychoanalysis, but also because it emphasizes one important aspect of the developmental approach which is central to our discussion. While basic, classically oriented concepts of development from the first three eras of psychoanalysis were taken for granted by the authors of the report, it was taken as self-evident that no developmental theory or set of theories are to be retained as unalterable or axiomatic. All tenets of psychoanalytic development need to be tested in the light of observations of infant and child behavior. Where found wanting, developmental theories should be altered or discarded, and replaced by more fitting and defensible formulations. As Gaskill (1976) wrote: "Further modifications in analytic theory are more likely to result from . . . developmental research from both within and outside analysis [which will lead to] further refinement of psychoanalytic theory. . . ." (pp. 573–574). Brody (1982) added: "A wealth of data are now at hand that can help to bring about a convergence of developmental, experimental, and psychoanalytic studies of infants. . . . Hypotheses about human psychological development based on reconstruction should be used sparingly, and preferably only when data of direct observation are not possible or available (p. 586).

EXPERIMENTAL STUDIES ON INFANTS: CHALLENGES AND CONTRIBUTIONS

It is in this spirit that we have chosen as a central theme of this paper an examination of the most prominent psychoanalytic theories of development in the light of experimental studies on infants. We will indicate congruent points in developmental progression that have apparently endured the test of neonatal, infant, and child research. In this context, we will refer to a previous attempt at integration of the developmental theories of Mahler and Kohut (Shane and Shane, 1980) and the objections that have been raised to such efforts at integration.

One group of experimental studies in the body of developmental research is important for the correction it offers of the approximate cognitive limits of psychoanalytic theories. After all, such theory should not postulate more (or less) psychic structure than is deemed likely by those who investigate the cognitive and affective development of infants and children.

Postulations of *more* psychic structure than is in evidence begin with a basic and far-reaching developmental postulate of Freud's: hallucinatory wish-fulfillment. Freud thought that an infant deprived of gratification of a drive will hallucinate that gratification, and will seek real gratification from the outside world only secondarily. This capacity for hallucination during early infancy was severely challenged as early as the late 1930's by experimental studies on the genesis of the capacity for psychic representation, which emerged from the work of Piaget and his school. He demonstrated that this ability develops slowly and is fully achieved only at eighteen months (Piaget, 1945).

Nevertheless, the young infant's capacity to hallucinate has been taken for granted and elaborated in some developmental theories. The Kleinian school, for example, (Klein, 1962) attributed to the baby during the first year not only cognitive capacities for hallucination, but such advanced psychic representations as imagining a body scooped out, a hidden fetus within, and poisons projected from the self to another. Much less blatant, but equally discordant with experimental findings, is Mahler's (1975) postulate of the separation-anxiety-prone infant's delusion of fusion at six or seven months in order to reestablish a lost symbiotic unity. Mahler also retains Freud's hallucinatory wish-fulfillment hypothesis, attributing such hallucinations to the young infant in the autistic state, described as "self-sufficient. in its hallucinatory wish-fulfillment." (p. 41). (See also Brody, 1982; Coen, 1981; Milton Klein, 1981.)

On the other hand, it has been discovered that considerably more is going on in the infant in other ways than had been conceived previously. Numerous empirical studies demonstrate that the infant is an active, eager learner, prewired and well equipped for communications and interactions with the environment from the very beginning. This has implications for Mahler's autistic phase of development, wherein the infant is viewed as unrelated to his or her caretakers, protected by a stimulus barrier through the first several weeks of life. Harley and Weil (1979), cognizant of some of these newer experimental findings, have amended Mahler's concept of autism to "quasi-autism." In the light of additional data, however, we must question the value of postulating even a "quasi-autistic" phase.

Mahler's symbiotic phase of development is also now being seriously questioned, with significant implications for psychoanalytic theory and treatment. In the symbiotic phase, the infant remains undifferentiated from and fused with the caretaker before beginning the important developmental task of distinguishing, over time, self from other. Based upon his own and others' experimental investigations and postulations, Daniel Stern (1980), a psychoanalyst and infant researcher, asserts that the infant probably never experiences an undifferentiated phase. He conceptualizes, rather — based upon sophisticated observational experiments — that the human being is equipped at birth with pre-designed emergent structures, which prepare the infant very early to develop totally separate cognitive schemas of self and other.

In terms of separation-individuation theory, this would imply that a truly symbiotic phase in normal development is improbable. Furthermore, the whole notion of separation-individuation may have to be modified. Weil and Mahler have always distinguished two distinct, although interrelated, processes: *separation,* which involves the infant's growing intrapsychic awareness of separateness; and *individuation,* which involves the infant's acquisition, over time, of a distinct and unique individuality. In order to integrate the data Stern presents, the process of separation as a major task in normal development, which has been seen as prone to failure, must be tentatively revised. However, a focus on the individuation aspect of separation-individuation does not mean leaving out the process of separation, for this would diminish our sensitivity to the important interactions in the mother-child unit, encompassed in the separation-individuation theory, which is generally consistent with all research data.

Helpful in this regard is Lichtenberg's (1982) concept of the infant's move from interdependence to independence, since this conception does not require fusion as a normal developmental phase preceding separation. Thus, we can view the infant as separating out of an interdependent state to a more independent state, rather than moving from a fused state to one where self-other boundaries are more distinct. In other words, during the first year of life, the infant is in an archaic, relatively interdependent condition within the infant-caretaker unit; during the second year, the infant moves away from archaic interdependence and assumes the relatively independent, initiating behavior of the toddler. By questioning the accuracy of such concepts as the autistic and symbiotic phases, and by suggesting that the separation process may need to be modified, we are not diminishing the basically sound contributions of Mahler's data on separation-individuation to our understanding of the developmental process. Later in this paper, we will discuss the integration of Kohut and Mahler in developmental theory. On Kohut and self psychology, all that need be said here is that Kohut's conceptualization of the selfobject and self-selfobject unit effectively captures the field-theory aspect of the infant-mother matrix, which is largely acknowledged in most infant research (including Stern's) to be of overwhelming significance during the infant's first year.

As a result of the findings of infant research, there is reason to question classical psychoanalytic theory concerning erotogenic zones and libidinal phases. The concept that in the infant and young toddler there are discrete libidinal phases, related to corresponding bodily parts, is unjustified by observation. As Lichtenberg, quoting Sander (1980), states: "Contemporary infant research assumes that the human, like all living systems, begins life in an organized state, with all senses operating in unison." (p. 6) Our notions about the oral phase in infancy, in which the mouth is seen as the primal cavity and the affective center of all perception and experience, around which drive organization forms, are not consistent with this research. Instead, the infant appears to be far more active, more broadly focused, and more stimulus-seeking than is suggested by our classical conception of the passively sucking, mouth-preoccupied baby. The infant not only sucks, but also looks, hears, smells, grasps, and seeks visual, auditory, olfactory, and tactile stimulation from the environment.

All of this experience is organized, not around the infant's mouth and gustatory activity, but around numerous inborn affect potentials or fundamental emotions, such as interest, excitement, enjoyment, anger, distress, shame, humiliation, rage, disgust, fear, and surprise (Basch, 1976; Tomkins, 1962, 1963). The oral phase as such is not the best designator of the infantile state; it may serve as an adequate reconstructive metaphor for affective experience in infancy in formation of a life narrative, but it should not be taken literally. We need to be reminded often that the reconstructed infant and child is not the same as the actual infant and child (Shopper, 1982). Moreover, the greater the discrepancy between the two, the poorer the resulting insight offered the patient.

This leads to a cental question concerning the relevance to the psychoanalytic situation of theories of development. If, contrary to the view just stated, analysis is seen exclusively as a reconstructive venture, where the reconstruction of a coherent narrative (Schafer, 1978) is the central task, with the analyst focusing on the here and now in the transference, then the exact events of the first several years of life — especially before symbolic and linguistic representation is possible — become trivial. Along with many others, we believe that the analyst's view of development from the inception of life is likely to influence understanding of the patient, the strategy of interpretation, and formulations or reconstructions regarding the patient's past experience, even if the analyst does (as he should) focus on the here and now in the transference. The fact that psychoanalytic theories of development have always been integral to understanding of the psychoanalytic process would seem to support this conviction.

Given the undeniable impact of infant research upon some of our most fondly held psychoanalytic postulates regarding development, much of the extensive body of that theory obviously remains intact — a good deal more than we can sketch out here. For example, our conceptions of development from the oedipal phase on have, for the most part, withstood the tests of both time and observation. It is preoedipal development that has been most challenged. We will therefore focus in the following pages on the preoedipal period, describing briefly a cursory line of development of self formation and dyadic object relationships from birth to about three-and-a-half years consistent with infant research to date and representing an integration of two influential developmental theories: separation-individuation theory and self psychology. First, however, we will describe the responses of Kohut and Mahler to an earlier attempt at integration of their theories (Shane and Shane, 1980).

THE PROBLEM OF INTEGRATION

Neither Kohut nor Mahler was enthusiastic about the value of finding similarities between their disparate systems of thought. In his discussion of this early attempt, Kohut (1980) identified two principal objections to the idea of integration. The first was a sweeping rejection of the formulations of Mahler, Winnicott, Spitz, and other psychoanalytic observers of infants and children, because of a difference in their "world view" from that of self psychology, which he had only hinted at in a footnote in his earlier work, *The Restoration of the Self* (1977, pp. 187–188). Kohut (1980) forcefully elaborated on this difference for the first time as follows:

> In the view of self psychology, man lives in a matrix of selfobjects from birth to death. He needs selfobjects for his psychological survival, just as he needs oxygen in his environment throughout his life for physiological survival.... Self psychology does not see the essence of man's development as a move from dependence to independence, from merger to autonomy, or even as a move from no-self to self.

Kohut thus clearly distinguishes himself from traditional psychoanalysis, and, specifically, from Mahler and separation-individuation theory, which views autonomy as an important, inevitable, and salutary aspect of normal development. In further personal communications on this point, Kohut was not open to the idea of a relative course of autonomy from supporting objects in succeeding phases of normal development; rather, he was intent upon maintaining as wide a gap as possible between his formulations and those of mainstream psychoanalysis in this matter. In his opinion, development toward independence is a bias of the Western world, which is inconsistent with Kohut's view of man. We feel, however, that the concept of relative autonomy is not inconsistent with a stand which posits selfobjects (and true objects, also) as necessary throughout the life cycle, since the quality of object ties, even in Kohut's theory, progresses from archaic to mature, from peremptory to the capacity for delay, from inflexible to flexible, and from primary to secondary.

To further support his view that integration between theories is not possible, Kohut pointed out a second distinction between his own world view and that of traditional psychoanalysis; differing views of aggression. Traditional psychoanalysis, he stated (1980), "emphasized the primacy of hostility and destructiveness in human nature, and consequently, man's propensity to be beset by conflict, guilt, and guilt depression" (p. 478). In contrast, self psychology posits aggression as secondary: "We do not disregard man's anxieties and depressions, in infancy, in adulthood, and when face to face with death. And ... we certainly do not ignore man's greed and lust or his destructive rage... [but] we see them not as primary givens but as secondary phenomena due to disturbances in the self-selfobject unit" (p. 479). Kohut saw no hope of integration with mainstream psychoanalytic theories of development based upon a conception of mankind as primarily hostile.

In response to Kohut's contention that destructuve aggression is a secondary, not a primary, phenomenon, reactive to disruptions in the self-selfobject unit, and stimulated by the separation-individuation-inspired observational research of Henri Parens (1979) on the development of aggression in the infant and toddler, we (Shane and Shane, 1982) made a further effort to integrate Kohut and Mahler (as modified by Parens) on the subject of aggression and aggressive sexuality. In brief, Parens classifies aggression into destructive and non-destructive varieties. The destructive kind was demonstrated to be principally secondary, or reactive, provoked by frustrations imposed on the child by the environment, whereas the child's non-destructive aggression, correlated with assertiveness, was viewed as innate and primary. Thus, in our opinion, the classically based, observational theory of Parens is consistent with Kohut's theory about the nature of aggression, and offers one area of integration between self psychology and separation-individuation theory.

Self psychologists also have a more generalized objection to the integration of developmental theories. This objection stems from their view that self psychology stands alone as an independent, new, and superordinate psychoanalytic theory (Basch, 1981; Goldberg, 1983), offering an adequate organization for all psychoanalytic data. Any attempt to incorporate self-psychological concepts within the larger psychoanalytic corpus is, they feel, a violation of the unity and integrity of self psychology's particular universe of discourse. To see, for example, the correspondence between self-cohesiveness and self-constancy is to ignore the theoretical context of each concept.

Despite these general objections to integration, we hold, along with others (Friedman, 1982), that self psychology is a supplemental theory, offering interesting alternative views within the current holistic-humanistic era of psychoanalysis. If one believes, as we do, that no one theory today stands independent of the main body of psychoanalysis, and that the newer theories, including self psychology, offer fruitful ways of conceptualizing aspects of the analytic process, then attempts at integration are neither sterile exercises nor needless violations of the integrity of specific theories. They are rather, necessary efforts, however imperfect, to do explicitly what all analysts do implicitly, in order to function in an integrated way.

PREOEDIPAL DEVELOPMENT, AN INTEGRATED VIEW

In the following discussion of preoedipal development, the focus is on the re-constructive theories of self psychology and the classically based observational theories of separation-individuation, as refined by findings of infant research. We believe it is appropriate to select these two bodies of theory for integration, because, despite areas of inadequacy, uncertainty, incompleteness, and con-troversy, they stand out as among the most ambitious and innovative theories regarding preoedipal development currently available in psychoanalysis. We focus, primarily, on formulations of these separate theories that are in agree-ment and have withstood the test of infant observation.

We would question, for example, both the quasi-autistic and the symbiotic phases of development postulated by Mahler. Self psychologists, however—particularly Basch (in press) and Tolpin (1982)—are more consistent with in-fant research when they speculate about the development of the emergent self in the early months of life. They see the infant as active, engaged, and intent upon communication (Basch), with a healthy cohesiveness (Tolpin), im-mersed within a self-selfobject unit. Neither Tolpin nor Basch postulates a normal developmental stage of psychological fusion; in this way, their conjec-tures fit in with those of Stern (1980), who sees separate schemas of self and the other developing from birth.

Kohut (1977) has described the earliest development of the nuclear self as a self that exists only in the mind of the mother. He terms this the "virtual self," the self in the process of becoming, as it is elaborated in the mother's imagina-tion. Wolf (1980) speaks of "virtual selfobjects," with an apology for this rather fanciful construction: how can a self that is, at this time, latent, have self-objects at all, even "virtual" ones? Nevertheless, the concept serves a heuristic purpose for Wolf. More recently, Goldberg (in a personal communication) talked of the emergence of the nuclear self at eighteen months, when symbolic, linguistic, and self-reflective capacities are possible. Before this time, by his definition, there is no self, and, therefore, little contribution from self psychol-ogy about its formation.

What we are able to say with some certainty about the earliest experience is that the infant functions in a perceptual-affective-action mode (Lichtenberg, 1982), by and large without representation; in this period, memory is organ-ized around motor and affective experiences. During the first year and well into the second, based upon data from separation-individuation research and self psychology reconstructions, one can conceptualize a dawning awareness of oneself as center of the universe, with intensely invested, recognizable, and separate others in the surround. Observations from separation-individuation research on sensorimotor egocentricity in the child during the practicing subphase are supported by reconstructions from self psychology that suggest a resonance to such a stage — however modified by subsequent development — in the almost unselfconscious assumption in many patients of grandiose centrality in the analytic situation.

During the second and third years of life, according to observation and reconstruction data, the child individuates and achieves, to an increasing extent, autonomy from an archaically idealized mother. Mahler and her colleagues see the toddler, struggling with separation and individuation, as unable to function continuously independent of the mother, requiring repeated "refueling" from her. Mahler's critically important rapprochement subphase lends, through its resolution, a meliorative developmental impact, centering around disillusionment with the idealized caretaker. Kohut and his colleagues see patients who do not function adequately separate and independent from the idealized analyst as reinstating the archaic self-selfobject matrix of toddler times. Such patients, therefore, require from the analyst — as they had previously from the archaic selfobject — soothing and approving functions. Kohut addresses the healing effects of the gradual disillusionment with the omnipotence of the analyst, leading to transmuting internalizations. In this sense, there is a rough confluence of hypotheses in these two theories.

In terms of the newer infant research, the postulates of separation-individuation theorists regarding the important rapprochement subphase need not be modified. We can continue to accept Mahler's convincing descriptions of the child's conflicts stemming from ambivalence toward the idealized mother, growing disillusionment with her, and the need for "refueling"; the process of individuation as she describes it does not require emendation. However, as indicated before, the process of separation may need to be understood as one that moves from relative archaic interdependence to relative independence, rather than from symbiotic merger to separateness. Therefore, the dangerous mother-after-separation and the fantasy of re-engulfment or intrusion will have to be reframed in terms of a continuing danger of archaic interdependence with the primary caretaker after the achievement of some relative autonomy.

Self psychologists view the second and third years of life as a period of development beyond the need for archaic selfobjects in the direction of a need for selfobjects at a more mature level. Such movement from archaic selfobject relatedness to more mature object relatedness is consistent with developmental research; and, while the self psychologist's timetable is rather vague, the findings are not inconsistent with Mahler's more precise, observationally based, empirical studies. However, separation-individuation theory perceives object relationships as more than relationships that serve the needs of the self in terms of self-esteem regulation and structure formation. Mahler's concept of relationships include the classically based true object relationships that are invested with libidinal and aggressive interest. Self psychology does not focus on such object relations, maintaining that true object relationships are essentially peripheral. Instead, self psychology focuses on objects that perform self functions.

According to Mahler, the attainment of self (as well as object) constancy takes place during the fourth year of life, indicating that self representations do not attain stability until that time. Kohut, on the other hand, postulates a cohesive self whenever the structures of the grandiose self and the idealized parent imago are discernible — structures that are generally reconstructed as deriving from an earlier period than the fourth year. However, Kohut perceives clinically a marked vulnerability to regression of the grandiose self and idealized parent imago structures. This would suggest that in his view of normal development, a further consolidation of self structure is required to obtain the degree of stable cohesiveness that can be equated with the relatively immutable self constancy postulated by Mahler. Kohut's stable self-cohesiveness and Mahler's self (and object) constancy can thus be seen as developing in roughly the same time period, which would suggest that they are different conceptualizations of the same phenomenon arrived at by different means.

Infant research and the theories of Mahler and Kohut do not significantly alter the classical understanding of the form and significance of the oedipal phase of development. Moreover, all psychoanalysts are basically in agreement that preoedipal development influences, to some extent, the oedipal phase, which in turn influences all subsequent development.

To correlate self psychology and separation-individuation theory in order to arrive at some coherent understanding of preoedipal development does not imply that these theories do not have important differences. One distinctive postulate of self psychology is the concept of separate lines of development of self and object relations. This allows its adherents to continue to focus on selfobjects and selfobject functions without attending to the possible centrality of true object relations or their close links with selfobject relations. As Mahler and McDevitt (1982) state their objection to this position, ". . . to try to speak of self-development separately from the development of object relations imposes an impossible strain on the data [of infant and toddler observation]."

Another sharp difference between self psychology and separation-individuation concepts is in the area of internalization. The transmuting internalization of Kohut is structure building without the identificatory tag inherent in the concept of identification. As we understand it, the shadow of the object does not fall upon the ego-self, but, rather, what falls upon the self is the shadow of the object's selfobject function. This permits the self psychologist to conceptualize the building up of self structure without the concomitant need for an invariable link to the libidinal object.

We should mention again a third persistent distinction between self psychology and classical analysis discussed previously: the self psycholgist's concept of the continuing need for selfobjects throughout the life cycle with the increasing number of such selfobjects required by the healthy person as he matures.

Such differences lead self psychologists to the belief that their body of theory cannot be subsumed within classical psychoanalysis. We maintain that what is needed ultimately in the field is a view of early life that is consistent with developmental observation and also stands a chance of achieving consensus among analysts. It is toward this goal that efforts at integration among developmental psychoanalytic theories should be directed. Today, psychoanalysis already has a serviceable developmental theory, based on obvious, though rough, confluences among theoretical viewpoints. However, we need to remain open to advances outside of and within the field.

CONCLUSION

We would like to reiterate two points here: First, classical psychoanalytic developmental theory, in particular preoedipal theory, is seriously flawed by its adherence to outmoded concepts. Psychoanalysts must accept the principle, however threatening to conventional views, that our theory cannot postulate more or less psychic structure than is found to be likely by researchers who investigate the cognitive and affective development of infants and children.

Second, efforts at integration of contributions to psychoanalytic theory-building should be encouraged rather than disparaged. While the newer theories may offer fruitful ways of conceptualizing aspects of the psychoanalytic process, no new theory can currently stand independent of the main corpus. Therefore, attempts at integration are neither sterile exercises nor needless violations of the integrity of particular theories; they are necessary efforts to create an indispensable unity. Without doubt, analysis needs its innovators, but we would argue that it also needs its integrators.

REFERENCES

Basch, M. F. (1981), *The future of psychoanalysis.* Paper presented at the Berkeley Conference on the Self, Berkeley, CA.

_____ (1976), The concept of affect: A reexamination. *J. Amer. Psychoanal. Assn.,* 24:759–777.

_____ (in press), The concept of "self": An operational definition. In: *Psychosocial Theories of the Self,* ed. B. Lee. New York: Plenum Press.

Brody, S. (1982), Psychoanalytic theories of infant development and its disturbances: A critical evaluation. *Psychoanal. Quart.,* 51:526–597.

Coen, S. J. (1981), Notes on the concepts of selfobject and preoedipal object. *J. Amer. Psychoanal. Assn.,* 29:395–411.

Erikson, E. (1950), *Childhood and Society.* New York: Norton.

Fairburn, W. D. (1952), *An Object-Relations Theory of the Personality.* New York: Basic Books.

Freud, A. (1965), *Normality and Pathology in Childhood: Assessments of Development.* New York: International Universities Press.

Freud, S. (1905). Three essays on the theory of sexuality. *Standard Edition,* 7:135–243. London: Hogarth Press, 1953.

Friedman, L. (1982), The humanistic trend in recent psychoanalytic theory. *Psychoanal. Quart.*, 51:353–371.

Gaskill, H. S. (1976), An assessment of psychoanalysis as a viewed from within. *J. Amer. Psychoanal. Assn.*, 24:553–589.

Gedo, J. E. (1979), *Beyond Interpretation. Toward a Revised Theory for Psychoanalysis.* New York: International Universities Press.

Gill, M. M. (1979), The analysis of the transference. *J. Amer. Psychoanal. Assn.*, 27:263–288.

Goldberg, A., ed. (1980), *Advances in Self Psychology.* New York: International Universities Press.

Goodman, S., ed. (1977), *Psychoanalytic Education and Research: The Current Situation and Future Possibilities.* New York: International Universities Press.

Harley, M., & Weil, A. P. (1979), Introduction to *The Selected Papers of Margaret S. Mahler,* Vol. 1. New York: Jason Aronson.

Hartmann, H. (1939), *Ego Psychology and the Problem of Adaptation.* New York: International Universities Press, 1958.

―――― (1950), Comments on the psychoanalytic theory of the ego. In: *Essays on Ego Psychology.* London: Hogarth Press; New York: International Universities Press, 1964, pp. 113–141.

Jacobson, E. (1964), *The Self and the Object World.* New York: International Universities Press.

Kernberg, O. F. (1976), *Object-Relations Theory and Clinical Psychoanalysis.* New York: Jason Aronson.

Klein, Melanie (1962), *Envy and Gratitude and Other Works, 1946–1963.* New York: Delacorte Press, 1975.

Klein, Milton L. (1981), On Mahler's autistic and symbiotic phases: An exposition and evaluation. *Psychoanal. Contemp. Thought,* 4:69–105.

Kohut, H. (1971), *The Analysis of the Self.* New York: International Universities Press.

―――― (1977), *The Restoration of the Self.* New York: International Universities Press.

―――― (1980), Summarizing reflections. In: *Advances in Self Psychology,* ed. A. Goldberg. New York: International Universities Press.

Lichtenberg, J. D. (1982), *Reflections on the second year of life.* Paper presented at the American Psychoanalytic Association, Spring Meeting, Boston.

Loewald, H. W. (1980), *Papers on Psychoanalysis.* New Haven and London: Yale University Press.

Mahler, M. (1968), *On Human Symbiosis and the Vicissitudes of Individuation, Vol. I: Infantile Psychosis.* New York: International Universities Press.

―――― Pine, F., & Bergman, A. (1975), *The Psychological Birth of the Human Infant: Symbiosis and Individuation.* New York: Basic Books.

―――― & McDevitt, J. B. (1982), Thoughts on the emergence of a sense of self. *J. Amer. Psychoanal. Assn.,* 30:827–848.

Parens, H. (1979), *The Development of Aggression in Early Childhood.* New York and London: Jason Aronson.

Piaget, J. (1945), *Play, Dreams and Imitation Childhood.* New York: Norton, 1951; London: Heinemann, 1951.

Rapaport, D., & Gill, M. M. (1959), The points of view and assumptions of metapsychology. *Internat. J. Psycho-Anal.,* 40:153–162.

Sander, L. (1980), *Polarity, paradox, and the organizing process in development.* Paper presented at First World Congress of Infant Psychiatry, Portugal.

Sandler, J., & Rosenblatt, B. (1962), The concept of the representational world. *The Psychoanalytic Study of the Child,* 17:128–145. New York: International Universities Press.

Schafer, R. (1976), *A New Language of Psychoanalysis.* New Haven and London: Yale University Press.

―――― (1978), *Language and Insight.* New Haven and London: Yale University Press.

Settlage, C. F. (1980), Psychoanalytic developmental thinking in current and historical perspective. *Psychoanal. Contemp. Thought,* 3:139–170.

Shane, M., & Shane, E. (1980), Psychoanalytic developmental theories of the self: An integration, In: *Advances in Self Psychology,* ed. A. Goldberg. New York: International Universities Press.

—— —— (1982), Psychoanalytic theories of aggression. *Psychoanal. Inq.,* 2:263–281.

Shopper, M. (1982), Report of the workshop on the developmental core curriculum. *J. Psychoanal. Education,* 2:1–3.

Spitz, R. A. (1965), *The First Year of Life.* New York: International Universities Press.

Stern, D. (1980), *The early development of schemas of self, of other, and of various experiences of self with other.* Paper presented at Symposium on Reflections on Self Psychology, Boston.

Tolpin, M. (1982), *Injured self-cohesion: developmental, clinical and theoretical perspective. A contribution to understanding narcissistic and borderline disorders.* Paper presented at Conference on Borderline Pathology, UCLA, Los Angeles.

Tomkins, S. S. (1962 and 1963), *Affect, Imagery, Consciousness,* Vol. 1 and 2. New York: Springer.

Wolf, E. S. (1980), On the developmental line of selfobject relations. In: *Advances in Self Psychology,* ed. A. Goldberg. New York: International Universities Press, pp. 117–130.

6

Change and Integration in Theoretical Concepts – Psychopathology

ROBERT R. NUNN, M.D.

Dealing with psychopathology is the way that psychoanalysis began, it is still the daily concern of most psychoanalysts, and it is the state in which almost all of our basic concepts are seen most clearly. For all those reasons, surveying the changes in views of psychopathology is central to understanding the changes in psychoanalytic concepts generally. Further, understanding the changes in psychoanalysis is the best way to understand present-day psychoanalysis.

However, before discussing change in psychoanalysis, I want to point up a paradox—that in two important ways there has actually not been much change. From the beginning, changes have been limited to progress along the same line, spelled out in *Studies on Hysteria* (Breuer and Freud, 1893–1895), where Freud delineated the general sequence: (1) a trauma, consisting of the "patient's ego" being approached by an incompatible idea; (2) an arousal of distressing affects by the trauma; (3) a reaction of psychological defense by the patient; and (4) a repetition of that sequence in successive episodes of the illness. It is my view that the progressive elucidation of the details of that schema has been the chief concern in the history of psychoanalytic psychopathology, and continues to be the challenge today.

The way we collect our data has also not changed much. The verbal free association of a patient, listened to with the naked ear, still constitutes our basic data, nearly a hundred years after psychoanalysis began. In that same period, medical pathologists have progressed from studying gross tissues, to examining tissue microscopically, to studying living cellular physiology, to molecular synthesis, so that now tissues can be studied by experimental arranging and tracing. Some may say that we can now subject psychopathological data to new techniques of analysis, such as electronic recording and statistical or linguistic analysis; and the data can be supplemented by observing physiological variables or even chemical effects during free association, or by accenting analysis of the analyst or the patient's family, as well as the patient. Many analysts, I know, would object that such supplements are not psychoanalytic data, which, in effect, limits change in our data collection methods, by definition.

HISTORICAL SURVEY

Beginning Period: 1880–1900

The beginning of psychoanalytic history is essentially contained in *Studies on Hysteria* and in the "Further Remarks on the Neuropsychoses of Defense." In these works, Freud characterized psychopathology as follows: (1) a psychologically traumatizing, overstimulating sexual seduction (active in obsessive cases and passive in hysterical cases) occurs; (2) anxiety is aroused; (3) the trauma, defended against by conversion, displacement, or projection, becomes unconscious; and (4) the whole sequence returns when a later event activates it.

However, toward the end of this early period, we know from his unpublished manuscripts and letters written to Fliess, that Freud's thinking was changing and enlarging. A different neurosis, melancholia, was addressed in "Draft G" (Freud, 1892–1899a) where Freud distinguished another type of trauma: a lack or loss of erotic psychic excitation. Other letters (Freud, 1892–1899b, 1892–1899c), expressed still another interest — in psychological developmental stages and their relation to the various pathological pictures, such as the relationships of trauma before four years of age to hysteria, of trauma between four and eight years of age to obsessional neurosis, and of trauma between eight and fourteen to paranoia. In "Letter 69" to Fliess (Freud, 1892–1899d), crucial determinants that later led to the next phase in conceptualization of psychopathology are described. Here, Freud gave four reasons why he no longer believed in his earlier theories of neurosis by traumatic seduction: the failure of patient treatments; the incredibility that so many fathers, including his own, could be perverts; the evidence that reality cannot be distinguished in unconscious thought; and the absence of such memories even in the delerium of the deep-going psychotic. This realization led to exposition in "Letter 71" (Freud, 1892–1899e) that the sexual events reported by Freud's patients were related to fantasies around the universal oedipus complex, rather than literal life history.

By this time, it was twenty years since the first case of hysteria had been studied, and Freud had become established as a psychoanalytic investigator, in addition to the recognition he had achieved before beginning psychoanalytic work by publishing twenty three articles about his studies in other areas of medical science.

Topographic Phase: 1900–1914

Realizing that his patients and he himself in his own self-analysis were usually not referring to historically accurate trauma in their associations, Freud devoted the next years to investigating and publishing his findings about the unconscious basis of their sexual fantasies of trauma.

The first report of his study was published in the *Interpretation of Dreams* (Freud, 1900) where the essential idea—found in its now famous "Chapter VII"—was that dreams can be explained as the product of three interacting systems of thinking—unconscious, preconscious, and conscious. Their interaction was described this way: During a night's sleep, an unconscious wish or impulse, stirred up by one of the preceding day's events, attempts to reach consciousness, but is worked over by the preconscious system before being allowed to do so, if the dream is what he called a "successful" one. As every analyst knows, the primary-process and secondary-process types of thinking, characteristic of the unconscious and preconscious respectively, the visual quality of dreams, the control of affect and motility and sleep disturbance, were all carefully explained. The larger purpose of the work, however, was to elucidate this interplay of mental systems, and to demonstrate that the compromise arrived at between them was also involved in psychopathological symptom formation. Freud went on to demonstrate the universality of his new view of mental functioning by arguing its existence in other evidence—in slips of the tongue and pen and bungled actions of all sorts (Freud, 1901), in jokes (Freud, 1905a), in literature (Freud, 1907), in anthropological study (Freud, 1913), and in two long case studies: "Little Hans" (Freud, 1909a) and the "Rat Man" (Freud, 1909b).

This work spread over approximately a fifteen-year period, interspersing an ample exploration of mentation, based on the topographic theory, with the other major theme of this period—the question of what was repressed. The major work on this other theme is found in "Three Essays on the Theory of Sexuality" (Freud, 1905b). Although the oedipus complex had first been described publicly in *The Interpretation of Dreams,* the essays on sexuality systematically explored sexual development in all its components from infancy through puberty, and explained how fixation of development at various stages resulted in either perversion expressing the fixation, or neuroses that defend against such expression. Here, Freud also presented theoretical formulations on the instincts, such as the libido theory, and concepts of source, aim, and object of each instinct. Later (Freud, 1915a, p. 138ff), he added the theoretical emphasis on separation of sexual from ego instincts and proposed that these were the respective instinctual bases for the affects of love and hate that may influence pathological development. In this work, he also confirmed the view that sexual instinct is the true motive for development of the psyche (Freud, 1915a, p. 118), rather than external stimuli, which can be escaped.

We may outline the explanatory steps of psychopathology in the neuroses, as updated in this period, as follows: (1) An immature and partial sexual instinct is incompatible with a preconscious repressive force (ego instinct); (2) whatever the affective reaction may have been originally, such as shame or anger (Freud, 1915b, p. 155), anxiety replaces it after repression; (3) symptom formation occurs to replace the anxiety; (4) a recurrence of anxiety takes place with any subsequent symptom failure.

The main problem of that formulation, as Freud realized later (Freud, 1923, p. 17), was that the repressive force was often unconscious. In addition, such a formulation implied that the pathology was in the instinct only, since the preconscious is realistic and logical; this kind of thinking did not promote investigation of the pathology of the repressive side, with its immaturities and partialities. Further, there was no explanation of the postulate that various qualities of affects were always reduced to the common coinage of anxiety, and no explanation of why sometimes others, such as depression, did not transform into anxiety. For these reasons, a stirring to further change in theories of psychopathology emerged. The topographic theory and the instinct theory of this period, however, had proved their usefulness, and the change that followed sought to supplement, not replace, these contributions.

Structural Phase: 1914–1940

Moves to supplement the topographic formulations were begun gradually and piecemeal. Freud's first transitional work, "On Narcissism" (1914), beautifully illustrates its place in history, because it explained narcissism both the old way and the future new way. Narcissism was accounted for instinctually as cathexis of the ego with libido, and also structurally as the ego's obtaining "satisfaction" by measuring up to and fulfilling the ego ideal. Similarly, in his *Mourning and Melancholia* (1917), the disturbance of narcissism was explained both ways. Freud accounted for melancholia instinctually as the ego instincts' original hatred of an object that turns against the ego after it is identified with the object; structurally, melancholia was explained as the conscience critically judging the ego. In *Group Psychology* (1921), Freud added that inferiority, as well as guilt, can be understood as expressing tensions between the ego and ego ideal. However, his dominant work of this period was the *The Ego and the Id* (1923). Here, he clearly enlarged his earlier concept of incompatibility between two opposing forces to a four-party arrangement — the ego reconciling the demands of the drives, the superego, and external reality. Descriptions of the superego, seen as consisting of both prohibitions and ideals — with stress on guilt when one's ideals as to one's own behavior are not achieved — are crucial to this time of change. Freud's *Inhibitions, Symptoms, and Anxiety* (1926) added important ideas: that anxiety is a reaction to danger, automatically if the ego is overcome, or as a signal if the ego is able to institute defense; and that anxiety consists of three parts — experience of unpleasure, discharge into the soma, and perception of the effects of those discharges. Finally, in Freud's posthumously published *Outline of Psychoanalysis* (1940), he defined the superego as the precipitate of the "long period of childhood during which the growing human being lives in dependence on his parents," expanded by "contributions from later successors and substitutes of his parents, such as teachers and models in public life of admired social ideals."

The view of psychopathology during this period might be described as follows: (1) The ego encounters difficulty in finding a way to make compatible the demands of the id, the superego, and reality; (2) a signal amount of anxiety is experienced; (3) defenses are instituted; and (4) failure of defense is signalled by recurrence of anxiety. Freud had already begun to complicate that scheme further by adding developmental stages. He described (Freud, 1926, p. 142) the different anxiety at each successive stage as the structures develop, and listed the sequence as fears of: psychical helplessness, loss of the object, castration, and superego punishment. The understanding of pathology had become much more sophisticated; yet, a number of problems still remained. The main one, perhaps, was the continuing clinical problem of dealing with complicated depressive (narcissistic) and borderline character pathology or psychosis. In fact, it is questionable whether we see a wider scope of patients today than Ferenczi (1950) and Abraham (1927) described, or whether we simply attempt to theorize in terms more useful than their instinct psychology. Individual analysts dealt with the problems skillfully and intuitively in this period, but the original structural theory did not explain why some ego-superego tensions resulted in anxiety, some in guilt, and some in depression.

CONTEMPORARY SURVEY

What are the contributions of the time since Freud's death? Foremost are the extensions of the structural theory of ego-psychology. Anna Freud (1946) began this process with her inclusive summary of the defensive activities of the ego. Hartmann (1964), with his careful detailing of ego functions in relation to instinct, superego, and reality, took the lead in the United States, along with

Kris and Loewenstein (Hartmann, Kris, and Loewenstein, 1962), his frequent collaborators. Arlow and Brenner (1964) gave a succinct description of structural theory, noting especially the utility of the concept of development as applied to the superego, and proposed that, in view of its contradictions of the topographic theory, use of the earlier theory should be discontinued.

Gradually emerging new additions to concepts of psychopathology have been made by three groups. One is made up of those who have added to our knowledge of developmental failures by studying children. Outstanding developmental researchers include Anna Freud and Melanie Klein in Britain, and Mahler and Spitz in the United States. Anna Freud, Spitz, and Mahler have elaborated and refined concepts more clearly in tune with the mainstream of psychoanalytic thinking. Melanie Klein, on the other hand, has theorized so differently that most analysts question her theoretical positions in support of representations derived from instincts instead of from experiences with objects, and her concept of oedipal events with structural precipitates in the first year of life, which would presume a psychotic core at the center of personality. Her development of play as a tool with children to augment free association is much valued, however. In addition, Benedek (1970) studied adult development, and Erikson (1959) integrated developmental studies over the whole life cycle into psychoanalytic theory.

A second group of researchers has studied the psychotic patient analytically, contributing to our knowledge of the early processes of development and pathology. Fromm-Reichmann (1950) and Searles (1965) in the United States, along with Rosenfeld (1954) and Bion (1965) in Britain, are foremost in this group. Many, perhaps most, analysts would dispute whether their therapeutic work is analytic; but, from the standpoint of understanding pathology as developmental failure with its symptoms and meanings, papers like "Chapter 18" in Searles' *Collected Papers On Schizophrenia* (1965) are unsurpassed.

The third, and much larger, group is made up of varied contributors who have formulated early psychopathology in terms of self-representations and object-representations. Some of these contributors emphasize aspects of the living, experiencing, whole psyche, in contrast to their view of Freud as having a mechanistic, fragmenting emphasis. Many have downplayed the sexual and unconscious aspects of mentation and favor a kind of inspirational view. Hartmann (1964, p. 127) has specifically suggested the usefulness of "self" as a concept in understanding narcissism. He believed that narcissism is best understood as the libidinal cathexis of the self, the whole person—in contrast to the cathexis of the ego, the superego, or the id, which he named as substructures of the personality. Jacobson (1964), in perhaps the most straightforward way, has attempted to trace the development of self-representations and object-representations from earliest psychophysiological states of the newborn through the contribution of such representations to the development of structures, and finally their reshaping through adolescence and adulthood. Sandler and Rosenblatt (1962) have tried to bring definitional clarity to self-representations and object-representations and their relations to structures, but they have, essentially, replaced structural relations with corresponding drive, moral, and organizational qualities of the self, in my opinion. Stressing the instinctual investment, both libidinal and aggressive, as contributing to self-development, Kernberg (1976) has offered criteria for differentiating grades of pathology — from borderline states to various levels of narcissistic personality disorder. Kohut (1971) has suggested differentiation of narcissistic personality disorders from transference neuroses, based on his opinion that narcissistic disorders are due to deficiencies in structure, whereas transference neuroses stem from conflicts between well-formed structures. Kohut stressed, additionally, that transferences of depressive affects and concerns about separation are diagnostic of narcissistic personality disorders. Winnicott (1965), of Britain, has earned mention as a member of this group with his writing about the normal transition between symbiosis and individuation, and about the false self that can emerge when transition occurs before an adequate symbiotic experience has taken place.

Great confusion has resulted from the fact that each contributor of this third group has felt impelled to develop an individual language to describe the pathology he was studying, because the view of many analysts, summarized by Gedo and Goldberg (1973), has opposed applying the topographic and structural models to the preoedipal period. The resulting dissent within this group — and between its members and the other contemporaries — has tempted some to suggest that we throw out all psychoanalytic theory at a level of abstraction higher than clinical theory. Schafer (1976) has challenged the usefulness of formulating psychoanalytic data in metapsychological terms. Alternatively, he has proposed a new language, called "action language," in which actions are described individually to explain their character and motivation, rather than using conventional psychoanalytic terms for emotional states, motivational structures, and levels of consciousness, to do so. Others, such as Peterfreund (1961), have challenged metapsychology from the standpoint of information theory and systems theory.

INTEGRATION OF HISTORICAL AND CONTEMPORARY THEORIES

Solomon (1982) has expressed in a recent article her view that all of the theories and formulations, past and contemporary, are pertinent to the work of psychoanalysts, if each is applied in the particular area that it explains best. However, the historical survey, presented here, suggests that, rather than combining past and present theories in patchwork fashion, a more genuine integration of them may be achieved. I believe that the attempt to improve our understanding about the pathologies related to earlier periods of development can best succeed by thinking of incompatibilities of internal structures rather than to regress, as Rangell (Richards, 1982, p. 727) has expressed it, to a psychology of composite wholes of the self and object. However, traditional structural theory requires modification in order to apply it to preoedipal conditions, and the modification needed is suggested by contemporary work.

First, Kohut (1971) has proposed, perhaps not an extension, but a new emphasis in relation to structural theory. In describing two narcissistic lines of development related to ideals, he has emphasized that we should pay equal attention to failures to achieve ideals of the superego as we have, traditionally, to transgressions of superego prohibitions. The term "incompatibility," Freud's original term, rather than "conflict," is used in this presentation to refer to both kinds of incompatibility of reality and the superego.

Second, we need to consider not only structures in the oedipal stage, but also primitive ideals and prohibitions of primordial stages that are incompatible with reality, as Freud was beginning to do in his last papers, when he added developmental considerations to his writings about the ego and the superego. A patient, who still idealizes symbiotic-stage gratification by an object, is frustrated and feels helpless failure at the incompatible reality of separation from the fantasied merged object. A patient, who has not completed the building of oedipal prohibitions, will feel anxiety at the incompatible reality of closeness to an erotic object. What I believe to be a false distinction between deficit and conflict pathologies is eliminated here, because the structure of each stage, oedipal as well as preoedipal, is deficient relative to a more advanced stage. It is relative deficiency that causes a particular incompatibility with the reality of life. Of course, in utilizing primordial structures to explain early pathology, we must keep in mind the distinctions classified as genetic fallacies (Hartmann and Loewenstein, 1962), and not confuse primordial structures with those that are fully developed.

Using primordial structural terms as a common language to describe preoedipal pathology also helps to explain the different qualities of affect disturbance as being related to different developmental stages. The helpless, hopeless feeling of depression reflects a failure to achieve the primordial superego ideal of gratification by another, conceived of as the competent part of oneself. It would be a contradiction in terms to conceive of anger or guilt, directed at an object, before the reality representations of the object—as an independent "center of initiative" (Kohut, 1971, p. 76)—are distinct from representations of the motives and functions (structures) that make up oneself. Analysts have, of course, long acknowledged that there can be no oedipal guilt until the prohibitions and idealizations of the oedipal superego are present.

SUMMARY

I have attempted to review the historic progressive sharpening of the basic and enduring conception of pathology as an incompatibility of the significant structures of the psyche, and suggested a way of looking at contemporary theorizing as an effort to extend that basic conceptualization to preoedipal related pathologies. It has been stressed here that, just as a developmental sequence of the instincts allowed the topographic model to explain more effectively the various conflicts that may occur, a developmental sequence for each structure will make the structural model more useful. We will then be able to address all the preoedipal findings of the contempoary period in universal concepts and terms rather than in many varying concepts and terms.

REFERENCES

Abraham, K. (1927), *Selected Papers on Psychoanalysis*. London: Hogarth Press.

Arlow, J., & Brenner, C. (1964), *Psychoanalytic Concepts and the Structural Theory*. New York: International Universities Press.

Benedek, T. (1970), Parenthood during the life cycle: In: *Parenthood: Its Psychology and Psychopathology,* ed. E. J. Anthony & T. Benedek. Boston: Little, Brown & Co., pp. 185–206.

Bion, W. (1965), *Transformations*. New York: Basic Books.

Breuer, J., & Freud, S. (1893–1895), Studies On Hysteria. *Standard Edition, 2*. London: Hogarth Press, 1955.

Erikson, E. (1959), Identity and the life cycle. *Psychological Issues,* Vol. 1. New York: International Universities Press.

Ferenczi, S. (1950), *Further Contributions to the Theory and Technique of Psychoanalysis*. London: Hogarth Press.

Freud, A. (1946), *The Ego and the Mechanisms of Defense*. New York: International Universities Press.

_____ (1965), *Normality and Pathology in Childhood*. New York: International Universities Press.

Freud, S. (1892–1899a), Extracts from the Fliess Papers, Draft G. *Standard Edition,* 1:200–206. London: Hogarth Press, 1966.

_____ (1892–1899b), Extracts from the Fliess Papers, Letter 46. *Standard Edition,* 1:229–232. London: Hogarth Press, 1966.

_____ (1892–1899c), Extracts from the Fliess Papers, Letter 32. *Standard Edition,* 1:233–239. London: Hogarth Press, 1966.

_____ (1892–1899d), Extracts from the Fliess Papers, Letter 69. *Standard Edition,* 1:259–260. London: Hogarth Press, 1966.

_____ (1892–1899e), Extracts from the Fliess Papers, Letter 71. *Standard Edition,* 1:263–266. London: Hogarth Press, 1966.

_____ (1896), Further remarks on the neuropsychoses of defense. *Standard Edition,* 3:162–185. London: Hogarth Press, 1962.

_____ (1900), The interpretation of dreams. *Standard Edition,* 4 & 5. London: Hogarth Press, 1953.

_____ (1901), The psychopathology of everyday life. *Standard Edition,* 6. London: Hogarth Press, 1960.

_____ (1905a), Jokes and their relation to the unconscious. *Standard Edition,* 6. London: Hogarth Press, 1960.

_____ (1905b), Three essays on the theory of sexuality. *Standard Edition, 7.* London: Hogarth Press, 1953.

_____ (1907), Delusions and dreams in Jensen's Gradiva. *Standard Edition, 9.* London: Hogarth Press, 1959.

_____ (1909a), Analysis of a phobia in a five-year-old boy. *Standard Edition, 10.* London: Hogarth Press, 1955.

_____ (1909b), Notes upon a case of obsessional neurosis. *Standard Edition, 10.* London: Hogarth Press, 1955.

_____ (1913), Totem and taboo. *Standard Edition, 13.* London: Hogarth Press, 1955.

_____ (1914), On narcissism. *Standard Edition, 14.* London: Hogarth Press, 1957.

_____ (1915a), Instincts and their vicissitudes. *Standard Edition, 14.* London: Hogarth Press, 1957.

_____ (1915b), Repression. *Standard Edition, 14.* London: Hogarth Press, 1957.

_____ (1917), Mourning and melancholia. *Standard Edition, 14.* London: Hogarth Press, 1957.

_____ (1921), Group psychology and the analysis of the ego. *Standard Edition, 18.* London: Hogarth Press, 1955.

_____ (1923), The ego and the id. *Standard Edition, 19.* London: Hogarth Press, 1961.

_____ (1926), Inhibitions, symptoms, and anxiety. *Standard Edition, 20.* London: Hogarth Press, 1959.

_____ (1940), An outline of psychoanalysis. *Standard Edition, 23.* London: Hogarth Press, 1964.

Fromm-Reichmann, F. (1950), *Principles of Intensive Psychotherapy.* Chicago: University of Chicago Press.

Gedo, J., & Goldberg, A. (1973). *Models of the Mind.* Chicago: University of Chicago Press.

Hartmann, H. (1964), *Essays on Ego Psychology.* New York: International Universities Press.

_____ Kris, E., & Loewenstein, R. (1962), Notes on the superego. *The Psychoanalytic Study of the Child,* 17:42–81. New York: International Universities Press.

Jacobson, E. (1964), *The Self and the Object World.* New York: International Universities Press.

Kernberg, O. (1976), *Object Relations Theory and Clinical Psychoanalysis.* New York: Jason Aronson.

Klein, M. (1948), *Contributions to Psychoanalysis.* London: Hogarth Press.

Kohut, H. (1971), *The Analysis of the Self.* New York: International Universities Press.

Mahler, M. (1968), *On Human Symbiosis and the Vicissitudes of Individuation,* Vol. 1. New York: International Universities Press.

Peterfreund, E. (1961), *Information, Systems, and Psychoanalysis. Psychological Issues,* Monogr. 1. New York: International Universities Press.

Richards, A. (1982), Panel: Psychoanalytic theories of the self. *J. Amer. Psychoanal. Assn.,* 30:717–733.

Rosenfeld, H. (1954), Psychoanalytic approach to acute and chronic schizophrenia. *Internat. J. Psycho-Anal.,* 35:135–140.

Sandler, J., & Rosenblatt, A. (1962), The representational world. *The Psychoanalytic Study of the Child,* 17:128–148.

Schafer, R. (1976), *A New Language for Psychoanalysis.* New Haven: Yale University Press.

Searles, H. (1965), *Collected Papers on Schizophrenia.* New York: International Universities Press.

Solomon, R. (1982), Man's reach. *J. Amer. Psychoanal. Assn.,* 30:325–343.

Spitz, R. (1957), *No and Yes.* New York: International Universities Press.

Winnicott, D. (1965), *The Maturational Process and the Facilitating Environment.* New York: International Universities Press.

7

Change and Integration in Theoretical Concepts: A Discussion

SHERWYN M. WOODS, M.D., Ph.D.

In Arnold Cooper's 1982 Presidential Address to the American Psychoanalytic Association entitled, "Psychoanalysis at 100: Beginnings of Maturity" (Cooper, 1982), he reviewed the evidence of increasing maturity in psycho-analysis, the inevitable resistance to change, the role of controversy in the evo-lution of ideas, and the growing importance of scientific data as it relates to theory–building. He points out — correctly, in my opinion — that one aspect of our profession's maturity is an increasing difficulty in defining the boundaries between psychoanalysis and other disciplines. Many of these issues are brought sharply into focus in any attempt to discuss the papers by Drs. Ekstein, Nunn, and Shane on the subject of change and integration in theoretical concepts.

Dr. Ekstein has shared his life with us. He chronicles a personalized view of his evolution as a psychoanalyst, dedicated to openness and receptivity to *all* languages involved in the interpretive process. The Drs. Shane remind us that theory–building based on reconstruction, as opposed to direct observation and research, can lead to therapeutically unprofitable flights of fantasy. Dr. Nunn's paper is a marvelous synthesis of the evolution of classical theory, and this leads him to suggest that there has been only modest change over the past nearly one hundred years. He implies that much current controversy may be a tempest in a teapot.

Since I find myself in the sharpest disagreement with his views of contemporary psychoanalysis, I shall begin with Dr. Nunn. By stating that, in our approach to psychopathology, change has been limited to progress along the lines of the concept of symptom–formation outlined by Freud in 1895, he effectively trivializes major contributions by both the object-relations school and the self-psychology school. This is particularly true with respect to character pathology and symptomatology, which are based less on structural conflict than on structural deficit or defect. The distinctions made by the self-psychologists between "tragic man" and "guilty man" or perhaps more accurately, the oedipal patient vs. the predominantly preoedipal patient — are, in my opinion, trivialized by translating Kohut's contributions as if they were merely a new emphasis in structural theory.

The concepts of deficit-induced psychopathology and the effects of archaic selfobject structures cannot be encompassed by postulating primordial superego structures and superego ideals. It is obvious that relative deficiency at any level of development, whether in structural terms or in terms of selfobject relations, produces incompatibility with or distortion of the tasks at the next level of development. However, the issue here is not the truth of that concept, but whether minor modifications of structural theory can best accommodate the wealth of clinical observation and research documentation about the nature of preoedipal life, and whether such modifications will lead to the most effective therapeutic intervention. This is a matter of great importance, and both Ekstein and the Shanes point out that the way you look at therapeutic dialogue strongly affects the process between patient and therapist. In other words, the issue is not whether the theory so well summarized by Nunn is a valid and necessary aspect of understanding psychopathology, but whether it is sufficient.

Ekstein reminds us that every theory is a covert description of the therapeutic instruments used by therapists, with different theories reflecting differences in the way we communicate with patients. He reminds us of Wittgenstein (1922), and the fact that vague and unclarified concepts or theories lend themselves particularly well to ideological warfare. The Shanes correctly point out that the concept of separate lines of development of self and object relations, the concept of psychic structure–building by "transmuting internalization," as opposed to identification, and the continuing need for an increasing number of selfobjects throughout the life cycle cannot be easily subsumed within classical psychoanalysis. In pure theory, though probably less true in actual practice, an orientation toward the central issue of conflict leads to interpretation of resistance and defense as the major therapeutic language to be derived from classical theory. The concept of intense exposure and relatedness to an empathic therapeutic selfobject, implicit disavowal of the primary role of conflict, and disavowal of aggression as a primary drive lead to a quite different emphasis. Such concepts go much further than Ekstein's focus on the process inherent in interpretation, although his process certainly includes some similar elements. To some degree, artificial dichotomies are drawn by different schools of thought. In clinical practice, I believe it is possible to integrate the various concepts far more than their proponents would have us believe.

To cite one clinical example, how does one best understand the intense erotic arousal and relief from depression which a bisexual male patient experiences with passive anal penetration? Is this a retreat from oedipal anxiety and guilt, the persistence of libidinal anal fixation, a warding off of primitive fantasies of annihilation and merger, or the search for a primitive selfobject, in order to avoid disintegration and to repair the fabric of self–cohesion? Utilizing the transference, do we proceed from the surface downward, moving through successively deeper levels of resistance and defense, and trust that rendering these conflicts conscious will build ego structure, modify superego structure, and ultimately achieve resolution. Or, do we proceed from the bottom upward by starting with the defects in primitive self and selfobject structures, creating an empathic, therapeutic, structure-building selfobject relatedness, which will catalyze psychic development and make such symptoms superfluous? This may, perhaps, be necessary, but will it be sufficient? Will we need to deal with drive– and structure–related developmental conflicts, stemming from later levels of development — dealing with these conflicts at a later time, after the patient has developed a sufficiently cohesive self to be able to do this effectively? And what of the process of working through? With adequately developed self–structures, with insightful consciousness of repressed conflicts, and with ego and superego structures correspondingly modified, will the patient then relinquish his symptom? Or, is it any longer truly a symptom, as opposed to a non–neurotic variant in sexual behavior? But what if the symptom is dystonic to the patient? What will be the effect of years of conditioned learning, highly reinforced by erotic pleasure, in the ego's attempt to extinguish its responsiveness to certain stimuli (Marmor and Woods, 1980). The complexities go on and on. I believe that it was not so complicated thirty or sixty years ago; and the complexity of contemporary psychoanalytic practice reflects significant changes in both theory and practice.

One of my esteemed professors had a great distrust of "eclecticism" and "integration," often referring to both terms as euphemisms for the garbage can. However, in the thirty years that I have been thinking seriously about psychoanalysis, as I acknowledge what I actually do with patients, I seem to be, increasingly, just such a garbage can. I have little trust in dogma, whether classical or neoclassical, although I confess to many moments when I yearn for the certainty and security such dogma might provide. Perhaps in another 500 years, or perhaps 5000, we shall have completed sufficient theory building to accommodate all the data and complexities. Until then, it behooves us to allow our cognitive structures, through which we organize our data, to be mindful of and open to alternative schemas for ordering such data, as well as to advances in related disciplines.

In their scholarly review of changes in developmental theory, the Shanes do not challenge the bulk of oedipal and postoedipal conceptualization. However, they do treat us to an exceptionally lively and comprehensive review of preoedipal theory as it is challenged or substantiated by infant research. This is, of course, the period around which most contemporary controversy rages. Validation of theoretical constructs does not come easily, and flights of theoretical fancy come all too easily, when we must rely on verbal communication and inferences about non-verbal behavior to capture the essence of that period of life before language and memory—an era when experiences are predominantly organized around affective and motoric structures, rather than around language and cognition (Basch, 1976; Lichtenberg, 1982). Those who are critical of the self-psychology point of view have noted the extreme vulnerability of empathic intervention to projective countertransference distortions. However, it should also be mentioned that classical interpretation and reconstruction, related to preoedipal conflict, is subject to the same vulnerabilities.

Taking the stand that direct observation should always take precedence over reconstruction in theory building, the Shanes summarize infant research. They find that it does *not* support the Freudian concept of hallucinatory wish fulfillment; the capacity for psychic representation prior to 18 months of age; the cognitive capacities attributed to infants by adultomorphic Kleinian theories; delusions of fusion, or even the existence of an undifferentiated and truly symbiotic early stage; the existence of a stimulus barrier during an autistic phase of development; or discretely libidinal phases related to corresponding body parts. Such infant observation *does* support the notion that there is a far greater than formerly suspected "pre-wired" capacity for communication and interaction from the beginning; emergent structures that prepare very early for the development of totally separate cognitive schemas of self and other; and organization of infant experience around numerous inborn affect potentials and motoric experiences.

To the degree that the Shanes have marshalled the evidence correctly, as I believe they have, there are major rents in the fabric of classical theory, object relations theory, and self-psychology. They believe, as I do, that both "deviationist" theories and classical theory are at their best when focusing on one or more particular aspects of the human condition, and at their worst when each theory insists on being a complete system, which can stand in splendid isolation from previous and concurrent contributions that focus on other aspects of being. What I find particularly refreshing about the Shanes' synthesis regarding preoedipal development is their willingness to integrate concepts derived from various schools, not merely for the purpose of collegiality, but with an eye toward validation at *both* the clinical and research levels. This is not a minor matter, since few would disagree that the greater the discrepancy between the theoretical and/or reconstructed versus the actual, the poorer the resultant insights and interventions offered to the patient. Ekstein's paper would support the Shanes' notion that the analyst's view of early development is likely to influence his or her understanding of the patient's material, the strategy of interpretation, formulations and reconstructions, and the nature of the therapeutic stance.

We should not leave the life cycle behind without acknowledging another change which has occurred in developmental theory building: the work extending from Erikson (1959) to the recent book by Colarusso and Nemiroff (1981), which describes continuing developmental tasks, influences, and effects on structure throughout the life cycle.

No discussion of change and evolution in psychoanalysis would be complete without considering changes in the theory of therapeutic action. Lawrence Friedman (1978), in his brilliant essay "Trends in the Psychoanalytic Theory of Treatment," points out that Freud considered understanding, attachment, and integration to be important factors in achieving treatment benefits. He goes on to document the historical emphasis on cognitive understanding and the resistance to conceptualizing the part played in therapy by the patient's personal attachment to the analyst. The object-relations school, Friedman points out, is united in belief that permanent changes are brought about when the therapist provides a relationship that the patient needs; its adherents are convinced that relationships structure, that good relationships integrate, and that psychoanalysis is, at least in good measure, a replacement therapy.

Both the object–relations school and the self-psychology school conceptualize a deficiency in the early development of psychic structures, which are necessary to provide secure self-esteem, although they differ about the nature of the pathogenic forces. In their therapeutic approach, they agree that childhood needs are gratified in treatment, and that the nature of the attachment to the analyst will effect ultimate psychic structure. This goes far beyond the concept of the therapeutic alliance and real relationship as elaborated by Greenson (1967); and I believe it goes beyond the concept of interpretive process as discussed by Ekstein. It does of course relate to Franz Alexander's theory of "corrective emotional experience." The emphasis on the nature and primacy of the therapeutic relationship as a force in psychic restructuring is a major change and a central issue in the contemporary debate about the workings of therapeutic action.

Psychoanalytic theory building must address itself—with an eye to the prerepresentational research data which is rapidly accumulating—to better conceptions of how the analytic technique may deal effectively with what Emde (1980) has called the affective core around which early experiences are organized. Whether we move in the direction of classical theory or self-psychology or object relations theory, the challenge is to assess the validity of the components of these theories in terms of both necessity and sufficiency for effective therapy.

Polarization between different schools, symbolized by the Kernberg-Kohut debate, serves a useful purpose in forcing a clarification of concepts. But it also recalls an unfortunate phenomenon associated with the evolution of psychoanalytic thought — the resistance of the main body of psychoanalysts to innovation and change and a tendency to exclude, rather than integrate, new knowledge and concepts. It is important to remember, as pointed out by Stolorow and Atwood (1976), that, in 1924, Otto Rank addressed himself to narcissism and narcissistic psychopathology in a fashion strikingly similar to modern self-psychology. He described the establishment and dissolution of a narcissistic transference: the therapeutic building of missing psychic structure by continuation of a developmental process arrested before the achievement of separation-individuation, followed by consolidation of a cohesive self-representation. Rank understood a great deal about narcissism — what we would now call ego and object splitting and the associated pathology. Why were his insights lost to the main stream of psychoanalysis for nearly fifty years? There were at least two important reasons: first, he was excluded and shunned for his audacity in challenging doctrine; and, second, because he insisted that his theories should stand alone as a whole new psychology. The adherents of Adler, Jung, and others have encountered the same response for the same reasons.

Should we congratulate ourselves on the rapid growth of theroetical concepts in our field, or should we be concerned about the resistance to growth and integration that has characterized our history? As psychoanalysts, we should probably do both! Cooper (1982) has pointed out that resistance to change, characteristic of all scientific thinking, has a positive side: it assures that new ideas will be subject to scrutiny and assimilated only after surviving the test of time. He identifies four particular factors underlying resistance of change in psychoanalysis: first, Freud's insistence on discipleship and adherence to a unitary view; second, a long-standing uncertainty regarding professional identity; third, a need for certainty and predictability in both theory and organizational life to contrast with our daily professional activities; and fourth, the tendency of all organizations to be threatened by and to resist change.

Ekstein's paper poses a fascinating question as to how much theoretical polarity may result from students and followers forcing leaders into a rigid position. Rothstein (1980) has addressed himself to the narcissistic professional investment in paradigm-making and the evolution of paradigms, pointing out that the resultant over-valuation isolates a theory and its proponents from colleagues who differ. It is a short step from such isolation to presenting these paradigms as the only organizing framework for all clinical data. An associated wish for uniqueness and immortality, I suspect, runs parallel to the fear that particular contributions may become diluted and lost with integration.

Whether speaking of the schools of Rank, Adler, Jung, Klein, or Kohut, one wonders at what point theory builders lose sight of the aim to truly understand patients (in the spirit of Ekstein's presentation), and begin to address themselves to making the theory stand alone.

If there has been resistance to change and integration within psychoanalysis itself, there has been an even greater resistance to the integration of scientific discoveries from related disciplines. Psychoanalysis has been slow to apply the extraordinary contributions from the social sciences, learning theory, neurophysiology, and neurobiology. We stand on the threshold of enormous breakthroughs in understanding basic brain biology and the neurophysiological structures and functions upon which human experience registers.

When biological intervention is primitive and non-specific, as in the past, it is easy to ignore in order to achieve purity in the analytic situation. Whether such purity is necessary or desirable in contemporary psychoanalysis is a matter of debate. However, as chemical interventions become more sophisticated — perhaps at the level of genetically determined defects in biological structure and function (as may be the case with Lithium and bipolar affective disorder) — it probably verges on malpractice to insist on such purity. Such specificity and sophistication of intervention on the biological systems involved with affects and anxiety will, undoubtedly, become increasingly common in the future. Even the issue of vulnerability to the effects of preoedipal psychic trauma, an important factor in understanding individual differences in response to similar developmental experiences, may in the future be understood in a far more sophisticated way than we have ever imagined, with an associated potential for biological intervention.

The brain is still a developing organ at birth. There is accumulating data that postnatal experience, including sensory pleasuring provided to the infant, affects brain development. For example, the degree of dendritic arborization and the anatomical development of certain brain pathways associated with pleasure (Prescott, 1970). Pleasure is a critically important phenomenon in virtually all theories of human development, including psychoanalysis and the learning theories. Are there biologically irreversible effects on brain structure created by the psychological environment in the first years of life? If so, what is the influence on subsequent developmental tasks? Do such differences in structure require modifications of psychoanalytic technique for effective intervention? These are exciting, but perplexing, problems for the future.

Freud believed — and I agree — that proof of the validity of psychoanalytic concepts will ultimately rest with research at the interface between neurophysiology and psychoanalysis. The challenge for the future will be found, not only in the evolution and integration of theory building, derived from psychoanalytic observation and research, but in the integration of our theories with scientific insights and discoveries of related disciplines. We must be willing to abandon dogma, discipleship, insularity, and even cherished (but outdated) concepts, and to address ourselves to scholarly inquiry, collegial interchange, and the uncertainties inherent in theory building, which is infinite rather than fixed.

REFERENCES

Basch, M. F. (1976), The concept of affect: A reexamination. *J. Amer. Psychoanal. Assn.,* 24: 759–777.

Colarusso, C. A., & Nemiroff, R. A. (1981), *Adult Development: A New Dimension in Psychodynamic Theory and Practice.* New York: Plenum Press.

Cooper, A. M. (1982), "Psychoanalysis at 100: Beginnings of Maturity," presidential address, American Psychoanalytic Association, midwinter meeting, New York.

Emde, R. N. (1980), Toward a psychoanalytic theory of affect: II. Emerging models of emotional development in infancy. In: *The Course of Life: Psychoanalytic Contributions Toward Understanding Personality Development,* Vol. 1, *Infancy and Early Childhood,* eds. S. I. Greenspan & G. H. Pollock.

Erikson, E. (1959), *Identity and the Life Cycle.* New York: International Universities Press.

Friedman, L. (1978), Trends in the psychoanalytic theory of treatment. *Psychoan. Quart.,* 47: 524–567.

Greenson, R. (1967), *The Technique and Practice of Psychoanalysis, Vol. 1.* New York: International Universities Press.

Lichtenberg, J. D. (1982), "Reflections on the Second Year of Life," presented at the American Psychoanalytic Association, spring meeting, Boston.

Marmor, J., & Woods, S. M. (1980), *The Interface Between the Psychodynamic and Behavioral Therapies.* New York: Plenum Press.

Prescott, J. W. (1970), Early Somatosensory Deprivation As An Ontogenetic Process in the Abnormal Development of the Brain and Behavior. Medical Primatology. Proc. 2nd Conf. exp. Med. Surg. Primates, New York 1969, pp. 356–375 (Karger, Basel 1971).

Rothstein, A. (1980), Psychoanalytic paradigms and their narcissistic investment. *J. Amer. Psychoanal. Assn.,* 28:385–395.

Stolorow, R. D., & Atwood, G. E. (1976), An ego-psychological analysis of the work and life of Otto Rank in the light of modern conceptions of narcissism. *Internat. Rev. Psycho-Anal.,* 3: 441–459.

Wittgenstein, L. (1922), *Tractatus Logico Philosophicus.* London: Kegan Paul, Trench Traubner.

8

Psychoanalysis as a Scientific Theory

HEINZ HARTMANN, M.D.

When some forty-five years ago Freud (1913) wrote for the first time about the philosophical interest in analysis, his main point was that philosophy could not avoid taking fully into account what he then called "the hypothesis of unconscious mental activities." He also mentioned that philosophers may be interested in the interpretation of philosophical thought in terms of psychoanalysis — adding, though, here as elsewhere, that the fact that a theory or doctrine is determined by psychological processes of many kinds does not necessarily invalidate its scientific truth. Since then, the knowledge of human behavior and motivation we owe to analysis has greatly increased, has become much more comprehensive but also more specific; and this development has certainly influenced not only social science, anthropology, and medicine, but also philosophy in a broad sense. This does not, though, necessarily mean that analysis can "answer" what one usually calls philosophical problems; it usually means that it leads to looking at them from a new angle. Some of its potentialities in this respect have been made use of only rather scantily so far. I am thinking, for example, of its possible contribution toward a better understanding of ethical problems. The interest psychoanalysis may have for philosophers has clearly two aspects: it resides partly in the new psychological findings and the-

Reprinted by permission of New York University Press from *Psychoanalysis, Scientific Method and Philosophy*, edited by Sidney Hook. Copyright © 1959 by New York University.

ories of analysis, but also in certain questions of methodology raised by Freud's and other psychoanalysts' approach to the study of man.

In speaking of psychoanalysis one often refers to a therapeutic technique. One may also refer to a method of psychological investigation whose main aspects are free association and interpretation; or, finally, to a body of facts and theories (Freud, 1913). In this last sense, we would certainly consider as psychoanalytical any knowledge gained directly by Freud's method of investigation; but many of us would today consider analysis to include related procedures such as the application of psychoanalytic insights to data of direct child observation, a field which has grown in importance in the last two decades. Of the three aspects just mentioned, it is the method of exploration that has undergone the least change; it is commonly used in a situation defined by a certain set of rules and referred to as the psychoanalytic situation or the psychoanalytic interview. The therapeutic technique has been repeatedly modified, and psychoanalytic theory has gone through a series of more or less radical modifications, by Freud and by others. I want to emphasize that the interrelations among these three aspects are, in analysis, a central topic — though in the context of this presentation I can refer to them only occasionally.

The theories of psychoanalysis follow principles of systematization, as do theories in other fields. Freud, however, did not speak of analysis as a "system," but rather accentuated its unfinished character, its flexibility, and the tentative nature of a considerable part of it. Actually, adjustments and reformulations of various aspects of theory have repeatedly become necessary. There are chapters such as the psychology of the dream, of libidinal development, of anxiety, and of symptom formation, that have been more systematically worked out than others. Psychoanalysis is obviously far from being a closed system of doctrines, though it has often been represented as such. Also, though some fundamental tenets of psychoanalysis are accepted by all (Freudian) analysts, agreement on all of them is obviously lacking.

There is in analysis a hierarchy of hypotheses as to their closeness to observation, their generality, and the degree to which they have been confirmed. It appears that a neater classification as to these points and a higher degree of systematization (considering the different levels of theorizing) than exist today would not only facilitate my task in discussing psychoanalysis as a scientific theory but also clarify the standing of analysis as a scientific discipline. Promising efforts in this direction have been made and are being made by analysts and also by nonanalysts, but as yet no complete and systematical outline drawn from this angle is available; a recent work by David Rapaport (1958) may come close to performing this task. This is probably the reason, or one of the reasons, that in more or less general presentations of psychoanalysis references to its history abound, and the reader will forgive me if they do in this paper too, at least in its first part. I shall mostly refer to the work of Freud, because most of the more general theories of analysis have their origin in it, and because he is in many ways more representative of psychoanalytic thinking than anybody else.

Often historical explanations are substituted for system; an attempt is made to clarify the function of propositions in their relation to others by tracing their place in the development of analysis. Also, without such historical reference it happens over and over again that analytical hypotheses are dealt with on one level, so to say, which belong to different phases of theory formation, and some of which have actually been discarded and replaced by others. Again, because of the comparatively low level of systematization, I think it is true that even to-day a thorough knowledge of at least some chapters of analytic theory cannot be acquired without knowledge of its history (Hartmann, 1948).

From the beginning, explanations of human behavior in terms of propositions about unconscious mental processes have been an essential part and one characteristic feature of psychoanalysis. I may, then, start by introducing Freud's concepts of unconscious processes. He makes a distinction between two forms of unconscious mental activity. The one, called preconscious, functions more or less as conscious activities do. It is not conscious, in a descriptive sense, but can become conscious without having to overcome powerful counterforces. Where such overcoming of resistances is necessary, as is the case with repressed material, we speak of unconscious processes in the stricter, the dynamic, sense of the word. The dynamic impact of these latter unconscious processes on human behavior — and not only in the case of mental disease — is one main tenet of Freud's theory of unconscious mental activities.

There is rather wide agreement that conscious data are insufficient for the explanation of a considerable part of behavior, and particularly of those aspects that were first studied in analysis. However, its critics have repeatedly claimed that the introduction of unconscious processes is superfluous. The explanation needed could be stated, or should be sought for, in terms of the more reliable data of brain physiology. The question here is not just whether, and why, explanations based on such data would be per se more reliable, nor why psychological hypotheses about mental processes ought not to be introduced in explaining human behavior. We have also to consider the fact that, given the actual state of brain physiology, many and even comparatively simple aspects of behavior of the kind we are dealing with in analysis cannot be explained. To rely on brain physiology alone would mean to renounce explanation of the greatest part of the field that psychoanalysis has set out to explain. Or, if one should insist on attempting an explanation on physiological grounds, the resultant hypotheses would of necessity be considerably more tenuous and more speculative even than psychoanalytic hypotheses are suspected to be by its critics today.

Freud, well trained in the anatomy and physiology of the brain, actually started out by attempting to devise a physiological psychology that could provide him with concepts and hypotheses to account for his clinical insights. But beyond a certain point this approach proved of no use. He was thus led to re-place it by a set of psychological hypotheses and constructs; and this step repre-sents probably the most important turning point in the history of psychoanaly-sis. It was the beginning in analysis of psychological theory, the heuristic value of which he found to be greatly superior — a point that, I think, has been cor-roborated by its subsequent development.

But it is true that even after this radical turn in his approach Freud held on to the expectation, shared by many analysts, that one day the development of brain physiology would make it possible to base psychoanalysis on its findings and theories. He did not think this would happen during his lifetime, in which he proved to be right. In the meantime certain, though limited, parallels be-tween analytic propositions and discoveries in the physiology of the brain have become apparent. Also, the usefulness of some psychoanalytic hypotheses for their field has been recognized by at least some representatives of brain re-search (Adrian, 1946). As to the psychology of unconscious processes, I think it can be said that Freud in developing that part of analysis was much less inter-ested in the ultimate "nature" or "essence" of such processes — whatever this may mean — than in finding a suitable conceptual framework for the phenom-ena he had discovered.

While Freud, after the first years of his scientific work, relinquished the at-tempt to account for his findings in terms of physiology, it is nevertheless char-acteristic of some of his psychoanalytic theorizing that he used physiological models. He was guided by the trend in German physiology which has been des-ignated as the physicalist school (Bernfeld, 1944) whose representatives were, among others, Helmholtz and Bruecke, the latter being one of Freud's teachers. Certain aspects of the psychology of neurosis, for example, led him to introduce into psychoanalysis the concept of regression (to earlier stages of de-velopment), which had been used in the physiology of his day; this concept, though, acquired new meaning in the context in which he used it. Also, in making "function" the criterion for defining what he called the mental systems (ego, id, superego), Freud used physiology as a model. But this no longer implies any correlation to any specific physiological organization (Hartmann, Kris, and Loewenstein, 1946). The value of such borrowings or analogies has, of course, to be determined in every single instance by confronting their appli-cation with tested knowledge (data and hypotheses). Physiological models (also occasionally physical models, as is obvious, for instance, in Freud's con-cept of a "mental apparatus") have been used also by other psychoanalysts (see Kubie in a recent lecture) in order to illustrate certain characteristics of mental phenomena or to suggest a new hypothesis. The use even of metaphors need not of necessity lead into muddled thinking once their place in theory has been clearly delineated. The danger that earlier implications of those model con-cepts might impair their fruitful use in the new context of psychoanalysis has on the whole been successfully avoided (Hartmann, Kris, Loewenstein).

The broadening of the scope of psychology that came about as the consequence of the inclusion of propositions about unconscious mental processes meant, first of all, that many aspects of a person's life history that had never been explained before — and that, as a matter of fact, one had not even tried to explain — could be accounted for in terms of the individual's experience and dispositions. Causation in the field of personality is traceable only at its fringes without this broadening of theory. Freud was a strict determinist and often stated that to fill that gap in earlier psychological approaches, partly because of which the study of personality had been unsatisfactory, was one of his primary aims in developing analytic theory. More recently it has been said, by the mathematician von Mises (1939), that the observations correspond rather to statistical than to causal relations. I may mention at this point that this interest in the causation of mental phenomena included, quite naturally, also the interest in what we call the genetic viewpoint, since Freud's attention had been drawn to many facets of early childhood which had been unknown, and regularities in the relationships between early childhood situations and the behavior of the adult had become apparent. With Freud, the investigation of highly complex series of experience and behavior, extending over long periods of time, soon moved into the center of interest. Developmental research was to become equally important for psychoanalytic theory and practice. It is significant that the reconstructive approach in analysis led not only to the discovery of a great wealth of childhood material in every individual case, but also to the ascertainment of typical sequences of developmental phases. The genetic approach has become so pervasive, not only in psychopathology but also in psychoanalytic psychology in general, that in analysis phenomena are often grouped together, not according to their descriptive similarities but as belonging together if they have a common genetic root (oral character, anal character). It was only much later that this predominance of a genetic conceptualization was counterbalanced by a sharper distinction between genesis and function, to which I shall shortly return in speaking of the structural point of view.

Here I want to add that while I just spoke of the study of the individual's "life history," it would be misleading (though it actually has been done) to classify this aspect of analysis as an historical discipline. This misinterpretation may be traceable to its comparison with archaeology, which Freud occasionally uses. It is true that most analytical knowledge has been gained in the psychoanalytic interview and that the concern with developmental problems refers primarily to the history of individuals. But this should not obfuscate the fact that the aim of these studies is (besides its therapeutic purpose) to develop lawlike propositions which then, of course, transcend individual observations.

At this point I should like briefly to summarize the role of psychoanalysis as a psychology of motivation, bearing in mind that nowadays psychoanalysis takes into consideration the interaction of the individual with his environment, as well as his so-called "inner-psychic" processes. The study of these psychic processes constitutes what, in analysis, we call "metapsychology," a term that signifies not (as it might seem) that which is beyond psychology altogether, but simply those psychological investigations that are not limited to conscious phenomena, and that formulate the most general assumptions of analysis on the most abstract level of theory. Metapsychology is concerned with the substructures of personality, with the ego, the id, and the superego which are defined as units of functions. The id refers to the instinctual aspect, the ego to the reality principle and to the "centralization of functional control" (to borrow a term from brain physiology). The superego has its biological roots in the long dependency on the parents and in the helplessness of the human child; it develops out of identifications with the parents; and it accounts for the fact that moral conflict and guilt feelings become a natural and fundamental aspect of human behavior. The theoretical and clinical advantage of the structural formulations, referring to the distinction of ego, id, superego, has several reasons. The most important is probably that the demarcation lines of the three systems, ego, id, superego are geared to the typical conflicts of man: conflicts with the instinctual drives, with moral conscience, and with the outside world. The paramount importance on neurotic *and* normal development of these conflicts, and of the ways to solve them, was one of the earliest discoveries of Freud and has remained central in psychoanalytic practice and theory ever since.

Critics of analysis often tend to underrate the wealth of individual data on which it is built. But on the other hand, it also happens that the theoretical nature of concepts like libido is not fully realized; for example, libido is often identified with sexual experience, or as a mere generalization of some observable connections.

In the beginnings of psychoanalysis (even after the importance of unconscious processes had been realized), Freud still adhered more or less strictly to associationism. But when he found conflict to be a primary motivating force of behavior, and specifically an important etiological agent in neurosis, he gradually developed the concept of mental tendencies and purposive ideas. Psychoanalysis became a psychology of motivation, the motives being partly, but not generally, considered in analogy with those consciously experienced. There originated the idea of wishes, in certain circumstances, warded off by defensive techniques. He discovered the role of repression and later of other defense mechanisms, like projection, isolation, undoing, and so on. The consideration of mental processes from this angle of synergistic or antagonistic motivating forces is what has been known since as the dynamic aspect of psychoanalysis. The systematic and objective study of conflict has remained one of its essential aspects and has proved a necessary and fruitful avenue to the explanation of human behavior. This was a second bold step in the development of psychoanalysis. The importance of "conflict" had, of course, been known in religious and philosophical doctrines and in literature, but scientific psychology before Freud had had no means to approach the subject.

The dynamic factors involved in both sides of a conflict were, for some time, rather poorly defined. It was, then, again primarily data of analytical observation that led to the realization of the dominance of the instinctual drives among the motivating forces. I am referring here to Freud's discovery of infantile sexuality. This discovery was, at the time, considered by many as the product of revolting imagination; today, it can easily be confirmed in every nursery.

Even at the period when instinctual motivation seemed to be pretty much ubiquitous, the basic fact of conflict was not overlooked. Self-preservative instinctual drives were, at the time, thought of as the opponents of sexuality. Besides this, the concept of overdetermination, referring to the multiple motivation of all human behavior, continued also through the phase in which motivation was, on the level of general theory, nearly always considered instinctual.

Again, to fit it to his field of observation Freud had to modify the concept of "instinct" commonly used in other fields. His term, in German, *Trieb,* in English, "instinctual drive," or "drive," is certainly not identical with what one refers to in speaking of the instincts of lower animals. His concept of drives had to prove its usefulness with respect to human psychology. Here, the sources of the drives are of much less importance than their aims and their objects. The lesser rigidity of the human drives, the comparatively easy shift of the aims, the freeing of many activities from a rigid connection with one definite instinctual tendency, the comparative independence from and variety of possible response to outer and inner stimuli have to be taken into account in considering the role of the drives in human psychology. Still, the psychoanalytic theory of instinctual drives is broad enough to show also many impressive parallels with the findings of a modern school of zoologists (ethologists).

The concept of a continuity of this driving force allows the consideration of a great variety of mental acts from the angle of their investment with drive energy. Also in this way it is possible to understand the close relationship of many mental processes which, looked at from the surface, would appear to be entirely heterogeneous. The capacity for displacement or transformation into various kinds of human activities; also the motivational role traceable through and specific on all levels of man's growth from birth to maturity; their central role in typical conflicts; and the fact that they involve relations to human objects — these are some of the psychologically essential aspects of the psychoanalytic concept of human drives. According to Freud, sexuality and aggression are, among all the drives one could describe, those that come closest fo fulfilling the demands psychoanalysis makes on a concept of drives.

The concept of mental energy was then elaborated in the sense that it is the drives that are the main sources of energy in what Freud calls the "mental apparatus." However, a strictly speaking quantifying approach to these energic problems has so far not been developed. Or rather: while it is possible to speak of a greater or lesser degree of, let's say, a resistance (against the uncovering of some hidden material), we have no way of measuring it. To account for the difference in the unconscious and the conscious (and preconscious) processes Freud postulated two forms of energy distribution, conceptualized as, respectively, primary and secondary processes. The primary processes represent a tendency to immediate discharge, while the secondary processes are guided by the consideration of reality. This distinction is again both theoretically significant and clinically quite helpful. The thesis that behavior is to be explained also in terms of its energic cathexis is what we call, in analysis, the economic viewpoint.

The regulation of energies in the mental apparatus is assumed to follow the pleasure principle, the reality principle (derived from the pleasure principle under the influence of ego-development), and a tendency to keep the level of excitation constant or at a minimum. There are parallels to this in hypotheses formulated by others, and again the use of physical and physiological models played a role in the Freudian concepts.

The three aspects of psychoanalytic theory I have mentioned so far — the topographical (conscious-preconscious-unconscious), the dynamic, and the economic (energic) — represent Freud's first approach to what he called "metapsychology." It is postulated that a satisfactory explanation of human behavior includes its consideration in relation to all aspects of metapsychology. The "meta" in this term points to a theory going "beyond" the investigation of conscious phenomena. The word, generally accepted in psychoanalysis, has proved misleading for many outside analysis. Actually, "metapsychology" is nothing but a term for the highest level of abstraction used in analytic psychology.

A fourth aspect of metapsychology, called structural, was explicitly stated considerably later, though it was implicit in earlier theoretical thinking on mental conflicts. The forces opposing the drives in typical conflict situations, warding them off and forcing them to compromise formations (of which the neurotic symptom may serve as an example), are today conceptualized as an essential aspect of what we call the ego. At the core of this concept formation is the recognition of the relevant differences between instinctual tendencies which strive for discharge, and other tendencies that enforce postponement of discharge and are modifiable by the influence of the environment. This means, of course, that the dynamic and economic viewpoints can no longer be limited to the vicissitudes of instinctual drives. The original concept of a defensive ego had to be broadened to include in the ego those nondefensive functions of the mental apparatus that are noninstinctual in character. Many of these are not, or not necessarily, part of the conflictual set-up; we call them today "the nonconflictual sphere of the ego" (Hartmann, 1951). Here belong (though they too may be involved in conflict, without, however, originating in it) perception, thinking, memory, action, and so on. It is likely that in man not only instinctual factors are in part determined by heredity, but also the apparatus of the ego underlying the functions just mentioned. We speak of the primary autonomous functions of the ego. It is true that analysis is, due to its method, directly dealing with environmental factors and with reactions to them, but this has never implied a denial, on principle, of heredity. It is in this sense that we speak of a drive constitution, and today also of constitutional elements in the ego, and of the role of maturational factors in the typical sequence of developmental phases.

To those noninstinctual functions that we attribute to the ego belongs also what one can call the centralized functional control which integrates the different parts of personality with each other and with outer reality. This function (synthetic function or organizing function) is in a way similar to what, since Cannon, we call homeostasis, and may represent one level of it.

The ego is, then, a substructure of personality and is defined by its functions. The instinctual aspect of personality is today conceptualized as the id. Through the development of the ego it becomes possible that the pleasure principle, dominant with the instinctual drives, can be modified to that consideration of reality, in thinking and action, that makes adaptation possible and is termed, as I said before, the reality principle. Through recent work, the relation between adaptation to outer reality and the state of integration of inner reality has become more accessible. This development in psychoanalytic theory has thus led to an improved understanding of man's relations to his environment, and to the most significant part of it, his fellowmen — which is, however, not to say that the socio-cultural aspects of mental functions and development had been overlooked in earlier analysis. Psychoanalysis, in contradistinction to some other schools of psychology, has never considered "inner-psychic" processes only, but also, and not only accidentally, includes the consideration of the individual's interactions with the environment. At any rate, the study of object relations in human development has more recently become one of the most fruitful centers of analytic interest ("new environmentalism," Kris, 1950). Ego psychology represents a more balanced consideration of the biological and the social and cultural aspects of human behavior. We may say that in analysis cultural phenomena are often studied in their biological context and significance, and biological phenomena in relation to the socio-cultural environment (Hartmann, 1956). But this aspect will be discussed more fully later.

Some of the functions of the ego have, in the course of development, to be wrested from the influence of the drives. Gradually, they then reach, through a change of function, a certain degree of independence from instinctual origins and of resistance against reinvolvement with the drives (secondary autonomy — see Hartmann, 1939, 1950a). A similar concept, though less specific in relation to psychoanalytic propositions, has been introduced by G. Allport (1937).

This relative independence of the ego is also energically conceptualized, with respect to the sources of energy at the disposal of ego functions. The necessity to distinguish function from genesis more clearly is one of the main implications of the structural viewpoint.

The third unit of functions, considered a substructure of personality, is called the superego. To it we attribute the functions of self-criticism, conscience and the formation of ideals. The acceptance of moral standards is considered a natural step in ontogenesis. Moral conflict, and the guilt feelings that are an expression of it, are, from the time when the superego has been instituted, one fundamental aspct of human behavior. The superego has a biological root in the comparatively long dependency and helplessness of the child of the human species, which also means increased importance of the parents for its development. The superego develops out of identification with them, to which, in subsequent layers of development, identifications with others are added. Also obvious in its genesis is a socio-cultural factor, which accounts for an important segment of tradition formation. The acceptance of certain moral demands, the rejection of others, the degree of severity of the superego and its capacity to enforce its demands can very frequently be traced in clinical investigation.

Structural hypotheses are in many ways more comprehensive, but also, if I may say so, more elegant than earlier formulations of partly the same problems. They have also a considerable value in clinical thinking, because they are particularly fit to account for what has remained dominant in clinical work, that is, the various forms of typical conflict situations. Actually, the demarcation lines of those units of functions, or systems, or substructures of personality are so drawn that they correspond to the main conflicts of man, which we now describe as conflicts between ego and id, superego and ego, and ego and reality. It was in this respect that Freud found the older topographical model, the layer model (conscious–preconscious–unconscious), rather disappointing, though in other respects it still retains a certain degree of significance. Defenses as well as drives can be unconscious; thus differences between conscious and unconscious processes cannot be used to account for these conflicts.

I thought it advisable to begin by giving a picture of certain fundamentals of psychoanalytic theory, and of the degree of its comprehensiveness, by indicating at least some of its dimensions, and also the relations between different parts of these theories. Its comprehensiveness means also its actual or potential importance in many neighboring fields. My survey shows also at least some of the points at which questions can be raised from the viewpoint of a philosophy of science. There would have been an alternative to the way of presentation I chose. I could have shown how, in the analysis of a symptom or a dream, our observations lead to anticipations, and how the various levels of our conceptual tools are brought to bear on them; also, how in this process theoretical thinking is constantly brought back to the observables. But this alternative would inevitably demand the introduction of a great number of variables and a discussion of the analytic method and the analytic situation much broader than I am able to give here. Of course, a sector of psychoanalytic propositions can be tested outside analysis, and some have been tested in this way; but it is still true that it is, in the field of analysis, extremely difficult to assay the suitability of the hypotheses for the purposes for which they have been primarily devised without the use, in the analytic situation, of the analytic method.

Since its beginnings analysis has struggled for a system of concepts fit to account for the peculiarities of the subject matter it had to deal with. Freud spoke of his endeavor to "introduce the right abstract ideas" and said, "We are constantly altering and improving them." This work has continued, and still not all concepts used are equally well defined. The distinction between independent, intervening, and dependent variables is often not clearly drawn. Also the different degrees of confirmation of the various parts of the complex network of psychoanalytic hypotheses are frequently not made apparent in analytic writings. Actually, there are many reasons for the lack of methodological strictness we often find in analysis. Some of them are encountered in every theoretical approach to the central aspects of personality. In addition, there is the fact that for psychoanalytic research there were no traditional methodological models available that could be used in its service; the differences in content as well as in method prevented a borrowing in this respect. To quote Freud again from a letter about Einstein who had paid him a visit: "He has had the support of a long series of predecessors from Newton onward, while I had to hack every step of my way through a tangled jungle alone."

Freud had a firsthand knowledge of experimental method and was thoroughly steeped in the philosophy of science of the great *Naturforscher* of his day. He was fascinated by the theories of evolution, which left their imprint on his thinking, and, of course, there must have been other factors in the intellectual climate of his "formative years" that influenced his development as a scientist. The heuristic character and value of hypotheses was well known to him, as well as the role of basic concepts and postulates. Though Freud was certainly not primarily interested in the philosophy of science, it is still true, and it has often been said by psychoanalysts and recently also by others (Frenkel-Brunswik, 1954) that his "sophistication" in this respect was much greater than early reactions to his work would let one realize. But we have to consider that logical clarification is not usually found in the early development of a science and is often not the work of the great explorers (Hartmann, Kris, and Loewenstein, 1946). It is only more recently that it has become, for the case of analysis, a subject of particular interest to a great number of workers.

Psychoanalysis was, of course, "new" not only because of its conceptual language, its method, and the methodological problems it posed, but "new" also as to content. The reorganization of commonly accepted knowledge, as a consequence of new data having been found and new modes of thinking having been introduced and of the replacement of old scientific, or old commonsense, or socialized, "truths" by the new ones, is mostly a slow and often a difficult process. In analysis, such new insights, which do not only add to our knowledge but also force upon us a revision of old ways of thinking, abound. There is also the additional difficulty that some (not all) of its discoveries could be made only under specific conditions (the analytic situation); and known facts often appeared in confrontation with such discoveries in a different light. On the other hand, looking at these discoveries from outside analysis, it seemed difficult to "place," if I may say so, these unexpected and apparently improbable insights, their real connections with other factors being hardly understood. Attitudes toward demands for reconsideration of what had appeared to be safely anchored knowledge do not of course always observe the lines of logical thinking. Psychoanalysis has systematically studied—has, indeed, to study in every single clinical case—this problem, that is, the conditions for the capacity or incapacity to observe new phenomena in the realm of psychology and to think rationally about them. At any rate, once the shock the content of Freud's discoveries had represented to his contemporaries had somewhat subsided, people started to take them more seriously and even to attribute to them a certain amount of scientific standing. This process of rehabilitation of analysis was then fortified by the confirmation of psychoanalytic findings in medicine or child psychology, and through the proven usefulness of analytic hypotheses in these fields, as well as in anthropology, and in other social sciences. This, naturally, led to a different evaluation of the psychoanalytic method, too, which was at the origin of these discoveries, and of the psychoanalytic theories of which these hypotheses were a part.

That the newness and the scope of the psychoanalytic findings and theories made changes of concepts and the introduction of new hypotheses imperative, does not seem surprising. In his tentative formulations, Freud occasionally did not even disdain to take models of motivation from common-sense psychology. But to these common-sense elements, confronted with new facts and subjected to analytic conceptualization, mostly rather uncommon sense has accrued. It also seems, from the perspective of a few decades of empirical work, that quite a few methodologically questionable formulations have proved their heuristic value. Given the state of the psychology of personality, risks as to the development of the method, as well as of hypothesis formation, had to be taken. One could not limit the field to those parts that could already be handled in an unobjectionable way. Knowing the inherent difficulties of the subject matter, one may well be inclined to postdict that without the courage and impetus of a genius this most comprehensive attack on the explanation of human behavior that we call analysis could hardly have come about.

I said before that even today some logical uncertainties persist. This may in part be due to the lack of trained clarifiers, as E. Kris (1947) has said. We have also to consider that the methodological demands made on science, the signposts which indicate which routes are open and which prohibited, which ways are likely to lead to dead ends, are generally geared to the logically best-developed branches of science. These we rightly admire as models of methodological clarity (which is not to deny that even there methodological controversies arise). Progress in physics, or in biology, has repeatedly led to demands on psychoanalysis for reformulation of its theories in accordance with these developments in other sciences. There is no reason of principle that such borrowings could not enrich the tools or the clarity of analytic thinking, as has happened with other models. But this question is less one of the theory of science, than of the, we could say, "practical" needs of a specific science — the empirical question of the fitness of certain elements of logically well-structured sciences for other less developed fields. There is also, of course, the question of the necessarily different consideration of different fields. There is the need to outline a fruitful methodological approach to the less systematized sciences, to allow maximal productivity on a given level of insight into the relations between fact and hypothesis and according to the degrees of formal organization.

Before discussing in a more general way the relations between data and theories in psychoanalysis, I next shall speak of one of the inherent difficulties of our field. Every psychologist is confronted with the problem of how knowledge of the mental processes of others can be achieved. (I am not speaking here of the possibility of knowing another person's subjective experience.) As to our own mental processes some do — and some don't — refer to "self-experience." For those who do, a further difficulty is introduced if, as is the case in psychoanalysis, self-experience is accepted on principle, but its cognitive value remains in doubt. That is, it is a question of further investigation as to what is the indicative value of a given element of self-perception in terms of mental process. Looked at from this angle, analysis can be termed a systematic study of self-deception and its motivations. This implies that thinking about our own mental processes can be found to be true or false. There is in analysis, as you know, the concept of "rationalization," to give you an example. While self-experience is obviously an important element in analysis, its theories, as I said before, transcend this level of discourse.

The lawlike propositions of metapsychology are not formulated on the level of self-experience. Generally, Freud's views on introspection have not always been clearly appreciated. They are, though, evident already in the kind of psychoanalytic thinking that is comparatively close to observational data, as in Freud's ideas on the psychopathology of everyday life. In a slip of the tongue, for instance, when, in place of a word we consciously intended to use, another one, not consciously intended, appears, we use the behavioral aspect in evaluating the psychological situation — we use it, that is, in taking the word actually spoken as an indication of an unconscious motivation that takes precedence over the conscious one.

The data gathered in the psychoanalytic situation with the help of the psychoanalytic method are primarily behavioral data; and the aim is clearly the exploration of human behavior. The data are mostly the patient's verbal behavior, but include other kinds of action. They include his silences, his postures (F. Deutsch, 1952) and his movements in general, more specifically his expressive movements. While analysis aims at an explanation of human behavior, those data, however, are interpreted in analysis in terms of mental processes, of motivation, of "meaning"; there is, then, a clear-cut difference between this approach and the one usually called "behavioristic," and this difference is even more marked if we consider the beginnings of behaviorism, rather than its more recent formulations.

As to the data, it is hard to give, outside the analytic process itself, an impression of the wealth of observational data collected in even one single "case." One frequently refers to the comparatively small number of cases studied in analysis and tends to forget the very great number of actual observations on which we base, in every individual case, the interpretations of an aspect of a person's character, symptoms and so on.[1]

By keeping certain variables in the analytic situation, if not constant, as close to constancy as the situation allows, it becomes easier to evaluate the significance of other variables that enter the picture. The best-studied example of this is what is called the "passivity" of the analyst, in contradistinction to the considerably more pronounced activity of the psychotherapist. This is not to claim that psychoanalysis is an experimental discipline. However, there are situations where it comes close to it. At any rate, there is sufficient evidence for the statement that our observations in the psychoanalytic situation, set in the context of psychoanalytic experience and hypotheses, make predictions possible — predictions of various degrees of precision or reliability, but as a rule superior to any others that have been attempted in the psychology of personality. Due to the emphasis on the genetic viewpoint, many predictions are what has been called "predictions of the past," (Hartmann and Kris, 1945) that is, reconstructions of the past which can often be confirmed in astonishing detail (Bonaparte, 1945). One obvious limitation of our predictive potential is, of course, the great number of factors determining, according to psychoanalytic theory, every single element of behavior — what Freud has termed "overdetermination." Still, our technique is constantly directed by tentative predictions of the patient's reactions. Also, studies in developmental psychology by means of direct child observation, such as have been conducted by E. Kris and other psychoanalysts (M. Kris, 1957), are guided by the formulation of expectations and their checking in individual cases. Here I just want to point to one way in which psychoanalytic hypotheses can be used vis-à-vis individual cases

---

[1]Thus every single clinical "case" represents, for research, hundreds of data of observed regularities, and in hundreds of respects.

and how they may be confirmed in clinical experience. I may mention here that problems of validation of psychoanalytic hypotheses ought not to be equated, as has too often been done, with the problem of therapeutic success.

A further difficulty results from the fact that psychoanalytic theory has also to deal with the relation between observer and observed in the analytic situation. There are personality layers, if you will excuse this term, that in the average case the observed cannot reach without the help of the observer and his method of observation. But the insight of the observer ought not to be confused with the insight of the observed. Some of these problems belong in a theory of psychoanalytic technique. But there is also the problem of the "personal equation" (Hartmann, 1950; Kris, 1950). The field of observation includes not only the patient, but also the observer who interacts with the former ("participant observation"). The interaction of analyst and analysand are accounted for in the theories of transference and countertransference. As to the potential handicaps of observations traceable to the mental processes of the observer, they are subject to the constant scrutiny of the analyst. Some such handicaps of psychological observation can certainly be eliminated by the personal analysis of the observer, and this is one of the reasons that a didactic analysis is an essential element in the training of our students of analysis. Thus, what I want to say here is not that in the psychology of personality objectivity is impossible. It is rather that psychoanalysis has discovered potential sources of error and found a way to combat them.

Distortions of self-observation as well as of observations of others that occur as consequences of instinctual pressure are clinically easily traceable, and can be accounted for by analytic theory. To one aspect of this problem we find a close analogy in the behavior of animals: the "speech" of the hungry animal is different from the "speech" of the same animal in heat. In man, following structure formation, the situation is more complex. How much we can perceive psychologically with respect to ourselves and others, and how we perceive it, is also determined by defensive and other functions we attribute to the ego; and the superego, too, can influence our perceptive range and lead to distortions. The influence of central personality factors — needs, desires, affective states — on perception in general (not just in the psychological field) has also been experimentally demonstrated; and how, despite this, "objective" perception is possible is an object of special study (G. Klein, 1958). The questions of objectivation and of "testing of reality," as Freud called it, are also accounted for in psychoanalytic theory and lead again to the concept of degrees of ego autonomy that I mentioned before.

The body of analytic theories on the "mental apparatus" must include, as an essential sector, hypotheses fit to explain the distortions of psychological observation. No doubt this involvement of the observer, and the potential sources of error of his perception and judgment, represent an added difficulty in analytic clinic and research. But it is well known that even in other fields, and often in a troubling degree, this problem plays a role. However, this complication we are confronted with in analysis is an essential feature of certain aspects of human behavior rather than a result of imperfections of the state of psychoanalytic theory. There is, as I have said, also a psychologically fruitful side to these same complexities that have led to some methodological discontent. Correction of at least some distortions of psychological observation and thinking are within the reach of our method. In the so far most comprehensive study of Freud's development, his biography by Ernest Jones, the role of his self-analysis in the unfolding of his thought has been emphasized. Now, self-analysis has this function only in exceptional cases; but we have similar experiences in great numbers from the analysis of others. In a more diluted way, this correction of blind spots can even occasionally be achieved outside analysis, as a consequence of changing attitudes toward certain factors that are essential for a psychology of personality.

It is very likely that in the work of Freud and other analysts such unaccountable insights have occurred. If so, it is clear that, certainly with Freud, his striving for scientific discipline, his patient accumulation of observational data, and his search for conceptual tools to account for them have reduced their importance to a stimulus factor in the formation of psychoanalytic theories. Many subjects approached in analysis, had, before Freud, been studied by so-called intuitive psychology only. But he was wont to oppose psychoanalytic psychology to intuitive psychology and the development psychoanalysis has taken bears out this point. Still the relation between data and theory is no doubt a rather complex one in psychoanalysis. There are the cases in which, mostly in the beginning, he approached a problem with what he called "a few psychological formulae," that is tentative hypotheses, whose heuristic value must be determined. To give you one example: certain clinical observations on hysterical patients had been made by Breuer before Freud, and also by Janet. But these discoveries were viewed from the angle of dynamic unconscious processes of conflict and defense only by Freud. It was with him and not with the others who had made similar observations that they opened the way to the understanding of mental conflict in general, which was later found to be an essential factor in normal and abnormal development. Here the introduction of fruitful hypotheses was decisive for the scientific momentum of a discovery (Hartmann). It led to an integration of the observed facts and also to the discovery of new facts. It is true in psychoanalysis as elsewhere that theories cannot be considered as mere summaries of observations. Actually, "the storehouse of pre-existing knowledge influences our expectations" and often "preconscious expectations . . . direct the selection of what is to be registered as observation and what seems to require explanation" (Hartmann, Kris, and Loewenstein). It is also obvious in psychoanalysis that the psychoanalytic investigator "must know that every step of his progress depends on his advances in the sphere of theory, and on the conceptual consistency, breadth and depth reached herein" (K. Lewin).

In dealing with new observations and often new hypotheses it has become unavoidable to redefine the meaning of many concepts in analysis and to add new ones. Some concepts that have meaningfully been used, let's say, in studying the psychology of lower animals in experimental situations are less fit if we deal with human behavior. Also, concepts common in everyday usage, in medicine, in philosophy, had to be redefined for psychoanalytic purposes. I mention this here, because it has sometimes made interdisciplinary communication more difficult. Thus, as I said before, the concept of instinctual drives has been radically modified. And there are redefinitions, in analysis, also of the concepts of libido, of anxiety and others. To this, I may quote W. Heisenberg's statement that "the transition . . . from previously investigated fields to new ones will never consist simply of the application of already known laws to these new fields. On the contrary, a really new field of experience will always lead to the crystallization of a new system of scientific concepts and laws."

The fact that the analyst's observations are made in a clinical setting has clearly, in more ways than one, determined the development of the scientific aspect of psychoanalysis. The psychological object is studied in a real-life situation: the patient comes to another person, the analyst, in the hope of being freed from limitations of his capacity for work and his enjoyment of life, imposed by changes in his personality that are considered pathological but remediable. This means readiness for hundreds of hours of work and for being confronted with his life history, with parts of his personality that have been repressed, and, generally, with many surprising and often unpleasant insights into his mental processes. In the therapeutic situation, motivations are mobilized that help to combat the natural resistance against objective scrutiny of one's self. Such motivations can hardly be expected to be available outside a real-life situation; actually the many attempts outside of analysis to create, for purposes of investigation, situations meant to mimic situations of real life, have not led very far. This point, then, refers chiefly to the superiority of analysis in making data available and creating a readiness for their observation.

On the other hand, it is good to remember Freud's reactions when after years of experimental work he decided to follow his research interests in the clinical field (and the quite similar reactions we meet today in young scientists turning to psychoanalysis). "He (Freud) confessed to a feeling of *discomfort*. He who had been trained in the school of experimental sciences was writing what read like a novel. Not personal references, he said, but the subject matter forced such a presentation on him" (Kris, 1947). He was confronted with a mostly unexplored field, with human motivations, human needs and conflicts. "Everywhere," he said later, "I seemed to discern motives and tendencies analogous to those of everyday life." Some concepts of common-sense psychology which, as I said before, were tentatively applied, had to be redefined, though the terms were sometimes retained. Thus common-sense psychology soon proved insufficient; nor could the scientific psychology of his day and its methodology be of great help. Freud had only what he called a "few psychological formulae," or hypotheses, to guide him. But it was only after the special and the more general theories of analysis had been developed that the full meaning could be extracted from the clinical data he had gathered.

There is always something ambiguous about the meaning of "clinical research" in general. There exists, so far as I know, no really satisfactory presentation of the subject in terms of the philosophy of science. I just want to say here a word about Freud's case histories, whose style of thinking is, however, unique and has hardly ever been successfully imitated. Every one of his comprehensive case histories is at the same time a study in psychoanalytic theory. I mention them at this point because they show the constant mutual promotion of observation and hypothesis formation, the formation of definite propositions which make our knowledge testable, and the attempts to validate or invalidate them.

Another aspect of the clinical origins of psychoanalytic theory is the fact that more was found, in the beginning, about pathological than about normal behavior. The etiology of neurosis was studied before the etiology of health, though psychoanalysis has, on principle, always aimed at a comprehensive general psychology. Also, as I mentioned, more became known, in the first attempts to deal with the field, about the instinctual drives, especially about sexuality and its development, than about the forces opposing the drives in the typical ego–id conflicts. This, however, has changed in the last two or three decades, and analysis thus has today come closer to what it always was intended to be, though not every aspect and not every implication of its very comprehensive conceptual frame has so far been actually developed.

In clinical work, one is used to being guided by signs and symptoms in forming an opinion on the presence or absence of a pathological process. But the question of the significance and the use of signs for purposes of explanation is, of course, logically of much wider relevance. Different meanings can be attributed to the terms sign, signal, expressive sign, symbol, and so on, and these differences are important also in psychoanalysis. However, I don't propose to deal with this problem here. Suffice it to say that a considerable part of psychoanalytic work can be described as the use of signs—a series of associations, a dream, an affect vis-à-vis the analyst—as indications of mental processes. In this sense one speaks of the psychoanalytic method as a method of interpretation (Hartmann, 1927; Bernfeld, 1932; Loewenstein, 1957). This has both a cognitive and a therapeutic aspect. They partly coincide, that is, in so far as a therapeutic agent of foremost significance in analysis is making the patient aware of, and capable of integrating, previously unconscious and, through defense, split-off processes. Some of those signs, for example, some of the symbols we find in dreams, have a rather ubiquitous meaning, while the interpretation of others requires a closer scrutiny of the individual under observation. At any rate, there are many situations in which the relation between a sign and what it signifies becomes easily recognizable, for instance in the associations immediately following the observation of some detail of behavior. In others, various levels of theory have to be introduced to explain the connection. Such sign systems are used today not only in the psychoanalytic situation, but also in the study by analysts, by means of direct observation, of child development. Many childhood situations of incisive significance for the formation of the adult personality have a low probability of direct manifestation. One tries to learn about the sign function of data of child behavior for a recognition of the central, and often unconscious, development that we know from the psychoanalytic interview (Hartmann, 1950). At this point it is possible, or even likely, that a misunderstanding may occur of what I have said about a low probability of manifestation outside analysis of certain processes investigated in analysis. I want, then, to add explicitly that this was not meant to be a general statement. Many phenomena first studied in the analytic situation could later be studied also in the direct observation of psychotics, in so-called applied psychoanalysis, or in the direct observation of children. What I want to emphasize in this context is that the comparative study of reconstructive data and data of direct observation of children leads, on the one hand, to the confirmation of analytic propositions; on the other hand it leads to the formulation of more specific hypotheses.

The essential importance of constructs for the coherence of the psychoanalytic system (or whatever we choose to call it) can be gathered already from the brief outline I have given in the first part of this discussion. Theories, or hypotheses of a different order, connect them with observational data. That these constructs, which are introduced because of their explanatory value, cannot be directly defined in terms of observational data, but that inferences from the constructs can be tested by observation, has long been known in psychoanalysis (Hartmann, 1927). Still, some of these constructs seem particularly suspect to many critics of analysis. An occasional lack of caution in the formulation of its propositions, or Freud's liking for occasional striking metaphors, has led to the accusation against analysis of an anthropomorphization of its concepts. But in all those cases a more careful formulation can be substituted which will dispel this impression.

There is, then, the question whether and in what sense such constructs are considered "real"; and, more specifically, the question has often been asked whether and in what sense Freud considered constructs like libido, the "system unconscious," and the substructures of personality in the sense of structural psychology, as real. He said that the basic concepts of science form rather the roof than the foundation of science and ought to be changed when they no longer seem able to account for experience; also that they have the character of conventions. But he certainly thought that what he meant to cover by these basic concepts had effects which could be observed. He was in no danger of confusing concepts with realities; he was a "realist" in a different sense. He does not seem to have thought that "real" means just "the simplest theoretical presentation of our experiences," but rather that those basic concepts pointed to something real in the ordinary sense of the word.

It is quite possible that Freud, as Frenkel-Brunswik (1954) has remarked on "scientists of great ingenuity," sometimes proceeded "from observation directly to hypothetical constructs and . . . derived the intervening variables later." But it is also evident from Freud's work that he by no means always spelled out the ways in which he had arrived at the formulation of his constructs. It is hard to say in a general way under what conditions a direct transition from data to constructs would seem legitimate or fruitful. It has been suggested by Ellis (1950) that "where intervening variables are of a limited usefulness in scientific theorizing, hypothetical constructs take in the widest range of relevant phenomena, lead to a maximum success in the prediction and explanation of behavior."

It is obvious that among the intervening variables "dispositional concepts" play a significant role in analysis. The term "mental disposition" has actually been used in analysis, but the same kind of concept is often also covered by different terms. It has been pointed out (Hartmann, 1927) that the concept of "latent attitudes" used by Koffka and others comes rather close to psychoanalytic thinking. The term mental tendency is ubiquitous in psychoanalysis, and many of these tendencies, as mentioned before, are understood to be not manifest but in the nature of a disposition.

Speaking now of the series independent–intervening–dependent variable, I want to quote to you a passage from Rapaport (1958) about a significant aspect of intervening variables in analysis, which states clearly the point I have in mind: "Let us assume that an aggressive drive is our independent variable and overt behavior towards an (actual or thought) object our dependent variable. It will be noted that in a certain subject at certain intensities of the drive we will observe aggressive behavior (in deed or thought) toward the object, at other intensities we will observe no overtly aggressive behavior but rather excessive kindness (reaction formation). In other subjects at certain intensities the aggressive behavior will be diverted from the object to other objects (displacement) or upon their own self (turning round upon the subject), or will be replaced by ideas and feelings of being aggressed by the other (projection). In these observations the defense of reaction-formation, displacement, turning round upon the subject, projection, etc., will be conceptualized as intervening variables." Here let me remind you of what I said before, that the explanation of manifest behavior presupposes in every single case the consideration of a great number of variables. The statement, current in analysis, that the same manifest action, attitude, fantasy may have different "meanings" (that is, may be the result of the interaction of different tendencies) has often been misunderstood. It has been said that it opens the door to bias or arbitrary interpretation. This argument seems to neglect the point I have just made. What the psychoanalytic approach has shown is a complex interdependence of a variety of factors, and of patterns of factors. I may mention too, in this context, that working with unilinear causal relations alone has not always proved satisfactory. The essential fact of interdependence of mental functions does not always allow a clear-cut answer to the question of which variable has to be considered as independent and which one as an intervening variable. A stimulus from the outside world will sometimes be considered an independent variable; but in another context it may be considered also an instinctual tendency or an autonomous tendency of the ego (Rapaport, 1958). We came across this problem of relative independence in speaking of the secondary autonomy of the ego, but it has a much wider significance in psychoanalytic psychology.

Turning now to the validation of psychoanalytic hypotheses, I shall follow Kris (1947) in distinguishing validations in analysis from validations outside of it. To begin with the former, I may repeat that the amount of time spent in the study of any single individual is vastly greater, and the wealth of data considerably richer, than in any other clinical set-up. This alone would make the use of the analytic method in the analytic situation the *via regia* to the psychology of personality. In this setting, data do appear which are not, or not easily, accessible to other methods. This asset as to fact-finding has, of course, a disadvantage in another respect: an observation an analyst makes may seem entirely credible to another analyst who possesses the necessary experience, an interpretation quite convincing, while the same observation may appear hardly credible, the same interpretation highly improbable or artificial, to one who approaches the field with a different method and in a different setting. For the analyst, one constant angle of his work is the observation of data and of sequences of data, the tentative interpretations (in search of the common elements in such sequences), and the checking of his interpretation against the subsequent (and past) material. It is safe to say that the greater part of evidence for the psychoanalytic propositions still lies with this work.

To broaden the reach of intersubjective validation beyond the relatively small group of workers in psychoanalysis, and also for teaching purposes and for comparing different techniques, the recording of interviews has been recommended by many (Kubie, 1952) and practiced by some. More recently, records of analytic interviews were submitted to other analysts, who were asked to predict the developments in subsequent sessions (L. Bellak). Such studies are likely gradually to attract a greater number of research workers, but, for the present, their potential contribution to the scientific status of analysis cannot yet be estimated.

As to the genetic propositions of analysis, the direct observation of children has not only become a rich source of information, but also given us the possibility to make our hypotheses more specific and to check their validity. A great number of Freud's hypotheses on childhood could be confirmed by direct observation of children. But to validate more completely our genetic propositions, "systematic observations of life histories from birth on" are necessary. "If the longitudinal observation in our own civilization were to be systematized and the study of life histories were to be combined with that of the crucial situations in Freud's sense, many hunches might be formulated as propositions, and others might be discarded" (Hartmann and Kris, 1945).

The literature on experimental research, both in animals and in man, devised for the purpose of testing propositions derived from psychoanalysis has become very extensive. It has been repeatedly reviewed (Sears, 1943; Kris, 1947; Benjamin, 1950; Frenkel-Brunswik, 1954; and others), and I do not think I should go into it in any detail here. The following remarks are, then, random remarks and do not attempt to be in any way systematic. The classical animal experiments of Hunt, Levy, Miller, Masserman are probably known to many of you. Many of the animal experiments were conducted with considerable insight and great skill. Where the experimental set-up is adequate, the frequency of "confirmation" is impressive. Or, as Hilgard (1952) states, "It has been possible to parallel many psychoanalytic phenomena in the laboratory. When this is done, the correspondence between predictions according to psychoanalytic theory and what is found is on the whole very satisfactory."

Of course, we would not expect that every psychoanalytic proposition can be tested in animal experiments (Frenkel-Brunswik, 1954). But there are also definite limitations to so-called "experimental psychoanalysis" in the human. It appears difficult (though it has been attempted occasionally) to study "real" conflicts with the tools that "experimental psychoanalysis" has at its disposal (Hartmann and Kris, 1945; Kris, 1950). And I may insert here that even experimentation that tends to remain close to "life situations," as does the work of K. Lewin, Dembo, Zeigarnik and others, is not quite free from those limitations.

A rather harsh criticism of Sears's "Survey" has been voiced by Wisdom (1953). But also with others who do not share his point of view, a certain amount of dissatisfaction has become apparent (A. Freud, 1951; Rapaport, 1958; Kubie, 1952). Sometimes in those experiments the hypotheses tested were not psychoanalytic propositions at all, though the author had meant them to be. Sometimes they were taken over literally from psychoanalytic writings, but the context in which they appear in analysis, and thus their function, being not sufficiently considered, the results had to be ambiguous. It also happened that, looked at from the vantage point of analysis, experiments could be considered as validations of certain points in analysis, though not of those the author had in mind. In evaluating the results of "experimental analysis," there is, in addition, the perspectival character of every method to be considered, highlighting certain aspects and throwing others into the shade. Every method implies a selection, and data are being centered in different ways, depending on our approach (Hartmann, 1950; Rapaport, 1958). That is, an analysis of the methods used, and an attempt to correlate them, becomes of prime importance.

On the whole, this field of research has not so far decisively contributed toward a clarification or systematization of psychoanalytic theory. As a rule, these studies do not go beyond what has been demonstrated in analysis before (Hilgard, 1952, and Kubie, 1952); they have often not achieved new insights nor stimulated research. But, at their best, they have a value as confirmatory (or nonconfirmatory) evidence. Apart from this, they have greatly contributed to bridging the gap between psychoanalysis and other psychological disciplines. Also, "experimental psychoanalysis" continues to expand, and there is the possibility that certain drawbacks of its beginnings will be overcome.

Another source of potentially fruitful contacts is the confrontation of psychoanalysis with learning theory. Thus Dollard and Miller (1950) have attempted "to give a systematic analysis of neurosis and psychotherapy in terms of the psychological principles and social conditions of learning." They concentrate their study on Freudian principles, and the theorist of analysis, though often disagreeing, will profit from this and similar ventures.

This review of experimental checking of psychoanalytic hypotheses is admittedly a sketch only. But even if it were not, even if I had given the full picture, it would remain beyond doubt that the main body of evidence does not rest on these studies, but on the wealth of empirical data gathered by the analytic method in the analytic situation. The task to better define his concepts, to work toward a higher level of clarification and systematization of his hypotheses, rests, in the main, still with the analyst. This is, of course, far from saying that attempts at validation using extra-analytic methods, or criticisms originating in points of view different from those of analysis, are not to be welcomed by analysis. It is to be hoped, though, in the interest of sound interdisciplinary communication, that these criticisms, more than has often been the case in the past, will be based on a close familiarity with the methods of analysis, with the special nature of its subject matter, and with the role theorizing has played and plays in its development.

REFERENCES

Adrian, E. D. (1946), The mental and the physical origins of behavior. *Internat. J. of Psycho-Anal.*, 27.

Allport, G. (1937), *Personality*. New York: Henry Holt.

Benjamin, J. (1950), Methodological considerations in the validation and elaboration of psychoanalytic personality theory. *Amer. J. Orthopsychiat.*, 20.

Bernfeld, S. (1932), Der begriff der deutung in der psychoanalyse. *Zeitschrift für Angewandte Psycholgie*, 42.

_____ (1944), Freud's earliest theories and the school of Helmholtz. *Psychoanal. Quart.*, 13.

Bonaparte, M. (1945), Notes on the analytic discovery of a primal scene. *The Psychoanalytic Study of the Child*, 1. New York: International Universities Press.

Deutsch, F. (1952), Analytic posturology. *Psychoanal. Quart.*, 21.

Dollard, J., & Miller, N. E. (1950). *Personality and Psychotherapy*. New York: McGraw-Hill.

Ellis, A. (1950), An introduction to the principles of scientific psychoanalysis. *Genetic Psychology Monograph*, 41.

Frenkel-Brunswik, E. (1954), Psychoanalysis and the unity of science. *Proceedings of the American Academy of Arts and Sciences*, 80.

Freud, A. (1951), The contributions of psychoanalysis to genetic psychology. *Amer. J. Orthopsychiat.*, 21.

Freud, S. (1913), The Claim of Psychoanalysis to Scientific Interest. *Standard Edition*, 13. London: Hogarth Press.

_____ (1922), Psycho-Analysis. *Standard Edition*, 18.

Hartmann, H. (1927), *Die Grundlagen der Psychoanalyse*. Leipzig.

_____ (1939), Ichpsychologie und anpassungsproblem. *Internationale Zeitschrift für Psychoanalyse*, 24. Partly translated in D. Rapaport, *Organization and Pathology of Thought*. New York: Columbia University Press, 1951.

_____ (1948), Comments on the psychoanalytic theory of instinctual drives. *Psychoanal. Quart.*, 17.

_____ (1950a), Comments on the psychoanalytic theory of the ego. *The Psychoanalytic Study of the Child*, 5. New York: International Universities Press.

_____ (1950b), Psychoanalysis and developmental psychology. *The Psychoanalytic Study of the Child*, 5. New York: International Universities Press.

_____ (1956), The development of the ego concept in Freud's work. *Internat. J. Psycho-Anal.*, 37.

_____ & Kris, E. (1945), The genetic approach in psychoanalysis. *The Psychoanalytic Study of the Child*, 1. New York: International Universities Press.

_____ Kris, E., & Loewenstein, R. (1946), Comments on the formation of psychic structure. *The Psychoanalytic Study of the Child*, 2. New York: International Universities Press.

Hilgard, E. (1952), Experimental approaches to psychoanalysis. In: *Psychoanalysis as Science*, ed. E. Pumpian-Mindlin. Stanford University Press.

Klein, G. (1958), Cognizant style and motivation. In: *Assessment in Human Motives*, ed. G. Lindzey. New York: Rinehart.

Kris, E. (1947), The nature of psychoanaltyic propositions and their validation. In: *Freedom and Experience*, ed. S. Hook & M. R. Konvitz. Cornell University Press.

_____ (1950), Notes on the development and on some current problems of psychoanalytic child psychology. *The Psychoanalytic Study of the Child*, 5. New York: International Universities Press.

Kris, M. (1957), The use of prediction in a longitudinal study. *The Psychoanalytic Study of the Child*, 12. New York: International Universities Press.

Kubie, L. (1952), Problems and techniques of psychoanalytic validation and progress. In: *Psychoanalysis as Science*, ed. E. Pumpian-Mindlin. Stanford University Press.

Loewenstein, R. (1957), Some thoughts on interpretation in the theory and practice of psychoanalysis. *The Psychoanalytic Study of the Child*, 12. New York: International Universities Press.

Mises, R. von (1939), *Kleines Lehrbuch des Positivismus*. The Hague.

Rapaport, D. (1958), The structure of psychoanalytic theory (A systematizing attempt). In: *Psychology: A Study of Science*, Vol. 3, ed. S. Koch. New York: McGraw-Hill.

Sears, R. (1943), Survey of objective studies of psychoanalytic concepts. Social Sciences Research Council *Bulletin*, 51.

Wisdom, J. (1953), *Philosophy and Psycho-Analysis*. New York: Philosophical Library.

III PSYCHOANALYSIS AS A PROFESSION

Introduction

The papers in Part III address the major aspects of psychoanalysis: treatment, research, and education.

The opening paper by Robert Tyson presents his views on the following elements involved in the treatment situation in psychoanalysis: management, application, remedies, and consideration or tact. Tyson's comprehensive review of these four components includes a discussion of the relevant literature.

In the second paper, Mardi Horowitz takes an encouraging approach to the need for more research by analysts, especially the kind that can be done in small groups — such as that done by Gill and Hoffman (1982) on transference. Studies by Windholz, Skolnikoff, and others, reported in Part IV of this volume, are also excellent, innovative examples of such research into the psychoanalytic process.

In the third paper of this section, Calvin Settlage pursues the question of a philosophy of psychoanalytic education from the viewpoint of psychoanalysis as a science. Based on a review of the literature, Settlage presents observations and thoughts of analysts on the purposes and problems of psychoanalytic education. After providing an outside perspective on the analytic scientific dialogue by comparison with other sciences, he focuses on recommendations for what he terms a "selectively open curriculum," where new and controversial ideas and concepts would be taught alongside traditional concepts in psychoanalysis. The objective is to bring the scientific dialogue, and its nature and criteria for evaluation of new ideas, into psychoanalytic education as an ongoing function for both faculty and analysts of the future.

Robert Wallerstein's discussion draws on his own extensive experience and expertise in offering an overall conceptualization of our topic, "Psychoanalysis as a Profession." Noting the diversified and changing climate of psychoanalysis today, Wallerstein emphasizes the healthy aspects of the ferment and change which have always been the essence of psychoanalysis as a science and a profession. In his hopeful and positive assessment of our humanistic science, Wallerstein sees a multiplicity of approaches, which will continue to pose a challenge to analysts.

Joseph Sandler's paper, part of the 1983 Madrid meeting of the International Psychoanalytic Association, was selected because it addressed many of the issues covered in this volume. Sandler deals with those concepts in psychoanalysis where he feels the distance between theory and practice is particularly wide, and he makes some suggestions for modification in our theory that would bridge the gap between theoretical concepts and clinical practice.

This section includes two historical papers rather than one because both uniquely address the process of integration and change in psychoanalysis from a historical perspective. Sandor Lorand's paper was published thirty-six years ago, and provides a comprehensive view of psychoanalytic theory and practice, particularly during the ten years following Freud's death. Ralph Greenson's paper was originally presented in 1969 as the Fourth Freud Anniversary Lecture of the Psychoanalytic Association of New York.

The Editors

REFERENCES

Gill, M. M., & Hoffman, I. Z. (1982), *Analysis of Transference: Vol. II: Studies of Nine Audio Recorded Psychoanalytic Sessions. Psychological Issues,* Monogr. 54. New York: International Universities Press.

9

Some Observations on Developments in Psychoanalytic Technique and Treatment

ROBERT L. TYSON, M.D.

Anyone who thinks psychoanalysis is a monolithic body of knowledge, theory, and therapeutic technique firmly adhered to by its devoted practitioners would find a corrective educational experience in reading the literature on these topics. Different views about the relationships between theory and technique, and various claims of therapeutic effectiveness, require an assessment of the evolution of psychoanalytic technique as it is applied in practice. In making such an assessment, special attention should be given to the periodic swings of enthusiasm or pessimism and to the fads and fallacies liberally sprinkled throughout the history of psychoanalysis. We need to make such assessments because, otherwise, the various contexts of historical development are lost, and errors are simply repeated. The long view highlights lines of development that might well be missed in a shorter view.

Perhaps the most concerted effort so far to examine all the facets of change in psychoanalysis was made at the 29th International Psycho-Analytic Congress in London in 1975, which was devoted entirely to that topic. In his concluding comments at the end of the Congress, Weinshel (1976) summarized it this way: "… many of the changes… are really different ways of presenting the same issues from somewhat different points of view" (p. 458). But he also saw psychoanalysis currently as being in a period of greater ferment, with greater diversity in theory and practice, than ever before. Chosen to present differing points of view (like psychoanalytic gladiators) Rangell (1976) saw desirable psychoanalytic change as an evolutionary process building on what had been previously achieved, while Green (1976) declared psychoanalysis to be in need of fundamental changes in theory and technique in order to do more with the new clinical problems that he saw confronting psychoanalysts.

So as not simply to repeat the arguments of that Congress, and in an effort to establish a fresh perspective, my aim in this presentation is to suggest a different framework within which the term "treatment" can be discussed. After a tentative and experimental redefinition of treatment, I will examine a few selected aspects of psychoanalytic technique that appear currently to be in some kind of transition. I will also outline some elements that seem not yet wholly integrated into psychoanalytic technique, but are at the periphery of the "average expectable treatment," as practiced or thought of by psychoanalysts. It is, of course, a useful but limiting simplification to refer to an "average expectable" anything, as Wallerstein (1973, p. 12) has pointed out. For present purposes, the term refers to the well-known features of the ordinary analytic setting and situation, and to work with a patient who suffers psychic pain or disability based primarily on inner, neurotic conflicts, whatever their origins or current status.

One aspect of this examination should be mentioned at the outset, especially regarding what is "expectable." Clearly, it is impossible to know what actually takes place behind the closed door, and so we must settle for what individual analysts report, or for what may be inferred from their descriptions and from what they advocate, or from the later reports of analysands. This limitation would appear to apply even within the confines of particular theoretical persuasions, or among those espousing the value of particular technical approaches. That is, even within an apparently homogeneous theoretical and technical framework in one city, different analysts do different things.

Glover (1955) made the first systematic effort to find out just what other analysts actually do. In 1938, he sent a questionnaire on psychoanalytic technique to (probably) the majority of British-trained analysts in England at the time. Twenty-nine forms were sent, twenty-four replies received, and a remarkable diversity of practices described. I agree with Weinshel (1976) that there is little reason to think that less diversity would be found today.

In spite of such diversity, psychoanalysts often talk about treatment and other technical matters with the apparent implicit assumption that everyone knows just what is meant by the terms they are using. Perhaps that is because of yet another assumption: that only psychoanalysts will be listening to or reading what we are saying. While this may have been true early in the history of psychoanalysis, it is no longer true today, a change evidently unrecognized by most analysts who, with few exceptions, continue to write primarily for other analysts.

However, a change that I believe does influence most psychoanalysts is the conceptual shift that occurs within all of us over the course of our training and careers. This shift is marked by the increment of meaning that our technical terms accrue as our learning and clinical expertise increase. We all experience such shifts in the course of our professional lives, changes that influence the way we understand the terms and concepts we employ and the way the analytic work is performed. A typical example would be in regard to the term "interpretation." Our understanding may begin with an almost magical view of interpretation as an *ex cathedra* declaration, and then move more toward a less rigid and less stereotypical position in which the analyst makes contributions or interventions as part of an ongoing interactional process (Stone, 1961, 1973, 1981).

In this perhaps more casual approach, it may be more difficult, in retrospect, to be precise about whether each and every intervention was a clarification, a reconstruction, or some other variety of interpretation. However, in good analytic work it should always be possible to provide an adequate and appropriate analytic rationale for any intervention. As another example, Anton Kris (1982) has described and discussed the change in meaning of the concept free association that takes place as the analyst grows in experience.

But, in addition to these personal shifts in meaning, there is another, broader and ongoing alteration characteristic of any scientific field as it develops. Among pertinent examples of such a profession-wide shift of meaning, the terms "transference," "resistance," and "ego" will call to mind important changes in ways of thinking and in technical procedures that are well marked in psychoanalytic history, at first integrated more by some and less by other analysts (Sandler, Holder, and Dare, 1973).

A DEFINITION OF TREATMENT

I suggest that the term "treatment" has undergone changes in both our understanding of the word and in the things we do that are called treatment. In pursuit of a different perspective, I turned to a source usually credited with objective and neutral authority, the *Oxford English Dictionary* (1971). There I found treatment defined as, among other things, "management in the application of remedies." The example offered (perhaps not so neutral) of the use of the term was from Bishop Berkeley, who was quoted as having said in 1744: "Many are even rendered incurable by the treatment of inconsiderate physicians."

Basing my experimental definition on this source, the elements of treatment may be listed tentatively as management, application, remedies, and by reversal of the good Bishop Berkeley, consideration. To discuss treatment according to these elements has the advantage of cutting across our usual ways of thinking about psychoanalytic treatment and providing a fresh perspective. One might say that *management* refers to things the analyst does, primarily conscious in motivation, including case selection, formulation of a treatment plan, and handling the treatment alliance; *application* covers certain aspects of technique in a more concrete sense; *remedies* would encompass specific interventions such as clarification, confrontation, interpretation, reconstruction, and whatever other elements are thought to be specifically responsible for the therapeutic action of psychoanalysis. *Consideration* is of great interest to analysts, for it is linked to matters of empathy, tact, countertransference, and therapeutic zeal; simply as a matter of convenience, I will use the term *tact* to cover all these components of consideration as they are involved in the psychoanalytic process.

Using this definition of psychoanalytic treatment, the individual-specific and profession-wide shifts of meaning may be classified into any one of the four categories: management, application, remedies, and tact. I propose to examine certain aspects of these categories, with an introductory glance at those influences that may impede or facilitate our integration of these elements into our professional activities. Throughout, some of the necessary connections with theory will be acknowledged but not explored.

Management

A generally neglected topic in psychoanalysis, management is not something currently taught as part of psychoanalytic technique; it seems, rather more often, to be viewed as equivalent to manipulation, which may be necessary in some instances, especially when circumstances require parameters. The term nowadays implies the imposition of standards by the therapist, arbitrary even if required (Greenson, 1967, p. 51). It is, however, a term with an orthodox pedigree; Freud (1915, p. 159) commented: "Every beginner... becomes convinced that the only really serious difficulties he has to meet lie in the management of the transference." More recently, it is applied to methods used by the analyst to help make transference manifestations more accessible to interpretive interventions so that the analytic work can proceed in the usual manner.

Brenner, for example, says: "... whether a transference in analysis is manageable by purely analytic means will depend very much on an analyst's ability to maintain an analytic attitude consistently" (1976, p. 125). Here Brenner seems to be considering not management of the patient so much as the analyst managing himself, and, therefore, it becomes a matter of countertransference. It may be in this sense that the term is used in discussions and reports of supervised analyses: the student is "managing the case well." Glover (1955, p. 92) referred to the "analytical 'toilet' [as] a necessary part of the analyst's routine," an ongoing act of self-management, which contrasts with the more superficial view of the work of the analyst as being totally passive in nature. Such activity as part of management is of course to be differentiated from what has been called "active technique" (Glover, 1955, pp. 165–184) on the part of the therapist vis-à-vis the patient. The kind of management that I see as an element of treatment seems to me compatible with the analyst maintaining free-floating attention and participation in the analytic process.

In addition to the countertransference implications of management, case selection, the treatment plan, the treatment alliance, and other aspects of technique are intrinsic to the analyst's directing himself and the various elements of the situation toward the goal of establishing and maintaining a psychoanalytic process. Take, for example, case selection and the treatment alliance. In the face of such external pressures as diminishing demand for psychoanalysis, criteria of case selection still appear to be of interest mainly in the selection of supervised training cases.

A situation recently came to my attention in which a young man sought more treatment following four years of supervised analysis in another city. That analysis had been preceded by six months of psychotherapy with the first candidate, followed by a year of psychotherapy with someone else. The case was discussed by a committee whose responsibility it was to approve only those cases most likely to offer a successful analytic experience for both the patient and the clinician in training. This patient, having been carefully evaluated and found acceptable by a capable senior candidate, was presented to the committee and approved for supervised analysis, after extensive discussion of the criteria for analyzability. While it was made clear that approval would not have been given had the application been for a candidate's first supervised case, nonetheless, the impression remains that what are seen as reality demands sometimes result in a "de-integration" of previously held principles. I doubt that such a case would have been accepted for training purposes in earlier times.

Unfortunately, it is extremely difficult to get comparable information about how analysts select their patients for analysis after they graduate from training. Without such information, one cannot document the reasons patients are taken into psychoanalysis, or determine the process by which they are selected, or the principles by which the evaluations are conducted.

Curtis (1979) has recently pointed to a tendency to see the therapeutic alliance as an end in itself, rather than as a means to an end. It was for this reason that Sandler and his colleagues (1973, 1980) preferred the term "treatment alliance." They wanted to emphasize that they viewed the alliance as designed to have a catalytic role, rather than being therapeutic in itself. In any event, among the criteria for selecting a patient — or for suggesting psychoanalysis to a patient — is the analyst's assessment that the patient has the capacity to establish such a treatment alliance. While this capacity is certainly important (and assuming it can be properly assessed before an analysis begins), many patients are accepted for analysis on the basis of this and other criteria which I believe to be aspects of *suitability* rather than of *analyzability* (Tyson and Sandler, 1971).

Among issues to be considered by the analyst in the process of assessment are the further distinction between suitability of analysis for the person in his or her present life situation, and the suitability of this person for such treatment. Suitability of the analytic treatment for the person at this time is to be preferred over recommending a particular individual as suitable for analysis. Otherwise, the attempt to fit some patients into the analytic situation may be more in the short-term interests of the analyst than in the long-term interests of the patient.

Other aspects of determining suitability of analytic treatment include such questions as whether the demands of the treatment can be met by the person's intelligence and motivation, financial resources, capacity for object-relatedness, for developing an alliance, for self-observation and psychological-mindedness.

In a narrow, concrete dictionary sense, analyzability refers to what can be understood by a study of parts or constitutents; but the term is used by psychoanalysts to connote also a positive therapeutic outcome. For example, a grossly disturbed patient may be analyzable in that he may be understood, his associations interpreted, and his unconscious meanings discerned; but in the more usual psychoanalytic sense, he is said to be unanalyzable when a beneficial result is not to be expected.

The importance of these distintions cannot be overstated, because, without sufficient attention to these issues, the therapeutic value of the treatment alliance and its contribution to analyzability are easily overestimated. Such an overestimation may well explain instances of patients in stalemated analyses, cases of failed analysis, as well as some analysts becoming disillusioned with the analytic process. Among these patients are some who may have been deemed suitable but who are not analyzable. There are special difficulties when considering the usefulness of analytic treatment for a child or for an elderly prospective patient, for whom the real object relationship may have considerable attraction and value, overwhelming and obscuring conflictual sources of psychic pain. In such cases, we may be led to attribute improvement to a non-existent analytic process rather than to the ongoing gratification of a significant need.

The concept of the alliance, it seems to me, has not yet been adequately integrated into psychoanalytic treatment. Indeed, there are some (Brenner, 1979) who feel that it is a hindrance better done away with, rather than helpful to the treatment, thus dispensing with what can be a valuable addition to our analytic understanding and technique.

Application

The act of application of remedies may be seen in two parts: the first results from an exercise of judgment in selecting a particular therapeutic element from among those available; the second part is the manner of its employment. A special aspect that combines both parts falls in the category of tact, to be discussed later. Clearly, any and all of these acts of judgment and selection may take place consciously, preconsciously, or unconsciously, and in various proportions, with all the vulnerabilities this connotes. On what basis is the analyst to make the necessary judgment about which element to select, and how is the manner of application to be decided?

Anna Freud (1936) made this first relevant clarification of the issue: "It is the task of the analyst to bring into consciousness that which is unconscious, no matter to which psychic institution it belongs. He directs his attention equally and objectively to the unconscious elements in all three institutions. To put it another way, when he sets about the work of enlightenment he takes his stand at a point equidistant from the id, the ego, and the superego" (p. 28). She points out that this requires the analyst "to change the focus of attention in the analysis" (p. 20), a technical dictum Ernst Kris (1938) refers to as an important "change in the mode of observation" (p. 139) as compared with previous technical views. She is not suggesting for the analyst a sole preoccupation with defense interpretation, as Schafer (1983, pp. 74–75) implies, but neutrality about the source of any aspect of the patient's participation in the analytic situation and its importance for analytic work. Neither is she advocating for the analyst a "listening perspective" which is related to either the "outside" or "inside" of the patient's experience (Schwaber, 1981); she is suggesting a level of participation that involves all aspects of the patient's experience simultaneously with those of the analyst.

This all seems simple and self-evident, because it has so often been taught and reiterated that resistance to this technique has hidden behind its apparent acceptance. Gray (1982) has made an elegant study of the reasons for what he calls this "developmental lag" in psychoanalytic technique, but limits the application of his ideas — unnecessarily, in my view — to the treatment of neurotic conflict. The arguments he marshals to support his thesis seem to apply to any use of the psychoanalytic method. He lists four factors (p. 640) that may influence the choice of therapeutic elements and the decision to employ them: 1) fascination with the id; 2) predilection for an authoritative analytic stance; 3) preoccupation with external reality, including past as external reality; and 4) counter-resistance to transference affects and impulses. One might add a fifth factor: preoccupation with internal reality. Gray emphasizes the unconscious influences on the analyst and his technique, while Rangell (1982) points up the analyst's conscious rationalizations evident in the espousal of particular theories to justify technical practices.

There is some overlap in my discussion of countertransference both in regard to management and as related to application. A further distinction can be made as follows: Whereas management encompasses aspects of countertransference in the analyst's self-management, in the course of application the analyst is profoundly affected by the unconscious aspects of his or her relationship to the patient—one of the more usual implications of countertransference (Tyson, in press).

The manner in which the analyst employs interventions (aside from those elements to be referred to under the rubric of "tact") needs some attention as an aspect of application. Schafer (1983, pp. 43–44) believes that many analysts are more at ease and more open in the analytic situation than they are in ordinary life. Anna Freud expressed a different opinion in a discussion on this point: "It would be easier if students were not taught the opposite somewhere, usually by their own analyst—because it is natural for human beings to be human. But if their analysts and teachers turn them into something wooden, and then try to turn them back into human beings, it becomes difficult!" (Sandler, Kennedy, and Tyson, 1980, p. 38). Brenner (1976, p. 32) devotes considerable effort to making a distinction between what is socially appropriate on the one hand, and what is psychoanalytically appropriate on the other. Whatever the ingredients of being human may be, apparently they cannot be taught, while aspects of what constitutes an analytic attitude can be conveyed from one person to another. However, the analyst's behavior in the analytic situation seems less effective if it derives automatically from dicta prescribed by authority than if it emerges from an adequately analyzed psychoanalytic "work ego" (Fliess, 1942), which the analyst utilizes in the involvement with the patient (Stone, 1981; Loewald, in press).

There are many aspects of psychoanalytic technique and practice which are perpetuated by analysts who do to their patients what has been done to them during training; other practices are employed on the basis of compliance rather than conviction or appropriateness to the needs of the particular patient. The dictum to say nothing for the first six months, for example, may be effective for one patient for whom relative silence from the analyst is useful in the course of the analytic work, but it may be totally inappropriate for another. One woman, for example, described her experience of two analysts, both women, both Viennese, both of the same generation. Since the first treatment had been a very silent one, the patient couldn't believe the second analysis was genuine, because her second analyst talked so much. We are accustomed to differences in style between analysts, and if the patient is in a second analysis, the different experiences are an important part of the analytic material. Relevant to this point, Loewald (1975) has persuasively described the analyst's skill as based on the nature of the responsiveness which "uses his own emotional experiences and resources for understanding the patient and for advancing the patient's access to his, the patient's inner resources" (p. 282). The optimal basis for differences in style would appear to be on skillful analysts' different responses according to the needs of their patients and of the analytic process at the time, rather than originating in different theoretical or technical principles.

Remedies

Remedies refer to those elements thought to be specifically responsible for the therapeutic action of psychoanalysis, including matters of insight and structural change. This is more familiar ground, which stretches all the way from Strachey's (1934) "mutative interpretation" and Kohut's (1971) "transmuting internalization," to Loewald's broad work (1960, 1970) on the nature of the identificatory processes and the resumption of ego development with the evolution of the transference. I confine myself here briefly to an area which some analysts have struggled to integrate and others have polarized.

During the 1975 International Psycho-Analytic Congress, Anna Freud (1976, p. 263) cogently summarized the relevant issues. She pointed out that some analysts maintain a conviction that analytic understanding always has and always will have a demonstrable therapeutic potential. In contrast, others maintain that this identity of exploration and cure (if it ever existed) was only true early in psychoanalytic history, and only in regard to a narrow scope of emotional disorders. The wider we make the scope of psychoanalytic inquiry and comprehension, in this view, the more we exceed our abilities to achieve a therapeutic result from the psychoanalytic method, since the ego can only change what it has done, and not what has been done to it.

Tact

The word "tact" is derived from the Latin *tactus,* referring to touch, on which is based our current meaning of a sense of what is fitting and appropriate. Freud (1898, p. 265) first referred to tact as one of the personal qualifications required for anyone who proposed to treat nervous or neurotic patients. By 1910, in *"Wild" Psychoanalysis,* he had become more specific, saying that "psychoanalysis provides . . . definite technical rules to replace the indefinable 'medical tact' which is looked upon as some special gift" (p. 226). One of the technical rules was spelled out in *The Question of Lay Analysis* (1926), where Freud discussed the issue of correct timing as a question of tact (p. 220).

This was taken further by Loewenstein (1951a), who added considerations of "dosage" (p. 8) and the selection or avoidance, sequencing, and wording of interpretations. He gave a now widely-known example of absence of tact: The analyst was awakened by his patient, who had noted the analyst's cigar quietly burning on the floor. In response to the patient's observation that the analyst had been asleep, he replied, "You always want everybody's attention." Loewenstein commented that, while this was true of the patient, he was certainly entitled to have the analyst's attention, that the remark was misused to displace the analyst's guilt onto the patient, and that at another time the patient's insight, rather than resistance, might have been increased by this remark. Loewenstein (1951b) has also made valuable contributions in the area of psychoanalytic tact with regard to developmental considerations, the meaning of abstinence in the analytic situation, and the technically appropriate use of humor (1958).

Poland (1975) has directly addressed the issue of narcissistic vulnerability, which is intrinsic to any consideration of psychoanalytic tact. Quite appropriately, Poland examines the relationship between empathy and tact, summarizing his views as follows: "Tact follows empathy. Empathy is one way we come to know the processes of the patient's mind. Tact is the way we then utilize this information in dealing interpretively with the patient. Empathy might be considered to be on the sensory end of the analyst's functioning as one source of insight. Tact is on the motor end. We learn with empathy and understanding, and we interpret with tact" (p. 156). I believe that Kohut's (1977) views, by contrast, underestimate the importance of tact in relation to empathy. He seems to have perceived the use of the term as a rationalization employed by some analysts for actions which he considered to be just appropriately empathic (pp. 72, 259).

CONCLUSION

Alexis de Tocqueville (1835) was speaking about Americans when he wrote the following; but he might have been speaking about some psychoanalysts today who, perhaps, would be too much in agreement about "perfectibility," and too little in agreement about change:

> They have all a lively faith in the perfectibility of man; they judge that the diffusion of knowledge must necessarily be advantageous, and the consequences of ignorance fatal; they all consider society as a body in a state of improvement, humanity as a changing scene, in which nothing is, or ought to be, permanent; and they admit that what appears to them today to be good, may be superseded by something better tomorrow.

Translated into the current psychoanalytic scene, this might read as follows: Some psychoanalysts persist in a lively faith in the perfectibility of psychoanalysis. They judge that learning more is advantageous, which is hardly disputable. They judge the consequences of ignorance to be fatal to the analytic aim, which is indeed likely. However, analysts differ on whether the body psychoanalytic is in a state of improvement — some holding that the changing scene is changing only for the worse, some more optimistically holding that our path is uneven but forward. There is a contrast between the extreme pole of those who, paradoxically, believe that analysis is perfectible (if not perfect), but that all change is deterioration, and the opposite pole of those who believe things are as bad as they could possibly be right now, and if we only would agree to throw everything out and start afresh with a new (and therefore better) view and understanding, we would have a chance to make a worthwhile contribution to the human condition.

The observations I have presented on developments in psychoanalytic technique and treatment are intended to promote a middle and optimistic view. This position permits the continued use of what has proved valuable, building on the past to improve psychoanalytic understanding and technique, without the curse of aiming for constant perfectibility.

REFERENCES

Brenner, C. (1976), *Psychoanalytic Technique and Psychic Conflict*. New York: International Universities Press.

_____ (1979), Working alliance, therapeutic alliance, and transference. *J. Amer. Psychoanal. Assn.,* 27(Suppl.):137–157.

Curtis, H. C. (1979), The concept of therapeutic alliance: Implications for the "widening scope." *J. Amer. Psychoanal. Assn.,* 27(Suppl.):159–192.

de Tocqueville, A. (1835), *Democracy in America,* Vol. 1. New York: Knopf, 1966, p. 393.

Fliess, R. (1942), The metapsychology of the analyst. *Psychoanal. Quart.,* 11:211–227.

Freud, A. (1936), The ego and the mechanisms of defense. In: *The Writings of Anna Freud,* Vol. 2. New York: International Universities Press, 1966.

_____ (1976), Plenary session, "Changes in psychoanalytic practice and experience: Theoretical, technical and social implications," reporters L. Shengold & J. T. McLaughlin. *Internat. J. Psycho-Anal.,* 57:261–274.

Freud, S. (1898), Sexuality in the etiology of the neuroses. *Standard Edition,* 3:263–285.

_____ (1910), "Wild" psychoanalysis. *Standard Edition,* 11:221–227.

_____ (1915), Observations on transference-love. *Standard Edition,* 12:159–171.

_____ (1926), The question of lay analysis. *Standard Edition,* 20:183–258.

Glover, E. (1955), *The Technique of Psycho-Analysis.* New York: International Universities Press.

Gray, P. (1982), "Developmental lag" in the evolution of technique for psychoanalysis of neurotic conflict. *J. Amer. Psychoanal. Assn.,* 30:621–655.

Green, A. (1975), The analyst, symbolization and absence in the analytic setting (on changes in analytic practice and analytic experience). *Internat. J. Psycho-Anal.,* 56:1–22.

_____ (1976), Plenary session, "Changes in psychoanalytic practice and experience: Theoretical, technical and social implications," reporters L. Shengold & J. T. McLaughlin. *Internat. J. Psycho-Anal.,* 57:261–274.

Greenson, R. R. (1967), *The Technique and Practice of Psychoanalysis.* New York: International Universities Press.

Kohut, H. (1971), *The Analysis of the Self.* New York: International Universities Press.

_____ (1977), *The Restoration of the Self.* New York: International Universities Press.

Kris, A. (1982), *Free Association: Method and Process.* New Haven: Yale University Press.

Kris, E. (1938), Review of *The Ego and the Mechanisms of Defense,* by Anna Freud. *Internat. J. Psycho-Anal.,* 19:115–146.

Loewald, H. (1960), On the therapeutic action of psycho-analysis. *Internat. J. Psycho-Anal.,* 41:16–33.

_____ (1970), Psychoanalytic theory and the psychoanalytic process. *The Psychoanalytic Study of the Child,* 25:45–68. New York: International Universities Press.

_____ (1975), Psychoanalysis as an art and the fantasy character of the psychoanalytic situation. *J. Amer. Psychoanal. Assn.*, 23:277-299.

_____ (in press), Transference and countertransference. *J. Amer. Psychoanal. Assn.*

Loewenstein, R. (1951a), The problem of interpretation. *Psychoanal. Quart.*, 20:1-14.

_____ (1951b), Ego development and psychoanalytic technique. In: *Practice and Precept in Psychoanalytic Technique.* New Haven: Yale University Press, 1982, pp. 30-39.

_____ (1958), Remarks on some variations in psychoanalytic technique. *Internat. J. Psycho-Anal.*, 39:202-210.

Oxford English Dictionary, Compact Edition, Vol. 2. Oxford: Clarendon Press, 1971.

Poland, W. S. (1975), Tact as a psychoanalytic function. *Internat. J. Psycho-Anal.*, 56:155-162.

Rangell, L. (1975), Psychoanalysis and the process of change: An essay on the past, present and future. *Internat. J. Psycho-Anal.*, 56:87-98.

_____ (1976), Plenary session, "Changes in psychoanalytic practice and experience: Theoretical, technical and social implications," reporters L. Shengold & J. T. McLaughlin. *Internat. J. Psycho-Anal.*, 57:261-274.

_____ (1982, May), On the theory of theory in psychoanalysis. Panel, "The relationship between psychoanalytic theory and technique." Annual Meeting, American Psychoanalytic Association, Boston, MA.

Sandler, J., Holder, A., & Dare, C. (1973), *The Patient and the Analyst.* London: Maresfield Reprints, 1979.

_____ Kennedy, H., & Tyson, R. L. (1980), *The Technique of Child Psychoanalysis: Discussions with Anna Freud.* Cambridge: Harvard University Press.

Schafer, R. (1983), *The Analytic Attitude.* New York: Basic Books.

Schwaber, E. A. (1981), Narcissism, self psychology and the listening perspective. *The Annual of Psychoanalysis,* 9:115-131.

Stone, L. (1961), *The Psychoanalytic Situation.* New York: International Universities Press.

_____ (1973), On resistance to the psychoanalytic process. *Psychoanalysis and Contemporary Science,* 2:42-73.

_____ (1981), Notes on the noninterpretive elements in the psychoanalytic situation and process: *J. Amer. Psychoanal. Assn.*, 29:89-118.

Strachey, J. (1934), The nature of the therapeutic action of psycho-analysis. *Internat. J. Psycho-Anal.*, 15:127-159.

Tyson, R. L. (in press), Countertransference evolution in theory and practice. *J. Amer. Psychoanal. Assn.*

_____ & Sandler, J. (1971), Problems in the selection of patients for psychoanalysis: Comments on the application of the concepts of "indications," "suitability," and "analyzability." *Brit. J. Med. Psychol.*, 44:211-228.

Wallerstein, R. S. (1973), Psychoanalytic perspectives on the problem of reality. *J. Amer. Psychoanal. Assn.*, 21:5-33.

Weinshel, E. M. (1976), Concluding comments on the Congress topic. *Internat. J. Psycho-Anal.*, 57:451-460.

10

Research in Psychoanalysis

MARDI J. HOROWITZ, M.D.

After some introductory statements on the nature of psychoanalysis and research in psychoanalysis, four topics will be addressed: psychoanalytic research on the developmental sequence; research on the outcome of psychoanalysis as a treatment; psychoanalysis as a system of explanatory description of phenomena derived from unconscious mental processes; and the process of personality change in psychoanalytic treatment.

These subjects were selected because they represent important opportunities for psychoanalytically oriented research. Research on the first two topics — psychoanalytic child development and psychoanalytic outcome — is difficult to conduct if one is engaged in full-time clinical practice and has no research facilities. Research on the other subjects — explanatory description of psychoanalytic phenomena and the process of change in psychoanalysis — can be conducted by small groups of psychoanalysts without major additional resources. Such studies could help revitalize theoretical and observational formulation in psychoanalysis during the next decade.

The following position statement on psychoanalysis as a scientific enterprise and on the meaning of the word "research" in relation to that enterprise is presented as a background to the discussion of the specific research topics.

The scientific status of psychoanalysis has been a subject of debate outside of psychoanalytic circles. Approximately thirty years ago, a book edited by the philosopher Sidney Hook (1959) presented varied points of view, but more or less concluded that psychoanalysis was not within the realm of science. More recently, Ricoeur (1970, 1974) asserted the acceptability of psychoanalysis as a hermeneutical discipline, or a science of how phenomena are interpreted. However, psychoanalysts such as Spence (1982) have challenged the scientific status of hermeneutics. Entering the debate, Blight (1981) has contributed an article aptly entitled "Must Psychoanalysis Retreat to Hermeneutics?" In essence, his question suggests that, even though Ricoeur has given psychoanalysis acceptable status in an interpretive domain, it does not mean that psychoanalytic theory has to reside within that "department." It can continue to be developed as a branch of psychology and psychiatry and, as such, a scientific enterprise.

According to the hermeneutical position, psychoanalysis can be seen as similar to the departments in a university. That is, the argument would not be whether psychoanalysis is "as scientific" as chemistry or social psychology, but rather that it be defined as a domain of systematic knowledge derived from the study of unconscious processes in individual human lives. The new department of psychoanalysis at the Hebrew University in Jerusalem, with the Sigmund Freud chair now occupied by Joseph Sandler, is an example of such departmental status.

Scientific research requires new observation and the comparison of earlier theories with inferences drawn from new observational studies designed to test hypotheses, which may thus be confirmed, modified, or disproved. Psychoanalysis can have a component of scientific research, which is scientific because it is based on objective and reliable findings, and may be called research because those findings are related to observed phenomena and pose a challenge to alternate explanations of these phenomena.

RESEARCH ON CHILD DEVELOPMENT

In the psychoanalytic treatment of adults, case formulation includes important developmental hypotheses, which rest upon a theory of psychosexual development through oral, anal, and phallic phases, and of how trauma, overindulgence, or other causes of fixation during a particular phase may lead to adult characterological patterns. The most important theoretical debates within psychoanalysis, debates that are an important domain of its scientific research, have concerned early development and how it can be inferred from observations made during the analysis of adults. These debates, reflecting a wide range of theories, are based on the work of many contributors, including Klein (1948), Jacobson (1964), Kernberg (1975), and Kohut (1971, 1977).

Psychoanalysts have also functioned as scientific investigators in the study of children, not only by analyzing them, but by observing them in systematic ways in other than treatment settings. These investigators include such analysts as Anna Freud (1965), Mahler (1975), Spitz (1950), Pine (1960), Wolff (1966), Bowlby (1969, 1973, 1980), Emde (1976), Fraiberg (1968), Freedman

(1969), and many others. As a result of this research, some discrepancy has emerged between the theory of childhood development as taught in psychoanalytic institutes, based on the reconstruction of childhood derived from the analysis of adults, and the concepts developed from direct observation of children (Shapiro and Stern, 1980). From such research, we may discover that there is one set of milestone developments in the sequential unfolding of attributes during childhood, and another type of layering that may unfold during regressions found in the development of such a transference neurosis during the analysis of an adult patient. A direct one-to-one correlation between these two kinds of observed sequences is probably not going to be found.

In the next decades, useful information on developmental sequences and alternatives will be provided by psychoanalytically-informed investigators of children. As noted before, this task probably cannot be performed by analysts in full-time clinical practice. The methodology of child observation is already advanced and requires years of study within its own scientific discipline. While it is important for investigators to have specialized in these methodologies, it is also useful for them to be psychoanalytically informed. Since this is not the type of research that most analysts can hope to conduct, there is a need to develop specialized theoreticians who combine knowledge in the area of adult clinical psychoanalytic practice with mastery of the methods of child observation, in order to develop a bridging theory that would be mutually beneficial or stimulating to either area of work. Research on the reconstruction of significant memories and fantasies explored in the analysis of adult patients can then be defined as a domain of study separate from the issue of actual transactions that occur between children and parents. At some point, of course, research in both domains will have to be unified into an appropriate general psychoanalytic developmental theory.

THE OUTCOME OF PSYCHOANALYSIS

For what kind of patients is psychoanalysis the best form of treatment? What may be expected in terms of change as the result of such treatment? Early leading scientific research on these questions was undertaken by members of the Berlin Psychoanalytic Institute. The most systematic study, however, has been conducted in this country in the Menninger Psychotherapy Research Project. It consisted of 22 patients who received psychoanalysis out of a larger 42-patient sample. The results, most recently reported by Wallerstein (1985), indicate the need for research on larger and more varied samples.

Supervised cases followed in psychoanalytic institutes, mostly low-cost analyses, undergo pre-analysis evaluations. It should be possible to conduct a nationwide systematic investigation of formulations of these cases before treatment, the rate of drop-outs, the rate of completion, and to add follow-up evaluations by the same people who did the pre-analysis evaluations. In practice, this is rarely done, because of resistance within most institutes to such an enterprise. It would be difficult to undertake such research efforts if investigators could not get the cooperation of faculty members at the institutes; in addition, they would need research money to fund the organization and examination of data. As with research on child development, this kind of clinical research methodology is already quite advanced, and investigators would need both psychoanalytic and research expertise.

This area of research is, probably, also too difficult for independent psychoanalytic practitioners. Despite these difficulties, however, imaginative approaches can be used by clinical practitioners to provide important data about outcome. One example is the work done in San Francisco by Norman, Blacker, Oremland, and Barrett (1976). They and their colleagues conducted a well-defined project by studying a group of patients who had already completed psychoanalysis, and who were felt by their analysts to have had a very good outcome. They interviewed the patients for several hours, in order to find out about the changes and processes of change in these patients. The results replicated and confirmed earlier findings by Pfeffer (1959) and others: It was found that even in such cases (with outstanding results), there was a recapitulation of transference reactions to the interviewer, who was an analyst but not the original treating analyst. This finding of recapitulation of transference reaction can be considered as well-supported (Pfeffer, 1961, 1963).

PSYCHOANALYTIC PHENOMENA AND EXPLANATORY DESCRIPTIONS

One of the signs of Freud's genius was that he chose to observe phenomena that were centrally appropriate to his evolving theory. These phenomena ranged from dreams to jokes and slips of the tongue in the normal realm, from phobias to perversions in the pathological domain. Fenichel's *Psychoanalytic Theory of Neuroses* (1945) is still used as an encyclopedic source book, a kind of Merck Manual of psychoanalysis. The explanatory description of phenomena caused in part by unconscious mental processes was one of the most exciting adventures of the early psychoanalytic pioneers. A metaphor has been used about this area of clinical research; it has been referred to as a gold mine from which all the ore had been stripped—a dead mine.

This is an unfortunate metaphor, since these phenomena still prevail in adults, and descriptive explanations of such phenomena need to be restated in contemporary language and revised according to new observations. As one example, the psychoanalytic theory of anxiety attacks is seldom discussed in the literature, and existing theory does not adequately describe either this phenomenon or its causes. This has been recognized by Leo Rangell (1954), by

Alan Compton (1972a, b), who has reviewed Freud's theory of anxiety in great detail in a series of three papers, and by Michels, Frances, and Shear (in press).

If the theory is not complete, then the observations are not all in, since theory guides observation as well as observation guiding theory. Reliability of observation then becomes a key issue. Can more than one clinician review the same phenomenon, classify it in the same way, and offer the same explanation? Study groups to examine the formation of such symptoms as anxiety attacks, phobias, perversions, and recurrent nightmares would be challenging to the participants and could lead to informative papers derived from a review of appropriate case material and a consensus of several psychoanalysts. This is a most enjoyable intellectual activity for the kind of person who chooses psychoanalytic training; yet in interviewing psychoanalysts, I have found that few participate regularly in such a systematic, clinically based enterprise.

Transference is probably the most important phenomenon to be studied in a clinical setting, and has been explored recently in a two-volume work by Gill and Hoffman (1982). Many of the theoretical issues in psychoanalysis could be dealt with by systematic review of evaluations and process notes of psychoanalytic sessions, in order to see if consensual agreement could be reached by groups of clinicians about what kinds of transference emerge. The classification of various transferences is in many ways the central concern in the field of psychoanalysis as a scientific discipline. Careful observational work would gradually lead to an elaboration of existing theoretical classifications of transference; positive and negative, maternal and paternal, mirroring and idealizing, and the like. Analysts engaged in such research reviews of process notes, actual transcripts, or analyst's reports, would find these immediately helpful in improving their own observational skills in clinical practice.

The work can be conducted by small groups willing to devote two to four hours a week to this activity. Keys to gathering significant data are: 1) select a particular, circumscribed clinical phenomenon; 2) follow a systematic discipline for making and recording inferences; 3) check inferences once they are made, by review of evidence. The degree of agreement revealed by that repetition — using different judges — may be quantified according to appropriate, available designs and statistical methods for such reliability judgments. To obtain statistical reliability, it is the reviewing clinicians who are quantified in terms of the degree of consensus on an observation or formulation.

SYSTEMATIC APPROACHES

In such scientific research efforts it is necessary to keep the level of discourse consistent in the effort to repeat inferences. In other words, the multiple points of view within psychoanalysis (topographic, structural, economic, genetic, adaptive, dynamic) have to be discussed *one at a time,* and *in relation to a specific clinical phenomenon.* This means that a working group has to develop an orderly discipline, focusing on one segment of a given phenomenon at a time for explanation, and one segment of the explanation. This systematic approach will be discussed further in the following pages.

THE CHANGE PROCESS IN PSYCHOANALYSIS

We know relatively little about the processes by which change may take place in psychoanalysis, and how these may compare or contrast with change processes resulting from psychotherapy or life experiences (Basch, 1981). There has been a range of salient research — from the psycho-historical approach exemplified by Erikson (1950) in *The Study of Lives over Time,* to Valiant's (1977) description of change over time in treatment, and a new contribution by Wallerstein in his forthcoming book. A team of investigators led by Weiss and Sampson (1977), at the San Francisco Psychoanalytic Institute and the Mount Zion Medical Center Department of Psychiatry, are currently studying the change process using quantitative methods, including the kinds of reliability assessments mentioned before. This is the type of research that can also be pursued by small groups of psychoanalysts working together, using the essential ingredients of maintained process notes. Windholz and Skolnikoff (this volume) have presented one method for such a project, called "consensual analysis."

In order to study change processes, one has to define the psychopathology as clearly as possible, explain why certain phenomena form, and then describe how these change at some later point in time. In the interval between how it was and how it became, there is a process that is explained by a series of inferences. Each of these intervals — the time before, the changing period, and the aftermath — can be approached by explanatory descriptions at various levels of abstraction, using varied points of view and languages.

A systematic approach is needed to keep clinicians talking about the same sector with the same agenda. This is discussed, in terms of describing change processes in a psychoanalysis, in a chapter by the present author in the volume *Hysterical Personality* (Horowitz, 1977), and more systematically in a review of a twelve-hour videotape of a time-limited psychoanalytically-oriented psychotherapy in his book *States of Mind* (Horowitz, 1979). This method is called "Configurational Analysis," and it has been applied to five video-recorded cases by two groups of three clinicians each (Horowitz, Marmar, Krupnick, Wilner, Kaltreider, and Wallerstein, 1984). Ideas about states and the transition between states were especially emphasized by Gaarder (1971) in his paper on control of states of consciousness.

The configurational analysis approach has ten steps (summarized in Table 1 at the end of this chapter) that are discussed in sequence. It is based on earlier work by Luborsky (1977), Knapp (1974), Loevinger (1976), Gedo and Goldberg (1973), Greenspan and Cullander (1973), as well as the Hampstead Index, a systematic approach to describing cases developed by A. Freud, Nagera, and W. Freud (1965). Work groups can modify the method to suit their particular aims, as a foil for finding a better system.

The memory of the analyst is not accurate enough for the task of carefully studying change processes. While recordings would be most desirable, in order to obtain eventual scientific reliability, process notes are sufficient at this stage of research. Some analysts accumulate many cubic feet of process notes, but rarely review them. Systematic review by a small group would provide enough intellectual stimulation to get past the initial confusion and into the fascinating area of discovery. The change process, I believe, is an optimum research task for practicing psychoanalysts.

SUMMARY

At the beginning of this chapter, psychoanalysis is posited as an area of knowledge expanded by scientific research, not one restricted to hermeneutics. Such research, it was indicated, should involve repeated observation in a systematic way. Four research topics were chosen for discussion — not meant to be all-inclusive.

The first two are probably beyond the scope of most practicing psychoanalysts, because they require extensive research training or substantial research support: 1) Careful *child development research* has advanced to a level where it is a sophisticated scientific field with its own discipline. 2) Systematic clinical investigations of the *outcome issues in psychoanalysis* also require a special research center. Existing psychoanalytic institutions, without substantial financial support, would find it difficult to mount these studies. University departments would also have difficulty in undertaking research on the outcome of psychoanalysis, and might better study the process and outcome of psychoanalytically-oriented psychotherapies.

In contrast to these two research areas, there are two other domains that are readily accessible to motivated, practicing, experienced psychoanalysts. Work in these domains would also allow clinical associates to gain research experience while they are still in training. One area involves descriptive explanation of particularly psychoanalytic phenomena. Much has already been done in this sphere, but it needs to be updated and revised. In that revision, on the basis of repetition, there is an opportunity to bring in new methodology. This would deal not so much with the quantification of the phenomenology itself, as with the quantitative assessment of the degree of reliability of clinicians seeking to agree that the phenomenon is present and to reach a consensus about certain dominant explanatory factors in the configuration of causes.

For those who are not yet interested in the issues of reliability of clinical inference, there is even more uncharted territory requiring careful investigation: the process of personality change in psychoanalysis. Systematic reviews of this process would advance knowledge beyond doctrinaire statements of what change "ought to take place" in psychoanalysis to finding out what changes actually do take place (in what way, at what rate, in relation to what sort of intervention, and in what type of patients). A small study group can take on part of the territory by defining the character type of patients to be considered, for example, examination of the change processes in compulsive characters. Several small study groups, taking on the same research topic, could perhaps gather at annual scientific meetings to compare findings. They would find this an invigorating experience!

Table 1.   Ten Steps for Configurational Analysis*

PRE-TREATMENT DESCRIPTIVE EXPLANATIONS

Step 1:   *Problem Analysis*

Describe major phenomena and relate these to the problems, environment and life style of the patient. Include a statement of difficulties or signs that the observer recognizes but the patient does not. Include a description of the time frame of the phenomena of special interest.

Step 2:   *State Analysis*

The goal is a language for brief description of the most important recurrent states of mind of the patient. Extended descriptions for each state are summarized by labels which can then be used for brevity in later steps. Extended descriptions should include observed behavioral patterns with summaries of reports of subjective experiences.

a. List first those states that contain the phenomena described in Step 1. Then list and describe states that occurred before the shift into the state with the phenomena, and those that occurred after it.

List these states in an order. To do so, begin with those states colored by intense and negative emotion, ones that seem overtly to be most undermodulated.

b. Next list states in which the subject seems overtly more controlled.

c. Complete the list of states by describing the qualities of overcontrolled states of mind, those that overtly appear to be used for purposes of concealment or conformity. This will result in a list of states from undermodulated, to those that are relatively well-modulated, to those that are overmodulated.

d. Discuss these states according to their defensive arrangements, in terms of problematic, dreaded, desired and compromise states of mind. Include and designate warded-off states that rarely occur but have a motivational function, such as when the patient seeks to remain in certain compromise states to avoid entry into the dreaded states. Include and designate any ideal states that are desired, even if they are rarely or never achieved.

e. Review the occurrence of each state in the context of the triggers or events that influence the subject to enter it or exit from it. Begin with triggers of entry into the state containing the phenomena of special interest. Include social, subjective and biological factors such as events, situations, dreams, drugs and fatigue. Where patterns are noted, derive a model of state transitions and cycles. Describe the nature of state transitions, noting abrupt disjunctions or smooth blendings from one state to another.

---

*Summarized from Horowitz, M., *Configurational Analysis Manual*. Formats and illustrations for the ten steps can be found in Horowitz, 1979, and in Horowitz et al., 1984. (Material from Horowitz et al., 1984 adapted by permission of Basic Books.)

Step 3:   *Self and Object Organization Analysis*

Describe each state in terms of underlying internal schemata of self-concepts, aims and concepts of others. Describe any repetitive story lines composed of sequences of these role relationship models. Derive a model of the conflicts or deficiencies embedded in maladaptive story lines. As with states, describe problematic, dreaded, desired and compromise self-concepts and role relationship models.

Describe the developmental basis for these self-concepts and role relationship models. Relate shifts in self-concept to recent life events, changes in social context or physical occurrences. A formulation of the level of supraordinate self and object conceptualization may be made here, with comments on stability and instability, as well as coherence or dissociation of elements:

Step 4:   *Motivational and Defensive Analysis: Processing Ideas and Emotions*

a. *Themes:* Indicate major constellations of memories and fantasies as composites of ideas, feelings and actions that influence current states of mind, especially those related to the phenomena described in Step 1 and the problem states described in Step 2. Describe trains of thought and emotions that activate the problematic self and object concepts described in Step 3. Relate these constellations to recent life events, environmental or physiological deficiencies, and object relationships. Derive a model of the degree to which outer reality accords with the subject's views, assumptions and schematizations, including self-concepts, role relationship models and values. Indicate how discrepancies between outer world, inner motives and inner critical or moral assessments evoke emotional responses and lead the subject to self-regulations and entry into various expressive or defensive states of mind. Also derive a model of how control operations influence the processing of themes consciously and unconsciously, awake or while dreaming.

b. *Habitual Styles:* Indicate the subject's typical use of specific information-processing strategies and how this leads to idiosyncratic use of any specific mode of expression, defensive operation and/or coping strategy. Relate different modes for processing or representing information and different levels of defense to different states of mind noted in Step 2. Include statements of any enduring attitudes that lead to maladaptive repetitions of a thought cycle, or inappropriate action responses to external contexts.

ANALYSIS OF PROCESS DURING TREATMENT

Step 5:   *States Analysis during Treatment*

Divide the treatment into phases according to when there are discernible changes in state patterns. For any phase, review the entry and exits from states of mind described in Step 2. Describe new states, shifts in the frequency or intensity of states, or modifications of state entry and exit situations. Describe the states of the analyst or psychotherapist, and relate these to states of the patient.

Step 6: *Relationships Analysis during Treatment*

For each phase of treatment described in Step 5 describe change processes affected by the patient's views of the relationship with the therapist, and the therapist's views of the relationship with the patient. Use the self and other concepts as defined in Step 3. Describe social alliances, therapeutic alliances, and transference-countertransference patterns. Describe progressive and regressive shifts in these role relationship models. Discuss interpersonal patterns outside the therapy as well, including acting-out of transference patterns. Note key separations and new attachments and group or ideologic commitments.

Focus on key dilemmas of nested transference relationship tendencies and resistance to tendencies. Discuss actual and potential errors of technique provoked by the patient or the therapist. Describe useful and unhelpful interpretive techniques. Include analysis of tests of transference relationship possibilities, as well as the occurrence of equivalent countertransference phenomena.

Step 7: *Analysis of Insight, Intervention and Learning Processes*

Classify interventions by the therapist in relation to the key themes in Step 4 and the key relationship dilemmas described in Step 3 and Step 6.

Focus as well on 1) work (or failure to work) on the main defensive styles described in Step 4; 2) explanations of the shifting state patterns in the phases of therapy as described in Step 5; 3) explanation of the process of changing relationship patterns as described in Step 6; and 4) how therapist interventions affected the patient's defensive control processes and core attitudes.

ANALYSIS OF OUTCOME

Step 8: *States*

Describe outcome in terms of changes in phenomena, signs, symptoms and states. Use the labels developed in Steps 1, 2 and 5.

Step 9: *Relationships*

Describe outcome in terms of modifications in self and object schemata and object relationship patterns described in Steps 3 and 6.

Step 10: *Information*

Describe outcome in terms of change in major themes and character patterns as described in Steps 4 and 7.

REFERENCES

Basch, M. (1981), Psychoanalytic interpretation and cognitive transformation. *Internat. J. Psycho-Anal.*, 62:151-173.

Blight, J. (1981), Must psychoanalysis retreat to hermeneutics? *Psychoanal. Contemp. Thought*, 4, No. 2:147-205.

Bowlby, J. (1969), *Attachment and Loss, Vol. I: Attachment.* New York: Basic Books.

———— (1973), *Attachment and Loss, Vol. II: Separation.* New York: Basic Books.

———— (1980), *Attachment and Loss, Vol. III: Loss.* New York: Basic Books.

Compton, A. (1972a), A study of the psychoanalytic theory of anxiety. I: The development of Freud's theory of anxiety. *J. Amer. Psychoanal. Assn.*, 20:3-44.

———— (1972b), A study of the psychoanalytic theory of anxiety. II: Developments in the theory of anxiety since 1926. *J. Amer. Psychoanal. Assn.*, 20:341-394.

Emde, R. N. (1976), *Emotional Expressions in Infancy: A Bio-Behavioral Study.* New York: International Universities Press.

Erikson, E. (1950), *The Study of Lives over Time.* New York: Norton.

Fraiberg, S. (1968), Parallel and divergent patterns in blind and sighted infants. *The Psychoanalytic Study of the Child*, 23:264-300. New York: International Universities Press.

Fenichel, O. (1945), *The Psychoanalytic Theory of Neuroses.* New York: Norton.

Freedman, D. (1969), The development of the use of sound as a guide to affective and cognitive behavior—a two-phase process. *Child Development*, 40, No. 4:1099-1195.

Freud, A. (1965), *Normality and Pathology in Childhood Assessment of Development.* New York: International Universities Press.

———— Nagera, H., & Freud, W. (1965), Metapsychological assessment of the adult person. *The Psychoanalytic Study of the Child*, 20:9-41. New York: International Universities Press.

Gaarder, K. (1971), Control of states of consciousness: I. Attainment through control of psychophysiological variables. *Arch. Gen. Psychiat.*, 25:429-435.

Gedo, J., & Goldberg, A. (1973), *Models of the Mind.* Chicago: University of Chicago Press.

Gill, M. M., & Hoffman, I. (1982), *Analysis of Transference, Vol. 1. Psychological Issues*, Monogr. 53. New York: International Universities Press.

Greenspan, S., & Cullander, C. (1973), A systematic metapsychological assessment of the personality. *J. Amer. Psychoanal. Assn.*, 21:303-327.

Hook, S., ed. (1960), *Psychoanalysis, Scientific Method and Philosophy: A Symposium.* New York: Grove Press.

Horowitz, M. J. (1977), Structure and the process of change. In: *Hysterical Personality*, ed. M. Horowitz. New York: Aronson.

———— (1979), *States of Mind: Analysis of Change in Psychotherapy.* New York: Plenum.

———— Marmar, C., Krupnick, J., Wilner, N., Kaltreider, N., & Wallerstein, R. S. (1984), *Personality Styles and Brief Psychotherapy.* New York: Basic Books.

Jacobson, E. (1964), *The Self and Object World.* New York: International Universities Press.

Kernberg, O. (1975), *The Borderline Conditions and Pathological Narcissism.* New York: Aronson.

Klein, M. (1948), *Contribution to Psychoanalysis.* London: Hogarth Press.

Kohut, H. (1971), *The Analysis of the Self.* New York: International Universities Press.

———— (1977), *Restoration of the Self.* New York: International Universities Press.

Knapp, P. H. (1974), Segmentation and structure in psychoanalysis. *J. Amer. Psychoanal. Assn.*, 22:14-36.

Loevinger, J. (1976), *Ego Development.* San Francisco: Jossey-Bass.

Luborsky, L. (1977), Measuring the pervasive psychic structure in psychotherapy: The core conflictual relationship. In: *Communicative Structures and Psychic Structures*, eds. N. Freedman & S. Grand. New York: Plenum.

Mahler, M., Pine, F., & Bergman, A. (1975), *The Psychological Birth of the Human Infant: Symbiosis and Individuation.* New York: Basic Books.

Michels, R., Frances, A., & Shear, M. (in press), Psychodynamic models of anxiety. In: *Anxiety and Anxiety Disorders,* eds. J. Maser & H. Tuma. Hillsdale, NJ: Lawrence Erlbaum Associates.

Norman, H., Blacker, K., Oremland, J., & Barrett, W. (1976), The fate of the transference neurosis after termination of a satisfactory analysis. *J. Amer. Psychoanal. Assn.,* 24:471–498.

Pfeffer, A. (1959), A procedure for evaluating the results of psychoanalysis: A preliminary report. *J. Amer. Psychoanal. Assn.,* 7:418–444.

_____ (1961), Follow-up study of a satisfactory analysis. *J. Amer. Psychoanal. Assn.,* 9:698–718.

_____ (1963), The meaning of the analyst after analysis. *J. Amer. Psychoanal. Assn.,* 11:229–244.

Pine, F. (1960), Incidental stimulation: A study of preconscious transference. *J. Abnorm. Soc. Psychol.,* 60:68–75.

Rangell, L. (1954), Similarities and differences between psychoanalysis and dynamic psychotherapy. *J. Amer. Psychoanal. Assn.,* 2:734–744.

Ricoeur, P. (1974), *The Conflict of Interpretations: Essays in Hermeneutics.* Evanston: Northwestern University Press.

_____ (1970), *Freud and Philosophy: An Essay on Interpretation.* New Haven: Yale University Press.

Shapiro, T., & Stern, D. (1980), Psychoanalytic contributions to the study of infancy. In: *Infancy and Early Childhood,* Vol. 1, eds. S. I. Greenspan & G. H. Pollack. Washington, DC: US Government Printing Office.

Spence, D. (1982), *Narrative Truth and Historical Truth: Meaning and Interpretation in Psychoanalysis.* New York: Norton.

Spitz, R. A. (1950), Anxiety in infancy: A study of its manifestations in the first year of life. *Internat. J. Psycho-Anal.,* 31:138–143.

Valiant, G. (1977), *Adaptation to Life.* Boston: Little, Brown.

Wallerstein, R. S. (1985), *42 Lives in Treatment.* New York: Guilford.

Weiss, J., Sampson, H., & Caston, J. eds. (1977), Research on the psychoanalytic process. I: A comparison of two theories about analytic neutrality. *Bulletin 3, San Francisco Mount Zion Hospital and Medical Center.*

Wolff, P. (1966), The causes, controls and organization of behavior in the neonate. *Psycholog. Issues,* 5:1–99.

11

Toward a Philosophy of
Psychoanalytic Education

CALVIN F. SETTLAGE, M.D.

*A knowledge of historic and philosophic background gives that kind of inde-
pendence from prejudice of his generation from which most scientists are suffering. This independence created by philosophical insight is — in my
opinion — the mark of distinction between a mere artisan or specialist and a
real seeker after the truth.*

—Albert Einstein

Psychoanalytic literature is distinguished by the absence of formal statements
articulating a philosophy of psychoanalytic education. Such a philosophy is
clearly inherent in the time-tested tripartite system of psychoanalytic education and is demonstrated by shared educational practice in the carrying out of
its three overlapping phases: the training analysis; the sequence of seminars
constituting the theoretical phase; and the supervised analyses of the clinical
phase (Goodman, 1977, pp. 11–47). Analytic writings also, of course, include
questions and views that point toward an educational philosophy.

In their *Psychoanalytic Education in the United States,* Lewin and Ross (1960)
compare academic and psychoanalytic graduate education noting that the outcome of both should be maturity, mastery, and scholarship, although scholarly
maturity has a different structure from the general personality change, produced by the training analysis, that is part of analytic maturity. In their definition, maturity also means that an individual has developed a self-conscious

philosophy (p. 40). Such a philosophy implies a quest for truth and wisdom that includes self-observation and the awareness that one's ideas originate in oneself. Their concept of syncretism underscores the problem of the training analysis as both therapeutic and part of an educational process, as well as the problem of simultaneously offering students training for professional practice and education for scientific endeavors (pp. 47–52). Lewin and Ross observe that institute faculties are trying to develop a philosophy of psychoanalytic education, and are beginning to raise questions not only about the goals of such education, but about broader issues, including at least three factors: the teachers, the courses, and the students (p. 297).

Writing on the meaning and purpose of curriculum planning, Lustman (1967) observes that the curriculum makes the difference between training and education. Beyond mastery of information and skills, analytic education, in his view, tries to provide a deeper level of knowledge of principles and basic ideas, going far beyond content. This deeper knowledge is productive in the sense that it can create new knowledge (pp. 868–869). Lustman feels that the thinking of analysts on fundamental issues of education is moving in the direction of a philosophy of psychoanalytic education (p. 871).

Addressing dilemmas in psychoanalytic education, Arlow (1972) writes that, regardless of the enunciated principles of a given training program, the real philosophy of education is empirically determined, eloquently revealed in the institutional practices, organization, and implementation of the curriculum. He also notes the phenomenon of "cultural lag." Whereas psychoanalytic education without a thorough knowledge of Freud's writings is obviously unthinkable, there is too great a tendency to cling to the past. Even within the framework of Freud's writings, the educational emphasis continues to focus on the earlier concepts to the neglect of Freud's own later contributions that superseded them (p. 557).

In his view of the future of psychoanalysis, Wallerstein (1972) emphasizes the dual purpose of psychoanalytic education: advancing the field as a profession and as a science. It transmits not only a body of knowledge to be used for amelioration of the sufferings of the mind, but a set of principles, assumptions, and propositions bearing on our still imperfect and incomplete scientific enterprise. The best teaching and learning requires a student body that is encouraged to question and to challenge in the Socratic sense (pp. 596–597). In a later publication, Wallerstein (Goodman, 1977) again emphasizes that psychoanalytic education needs to protect both of Freud's legacies: the central basic truths of psychoanalysis that underlie psychoanalytic treatment and Freud's stewardship of science (pp. 309–310). In this connection, he echoes Lustman's educational objective of integrating research and treatment in the mind of today's analyst, as they were in Freud's mind (Lustman, 1967, p. 872).

Also looking to the future, Solnit (Goodman, 1977, pp. 302–303) conveys his impression that psychoanalysis has failed to find and foster the development of analysts with the enthusiasm, curiosity, originality, versatility, and productivity of the original European-trained group. Wondering how to anticipate the next twenty to thirty years of learning and practicing psychoanalysis, he states two prevailing concerns among psychoanalysts: the risk of diluting our science, diffusing our energies, and losing the vigor and productivity of the analytic method as it is used in the treatment of adults with the so-called classical neuroses; and the implication (if we limit ourselves by this fear) of an equal or greater risk of becoming specialists in treating only one kind of patient. This concern was voiced much earlier by Ernst Kris (Goodman, p. 303) in the first discussions on the widening scope of indications for psychoanalysis (Stone, 1954).

In his summary of trends at the 1974 Conference on Psychoanalytic Education and Research, Goodman (1977) frames related issues of concern voiced during the meeting. He notes that the analysts' discussion sought to balance the interplay of several tendencies: the wish for growth, the urge for constructive change, respect for the principle of flexibility, the wish to conserve the core, the need to achieve and preserve high scientific and professional standards, and the opposition to change for the sake of change (p. 355).

At the same conference, the Preparatory Commission on the Tripartite System of Psychoanalytic Education, chaired by Joan Fleming, posed a series of cogent questions that extend the Lewin and Ross (1960) questions about educational goals and the educational situation (Goodman, 1977, p. 14). Should analyst educators remain primarily educators of professional therapists? What is needed to educate a psychoanalyst who can continue to recognize unanswered questions about behavior and is motivated to try to find answers? Can such learning goals be built into the program for psychoanalytic education? Can analysts construct an educational track that provides both professional learning experiences and continuing educational opportunities and support for scientific exploration?

The various questions and views presented above pose the dilemma and challenge confronting any scientifically-based endeavor: reacting to, processing, and possibly accommodating to new ideas that have the undetermined potential of advancing or temporarily misleading the field. Within psychoanalysis, this dilemma and challenge have created tensions and internecine conflicts (sometimes of unmanageable proportions) from the early years to the present. Even within mainstream Freudian analysis in Freud's day, the extension of psychoanalytic theory beyond depth psychology caused great conflict and concern. Anna Freud (1936), in her introduction to *The Ego and the Mechanisms of Defense,* writes that whenever research was deflected from id to ego, it was seen as the beginning of apostasy against psychoanalysis. But with the publication of Freud's studies on the ego (Freud, 1921, 1923), the odium of unorthodoxy was no longer attached to the study of the ego, and interest was seriously focused on ego-institutions (p. 4).

In his discussion of conflicts engendered by new ideas within psychoanalysis, Greenson (1969) reminds us of Freud's scientific attitude — of his ability to relinquish and change his ideas when faced with new information and newly emerging problems:

> No preconceived idea precluded the possibility of discovering new insights, new techniques, and new theories. Obstacles and adversities prompted [Freud] to try new approaches and led to new discoveries, new formulations, and new theories. Just as dramatically, new discoveries did not lead automatically to the elimination of old ideas (p. 507)....Freud, clearly, was no Freudian in the narrow sense (p. 510).

Insightful statements about the problem of ideological and interpersonal conflicts in psychoanalytic education have been offered by Keiser (1972) and Arlow (1972). On the basis of his extensive experience as a first-hand observer of the functioning of training institutes in site visits, Keiser expresses the view that

> students and faculty can only profit from exposure to ideas which vary from the supposed "majority." The acceptance of theoretical instruction by majority vote cannot be construed as an absolute or scientific validation. If this were so, the acceptable spectrum too easily becomes constricted....obliteration [of ideas perceived to be unacceptable] frequently produces disastrous side effects by initiating the polarization of groups within an institute. The smoldering resentment builds into a conflict which interferes with the educational experience and advancement of the students. Whatever disadvantage may result from allowing free expression of contradictory opinion would be infinitesimal compared with the harm caused by their suppression.

> Must we reject differences of opinion? Do faculties hide behind the rationalization that it will be confusing to students to hear contradictory opinions espoused by teachers? Won't they be better educated if allowed a modicum of confusion rather than the disastrous fantasy that theories are unquestioned facts? (p. 528).

With regard to the polarization of groups within an institute, Arlow (1972) observes that

> the implications of splitting are weighty indeed for psychoanalytic education. First of all, they signalize the inadequacy of the training atmosphere and the failure of the educational program. Secondly, such an unhappy turn of events bodes ill for the future development of the candidates as well as for the analysts who are caught in the midst of the struggle. Faced with the need to take a firm stand on one side or the other of the conflict, the individual analysts are usually propelled either in the direction of dogmatism, or, contrariwise, toward rebellious distortion of psychoanalysis, neither of which is healthy (p. 559).

Along the same lines, Keiser (1972) notes that an atmosphere conducive to partisanship and fear tends to preclude a free academic environment. "One sees passive agreement in order to avoid retaliatory hostility and banishment...At a society meeting, even fear of speaking...exists. Some members [and particularly students and recent graduates] believe that if their remarks are not acceptable...they will forever be marked down....To avoid this...[they] believe it best to remain quiet and passive" (p. 533).

From this review of thoughts and observations about psychoanalytic education, it is clear that problems arise from the fact that psychoanalysis is both a science and a profession. From psychoanalysis as a science — as in all sciences — there emerge new discoveries and new ideas that need to be understood and then assessed and tested for their practical value. For psychoanalysis, the ultimate arena for testing is in the analytic situation. The tension between the scientific idea and its professional, technical application was well-defined by Weinshel (McLaughlin, 1973). Weinshel observed: "The worse conflicts, within and between institutes and the American [Psychoanalytic Association]...are over how theory and concept become translated into psychoanalytic therapy. Despite the truth that there is no one psychoanalytic technique or single set strategy for applying theory to technique, differences in technique are especially capable of mobilizing factions and passionate dissension" (p. 588).

In keeping with Einstein's comment on the value of historical and philosophical perspective, it is important for psychoanalysts to be mindful that the problems of psychoanalytic research pervade sciences generally. Thomas Kuhn (1962), an American historian of science, notes that Einstein's ideas were strongly resisted, as were those of other scientists in widely diverse fields. He observes:

> The invention of other new theories regularly, and appropriately, evokes the same response from some of the specialists on whose area of competence they impinge. For these men the new theory implies a change in the rules governing the prior practice of [their] science. Inevitably, therefore, it reflects upon much scientific work they have already successfully completed. That is why a new theory, however special to its range of application, is seldom or never just an increment to what is already known. Its assimilation requires the reconstruction of prior theory and the re-evaluation of prior fact, an intrinsically revolutionary process that is seldom completed by a single man and never overnight (p. 7).

Kuhn (1962) distinguishes between normal science and scientific revolution or breakthrough and sees the concept of paradigm or model as serving both (pp. 10–12): "Men whose research is based on shared paradigms are committed to the same rules and standards for scientific practice. That commitment and the apparent consensus it produces are prerequisites for normal science, i.e., for the genesis and continuation of a particular research tradition" (p. 11). Transformational paradigms, such as Einstein's theory of relativity and Freud's theory of unconscious mental processes, present major innovations that initiate and ultimately effect scientific revolutions, transforming these sciences. When accepted by most scientists in that field, Kuhn reminds us, the once revolutionary paradigm becomes a shared paradigm that is then subjected to the usually long-ensuing "mop-up" work of normal science. This work is essential to achieve actualization of the paradigm through detailing its structure and application (pp. 10–14), mostly by the "determination of significant fact, matching of facts with theory, and the articulation of theory" (p. 34).

The nature of normal science accounts for its lack of truly revolutionary innovation. Kuhn (1962) states:

> one of the things a scientific community acquires with a paradigm is a criterion for choosing problems that, while the paradigm is taken for granted, can be assumed to have solutions. To a great extent these are the only problems that the community will admit as scientific or encourage its members to undertake (p. 37)....A paradigm can, for that matter, even insulate the community from certain socially [or clinically] important problems because they cannot be stated in terms of the conceptual and instrumental tools the paradigm supplies (p. 44)....No part of the aim of normal science is to call forth new sorts of phenomena; indeed those that will not fit the box are often not seen at all. Nor do scientists normally aim to invent new theories, and they are often intolerant of those invented by others (p. 24)....Extraordinary problems and revolutionary paradigms emerge only on special occasions, as prepared, though, by the advance of normal research (p. 34).

The "rules" or established viewpoints of normal science also contribute to its conservatism. Kuhn states that the most obvious, and probably most binding, of these rules are explicit concepts and theories, which tend to limit acceptable solutions. At a lower and more concrete level, there are a multitude of commitments to preferred types of instrumentation and to ways that accepted techniques may be employed. Less concrete and temporary are the higher level metaphysical commitments.

Kuhn also notes, however, that there are still higher level commitments which do favor innovation: The true scientist is motivated to understand the world and to extend the precision and scope of its order; to scrutinize some aspect of nature in great empirical detail; and to be challenged by this scrutiny to a refinement of observational techniques or to further development and articulation of theories (Kuhn, 1962, pp. 38–42).

With regard to scientific progress, Kuhn observes that resistance to change can be useful. By insuring that the paradigm will not be too easily modified or surrendered, such resistance guarantees that scientists will not be easily distracted, and that paradigm change will penetrate existing knowledge to the core (Kuhn, 1962, pp. 64–65). Significant scientific change, Kuhn points out, is inaugurated by a growing sense — usually among relatively few members of the scientific community — that an existing paradigm that previously led the way is no longer fully adequate. This sense of ferment usually precedes both revolutionary and non-revolutionary paradigm change (p. 92).

Michael Polanyi (1958), a European chemist and philosopher, observes that a true understanding of science includes the capacity for a contemplative experience of it, and the teaching of science must aim at imparting this capacity to the student (pp. 195–196). In speaking of contemplative experience, Polanyi is emphasizing the personal, intuitive, internal dimension of discovery and the creative process. He makes the psychoanalytically compatible statement that the satisfaction of gaining intellectual control over the external world is linked to the satisfaction of gaining control over ourselves:

> The urge toward this dual satisfaction is persistent; yet it operates by phases of self-destruction. The construction of a framework which will handle experience on our behalf begins in the infant and culminates in the scientist. This endeavor must occasionally operate by demolishing a hitherto accepted structure, or parts of it, in order to establish an even more rigorous and comprehensive one in its place. Scientific discovery, which leads from one such framework to its successor, bursts the bounds of disciplined thought in an intense moment of heuristic vision. And while it is thus breaking out, the mind is for the moment directly experiencing its content rather than controlling it by the use of any pre-established modes of interpretation (p. 196).

> [Scientific discovery] sets out not to conquer, but to enrich the world. Yet such a move is also an attack. It raises a claim and makes a tremendous demand on other men; for it asks that its gift to humanity be accepted by all. In order to be satisfied, our intellectual passions must find a response. This universal intent creates a tension: we must suffer when a vision of reality to which we have committed ourselves is contemptuously ignored by others. For a general unbelief imperils our own convictions by evoking an echo in us. Our vision must conquer or die (p. 150).

With Kuhn, Polanyi (1958) underscores the fact that "major discoveries change our interpretive framework. Hence it is logically impossible to arrive at these by the continued application of our previous interpretive framework. So we see...that discovery is creative, in the sense that it is not to be achieved by the diligent performance of any previously known and specifiable procedure...The application of existing rules can produce valuable surveys, but does not advance the principles of science" (p. 143). Referring to Einstein's description of scientific research as "ein intuitives Heranfühlen an die Tatsachen" (a groping for the meaning of the facts), Polanyi states that empirical guidance of such groping accounts for the difference between a merely formal advance and a new insight into the nature of things (p. 150).

In presenting the historian-philosopher view of the problems of scientific advance in other sciences, my intention is to demonstrate the universality of such conflicts, which are not unique to psychoanalysis. I also want to draw an analogy: It is recognition and understanding of transference that allows the analyst to maintain a posture of non-reactiveness and objectivity by not taking the transference personally. Perhaps a recognition and understanding of expected reactions to scientific and methodological-technical issues can help us maintain a similar posture of objectivity in this area. This should help sustain a scientific dialogue in our field in the same way that non-reactiveness to the transference sustains the analytic dialogue.

The realization that any one of us could, conceivably, be in one or the other of the conflicting positions noted by Kuhn should be an important deterrent to escalating conflict among various psychoanalytic groups. We could be immersed in the normal science process, pursuing and protecting the once revolutionary (but now established) paradigm; or we could be pursuing new ideas that pose a threat because they may challenge the established paradigm.

My views on the question of a philosophy of psychoanalytic education have been derived from observations and thoughts based upon my own experience. As chairman of the education committees of two institutes of the American Psychoanalytic Association, I had first-hand experience of the pervasiveness, complexity, and affective intensity of the issues, and a close look at the personality factors and conscious and unconscious resistances to solutions.

In psychoanalysis and in the sciences generally it has always been difficult to maintain a scientific dialogue. My own experience convinces me of the dialogue's vital importance for processing ideas to decide what consitutes an acceptable or an unacceptable idea. An overriding principle that we need to bear in mind in this process, although not immediately evident, will become known in time through its usefulness ultimately in the analytic situation. This principle is more likely to be borne out in an ongoing dialogue among a scientifically-based heterogeneous professional group than in individual beliefs or in dialogues within a homogeneous group consisting of the advocate of an idea and like-minded colleagues. Since the early days of psychoanalysis, every psychoanalytic society, institute faculty, and education committee, sooner or later embodies a range of views on general theory and on the theory of treatment and its technical application. Because of this diversity of views, a dialogue-based validation process is potentially available; but, as we have seen, the well-tempered dialogue is difficult to sustain.

As explained by Polanyi (1958), a dialogue can be sustained only if the participants belong to a community accepting basically the same teaching and tradition for judging their own affirmations (p. 378):

> The two conflicting systems of thought are separated by a logical gap, in the same sense as a problem is separated from the discovery which solves the problem.

Formal operations relying on *one* framework of interpretation cannot demonstrate a proposition to persons who rely on *another* framework. Its advocates may not even succeed in getting a hearing from these, since they must first teach them a new language, and no one can learn a new language unless he first trusts that it means something (p. 151).

On the same point, Kuhn (1962) draws an analogy between this kind of dialogue and political discourse, speaking of the polarization of scientists belonging to different schools of thought who talk through each other when debating the relative merits of their respective paradigms (p. 109).

Polanyi (1958) remarks further:

> The refusal to enter an opponent's way of arguing must be justified by making it appear altogether unreasonable. Such comprehensive rejection cannot fail to discredit the opponent. He will be made to appear as thoroughly deluded, which in the heat of the [debate] will easily come to imply that he was a fool, a crank or a fraud. And once we are out to establish such charges we shall readily go on to expose our opponent as a 'metaphysician,' a 'Jesuit,' or a 'Jew,' or a 'Bolshevik,' as the case may be — or, speaking from the other side of the Iron Curtain — as an 'objectivist,' an 'idealist,' and a 'cosmopolitan.' In a clash of intellectual passions each side must inevitably attack the opponent's person (pp. 151–152).

Even without the critic's regression to the *ad hominem* mode, the advocate of a new idea, in Polanyi's (1958) analysis has separated himself from others who embrace the old and do not entertain the new theory. Like the heuristic passion from which it flows, the persuasive passion of the discoverer is thus intensified and he seeks to convert everybody to his way of seeing things (p. 150). Opposition, and particularly what is experienced as hostile, personalized opposition, tends to cause the attacked scientist to withdraw from the dialogue and set about recruiting allies and followers. When this occurs, factionalism is in the making.

Another consequence of withdrawal from the dialogue as the means of resolving differences is the resort, by either side, to manipulations designed to lock in one's own and freeze out the opponent's ideas. Relatively quiescent personal and group strivings for power — for organizational control, and for protection of vested interests — tend to burgeon, marked by self-righteous exploitation of stalemated ideological differences.

There is, however, also a positive reaction to new ideas that bears directly on the philosophy of psychoanalytic education. Kuhn (1962) observes that if a new viewpoint endures for a time and becomes fruitful, the reported results will grow in number, motivating some scientists, who perceive the explanatory potential of the new ideas, to begin testing them through application. "That reaction," he notes, "comes particularly easily to men just entering the profession, for they have not yet acquired the special vocabulary and commitments of [a particular] group" (p. 203). Kuhn quotes Darwin on this subject:

Although I am fully convinced of the truth of the views given in [*The Origin of Species*], I by no means expect to convince experienced naturalists whose minds are stocked with a multitude of facts [gained] from a point of view directly opposite to mine. [But] I look with confidence to the future — to young and rising naturalists who will be able to view both sides of the question with impartiality (Kuhn, p. 151).

The philosophy of psychoanalytic education that I am proposing would require in-training exposure of analysts of the future to significant new analytic ideas within the curriculum. The established, time-tested ideas would generally be taught early and the new ideas later in the seminar sequence. The exposure would include a considered appraisal of the ideas and their value in terms of both theory and clinical application. This philosophy is not totally new; it has been espoused and in some measure practiced. But, to my knowledge, its rationale and implementation have not been formally defined. The central objective of this philosophy is to develop an analyst whose therapeutic work and scientific observation are mutually informed.

The application of this philosophy in the educational experience is intended to demonstrate the scientific approach to theory and practice, including the acceptance of established ideas and the assessment and testing of new ideas. Since the faculty of any given institute usually embodies a range of differing views, the teaching is likely to provide (or can be structured to provide) an appropriate pro-and-con view of new and established ideas. This spectrum of opinion would lean on what is known — the tried and true — and reflect both the tension and the affirmational growth potential in the interplay of the known and the new.

The inclusion of significant new ideas in the psychoanalytic curriculum should diminish the tendency toward proselytizing in other arenas. It also avoids the need to make difficult curricular decisions and the negative consequences of a policy of exclusion by majority vote of ideas felt by some analytic faculty to be worthy of consideration (Keiser, 1972). What one might call *a selectively-open curriculum* has two further advantages. One is that theoretical and technical differences are confronted and discussed in the educational forum, rather than in extra-curricular exposures. Such experiences often occur under unfavorable learning conditions where the student is entirely on his own in assessing persuasively presented, complex, controversial ideas. The other advantage of having a dialogue about different views in the educational forum is that it counteracts the tendency of polarized forces to view theories as categorically "good" or "bad." The analyst-in-training and the newly graduated analyst are thus relieved of the burden of choosing between one or the other viewpoint, which they feel will affect their analytic careers (Polanyi, 1958).

In the implementation of this educational philosophy, new and controversial ideas would be identified as such. They should, preferably, be taught by faculty members who fully understand the concepts and are attempting to perceive or test their application, rather than by someone who has rejected them *a priori* or is categorically opposed to these ideas. With both traditional and new theories taught in the curriculum, students will have the opportunity to discuss them with instructors of varying views. New ideas will also be brought to supervised analyses where the supervisor can comment and compare them with established approaches, favorably or negatively, depending upon his or her point of view. In this regard, students should be exposed to as many different supervisors as possible. Another curricular approach is to hold a seminar on current psychoanalytic literature where the focus is on new ideas and their usefulness — again in comparison with established concepts.

In my view, a selectively-open curriculum is in keeping with the optimal development of both the clinical and the scientific analytic function. The clinical function requires freedom in the associative processes of the analyst and the capacity to entertain all possible ideas in seeking to understand and help the patient. The same is true for the scientific function of the analyst (Polanyi, 1958). For both purposes, the garnered ideas would initially be used as tentative hypotheses to be evaluated for their fit with available data and, if promising, to be tested in application. In clinical psychoanalysis, the test would be applied in the interpretive and analytic process.

Freedom of thought and associative processes in the analyst and the capacity to reality-test different ideas rest on relative freedom from pathology, determined by the success of the training analysis. Both the scientific breakthrough (Polanyi, 1958; Kuhn, 1962) and the analytic insight involve a temporary escape from mental constraint. It seems to me that the analyst and analytic functions can best be developed in an educational atmosphere that is characterized by open-mindedness combined with the scientific attitude. The proposed structuring of the curriculum can integrate research and treatment in the mind of the future analyst as they were integrated in the mind of Freud.

REFERENCES

Arlow, J. (1972), Some dilemmas in psychoanalytic education. *J. Amer. Psychoanal. Assn.,* 20: 556–566.

Freud, A. (1936), *The Ego and the Mechanisms of Defense.* New York: International Universities Press.

Freud, S. (1921), Group psychology and the analysis of the ego. *Standard Edition,* 18:69–143. London: Hogarth Press, 1955.

———— (1923), The ego and the id. *Standard Edition,* 19:13–66. London: Hogarth Press, 1961.

Goodman, S. (1977), *Psychoanalytic Education and Research: The Current Situation and Future Possibilities.* New York: International Universities Press.

Greenson, R. R. (1969), The origin and fate of new ideas in psychoanalysis. *Internat. J. Psycho-Anal.,* 50:503–515.

Keiser, S. (1972), Report to the Board on Professional Standards. *J. Amer. Psychoanal. Assn.,* 20:518–539.

Kuhn, T. S. (1962), The structure of scientific revolutions. *International Encyclopedia of Unified Sciences: Foundations of the Unity of Science,* Volume 2, Number 2, ed. O. Neurath, R. Carnap, & C. Morris. Chicago: University of Chicago Press, 1962, 1970.

Lewin, B. D., & Ross, H. (1960), *Psychoanalytic Education in the United States.* New York: W. W. Norton.

Lustman, S. L. (1967), The meaning and purpose of curriculum planning. *J. Amer. Psychoanal. Assn.,* 15:862–875.

McLaughlin, J. T. (1973), Panel report: Committees of the Board on Professional Standards. *J. Amer. Psychoanal. Assn.,* 21:576–602.

Polanyi, M. (1958), *Personal Knowledge: Towards a Post-Critical Philosophy.* Chicago: University of Chicago Press, 1962.

Stone, L. (1954), The widening scope of indications for psychoanalysis. *J. Amer. Psychoanal. Assn.,* 2:567–594.

Wallerstein, R. S. (1972), The futures of psychoanalytic education. *J. Amer. Psychoanal. Assn.,* 20:591–606.

12

Change and Integration in Psychoanalysis as a Profession: Discussion

ROBERT S. WALLERSTEIN, M.D.

The three preceding presentations have highlighted important issues in three distinctive areas, each vital to our discipline: psychoanalysis as a therapy, psychoanalytic education, and psychoanalytic research. I will discuss them separately, each for what I believe is the central message that I want to extract in my effort to develop a unifying theme from my perspective. At the same time, I will present my own explicit ideas for thematic and programmatic integration in the profession of psychoanalysis.

In Robert Tyson's reflections on psychoanalysis as treatment, he has used as his organizing context the kaleidoscope of change and flux in our profession within which he has tried to discern enduring guiding threads. He has bracketed his observations as referring to the century and a half between Edward Weinshel's statement at the International Psychoanalytic Association Congress in London in 1975 that psychoanalysis was then in a period of greater ferment and diversity than ever before, and Alexis de Tocqueville's statement about Americans (if not yet American psychoanalysts) in 1835 that "they all consider society as a body in a state of improvement, humanity as a changing scene, in which nothing is, or ought to be, permanent." The implication is again one of constant ferment, and with it inevitable diversity.

The conclusion I have been reaching over my own scientific lifetime in psychoanalysis is that ferment, change, and diversity have always been of the es-

167

sence in psychoanalysis as a science and profession; and it is not necessarily more so now, or in 1975, than it was in the earlier days: Witness the deviations of Jung, Adler, Rank, Ferenczi, and Stekel in the first generation around Freud, and those of Horney, Alexander, Fromm-Reichmann, and Harry Stack Sullivan in a later generation. Although change, development, and diversity are central to the scientific enterprise everywhere, it is more plainly evident in our field than it is, for example, in physics, where, despite all the bewildering changes in the modern-day physics of relativity and quantum theory, I think there is greater consensus among physicists on what their field is all about (at least at any given point in historic time). That consensus was a different one, of course, in the nineteenth-century world of Newtonian, pre-Einsteinian physics than it is today.

In psychoanalysis, by contrast, though we have been living under the monumental imprint of our founding genius, Sigmund Freud (who almost more than any other man in human intellectual history brought into being single-handedly an entire field of knowledge and its organizing world view), there has been among us, at all times, much less agreement on the nature of our field—as a theory, as a technique, and as a treatment. And I don't think that that is necessarily a function of our young, still uncrystallized science; this lack of consensus may be just a matter of the essential nature of our field, and perhaps the search for greater clarification of conceptual differences that will lead to more precise understanding of the scope, nature, and defining parameters of psychoanalysis is a chimerical and ultimately futile quest. Drawing on what I have gleaned from Tyson's paper, I would like to clarify what I mean by all this.

Tyson talks about how presumptuous it would be to pretend to speak for the profession as a whole. Not only does he remind us of how impossible it is to know what actually takes place behind the closed doors of other analysts' consulting rooms, but he implies that even if we transcend that limitation (for example, by videotapes of sessions with our patients shared with one another) and transcend as well that other limitation of the endless variations in individual personal styles, we would still be left with major, and not just incidental, national, regional, and local variations that make psychoanalysis quite palpably different in different areas of its practice throughout the world.

Years ago we ascribed these differences to the great internal schism between the Freudians and the Kleinians, passionately promoted, of course, by both sides. (A famous aphoristic statement from the side of the American version of modern-day ego-psychology was Rapaport's quip that the Kleinians had just substituted an id mythology for an ego psychology.) The Freudian-Kleinian controversy did split the psychoanalytic ranks in its heyday—with the largest group in England, and most of Latin America stalwartly Kleinian, and an American enclave subsequently developing in Los Angeles; but the overwhelming part of psychoanalysis in the United States, much of the European continent, and, to some extent, in England, remained staunchly Freudian, however each of the local or regional groups defined that rubric. However, I need only mention some major instances of our *continuing* proliferation of ideologies and ideological divisions to indicate that this was just the beginning: the English object-relations middle group of Fairbairn, Guntrip, and others; Bion starting in England, spreading somewhat to the United States, and now quite the rage in Latin America; Lacan in France, spreading a little to the United States, and now competing with Bion on a large scale for influence in Latin America; and of course our indigenous American phenomenon of Kohut's self-psychology as a potential ultimate replacement for psychoanalytic conflict psychology. Except for the Lacanians (who withdrew originally from the International Psychoanalytic Association but are now in some places returning), all of these ideologies have grown within, and remained within, the body of psychoanalysis, organized worldwide in the International Psychoanalytic Association (IPA).

Yet, these distinctive theoretical or ideological positions are not the only kinds of differences among us; they are just the most obvious. There are also national and cultural and language differences that I have become increasingly aware of in my years as an officer in the IPA, so that I have had to develop perspectives on psychoanalysis that reach beyond our national borders to include England, the European continent, and Latin America. I don't have the space here to develop the fullness of this argument, but all of us who have been party to the international dialogue at IPA Congresses know that French analysts talk a very different language than we do—not just linguistically but, more important, conceptually. Their psychoanalysis is more fluid—some would call it less precise—grounded in philosophical, linguistic, and literary conventions, with a powerful hermeneutic emphasis, difficult for Americans to comprehend. They, in turn, look upon the whole American ego-psychology explanatory edifice so carefully constructed by Hartmann, Rapaport, and their followers as but a mechanical application of a deadening pseudo natural science squeezing all semblance of the soul out of the psychoanalytic encounter. This is familiar enough to many of us, and we often comfortably put it down to cultural and language differences with the French. That is an important part, to be sure, but then we would be surprised to find that many English analysts—middle group and Freudians alike as well as, of course, many Kleinians—see eye to eye with the French.

From this French and English combined perspective, psychoanalysis here in North America is a very different, often quite unflatteringly a rather lifeless and mechanistic thing. I had this point tellingly brought home to me when I participated in a panel discussion with Jacob Arlow and Roy Schafer at the December, 1982 meeting of the American Psychoanalytic Association in New York; the topic was the nature of psychic reality. I felt that the panel was worthwhile and productive enough; and our overflowing audience was quite enthusiastic. Afterward, a good English friend and colleague (a very proper B-group Freudian psychoanalyst) who had attended the session commented to me privately about how different—and by clear implication how impoverished—American psychoanalytic thinking is on this issue compared with the thinking within the British Society.

I turn now to the related, and additionally complicating, point made by Tyson about individual differences in style or idiosyncrasy, even among those of us in the most cohesive and homogeneous small-group cluster. In this connection, I will quote from Anna Freud as an acknowledged pillar of psychoanalytic orthodoxy. In her 1954 discussion of Leo Stone's paper on the widening scope of indications for psychoanalysis she said:

> There are . . . individual variations in dealing with material. . . . Years ago, in Vienna, we instituted an experimental technical seminar among colleagues of equal seniority, and equal theoretical background, treating cases with similar diagnoses and therefore supposedly similar structure. We compared techniques and found in discussion—not only, as Stone put it today, "that no two analysts would ever give precisely the same interpretations throughout the analysis," but more surprisingly still, that such uniformity of procedure was never kept up for more than a few days in the beginning of the analysis.

And then after describing some of these ways in which these analyses began to run so very differently, she went on to say:

> So far as I know, no one has yet succeeded in investigating and finding the causes of these particular variations. They are determined, of course, not by the material, but by the trends of interest, intentions, shades of evaluation, which are peculiar to every individual analyst. I do *not* suggest that they should be looked for among the phenomena of countertransference [emphasis added]. . . . Just as "no two analysts would ever give precisely the same interpretations," we find on closer examination that no two of a given analyst's patients are ever handled by him in precisely the same manner. With some patients we remain deadly serious. With others, humor or even jokes, may play a part. With some the terms in which interpretations are couched have to be literal ones; others find it easier to accept the same content when given in the form of similes and analogies.

I think I have now made my point (perhaps even overstated it), probably taking it far beyond what Tyson might feel could properly be extrapolated out of his paper: It is, simply, that there may not be one true and correct psychoanalysis that we try to approximate as best we can; there may be, rather, many psychoanalyses—ideological, regional, linguistic, cultural, local, and even uniquely idiosyncratic. One major implication of all this is that in the search to delineate the elements of management—applications, remedies, and tact—as defining parameters of the psychoanalytic treatment process, each of us could offer a very personal approach, espousing different ingredients and different emphases; and I am sure that Tyson is prepared for that kind of divergence and diversity of response. Other, even more important, implications that I want to discuss include the consequences of such thinking for our educational and research enterprises, which I will try to outline in the context of my discussion of the papers by Calvin Settlage and Mardi Horowitz.

Before proceeding to this discussion, however, I want to comment briefly on the thoughtful and sobering questions raised by Tyson on the issues of suitability, analyzability, and indications for analytic treatment. We have lived for a long time in a world of the "widening scope" of psychoanalytic indications, thoughtfully discussed in so balanced and complexly nuanced a way by Leo Stone in 1954 — three decades ago. Today, with the work of Kohut and his followers with narcissistic personalities and Kernberg's work with borderline personality organizations, this trend seems, if anything, to be intensifying. It was Anna Freud who, in her discussion of Stone's paper, presented the case for a return to classical, i.e., narrowing, indications. Currently, in my own book, *42 Lives in Treatment* (1985), based on the Psychotherapy Research Project of The Menninger Foundation (to which Horowitz has referred), I strongly underline Anna Freud's position on the basis of a thirty-year-long observation of these forty-two patients throughout their treatment courses and their subsequent life courses.

Tyson hints, I think quite unmistakably, that the search for a wider scope of psychoanalytic application may be, in part, economically, rather than just scientifically motivated — an understandable response to the growing scarcity of classically suitable psychoanalytic patients, in part lured away by rival, mostly quick-fix treatment offerings, in part, perhaps, driven away by our escalating fee structures.

I turn now to Settlage's scholarly and very thoughtful presentation, drawing as it does on philosophy of science and philosophy of education considerations, with special attention to the relevant concerns of such central figures in the modern discourse on these issues as Thomas Kuhn and Michael Polanyi. In his presentation Settlage deals with all the complex, unresolved issues and problems that have beset psychoanalytical education since its inception, with its rapid crystallization into the familiar tripartite structure, consisting of the training analysis, the seminar sequence, and supervised treatment of psychoanalytic cases. Settlage has reminded us of the major, substantial discussions of these many-sided issues, at least here in America: the Lewin and Ross book published in 1960; the plenary session of the American Psychoanalytic Association in celebration of ten years' work by its Committee on Psychoanalytic Education (COPE); and the special Conference on Psychoanalytic Education and Research, sponsored by the American Psychoanalytic Association in 1974.

Throughout the surveys, conferences, and writings, the *same* statements of issues and problems have repeatedly appeared, for example, the problems of our part-time training system usually run as a night school, on the tired energies of tired men and women after full working days of clinical practice. (Anna Freud addressed herself explicitly to this issue in her Chicago talk on the "Ideal Psychoanalytic Institute: A Utopia," which would be a full-time school like her Hampstead Clinic tried to be.) Central to all the weighty problems of our educational enterprise have been what I regard as the cluster of interrelated problems (not usually disentangled and separately identified) that Lewin and Ross rather globally identified as the syncretistic dilemmas of the training system. Most important among these is the issue of the training analysis as having to be simultaneously a valid and productive therapeutic experience and at the same time a vital, monitored aspect of the educational process. Linked to this has been the problem of the candidate's pursuing (as much as possible) personal goals in the personal analysis, while squaring these with professional goals in the other two components of the tripartite training curriculum. In addition, there has always been the dilemma of both the institute and the candidate of serving two purposes in psychoanalytic training for a profession and psychoanalytic education for a science.

This last is, of course, a dilemma shared with all the so-called "learned professions," those callings, the education for which has been properly identified as the appropriate purpose of the university, with medicine and the law, for example, being among the original cluster of faculties in the very first medieval universities of Bologna and Salerno. The issue here, to put it dramatically, is the conflict between staunchly conservative and disruptively radical goals pursued at the same time and within the same learning context. On the one hand, part of the educational enterprise, which is committed to professional training, rests on a solidly conservative core. The established wisdom of the field must be conserved and transmitted to new generations of students in order to maintain the highest standards that the profession has achieved in its ministrations to the public it serves. In this context, Settlage has referred to the educator's natural and proper resistance to change. On the other hand, the same educational enterprise is committed to new scholarship and scientific advance — at least equally necessary if the whole discipline is not to stagnate and ultimately atrophy. Within this framework it must be ever on the lookout for, and receptive to new ideas and to their appropriate testing in the crucible of clinical experience, and yet in ways that safeguard the therapeutic interests of the patients who commit themselves to our care.

In this context, Settlage has referred to the struggle over the proper, responsible integration of new ideas into our educational system, drawing upon Greenson's article about the origin and fate of new ideas in psychoanalysis. Settlage's own prescription comes out of his conviction that the educational pendulum has swung too far toward a conservative hardening of our educational structure, which makes what he felicitously calls the "well-tempered dialogue" difficult to sustain. He calls for a "selectively open curriculum" which, given what he accurately enough identifies as the range of differing views that is usually embodied within the faculty of any given institute, would inherently be likely to provide the "appropriate pro-and-con view of new ideas in relation to established ideas."

Clearly, in the context of the thesis that I have sketched out — the view of our field as comprising many psychoanalyses, sharing a common core but almost unendingly variable, perhaps for reasons inherent in the nature of the enterprise — I support and underline Settlage's thinking: that there will inevitably be "the range of differing views" within the faculties of all but the smallest institutes, and that none has a corner on what psychoanalysis is, because it just isn't one monolith that we all try imperfectly to approximate. This is the message that I read into Settlage's paper, and I see it as a logical extension into our educational system of the views on the nature of psychoanalysis that I have presented in such preliminary and not yet developed fashion.

I turn now last to Mardi Horowitz's characteristically lucid presentation of the areas of viable and vital psychoanalytic research, including a seductive call to all of us, as curious practitioners, to immerse ourselves in the field's exciting research frontiers — not just the few of us, like Horowitz himself, in academic research positions in departments of psychiatry at medical schools. His always upbeat presentation of the thriving (or, anyway, potentially thriving) state of research in psychoanalysis is bolstered by his rather optimistic portrayal of the capacity and readiness of his analytic practitioner colleagues to surmount all the obstacles, logistical and psychological, that keep them from joining him in the research endeavor to the best of their abilities.

In my discussion of Horowitz's paper, I would like to bypass his remarks about psychoanalytic child development research. I agree with him completely that this is, technically, a highly refined field, not only in its conceptualization but in its complex and detailed data-gathering, which often involves complicated psychophysiological monitoring as well as close interactional behavior observation. It is truly a field for the special expert, who can devote almost full time to such research. Happily, we have a number of such experts in the ranks of psychoanalytic developmental researchers — for example, Justin Call, Anneliese Korner, and the late Selma Fraiberg here in California, Robert Emde and Lou Sander in Colorado, Billie Escalona, Eleanor Galenson, Herman Roiphe, and Dan Stern in New York, and Peter Wolff in Boston are among those who immediately come to mind, not to speak of Margaret Mahler and all of her coworkers in New York and Philadelphia — so that our special psychoanalytic perspective is well represented in this busy field, and many findings of major psychoanalytic interest are being fed back into our ongoing clinical and theoretical enterprise. I will focus on the three other areas of psychoanalytic research that Horowitz has outlined: outcome studies applying state-of-the-art assessment methodology that has advanced so spectacularly over the past two decades in the field of psychotherapy research; the study of what he terms "psychoanalytic phenomena and explanatory descriptions" calling for detailed phenomenological descriptions of discrete psychopathological phenomena such as anxiety or panic attacks, which are all too often neglected in favor of theoretical metapsychological expositions on such intricacies as Freud's anxiety theory, whether for example a unitary theory can conceptually encompass both what is designated as signal and as traumatic anxiety; and lastly studies of the psychological change process in analysis where he mentioned our own thirty-year-long Menninger Psychotherapy Research Project which I am bringing to its final summary clinical accounting in my forthcoming book, *42 Lives in Treatment: A Study of Psychoanalysis and Psychotherapy* (1985), along with his mention of the "consensual analysis" studies of Emanuel Windholz and his group, and of course the mention of his own group's "configurational analysis" studies reflected by now in several published books.

Psychoanalytic outcome studies were initially started not only in Berlin, but also in London and Chicago; but they were crude and oversimplified by today's research standards. The most complexly comprehensive outcome study to date was in the Psychotherapy Research Project at The Menninger Foundation in Topeka started back in the early 50s. In this project, conditions were in some senses "ideal," with ample time and money and the cooperation and involvement of the total clinical psychoanalytic community — made possible within a full-time clinical community with everyone on the same payroll, and psychologically even more important than that, with a consequent shared commitment to a common institutional professional purpose. However, it need not take all of that to do and the necessary conditions can at least be approximated at low-cost treatment clinics affiliated for training purposes with most psychoanalytic institutes. Within any institute this kind of research could be an important and exciting collective contribution to our field, which could be sparked by a few committed local psychoanalytic researchers. Along these lines, Horowitz mentioned the influential and interesting outcome studies pioneered by Arnold Pfeffer in New York on a clinical private practice base, just with access to some of the patient population treated at the New York Institute's low-cost treatment center. Similar studies have been undertaken by Schlessinger and Robbins in Chicago and by Norman, Oremland, Windholz, Blacker, and Hoch in San Francisco. The point I am making is simply that outcome research can be done to some extent by us all and that it does not require much more in the organization of one's professional life than do studies of psychoanalytic phenomena or the change process in analysis, to be next discussed.

I strongly agree with Horowitz about the need for research on "psychoanalytic phenomena" and "explanatory description," and I want to underline the need for a phenomenology that is at least as good as, and that precedes, the metapsychology. Such studies also happen to follow the time-tested and old-fashioned clinical case-study method—the method, after all, innovated by Freud to create single-handedly the entire discipline of psychoanalysis, conceptually and technically. Kohut's careful delineation over more than a decade of the mirroring and idealizing self-object transferences and the counterpart countertransferences that they characteristically evoke is but one recent significant example of the continuing scientific fruitfulness of this approach. (This is a vital contribution to psychoanalytic knowledge recognized by many of us who disagree thoroughly with the divisive theory of self psychology in what Kohut calls the "broader" sense that I feel he unnecessarily creates upon it.)

I wish that Horowitz had mentioned under this same heading the small study group model, linking concept development to empirical data under scrutiny, that was developed at the Hampstead Clinic in the "Concepts" groups working there with accumulated data from cases treated analytically at the clinic and summarized according to the categories of the Hampstead Index. It is, of course, a model with all the pitfalls of trying to resolve the "consensus problem" in psychoanalytic research, about which Seitz wrote so cogently a few decades back in his evaluation of the psychosomatic research by Franz Alexander and his group in Chicago. Such pitfalls inevitably confront all efforts to achieve a meaningful clinical consensus, a kind of clinical reliability in areas where rigorous research-adequate reliability is not yet attainable nor yet the goal. As an aside, I will just allude to a data-base issue mentioned by Horowitz: the differential values and need for verbatim recorded tapes and transcripts versus comprehensive process notes written after the treatment hour. Suffice it to say that there are interesting comparative studies by Peter Knapp in Boston and by Harold Sampson, Joseph Weiss, and their group in San Francisco about how well the themes that emerge in the full transcript are actually captured and presented in "good process notes."

Lastly, turning briefly to what Horowitz calls studies of the change process in psychoanalysis, which most clinical psychoanalysts would see as what should be the heart of psychoanalytic research, I will just say that the model here can cover a wide range: from individual case studies by a Kernberg investigating borderline personality organization or a Kohut doing the same with narcissistic character organization, to group-consensus studies of the Hampstead Index, such as the "Diagnostic Profiles" mentioned by Horowitz, all the way to formal, systematic, logical, and even quantitative computerized studies. These would include the research of Merton Gill and Irwin Hoffman in Chicago on their conception of the psychoanalytic transference and Hartvig Dahl's studies in New York on the minute linguistic syntactics of moment-to-moment psychoanalytic transactions as clues to the dissection of evolving transferences and countertransferences.

Horowitz's purpose in describing the whole potential research smorgasbord is, I believe, frankly to proselytize, to draw as much of the clinical psychoanalytic world as possible into the psychoanalytic research enterprise, because he is convinced that this is more feasible than we usually think and vitally important to our long-term survival as a growing science. The rich potential research smorgasbord, to stick with that metaphor, appeals to me particularly because of the main thematic line I have tried to draw, the perspective outlined in this paper as a heuristic and provisional viewpoint, yet one that I wish to have you think about with me. From this perspective of many psychoanalyses—ideologically and regionally and culturally and linguistically and even individually idiosyncratically colored—which I am convinced is valid to a substantial degree, not only must our educational system offer a more "selectively open curriculum," but our research enterprise must be more committed to vigorous and sustained activity along all potentially workable research facets. Yet, at the same time we need to accept the sobering fact that agreed-upon data and findings will be harder to come by in the field of psychoanalysis, and will be much slower to build toward the accumulating knowledge edifice of other sciences—if psychoanalysis can, indeed, ever approximate that goal at all.

In the context of my discussion of the three preceding presentations on the topic of "Change and Integration in Psychoanalysis as a Profession" (I would prefer to substitute the word "discipline" that encompasses the concepts of both profession and science), I have offered my own argument or perspective on the nature of psychoanalysis—or psychoanalyses as I prefer to call it. I would hope that this perspective may be considered as part of the "selectively open curriculum" that Settlage calls for within our educational training institutes. It can also serve as underpinning for a more intensive, more diversified, and a more widely involving research enterprise as proposed by Horowitz, and can be factored then also into the assessment of all of our research findings. The point of view expressed in this paper is obviously itself part of the clinical difference and diversity that marks the worldwide psychoanalytic clinical community and that has so much room for individual reflections such as Tyson's, which show how he conceptualizes our discipline as a therapy and invites then our own individual resonant or dissonant response.

REFERENCE

Wallerstein, R. S. (1985), *42 Lives in Treatment: A Study of Psychoanalysis and Psychotherapy.* New York: Guilford Press.

13

Reflections on Some Relations Between Psychoanalytic Concepts and Psychoanalytic Practice

JOSEPH SANDLER, M.D.

I am reminded of something my father said... when he spoke of how we bring up our children. He said we supply them with a map of the Italian lakes and send them to the North Pole.

—Anna Freud, 1973

I

If one looks carefully one can find an implicit unconscious assumption in many psychoanalytic writings that our theory is essentially complete and or-ganized, with each part being fully integrated with every other. Imperfections in the theory, some of them major, are clearly recognized, but are seen as blemishes that have to be remedied. Gaps in our formulations have to be filled and definitions made much more precise, so that ultimately the pieces of the theoretical jig-saw puzzle will fit neatly together. Freud's ideas are seen as the

Prepublished paper for the 33rd International Psychoanalytical Congress, Madrid, July 1983. Reprinted by permission from the *International Journal of Psycho-Analysis,* 64: 35–45. London: Inter-national Psychoanalytic Association.

core of existing theory, and acceptable later developments are viewed as amplifications and additions which are consistent — or at least not inconsistent — with Freud's thoughts. Those who think in these terms will, when they disagree with other writers, do so on the grounds that the others have misunderstood, misinterpreted or misapplied Freud, and will turn back to Freud's writings to find supporting evidence for their own ideas.

This particular standpoint fits well with a very necessary conservative trend in psychoanalysis, one which functions to support and to protect fundamental psychoanalytic propositions and which has a significant stabilizing function. Yet, in contrast, we can look at psychoanalytic theory as a body of thought which has been in a state of continuous organic development since the beginning. As ideas have developed on one front, so there have been repercussions in other areas, and theoretical strain has constantly been — and is being — generated. Every new definition, every new gain in precision, puts pressure on other aspects of theory. In particular, concepts become stretched to encompass new insights and new ideas. Often such an expansion of the meaning of a conceptual term is not explicit, and one writer after another will attempt to define it in some specific way, or will reiterate the "standard," "official" or "public" formulation, taking it for granted that any respectable psychoanalytic concept will have one proper meaning only. The reality is, of course, that conceptual terms in psychoanalysis often have multiple meanings which vary according to the context in which the term is used. We have only to think of such notions as fantasy, trauma, identification, resistance, acting out — the list can be made very long indeed — to become aware that each possesses elasticity, is pliable in its usage, having a whole spectrum of context-dependent meanings.

There are advantages to emphasizing the developmental-historical dimension in psychoanalysis when we think of theoretical matters. It allows us to escape — if we want to — quarrels about which theory is "right" and which is "wrong." Rather, it puts us in the position of asking "Why was this, that or the other formulation put forward?" and "What did its authors mean?" It is of some interest that whenever an aspect of theory has emphasis transferred from it to some new formulation, so the hiatuses and weak areas in the theory which follow (if only because the new theory never encompasses exactly the same area as the old) attract counterforces aimed at filling the gaps or remedying the weaknesses. It is characteristic of these counterforces that they inevitably push forward a core of ideas which are useful and important; equally inevitably they represent an over-reaction, and over-filling of the empty spaces. Gaps and weaknesses in theory also follow changes in specific areas resulting from advances in clinical psychoanalysis and in technical procedures; again, sooner or later over-reactions occur. And if the proponent of the new ideas is a charismatic leader, then a new "movement" in psychoanalysis may result. It may split from the mainstream of psychoanalysis, or remain within it, contributing to the dialectic of theoretical development.

If one takes a combined developmental and functional point of view, and if we abandon our search for the pot of theoretical gold at the end of the rainbow, then we may perhaps allow ourselves a greater degree of tolerance of concepts which are unclear and ill-defined, particularly those which have been created by people who have a different psychoanalytic background. Moreover, the examination of the reasons for dissatisfaction with older ideas and for the formulation of new ones should prove at least as profitable, if we want to understand the processes occurring in the development of psychoanalytic theory, as the stringent examination of the structure and formal qualities of the new concepts. (In searching for causes for dissatisfaction with existing theory, we ought to treat the manifest reasons given by the authors of new theories with a great deal of caution.) It is interesting in this context to look at Glover's scathing critique of Melanie Klein's ideas (1945). Certainly her ideas had (and still have) many flaws but their importance in the development of psychoanalysis cannot be disputed. Similarly, we can examine with profit the technical and theoretical ideas of Heinz Kohut (1971, 1977), in order to make ourselves aware of *the nucleus of appropriateness* contained in them, rather than dismiss his approach as a whole because of theoretical imperfections and the limitations of one-sided technical procedures.

Elastic concepts play a very important part in holding psychoanalytic theory together. As psychoanalysis is made up of formulations at varying levels of abstraction, and of part-theories which do not integrate well with one another, the existence of pliable, context-dependent concepts allows an overall framework of psychoanalytic theory to be assembled. Parts of this framework are rigorously spelled out, but can only articulate with similar part-theories if they are not tightly connected, if the concepts which form the joints are flexible. Above all, the value of such a loosely jointed theory is that it allows developments in psychoanalytic theory to take place without necessarily causing overt radical disruptions in the overall theoretical structure of psychoanalysis. The elastic and flexible concepts take up the strain of theoretical change, absorbing it while more organized newer theories or part-theories can develop. One of the best examples of this is Susan Isaacs' use of the concept of unconscious fantasy to absorb a view of fantasy which was radically different from Freud's.

Such an approach to psychoanalytic concepts regards each as having a set of *dimensions of meaning,* as existing in a meaning-space, in which it moves as its context and sense changes.[1] The examination of the different dimensions of our major psychoanalytic concepts may then prove to be as profitable as the search for precise definitions — possibly even more profitable, for some of our most useful concepts are incapable of being pinned down by being defined, and today's precision may be tomorrow's rigidity.

---

[1]Indeed, most of the words in our everyday language are moved around within their own meaning-spaces as we communicate with one another.

To the extent that different psychoanalysts share the same meaning-space for a concept or theoretical term, they can communicate relatively satisfactorily in that particular area. However, it may happen that their meaning-spaces for the concept are different, and then problems of lack of communication or pseudo-communication may arise. Thus, while the search for a clearer understanding of the dimensions of meaning of psychoanalytic concepts is appropriate in regard to the meaning-space common to all psychoanalysts or to groups of analysts, it is also possible to look with profit at the dimensions of meaning of a theoretical notion or term *within the mind of any individual psychoanalyst.*[2]

Reference was made at the beginning of this paper to the implicit assumption that an essentially complete and organized psychoanalytic theory should be aimed for, and that such a view has a conservative and stabilizing function. But the striving towards a *complete* theory is also an outcome of many other factors. Contradictions make for dissonance, and dissonance is uncomfortable and has to be avoided. The idea that there might be a not-fully-integrated *body* of theory does not seem quite respectable, especially if we take the search for unified theories in the physical sciences as our ideal. We can add to this the fear of disagreeing with Freud, or of appearing to disagree. This latter factor touches on the desire to be a "good" member of the psychoanalytic hierarchy so that the local Institute's or Society's seal of approval is retained.

George Klein (1976) has referred to a particular strand of psychoanalytic theory which has as its intent "to place psychoanalysis in the realm of natural science" and mentions a number of further factors creating "a momentum for a mode of theoretical explanation quite different from the clinical mode, to the point where it is no longer clear which mode of explanation has priority in the development of the theory." Klein amply demonstrates the lack of value of metapsychology in relation to psychopathology and clinical work, and argues cogently for a clinical theory. The difference between the two theories "is not in degree of abstractness but in explanatory intent." Part of the "intent" in metapsychology is to provide a general psychology within psychoanalysis, and I agree with Klein that while psychoanalysis can be considered to be a part of psychology it is "by no means the overall structure which incorporates the rest of psychology." I am unhappy, however, with the idea that psychoanalytic theory has to be reformulated as a fundamentally *clinical* theory, partly because I do not think psychoanalysis will ever be a complete theory, and partly because as a theory it encompasses — and needs to encompass — more than the clinical or the pathological. To try to satisfy all "explanatory intents" with one comprehensive theory is clearly impossible, and I would urge the view that we have *a body of ideas,* rather than a consistent whole, that constitutes psychoanalytic theory. What is critical is not what psychoanalytic theory *should* be, but what should be *emphasized* within the whole compass of psychoanalytic thinking. *And what should be emphasized is that which relates to the work we have to do.* This

---

[2]This task poses certain methodological problems, but they can be overcome (see Fonagy, 1982).

means that for most of us the theory needs to be a clinically, psychopathologically and technically oriented one, which also includes a central preoccupation, not only with the abnormal, but with the normal as well.

Of course we cannot ignore adjacent disciplines and the need to build bridges, where we can, between psychoanalysis and its neighbours. But we need not tear down or reconstruct our psychoanalytic structures in order to build such bridges. A psychoanalytic "normal" psychology needs to be first and foremost psychoanalytic, and should not aspire to be a "general" psychology. This means accepting the view that there can be many legitimate co-existing psychologies, for different purposes, constructed from different points of view. And a psychoanalytic normal psychology, a psychoanalytic developmental psychology, or any other form of psychoanalytic psychology needs, I believe, to be as congruent as possible with psychoanalytic clinical theory. Psychoanalysts and others who are interested in constructing a general psychology are concerned, in regard to this interest, with aspects and levels of theory which are very far from those which normally concern psychoanalytic practitioners. In spite of this there are still psychoanalytic training institutes where substantial quantities of metapsychology (of the "Chapter 7" variety) are taught to beginning students, as an end in itself rather than as one aspect of the history of ideas in psychoanalysis. For how long will we need to expound the vicissitudes of cathexes and the acrobatics of energy transformation to our clinical students, as if these matters had direct relevance to their clinical work?

The fledgling psychoanalyst will bring with him into his consulting room what he has learned from his own analyst, from his supervisors and other teachers, and from his reading. He will carry in his head the theoretical and clinical propositions that he has gathered from these various sources, and these propositions will be, for the most part, the official, standard or public ones. The human mind being what it is, he will continue to underestimate the discrepancies and incongruities in the public theories and will learn to move from one part of his theory to another without being aware that he has stepped over a number of spots in this theory that are conceptually weak.

With increasing clinical experience the analyst, as he grows more competent, will preconsciously (descriptively speaking, unconsciously) construct a whole variety of theoretical segments which relate directly to his clinical work. They are the products of unconscious thinking, are very much partial theories, models or schemata, which have the quality of being available in reserve, so to speak, to be called upon whenever necessary. That they may contradict one another is no problem. They coexist happily as long as they are unconscious.[3] They do not appear in consciousness unless they are consonant with what I

---

[3]I am referring to theories and schemata which are the products of secondary process activity, reflecting the work of the Preconscious system of the topographical model, or of the unconscious ego of the structural theory. The absence of contradiction is *not* that which is ascribed to the contents of the system Unconscious or to the Id.

have called official or public theory, and can be described in suitable words. Such partial structures may in fact represent better (i.e. more useful and appropriate) theories than the official ones, and it is likely that many valuable additions to psychoanalytic theory have come about because conditions have arisen that have allowed preconscious part-theories to come together and emerge in a plausible and psychoanalytically socially acceptable way.

I suggested earlier in this paper that it might be possible to look with profit at the dimensions of meaning of specific concepts within the minds of individual psychoanalysts. This must, of course, include the study of *unconscious* conceptual structures, and such investigations may, I believe, accelerate the development of psychoanalytic theory. In this way the psychoanalyst can be regarded as an instrument, a sort of probe into the psychoanalytic situation, that organizes the experience the analyst has in interaction with his patients through the formation of unconscious theoretical structures. The probe can be withdrawn from the situation and the theories which have been formed can be examined.[4] It is my firm conviction that the investigation of the implicit, private theories of clinical psychoanalysts opens a major new door in psychoanalytic research. One of the difficulties in undertaking such research is that posed by the conscious or unconscious conviction of many analysts that they do not do "proper" analysis (even though such a conviction may exist alongside the belief that they are better analysts than most of their colleagues). The conviction that what is actually done in the analytic consulting room is not "kosher," that colleagues would criticize it if they knew about it, comes from the reality that any analyst worth his salt will adapt to specific patients on the basis of his interaction with those patients. He will modify his approach so that he can get as good as possible a working analytic situation developing. To achieve this, he needs to feel relaxed and informal with his patient to an appropriate degree, and at times he might have to depart quite far from "standard" technique. He may be very comfortable with this as long as it is private rather than public, especially in view of the tendency for colleagues to criticize and "supervise" one another in clinical discussions, and the ease with which analytic material can be seen and interpreted in different ways. I believe that the many adjustments one makes in

---

[4]In a study of the implicit meanings of the trauma concept carried out by the author in collaboration with a research group at the Sigmund Freud Institute in Frankfurt (H. Vogel, S. Drews, R. Fischer, W. Grissmer, R. Klüwer, M. Muck and C. Will) it has become clear that the private, largely unconscious concepts of trauma held by psychoanalysts almost always differ from the public definition. For many, the trauma is conceived of, not only as an event or an experience, or as a memory, but as a sort of foreign body which has been implanted in the individual from outside, which continues to exert an ongoing and threatening effect and which carries with it the danger of overwhelming the individual at any time. It is something to which the person adapts, and continues to adapt, and can only be negatively defined as that emotionally-charged "something" which links certain antecedent experiences with subsequent effects; and if treatment is successful, the "trauma" has been removed!

one's analytic work, including the so-called parameters that one introduces, often lead to or reflect a better fit of the analyst's developing intrinsic private preconscious theory with the material of the patient than the official public theories to which the analyst may consciously subscribe. Often (I hope very often) the analyst "privately knows better," and the more access we can gain to the preconscious theories of experienced analysts, the better we can help the advancement of psychoanalytic theory.

II

Mention was made in the previous section of the way in which concepts may broaden and expand as clinical experience is gained and observations are sharpened and refined in the minds of psychoanalysts. The making of new clinical observations and the gaining of clinical experience very often goes hand in hand with some degree of modification of technique, for no psychoanalyst can follow exactly the same technical procedure with each of his patients. Within certain limits he will adjust what he does to what he feels is necessary for any one patient, and his interaction with his patient will affirm or disaffirm his technical procedures (unless he is completely out of touch with what is going on). I have suggested that a consequence of this dynamic interaction with the patient may be that the analyst will gradually form organized part-theories that will remain unconscious unless conditions are suitable for their emergence. What determines the emergence of new theories on the basis of clinical experience is a matter for further research.

In this section I want, for purposes of demonstration, to look specifically at the concept of *transference* from the point of view of the strain which began to be imposed on the concept before the second world war, a state of strain which remains even today. The suggestion will be put forward that this conceptual strain is the direct outcome of changes in clinical understanding and corresponding changes in technical procedures.

The concept of transference arose, as is well known, from Freud's observations of the way in which a patient's feelings towards his analyst can derive from a "false connexion" between an important figure of the past and the person of the analyst. The repetition of the past may represent a "revised edition" of the older relation, but is not known by the patient to be such. First regarded as a source of resistance in the analysis, transference came to be seen as playing "a decisive part in bringing conviction not only to the patient but also to the physician."

The view of transference as a repetition of the past in the present remained as the main public definition of transference (see Sandler et al., 1973). However, it is possible to see in retrospect that a stretching of the concept of transference was beginning to occur over half a century ago. As long ago as 1930, a British analyst, Ella Freeman Sharpe, wrote:

> Transference begins with the very first analytical session . . . just because every-
> one has thoughts about another human being when brought into close contact
> . . . In analysis . . . we have potentially the freest field for phantasy concerning
> the analyst . . . From the first hour the patient will have thoughts and opinions
> about the analyst as in ordinary contact, but the very fact of the phantasy-
> situation, the detachedness and isolation of the hour, the unknownness of the an-
> alyst, activates phantasy; and this, with the stimulus of dream-life and recollec-
> tions of the past, brings about a very special relationship with the analyst. This
> relationship is the transference.

It is not difficult to detect a shift of emphasis here from the repetition of the
past to the patient's fantasies within the very special relationship of patient to
analyst that Sharpe refers to as transference. What we can also infer, I believe,
is that there must have been first a shift of emphasis in Ella Sharpe's clinical
work which led her to pay special attention to the "field of phantasy concerning
the analyst." But even though what she called the transference referred to something more than the repetition of the past in the present, no other concept came
closer to encompassing the new thoughts than that of transference, and the concept or term was the natural one for her to use. As a consequence, even at that
time, strain was beginning to be put on the concept. The particular emphasis
given by Ella Sharpe to the transference relationship is also discernible in the
early works of Melanie Klein, who was by then an active member of the British
Society. However, Klein tended to view all behaviour as the *repetition* of very
early fantasy relationships.

In 1936 Anna Freud published *The Ego and the Mechanisms of Defence*, and followed Freud in defining transference as a repetition of the past, seeing such
repetitions as being "of incomparable value as a means of [gaining] information about the patient's past affective experiences." While keeping explicitly to
the view of transference as repetition, her special interest in the analysis of the
defences led her to postulate two categories of transference. The first was the
well-established "transference of libidinal impulses," while the second was
"transference of defence." The latter represented the repetition in the analysis
of "former defensive measures against the instincts." These defences show
themselves as resistance, and have to be analysed. "The more correct method,"
said Anna Freud, in speaking of the analysis of resistance, "is to change the focus of attention in the analysis, shifting it in the first place from the instinct to
the specific mechanisms of defence, i.e. from the id to the ego."

It seems likely that what was put forward in theoretical terms stemmed from
Anna Freud's clinical experience of the necessity to handle resistances in analysis differently from the way they had formerly been treated. This is borne out
by a comment she made later (1972) in connexion with the transference of
defence:

> Of course, many of the things I said in the chapter . . . were common knowledge
> at the time I wrote it, but the idea of the transference of defence was not common

knowledge. It was a really new aspect. My idea was that the resistance is so extremely valuable for us because it makes use of the defences within the analytic process, for specific purposes. This was for some reason not generally recognised at the time.

Close reading of Anna Freud's book makes it clear that the defences were regarded by her as having achieved a certain autonomy during development, and that while their use may be a repetition of the past, they are in the present not necessarily historically connected with the impulses they were directed against. At times Anna Freud even used the term "transference" more-or-less synonymously with analytic relationships, perhaps because by then a wider, more colloquial use of the term was emerging. For example, she says "From the theoretical standpoint, analysis of the process of 'identification with the aggressor' . . . enables us to distinguish in the transference anxiety attacks from outbursts of aggression." But, unquestionably, she still held fast, when a definition was required in the text, to the official or public definition of transference.

In 1936 Anna Freud extended the existing list of defences (regression, repression, reaction formation, isolation, undoing, projection, introjection, turning against the self and reversal) by adding, among others, two special forms of defence — identification with the aggressor and what she called "a form of altruism." What is special about these mechanisms is their propensity to *make use of another person for purposes of defence.* [5] In describing identification with the aggressor Anna Freud quotes the case of:

a boy who had the habit of furiously pealing the bell of the children's home where he lived. As soon as the door was opened, he would scold the housemaid loudly for being so slow and not listening for the bell. In the interval between pulling the bell and flying into a rage he experienced anxiety lest he should be reproved for his lack of consideration in ringing so loudly. He upbraided the servant before she had time to complain of his conduct . . . The reversal of the roles of attacker and attacked was in this case carried to its logical conclusion.

In another case a young patient used to reproach her analyst bitterly for being secretive. It emerged that at times she kept certain material secret from the analyst, expected the analyst's reproaches, and dealt with this expectation by reversing the roles. "She criticized the analyst for the very fault of which she herself was guilty." Identification with the aggressor is referred to in this context as a "peculiar combination of introjection and projection."

The form of altruism or "altruistic surrender" described by Anna Freud in 1936 is also referred to by her as a "combination of projection and identifica-

---

[5]It could be argued that projection, as described by Freud, does this as well. But projection on its own represents the distortion of one's image of another person by attributing to that image an unwanted aspect of oneself. It does not, in its simple form, involve the wish to create or evoke a particular response in the other person; it is rather an illusion about that person.

tion for purposes of defence." Through the use of this mechanism the person succeeds in abandoning internally forbidden wishes by aiding the gratification of such wishes in others. The example is given by Anna Freud of a young governess, who, as a child, wanted very much to have beautiful clothes and many children. She also wanted to do better than others and be admired. As an adult she came to analysis appearing unassuming and modest, unmarried, childless and dressed rather dowdily. "She showed little sign of envy or ambition and would compete with other people only if she were forced to do so by external circumstances." But it emerged that she had "an affectionate interest in the love life of her women friends and colleagues," she was "an enthusiastic matchmaker," "she was devoted to other people's children" and "ambitious for the men she loved and followed their careers with the utmost interest." As Anna Freud pointed out "She lived in the lives of other people, instead of having any experience of her own."

In describing the mechanism of altruistic surrender Anna Freud made use of the idea of another person acting as a proxy for one self, of being a "respository" for warded-off impulses. And the governess patient "felt that there was an extraordinarily strong bond between these people and herself."

What Anna Freud did at this time was to introduce a whole class of what might be called object-related defences, which involved reversal of roles or some combination of identification and projection. These are defences in which there is an active interchange between aspects of the self and of the object, the unacceptable aspects of one's own self being dealt with by producing (or attempting to produce) their appearance in the external object. Often, simultaneously, frightening or admired aspects of the object may be taken into the self.

Not long after this, Melanie Klein, who had been developing her own line of thought since the twenties, introduced the concept of projective identification (1946), which took the process described a step further. She couched her formulations in terms of concrete infantile fantasies, and defence mechanisms were seen as the operation of particular fantasies (e.g. the fantasy of getting rid of bad parts of the self by pushing them into the mother or her breast). It would seem that what she emphasized, in other words, was the forcible allocation of aspects of the self to the object, and through controlling the object, achieving control over the projected or externalized aspects of the self.[6]

It seems clear that the introduction and description of these object-related processes, particularly the object-related defences, reflected a major new di-

---

[6]For many years Kleinians and non-Kleinians could be distinguished by the fact that the more classical analysts would speak of "projecting on to the object," and Kleinians would say "projecting into the object." The concept of projective identification should also be taken to refer to a whole class of object-related processes, many of them defensive (see the later extensions of the concept by Bion, 1959; Segal, 1964 and Rosenfeld, 1969).

mension in the analytic work and in the concept of transference. The analysis of the here-and-now of the analytic interaction began to take precedence, in terms of the timing of interpretations, over reconstruction of the infantile past. If the patient used defences within the analytic situation which involved both him and the analyst, this was seen as transference,[7] and increasingly became a primary focus of attention for the analyst. The question "What is going on now?" came to be asked before the question "What does the patient's material reveal about his past?"

In other words, the analytic work became more and more focused, in Britain certainly, on the patient's use of the analyst in his unconscious wishful fantasies and thoughts as they appeared in the present — i.e. in the transference as it is explicitly or implicitly understood by most analysts, in spite of the limited official definition of the term.

My aim in this section has been to put forward the argument that major changes in technical emphasis brought about the extension, the stretching of a concept such as transference, so that it came to include a variety of object-related activities which need not be repetitions of relationships to important figures in the past. (This may not make much impression on those who still believe that everything that happens in the present is a close reflection of what happened or what was fantasied in early infancy.) Such a stretching of a concept is inevitable (and therefore legitimate) and elastic context-dependent concepts, of which transference is only one example, are of the greatest value in articulating, as I tried to show in the previous section, the various aspects of psychoanalytic theory. Let me add, nevertheless that attempts to clarify such concepts are equally important. And without disagreement psychoanalytic theory would be dead.

III

To round this paper out I want to point to three of the many areas in psychoanalysis where the distance between theory on the one hand and clinical practice and experience on the other is particularly wide, and to take the liberty of suggesting possible directions of theoretical clarification or modification.

1. Drives and Motives

However important the instinctual drives may be in our psychoanalytic thinking — and they will certainly always occupy a central position — the need for psychoanalysts to defend the significance of sexual and aggressive wishes has led to the building of theories in which everything tends to be brought back

---

[7]A process probably accelerated as a consequence of James Strachey's contribution to the Marienbad symposium (1934).

to the drives. I am convinced that for most psychoanalysts such reductionism plays a less significant part in their analytic work than in their theory. What they are often much more concerned with are the variety of *motives* for the use of defences, for the construction and development of fantasies and transference, and for many other phenomena with which we concern ourselves as clinical psychoanalysts. Certainly sexual and aggressive drives provide highly important motives, but so do threats to our feelings of safety (to the "integrity of the ego"), injuries to our self-esteem, feelings of guilt and shame, and threats from the real ("external") world. Above all, *anxieties* of all sorts provide motives which are of central clinical significance. I believe that we need to accept into our theory, for example, the proposition that the latent content of a dream or of a piece of transference behaviour can be an unconscious wish or fantasy created to deal with anxiety, pain, or any other unpleasant affect from any source, and not necessarily to "discharge" libidinal or aggressive drive energies. *Not all unconscious wishes derive from the instinctual drives.* Even if they may have done so in the past, such wishes need not be impelled by drives in the present. They may have other causes and other motivating forces.[8]

2. Conflict

For how long will psychoanalysts continue to speak of conflict between id and the ego, between id and superego, between ego and superego, when clinically we address ourselves to the person who is in conflict? Certainly he may experience conflict between a sexual wish and his conscience, but what this means is that *he* is in conflict about *his* wish to gratify a sexual urge and *his* wish to avoid feelings of having done wrong (see Sandler, 1974). Moreover, from the point of view of the sorts of conflict which are clinically significant, what we usually see (and, I hope, interpret) is conflict over derivatives of wishes or wishful fantasies that have been, at some time, acceptable to the person — we might say consciousness-syntonic — but have become, in the course of development, unacceptable, i.e. consciousness-dystonic. The best examples of such conflictual wishes in ordinary everyday analytic experience are transference wishes. These often represent (often quite complicated) ways of interrelating with objects that were once acceptable but had later to be defended against, as a result appearing again in the transference in disguised form. Thus a patient who, as a child, developed a strong clinging tendency, might have turned against this later on. The transference might show a heightened wish to reject or move away from the analyst, for purposes of defence, and the conflict behind this might be over the wish to cling. The impulse to cling, in its turn, might have been a way of dealing with anxieties about losing the mother, and it

---

[8]I would remind any reader who might be shocked by such statements, of Hartmann's ideas about "change of function" and the "genetic fallacy."

would be a great error, both clinically and theoretically, to equate it automatically with an oral instinctual wish. If we take such a view of conflict, then we should have no problem over analysing conflict in our patients with so-called narcissistic character disorders. Whether or not an early defect in object relationships exists, whether or not the pathology is rooted in the pre-oedipal years, childhood wishes (and solutions to the problems caused by these) bring about future conflicts during development, which are then adapted to in turn, and show themselves in the narcissistic adult.

In this connexion I should like to suggest that every solution (defensive or otherwise) to a conflict, because it solves a problem during development, acquires a peremptory and urgent quality, and the urge to impose it in the face of renewed or revived conflict becomes the content of unconscious wishes driven towards actualization. Such wishes may then cause further conflict that might well be reflected in the here-and-now of the analytic situation. As solutions to conflict, both early and late, for the most part involve relationships to real or fantasied objects, conflict over such solutions will tend to reflect itself in the transference, even in the most narcissistic of our patients.

3. Object relationships and transference

Classical theory holds that object relationships reflect the cathexis of the object with instinctual energies, or with aim-inhibited drive energies. The inadequacy of such a view must be self-evident, and although there may still be some who pay lip-service to formulations like the one just given, most analysts conceive of object relationships in some very different way. My own preference is to regard the object relationship, inasmuch as it involves some external person, as a valued type of interaction with that specific person, in which the object plays as big a part as the subject. Such an interaction may satisfy instinctual needs, but (at least equally) satisfies needs for security and familiarity, for reassurance and affirmation of one's own value and identity. Needs of this sort develop from what Mahler (Mahler et al., 1975) has called processes of separation-individuation, and the satisfaction of these needs through an interchange of signals with the object, a dialogue with the object, is a vital part of our existence. As development proceeds, the external objects (together with their distortions by wishful fantasies and defences) are internalized, and the resulting introjected objects form the basis for dialogues with the objects in unconscious fantasy life.

It may be relevant to our understanding of transference if we consider that introjects are constantly being externalized, in a sense being *actualized,* so that they can be related to as external objects rather than as internal ones. Such a tendency to externalize one's introjects is probably a fairly general one, and deserves closer investigation. It is a tendency which can be observed particularly well in the psychoanalytic situation and we regularly see attempts to force, manipulate or seduce the analyst into taking over the role of one or other introject so that an internal fantasy scenario involving a dialogue between self and introject can be enacted. This externalization is as much what we mean by transference as anything else, and the analyst's experience of, and reaction to, this externalization of the introject (extrojection?) is part of his countertransference. I believe that this is implicitly if not explicitly understood by many analysts, who take such processes into account in their work. From the point of view of our theory, however, we should recognize that it is a gross mistake to regard the externalization of inner object relationships, the unpacking of mental furniture as the patient settles into the analysis, as simply the direct or indirect fulfillment of unconscious instinctual wishes, once directed to a figure of the past, and now transferred to the analyst in the present.

As a concluding remark I want to say that I am aware that the ideas in this paper are argued as much against an aspect of my own self as against the views of others — and I hasten to make this comment before others do!

SUMMARY

This paper adopts the standpoint that psychoanalytic theory has been in a state of continuous organic development from the beginning, with states of theoretical strain being generated with each new advance in theory. The meaning of concepts becomes stretched, and psychoanalysts develop implicit theories, concepts and definitions that differ from the "official" or "public" formulations.

While flexible concepts play an important part in psychoanalytic theory, it should be accepted that each may have a number of dimensions of meaning, and that these dimensions may differ from one psychoanalyst to another. Research should be directed towards making explicit the implicit concepts of practising psychoanalysts, and it is suggested that this process will result in the accelerated development of psychoanalytic theory. The essentials of that theory must be those aspects which relate to the work the psychoanalyst has to do, and therefore its main emphasis needs to be clinical.

In the second part of the paper, the expansion of the concept of transference with the introduction of defence analysis is discussed, with particular reference to the class of object-related defences, which involve some combination of identification and projection. It is argued that major changes in technical emphasis brought about the extension of the transference concept, which now has dimensions of meaning which differ from the official definition of the term.

Finally, three areas among many in which there is a significant distance between theory and practice are discussed. The public and official theories relating to drives, conflict, and internal object-relationships and transference are discussed, and suggestions made in regard to possible developments which might lessen the gap between the public theories and the implicit private clinical formulations of the practising psychoanalyst.

REFERENCES

Bion, W. (1959), Attacks on linking. *Internat. J. Psycho-Anal.,* 40:308–315.

Fonagy, P. (1982), The integration of psychoanalysis and experimental science: A review. *Internat. Rev. Psycho-Anal.,* 9:125–145.

Freud, A. (1936), *The Ego and the Mechanisms of Defence.* London: Hogarth Press.

_____ (1972), In Sandler, J. with Freud, A. (1981), Discussions in the Hampstead Index on "The Ego and the Mechanisms of Defence": II. The application of analytic technique to the study of the psychic institutions. *Bull. Hampstead Clin.,* 4:5–30.

_____ (1973), In Sandler, J. with Freud, A. (1982), Discussions in the Hampstead Index on "The Ego and the Mechanisms of Defence": VIII. Denial in word and act. *Bull. Hampstead Clin.,* 5:175–187.

Glover, E. (1945), Examination of the Klein system of child psychology. *The Psychoanalytic Study of the Child,* 1:75–118.

Klein, G. (1976), *Psychoanalytic Theory.* New York: International Universities Press.

Klein, M. (1946), Notes on some schizoid mechanisms. In: *Developments in Psychoanalysis.* London: Hogarth Press, 1952, pp. 292–320.

Kohut, H. (1971), *The Analysis of the Self.* New York: International Universities Press.

_____ (1977), *The Restoration of the Self.* New York: International Universities Press.

Mahler, M., Pine, F., & Bergman, A. (1975), *The Psychological Birth of the Human Infant.* New York: Basic Books.

Rosenfeld, H. (1969), Contribution to the psychopathology of psychotic states: The importance of projective identification in the ego structure and the object relations of the psychotic patient. In: *Problems of Psychosis,* Vol. 1, ed. P. Doucet & C. Laurin. Amsterdam: Excerpta Medica, pp. 115–128.

Sandler, J. (1974), Psychological conflict and the structural model: Some clinical and theoretical implications. *Internat. J. Psycho-Anal.,* 55:53–62.

_____ Dare, C., & Holder, A. (1973), *The Patient and the Analyst.* New York: International Universities Press.

Segal, H. (1964), *Introduction to the Work of Melanie Klein.* London: Heinemann.

Sharpe, E. F. (1930), *Collected Papers on Psycho-Analysis.* London: Hogarth Press, 1950.

Strachey, J. (1934), The nature of the therapeutic action of psycho-analysis. *Internat. J. Psycho-Anal.,* 15:127–159.

14

Comments on the Correlation of
Theory and Technique

SANDOR LORAND, M.D.

Freud's basic principles of therapeutic technique, which were evolved from clinical experimentation, have remained the fundamental guide in present day analytic therapy. But his theoretical formulations and those of his early co-workers concerning technique and therapy were gradually subjected to re-examination as time went on, by Freud himself, as well as others. Attempts at re-examination began on a large scale in 1924 with Ferenczi's *Entwicklungsziele der Psychoanalyse.* In 1936 at the Marianbad International Congress there was a symposium which dealt with the interrelationship between theory and therapy. The contributions of the symposium are well known, as are the participants; however, contrary to expectations, this wide-scale discussion brought little clarification to the problem. It did make plain, however, that there were many questions in the minds of the analysts, and differing views on the relationship between theory and technique. One important contribution of the symposium was to bring to the foreground of attention the necessity for discussing these problems. From that date, we more frequently find in analytic literature attempts at fresh orientation, and trials at finding and formulating new correlations between technique and theory. It became apparent in these

Presidential address to The New York Psychoanalytic Society, October 1947.
Reprinted by permission from *The Psychoanalytic Quarterly,* 17: 32–50, 1948. New York: The Psychoanalytic Quarterly.

publications that although there was agreement on many basic principles, there was sharp disagreement about various others.

We are all familiar with the comprehensive work pertaining to the problem done by the Institute on Psychoanalysis in London, edited by Edward Glover, entitled: An Investigation of the Technique of Psychoanalysis. The volume represents an attempt to systematize and correlate knowledge and opinion on the technique of psychoanalysis. Glover hoped as a result "That problems requiring further investigation [would] be made to stand out more clearly." The book was intended also as a stimulus for further investigation in order to settle both old and newly arising problems of technique.

The questionnaires from which the book was compiled brought into the open comparatively wide differences in the application of analytic principles which obtained mostly among British analysts, but in my opinion apply to analysis wherever it is practiced. In summarizing the information contained in the replies, Glover pointed out that the answers justified the view held by many analysts that it was "very desirable to make fresh investigations of technique from time to time." Scattered throughout the book are references to various theoretical differences which interfere with standardization of technique. The answers to several questions showed that many analysts are concerned about the relation of theory to practice. Glover grouped the replies according to marked differences of opinion, resulting in twenty-one headings, with an addition of nineteen individual opinions which did not fall into any of the twenty-one categories.

In general, the belief that there was need for reformulation of various subjects was expressed by many authors and several members of our Society made contributions towards the solution of the problem, among others Zilboorg's (1939) paper, The Fundamental Conflict with Psychoanalysis, and Kubie's (1939) work entitled, A Critical Analysis of the Concept of a Repetition Compulsion.

In 1943 Oberndorf published a report of his investigation, using the questionnaire method, of the results of psychoanalytic therapy. Replies to the questionnaire received from eighteen established psychoanalysts, each having more than twenty years' experience, revealed a disconcerting divergence of opinion on such topics as the type of case considered most favorable for analysis, criteria for termination, percentage of patients who discontinued analysis, etc. In 1946 in a paper entitled, Constant Elements in Psychotherapy, Dr. Oberndorf (1946) stated that "In addition to and aside from the physician's personality we must include the content, the timing and the manner of presentation of his suggestions, explanations and analytic interpretations, and . . . further investigation of these elements will lead to a broader . . . application of freudian principles in psychotherapy and psychoanalysis to the innumerable medical conditions affected by or consisting of the psychic attitude of the patient."

In the short symposia held during our Society's meetings in 1946 the need for re-examination, clarification and reformulation was expressed by Hartmann, Eidelberg, Kris, and Waelder. Hartmann, Kris and Loewenstein (1946), in a paper entitled Comments on the Formation of Psychic Structure, drew attention to the fact that there was a lack of adequate communication among various groups of analysts. They brought out the fact that because of this situation students are not adequately informed about the development of various hypotheses and formulations. They further emphasized the need for verification in many areas of theory and construction.

Spitz (1946) discussed theoretical assumptions concerning melancholia in a study called Anaclitic Depression. He examined the concept of early depression in the literature and offered some critical remarks on Melanie Klein's theories. Van Ophuijsen's paper, The Psychoanalytic Rule, presented in the spring of 1947, brought to the fore a discussion of various views on free association in therapy.

All the papers and discussions cited point to the fact that interpretation of fundamental rules, both of theory and technique, varies considerably. There is need for organizing and bringing into harmony various opinions regarding basic technical proceedings. A sharper, clearer, more detailed definition of them is needed. This can only be done if differences of opinion in therapeutic procedures, which are arrived at through one's clinical observation, are compared. The comparison of therapeutic progress in types of cases which present basically similar problems might conceivably be used ultimately to verify the various claims of needs for reformulating theory. It may lead finally to a more useful formulation and to a greater uniformity in the application of theoretical concepts.

Freud's explorations and theoretical formulations gave us the basic scientific explanation for the understanding of neurosis. This theoretical understanding in all its ramifications is essential to acquiring skill in therapy and in bringing about the dynamic alterations in the neurotic conflict. But theoretical considerations may be overemphasized and may lead to error in judging the dynamic structure of the patient's symptom. We all agree that the theoretical orientation of the analyst may influence his therapeutic work. It may lead to preconceived ideas which may enter into the manner of conducting analysis. The therapist may hastily interpret unconscious material and unconscious conflicts, but if they are not recognized by the patient as a part of his unconscious struggle, it will be no more effective than naming or describing something to the patient of which he cannot conceive. An analyst can discuss and interpret developmental phases, the meaning of drives and fixations, but may fail, if he gets lost in theoretical concepts, to link the developmental phases with present behavior of the patient.

Finding out and informing the patient that something went wrong in his early psychological development has no therapeutic influence unless it is connected with the patient's affects in analysis in the transference, and referred back from the actual analytic situation to the repressed affects of the early developmental period. Emphasis on theory may give the patient superficial knowledge but too often interferes with therapeutic progress. Guiding one's self solely by theory can create uncertainty in the analyst, and prevent the proper handling of transference and resistance. It interferes with objectivity and intuitiveness, both of which are so important in therapy.

The first theoretical constructions of Freud were derived empirically through clinical experience and many analysts are prone to do likewise, namely, to form their own theoretical ideas as a result of their individual experiences. This is perfectly understandable, but it is important that such views be exposed to general review and criticism in order to evaluate them properly. Working methods of one analyst may differ slightly, or to a great degree, from other analysts. Ferenczi was of the opinion that analysts fall into two groups, one to whom therapy is more important, who consider psychoanalysis a branch of medicine, and the analyst as a medical healer; for this group theory is a by-product. The other group consists of those who look upon analysis as a research laboratory in which they can prove some psychological truth or the existence of some unconscious factors. For the latter, the exploring of the unconscious and testing of scientific findings is of primary importance, therapy being looked upon merely as a concomitant of research. Many clinicians feel that having a favorite theory may result in a tendency to mold observations to fit the theory. In this connection Glover says, "The pure clinician will maintain that theoretical orientation is a fertile source of mistakes due to bias."

In the course of many years of analytic work, I have had the opportunity to observe, in working with younger colleagues who are in the process of being trained, the influence upon them of the changes of training programs, expansion of subjects and also the shifting of their theoretical orientations. With students or patients who have transferred from another colleague, one often meets ideas which differ from one's own and from those generally accepted. Sometimes an analyst favors a particular theoretical point of view and repeatedly refers to it. An analyst may be led on by scientific interest to prove the validity of a concept to which he feels a predilection. In some cases it can be an emotional attitude based on "training transference" which causes an analyst to over-emphasize one viewpoint.

It is essential to theorize a certain amount but one must beware of the danger of neglecting the clinical aspects. Since theoretical orientation may determine procedure, there is always the possibility that preconceptions will be the guide in technique.

The following short example is given to illustrate the misguidance of therapeutic effort because of adherence to a favorite theory. A student in supervised clinical work happened to be treating an artist, with whom he worked into a long-lasting period of resistance and stagnation of analysis, as a result of interpreting the unconscious factors in the artist's creations and his neurosis entirely on the basis of theory. He wanted to prove that his patient's artistic productions were projections into his art of early introjected objects. It was true that the patient's basic problems were connected with scoptophilic tendencies, but in the analyst's opinion, these tendencies resulted in introjection of the external world by oral destruction. He believed that looking was equated with devouring, being very much impressed by that bit of theory, which was Fenichel's construction. Fenichel extracted the idea from Ella Sharpe's (1930) paper, Certain Aspects of Sublimation and Delusion, in which she expressed her belief that representation of objects in artistic creation is primarily an unconscious attempt at "making reparation" for criminal fantasies and tendencies. In her opinion the work of art aims to reanimate persons whom one has killed with his omnipotent thoughts. The killing having been effected by introjection, the introjected object is projected into art and thus reanimated.

This young analyst pursued his therapeutic goal entirely through one avenue of approach. There were abundant, obvious factors in the complicated neurosis of the artist which should have been interpreted and followed up, but the therapist chose the most remote as a result of his attraction to a particular theory. In other words, his clinical evaluations were based mainly on theoretical considerations.

We are all inclined to place emphasis on some aspect of therapy and theory, this emphasis depending more or less upon our personality. But if one of us wishes to present a new discovery or a new theory which he considers superior to a previous formulation, and especially if he is in a position to indoctrinate younger colleagues, then it is time to investigate these private views and compare them with the accepted ones.

I do not mean to suggest systematizing therapeutic technique in analysis. It is hardly feasible. But the teaching of technique of analysis should be better organized and systematized. The logical step at which to begin reorienting ourselves in the teaching of analysis would be objectively to review the subject matter and our method of teaching it. An evaluation of both comes to us indirectly occasionally through seminars and supervised clinical work with students. It is not enough in teaching to emphasize the importance of analyzing resistances. For instance, properly timing the analysis of the resistances and the interpretation, and even the correct expression and wording of interpretation, are of equal importance. This topic requires further detailed study. Not enough has been written in concrete terms about methods of interpreting. Very little has been said on the form of interpretation or about content, which is of paramount importance. Should one place the greater emphasis on the pregenital phase, as in the English school? When should interpretations be given? What are the drawbacks of interpreting in terms of particular developmental levels, a practice with which one still meets.

The meaning of the term "deep interpretation" also has to be clarified. Glover's questionnaire sought opinions regarding it, and the replies indicated that to most analysts deep interpretation connoted theoretical description, topography. But the term is also frequently used in reference to dynamic interpretation. Efforts to give deep interpretation we often see in younger colleagues who overlook the obvious, it seems so easy, and reach for the far-fetched, sometimes obscure interpretation. In Glover's book he actually refers to "deep groups": those who feel that anything but deep interpretation is ineffective. For instance, for states of anxiety they would consider reassurance or gradual interpretation ineffective; furthermore, this group believes that reassurance can become a handicap in analysis.

Younger colleagues are sometimes afraid to interpret because the interpretation may serve also as reassurance, or carry some suggestion to the patient. They are not quite aware of the fact that the analysis of the transference relationship always contains suggestions; moreover, they consider interpretation to be generally the same for all cases, whereas our clinical experience, which is now much greater than it was when fundamental rules were established, warrants various attitudes about interpretation in special cases. Observation of the technical handling of compulsion neurosis, for instance, points to the fact that the greatest progress is made in therapy through proper interpretation of the transference. But in this instance also, various views are held about the line of therapeutic approach. Comparison and discussion of empirical observation by a number of analysts is needed because observation of technical procedure has not been adequately and sufficiently described, and in their courses of study our younger colleagues have little chance to hear about it in detail.

There are many and varied theories about the interpretation of transference. Some analysts advocate interpretation of transference only when original emotional situations are being relived and re-experienced in relation to the analyst. Opinions are divided concerning the handling of early phases in the development of transference, and the fully developed transference. Fenichel referred to "silently developed" transference. Some immediately interpret the patient's feelings about the analyst and analysis in early sessions. Others believe that early interpretation of the transference may help the patient to hide and repress the relationships to the real objects in early life and cause him to dwell on the interpreted transference of analytical relationship. The interpretation of transference on the basis of introjected and projected objects of the pregenital phase is also open to much criticism.

In my opinion, the most favorable time to start interpretation is when sufficient material has been produced by the patient to convince him of the validity of the interpretation. Interpretation which includes the patient's productions reassures him, whereas badly timed and nonspecific interpretations may be upsetting. By proceeding without haste, step by step, affects in interpretation will be relived and the emotions produced by the interpretations will become dynamic. Through it, the analysis of early patterns of emotional reaction is made possible. Love, hate and anxiety related to the transference and to reality situations will be easily connected with the patient's childhood pattern of reaction. The practice of giving anamnestic interpretations, of relating everything to the patient's childhood, is of little value unless the interpretation is dynamic (related to the present). I feel that it is important to emphasize the emotional reactions to the analyst or to the analysis and then interpret the pattern of reactions which brings about such feelings in regard to analysis.

In the teaching of analysis some way must be found of correlating the various views to avoid theoretical indoctrination which leads to confusion — to interpreting what seems theoretically correct but misses the obvious. We find too often in supervised clinical work a lack of up-to-date knowledge of the progress of theory. The students work with theories based on early concepts of Freud and have not enough information about additional material or changes of those early views; for whenever clinical evidence called for modifications, Freud altered his earlier concepts.

I frequently encounter young colleagues who will not analyze dreams which are fragmentary. If there are parts which the patient does not recall, instead of asking for associations to the remembered parts, they ignore the dream entirely. In response to my inquiries into the origin of this attitude, I have received the reply that Freud said that many dreams are untranslatable. But Freud (1923) also said that untranslatable dreams can be of use for introducing thoughts and evoking memories, even if their manifest content cannot be interpreted; also, that one can at least draw conclusions as to what the dream wish is. This, these students do not know.

The four methods of starting dream interpretation described by Freud are:

1. Associations in accordance with the manner in which the dream is presented, which he terms classical technique.
2. Selecting one part of the dream which seems important and starting associations from it.
3. Starting the dreamwork with the day's residue without taking the manifest content into account.
4. When the patient knows enough about dream interpretation, leaving it to him to begin his associations as he chooses.

Freud stated that it was up to the analyst to decide which of these techniques was the most suitable for the situation at hand. He further stated that if the dream resistance was strong, resulting in fragmentary dreams or forgetting of parts, one must be satisfied with interpreting some symbolic meaning (symbol translation).

The teaching of dream interpretation is another area where varied opinions must be brought into closer harmony.

In 1936, in an address entitled, The Future of Psychoanalysis, which was delivered to the Vienna Psychoanalytic Society, Jones (1936) said, in referring to interpretation: "What I look to is rather a steady progress in thoroughness, a greater polish and accuracy leading to far more sureness than we now possess. Special studies are needed on the precise criteria for the trustworthiness of our interpretations and also on the extraordinarily difficult subject of the correlation between technique and theory in psychoanalysis."

Theoretical formulations reached through practical clinical experiences may serve as a hint, but not as a definite guide for therapeutic practice. Individual cases demand special treatment at times, quite apart from one's theories. Theory can always identify the mechanism of the neurosis, but it cannot be the sole guide in therapy. This fact must be constantly emphasized, especially in teaching and training.

Masochism is another important problem which has given rise to much discussion and needs to be clarified. It was discussed from a seemingly new theoretical angle in the spring of 1947 by Dr. Berliner at the meeting of the American Psychoanalytic Association. Freud's concept of primary masochism as being connected with death instinct is not applicable in technique. The workable hypothesis is his earlier view expressed in Three Contributions to the Theory of Sex wherein he showed that masochism is the result of sadistic drives turned against the ego. His early paper, A Child is Being Beaten, is based on clinical observation: the fantasy of being beaten follows the wish that the hated rival should suffer. In our clinical work we also find aggression turned against the ego, and carrying with it sexually charged drives.

Dr. Berliner elaborated his concept that masochism is a deep plea for affection. He endeavored to prove that masochism represents chiefly the person's wish to bear pain in order to attain pleasure and that the masochist's suffering has as the deepest aim the re-establishment of the unconscious wish to get attention from the beloved person who in the past caused him pain; further, that it orginates in the oral stage of development. Certainly one of the aims of masochism is the securing of love, but to claim as Dr. Berliner does that all masochism originates on the oral level is giving undue emphasis to one factor, and theoretically substantiating something which clinical experiences do not, on the whole, bear out. Masochistic fantasies, as we all know, can originate in any developmental level.

Eidelberg (1934) is of the opinion that masochistic mechanisms permit the individual to render frustrations harmless by creating some active frustration himself instead of tolerating them passively. According to Eidelberg, this mechanism belongs with those of projection, introjection, repression and reaction-formation. He found masochistic perversion least amenable to scientific research and therapy in isolation but when present with other neurotic difficulties therapy is more fruitful. He also emphasized the importance of the rôle of childish megalomania and strong aggressive drives in cases of masochism.

The controversial aspects of the problem of sado-masochism are far from clear theoretically; however, in therapy we are fairly well able to cope with masochism through the understanding of its relation to general aggression.

The puzzling fact that fantasy and reality are so peculiarly mixed in masochism and that it seems contrary to pleasure-seeking tendencies led to numerous attempts on the part of various analysts to clarify the problems of theory involved, but no one has been completely successful. Fenichel, one of many who studied the problem, described four mechanisms, all of them valid but yet not constituting a comprehensive explanation of the phenomenon. To try to simplify the problem theoretically and to teach it that way will not advance progress in understanding of it, as he himself pointed out. The solution lies in clinical case studies. Theoretical formulations should be appraised in the light of clinical findings in a variety of cases.

However, one cannot fit a patient into a category formed from ideas drawn from the analysis of other patients or from the writings of other authors. We can use theory and the findings of others to guide us in situations where it is necessary to formulate an idea as to the trend in which we are likely to be led by the patient or to explain some structure in the patient's neurosis. But we must wait for material from the patient which will tell us whether or not we have been correct in our hypothesis. Theoretical formulations will help us to schematize and keep in mind the relationships in the personality structure and the variety of factors entering into that structure. Thus it will be of help in describing the analytic process or changes which have to take place in the different parts of personality as a result of therapy. But in teaching, the greater emphasis must be put on what takes place in the therapeutic process. Then one can check his theoretical knowledge by his findings in treatment.

It is advisable that an analyst be well oriented in theory, but he should guard against trying to rediscover and apply in all his work some specific theoretical ideas. One can be a good analyst by adhering to fundamental principles and bearing in mind the fact that the analytical process is an affective one permitting elasticity in the application of rules, and that it is not chiefly an intellectual process.

The progress of technique, the evaluation of data, and further knowledge gained by practical experience necessitate new formulations and the reformulated theories can be applied with greater precision to the therapeutic technique than they now are. Rather than substitution of the old theory, there should be reconstruction of the old on the basis of new clinical and therapeutic experiences. We are now in a better position to do that than in past years because of the greatly increased number of analysts and the number and variety of cases which can be compared. Technique has of course run ahead of theory, and attempts towards clarification of their mutual relationship have to be undertaken from time to time.

What we find in the majority of cases is that such new theories and formulations often obscure rather than clarify. They attempt to replace the old theory without having sufficiently substantiated new hypotheses and methods. The missing factor is testing on a large scale, which can only be done through a comparison of clinical results.

The theory of instincts is another important topic which many have attempted to explain and which still requires more comprehensive interpretation. Therapy aims to recognize instinctual drives towards more harmonious functioning. This is accomplished indirectly by re-establishing the original line of functioning, biological in origin, which we feel was disturbed by environmental influences. What we can observe are the effects of the instinct; hence so much speculation about the nature of the instinctual energies.

The last reference to instinct made by Freud is to be found in a paper entitled, An Outline of Psychoanalysis (translated from his unfinished work which was started in 1938). In this paper Freud (1940) stated that the instincts represent the somatic demands upon the life of the mind, and that with regard to the specific instinctual factor, there is a discrepancy between theory and experience; moreover, "The gap in our theory cannot at present be filled."

There have been many attempts, if not to fill, at least to narrow the gap. Loewenstein (1940), in "The Vital or Somatic Instincts," re-examines the classification of the instincts. He emphasizes a distinction between sexual and somatic instincts. Fairbairn (1944, 1946) in a series of involved papers attempted a complete revision of the theory of mental structure and instincts. He proposes to replace Freud's classical theory with his own, and begins by examining the classical libido theory of pleasure seeking. According to Fairbairn, libido is object-seeking and the libidinal aims which Freud describes in terms of erotogenic zones to him are not libidinal aims but modes of dealing with objects: "The zones in question should properly be regarded not as the dictators of aims, but as the servants of aims." He changes instinct to instinctive tendency, declares that Freud's ego, id and superego are not dynamic structures, that his (Fairbairn's) psychic structure includes all energies in contrast to Freud's psychic energy. Fairbairn's entire theory is based on Melanie Klein's hypothesis of good and bad objects. His revision of the theory of instincts and mental structure presents a very obscure picture when one tries to think of its possible application to therapeutic work. It is perfectly obvious that pleasure-seeking tendencies in therapy are always attached to objects, and the libidinal aims themselves which are attached to erotogenic zones are always directed towards objects. Fairbairn's theoretical formulation seems rather twisted and certainly it would be difficult to prove its validity in clinical application.

At the meeting of The American Psychoanalytic Association in 1947, Dr. Kubie, in a paper on Instinct and Homeostasis approached the problem from a more clinical angle. Following is his own short abstract of the paper.

> We find that in discussing instincts Freud made two important points which have been largely neglected, partly by himself, and in part by other workers:
>
> (a) that a classification of instincts must rest on a physiological rather than a psychological basis;
> (b) that instincts represent the demand which the body makes on the mental apparatus.

Our discussion supports Freud's position.

All instincts consist of (a) the direct or indirect expression of biochemical body processes, through (b) inherited yet modifiable networks of neuronal synaptic patterns, which (c) are molded in turn by superimposed, compulsive and phobic mechanisms. These are seen to operate in normal psychology as in psychopathology. The relative rôles of the three components of instinctual activity vary in different instincts and in different species. Therefore, it is impossible to make any absolute distinction between instinct and drive (*Trieb*). The differences are quantitative rather than qualitative, and are due to the different rôles played by the three components mentioned above.

In many of the instinctual processes the biochemical source of energy is converted into behavior through deprivation because deprivation synchronizes the continuous asynchronous flux which in states of rest goes on in body tissues. The biochemical processes, however, are linked to warning mechanisms, which under ordinary circumstances come into play before any actual tissue deprivation occurs; therefore, in higher animals, instinctual patterns are triggered off by warning mechanisms rather than by tissue hungers; therefore, on the psychological level, instinctual aims and objects are also built around the warning mechanism.

This paper points the way to a more profound clinical observation of the derivatives of instincts, the observation of which may enable us to form clearer ideas about the way instincts work.

At a recent meeting of the New York Psychoanalytic Society, Dr. Hart expounded some ideas in relation to the problem of narcissism. He spoke about the concept of narcissistic equilibrium and its therapeutic aspects, and discussed the disturbing effect of the various id drives upon the equilibrium, maintaining that they can gradually be repaired by the substitution of sublimatory equivalents.

To return to the main point of this paper: we are all agreed that the interpretation of fundamental rules varies considerably. Freud (1914), in Remembering, Repeating and Working Through, writes: "It seems to me not unnecessary constantly to remind students of the far-reaching changes which psychoanalytic technique has undergone since its first beginnings." In a paper published in 1938 dealing with technical rules he mentions a type of patient who must be analyzed like a child because he cannot be made to adhere to rules. "Many neurotics have remained so infantile that in analysis too, they can only be treated like children," and "the amount of influence which the analyst may legitimately employ will be determined by the degree of inhibition in the development of the patient."

When we think of fundamental rules in the technique of psychoanalysis we should bear in mind such changing attitudes of Freud himself, who advocated even such extreme elasticity in their application. Fundamental rules cannot become rules of theory but must be thought of always as fundamentals for technique. To treat is more important than to adhere to specific rules and theoretical concepts. The technique should be adapted to the patient, not the patient to the technique. Some patients cannot comply with rules, and we still have to treat them.

Dynamic interpretation is ineffective unless it carries feelings which concern both reality situations and transference, which means that practical problems must be discussed objectively by the analyst and the subjective feelings of the patient in relation to his problems must be tested.

One may question to what extent the early biography of the patient enters into the creation of the neurosis. One may argue as to just when the oedipal phase is in progress and at what age the superego organization begins. The exact course of the early object development of the individual may also be a ground for disagreement among analysts. However, I do not deem it of great importance to determine the exact date of development of definite object relationships. Our ability to study infantile development is considerably limited. Descriptions of these very early stages are mostly theoretical hypotheses. We cannot arrive at an accurate appraisal of the psychic apparatus of the infant. In my opinion the outstanding importance of this early period is that it forms the basis for identification through object relationships and within it is to be found the origin of conscience.

The early object relationships are the ones which are emotionally reactivated in the transference relationship, enabling unconscious impulses to be brought into consciousness. To be sure, there are diversities in technique, but if the difference arises from an emotional bias or a bias in favor of a particular theory, it will prove to be a source of trouble. We know that therapeutic results were achieved even when theories about etiological factors in neurosis were changing. During that time the therapeutic process served a second purpose as well, that of research, and as more knowledge was gathered about technique, the theory was reformulated in conformity with it. The best example of an extreme change in theory is to be found in Freud himself. He originally warned analysts to be cool and detached in observing the patient, acting as a mirror, merely reflecting to the patient his own actions and feelings. Later he made the above-mentioned statement in regard to treating certain types of patients as children — the extreme of elasticity. Therefore, many of us advocate pooling our therapeutic results in order to formulate new theories about treatment. New theories which survive objective examination will be utilized in practice.

Another important phase of treatment which would profit greatly from a comparison and re-examination of therapeutic results is the matter of the final aim of analytic therapy. Criteria of degree of adjustment attained through therapy differ. Some analysts are inclined to overestimate therapeutic possibilities, others to underestimate them, especially in certain types of neuroses; hence the growing tendency toward specialization. There are analysts who will treat only certain types of cases, others while accepting all types will always have greater success with a particular kind of neurosis.

As to criteria of results in therapy, some therapists emphasize improved object relationship, others improvement in social contact and elimination of anxiety. Still others consider sexual adjustment of primary importance as a criterion of well-being. Such differences of opinion may be influenced by theoretical orientation. Clinical evidence must be lined up so that we can arrive at some kind of uniformity in our theory as to when termination is at hand.

In clinical conferences and in supervised clinical work one receives the strong impression that criteria for and method of termination are outstanding problems for the young analyst. In the answers to his questionnaire, Glover found broad disagreement regarding termination of analysis. He saw an urgent need for a "detailed list of the practical indications for terminating an analysis, a list that will allow for variations in the clinical type of case."

Etiological views play a part in the various opinions held regarding length and thoroughness of analysis. These marked divisions of opinion undoubtedly enter into our teaching and they must be reduced if we want better therapists and to improve our therapeutic results.

The impression is inescapable that the handling of the final phase of treatment is entirely an individual matter. Since very little has been written on the subject, young analysts have nothing to guide them except the manner of termination of their own analyses, or they are reduced to experimenting with their patients.

I do not underestimate the need for theoretical knowledge. It is necessary for scientific research and in varying degrees every therapeutic process contains some elements of research. But the usefulness of hypotheses can only be judged by adequate description of the phenomenon investigated. The various forms of neuroses, mechanisms which are common to particular types of cases, differences in technique, modifications by individual analysts, all should be subjected to detailed study and comparison.

I believe that many discrepancies among the various formulations can be eliminated. In the process, theories can be substantiated or changed through observing effects in practice, for it is undeniable that in psychoanalytic work practice influences theory.

After all, it was interest in technique of therapy which led Freud to therapeutic experimentation, the results of which ultimately yielded the theory of the unconscious, with all its dynamics, as we know it today.

REFERENCES

Berliner, B. (1947), On some psychodynamics of masochism. *Psychoanal. Quart.*, 16:459–471.
Eidelberg, L. (1934), Beiträge zum studium des masochismus. *Int. Ztschr. f. Psa.*, 20:336–353.
Fairbairn, W. R. D. (1944, 1946), Series of papers. *Internat. J. Psycho-Anal.*, 25 & 27.
Freud, S. (1914), Remembering, repeating and working through. *Standard Edition*, 12:147–156. London: Hogarth Press.

_____ (1923), Bemerkungen zur theorie und praxis der traumdeutung. *Int. Ztschr. f. Psa.,* 9.

_____ (1940), An outline of psychoanalysis. *Internat. J. Psycho-Anal.,* 21.

Hartmann, H., Kris, E., & Loewenstein, R. (1946), Comments on the formation of psychic structure. *The Psychoanalytic Study of the Child,* 2:11-38. New York: International Universities Press.

Jones, E. (1936), The future of psychoanalysis. *Internat. J. Psycho-Anal.,* 17.

Kubie, L. (1939), A critical analysis of the concept of a repetition compulsion. *Internat. J. Psycho-Anal.,* 20, Nos. 3-4.

Loewenstein, R. (1940), The vital or somatic instincts. *Internat. J. Psycho-Anal.,* 21.

Oberndorf, D. P. (1946), Constant elements in psychotherapy. *Psychoanal. Quart.,* 15:435-449.

Sharpe, E. (1930), Certain aspects of sublimation and delusion. *Internat. J. Psycho-Anal.,* 11.

Spitz, R. (1946), Anaclitic depression. *The Psychoanalytic Study of the Child,* 2. New York: International Universities Press.

Zilboorg, G. (1939), The fundamental conflict with psychoanalysis. *Internat. J. Psycho-Anal.,* 20, Nos. 3-4.

15

The Origin and Fate of New Ideas
in Psychoanalysis

RALPH R. GREENSON, M.D.

In the first issue of the *International Journal of Psycho-Analysis,* Freud (1917a) contributed a paper, "A Difficulty in the Path of Psychoanalysis," which I believe is particularly relevant today in understanding the developments in psychoanalysis in the last 50 years. In that essay Freud attempted to demonstrate how psychoanalysis, like other scientific research, has alienated most men by hurting their narcissism, their self-love. He described the three most hurtful blows to human narcissism as follows:

> In the early stages of his researches, man believed at first that his dwelling-place, the earth, was the stationary centre of the universe, with the sun, moon and planets circling round it. In this he was naively following the dictates of his sense-perceptions, for he felt no movement of the earth, and wherever he has an unimpeded view he found himself in the centre of a circle that enclosed the external world. The central position of the earth, moreover, was a token to him of the dominating part played by it in the universe and appeared to fit in very well with his inclination to regard himself as lord of the world.

Copernicus and his forerunners put an end to this illusion and proved the earth was much smaller than the sun and moved around that celestial body. That was the *cosmological* blow to man's narcissism.

Presented as the Fourth Freud Anniversary Lecture, the Psychoanalytic Association of New York, 19 May 1969. Reprinted by permission from *International Journal of Psycho-Analysis,* 50:503–515, London: International Psychoanalytic Association.

Freud then went on to define the second narcissistic wound, the *biological* one:

> We all known that little more than half a century ago the researches of Charles Darwin and his collaborators and forerunners put an end to this presumption on the part of man. Man is not a being different from animals or superior to them; he himself is of animal descent, being more closely related to some species and more distantly to others.

The third blow to man's self-love, the *psychological,* Freud considered the most wounding:

> Although thus humbled in his external relations, man feels himself to be supreme within his own mind. Somewhere in the core of his ego he has developed an organ of observation to keep a watch on his impulses and actions and see whether they harmonize with its demands. If they do not, they are ruthlessly inhibited and withdrawn.

Freud then went on to portray how illusory this strength was. It is in his neuroses that man is forced to recognize the limits of his ego's powers. Freud then describes for us an imaginary talk to the ego:

> You over-estimated your strength when you thought you could treat your sexual instincts as you liked and could utterly ignore their intentions. The result is that they have rebelled and have taken their own obscure paths to escape this suppression; they have established their rights in a manner you cannot approve . . .

> What is in your mind does not coincide with what you are conscious of; whether something is going on in your mind and whether you hear of it, are two different things . . .

> You behave like an absolute ruler who is content with the information supplied him by his highest officials and never goes among the people to hear their voice. Turn your eyes inward, look into your own depths, learn first to know yourself!

Freud concludes this paper with the following:

> It is thus that psycho-analysis has sought to educate the ego. But these two discoveries — that the life of our sexual instincts cannot be wholly tamed, and that mental processes are in themselves unconscious and only reach the ego and come under its control through incomplete and untrustworthy perceptions — these two discoveries amount to a statement that *the ego is not master in its own house.*

Ernest Jones (1920), in an editorial in that same first issue, depicts how mankind uses two main methods of defense against disagreeable truths:

the first, more obvious, and therefore less dangerous one is direct opposition, the new truths being denied as false and decried as obnoxious; the second, more insidious, and much more formidable one is to acquiesce in the new ideas on condition that their value is discounted, the logical consequences not drawn from them, and their meaning diluted until it may be regarded as "harmless."

Jones also mentions that this opposition may not only be displayed by outside antagonists, but may assume subtle forms within psychoanalysis itself.

As I review the developments in psychoanalysis during the last 50 years, I have the impression there is much evidence which indicates that similar conflicts concerning their narcissism have influenced psychoanalysts and have become an important factor impeding the progress of psychoanalysis. I believe that unresolved problems with narcissism have resulted in a dearth of creativity in psychoanalysts and also to the establishment of separate psychoanalytic "schools." I believe that both of these developments are interrelated and are obstacles to the furtherance of new ideas and the advancement of psychoanalytic knowledge.

Anna Freud apparently had something similar in mind when she is reported as saying, in the Annual Freud Memorial Lecture to the New York Psychoanalytic Society in 1968, that an *ad hoc* committee of the International Psychoanalytic Association was examining the lack of creativity among analysts today (Shapiro, 1968). She is also quoted as having said that the analyst is basically not a creative person but rather an explorer using analytic technique as a tool to help him in his task. I myself have noted how few new faces appear on our scientific programme and that many papers do not contain new ideas. Above all, I have been impressed and depressed by the observation that applicants for training often seem to be more creative than the psychoanalysts who graduate from our training institutes. Perhaps our method for selecting candidates is faulty, but in all candour, we must also face the possibility that our training programmes and the atmosphere of our institutes may stultify the creative imagination of our students.

It has often been said by certain enemies of psychoanalysis that psychoanalysis is dead, but that is the tongue of ignorance being wagged by envy and wishful thinking. It does seem to be true, however, that the psychoanalytic movement is no longer moving very quickly; it is not very lively. I believe that some of the reasons for this relative inertia are related to factors which are involved in the origin and fate of new ideas.

In this presentation I shall try to explore some of the rudiments which seem to serve as the source and stimulus for new ideas in the psychoanalyst. Then I shall attempt to describe what may happen to the innovation in the psychoanalyst himself and also in the psychoanalytic community. I shall try to demonstrate that the forces which make for new ideas contain elements which may lead to both constructive and destructive developments in the analyst and in psychoanalytic groups. It should be emphasized that this paper deals in the main with new ideas, not great ideas or the ideas of geniuses. And while I do touch on the origin of such ideas, in the end I shall be more concerned with their ultimate fate.

THE ORIGIN OF NEW IDEAS

I always prefer to begin a psychoanalytic paper by presenting clinical material, because I have found that clinical data offer the presenter and the reader the clearest basis for understanding and discussion. In this instance, however, there is a dilemma. My major embarrassment is that of necessity I must use my own personal experiences in the analysis of a patient as my source material. I find myself having to reveal my immodesty publicly, for the sake of providing clinical data. I shall present some of the pertinent highlights from a paper I wrote in 1949, "The Mother Tongue and the Mother" (Greenson, 1950).

In 1946 I began the psychoanalytic treatment of an intelligent and attractive 35-year-old married woman, who sought help primarily because of a sleep disturbance. She was born and raised in Vienna until the age of 18, when she moved to the United States. The first year of psychoanalytic therapy proceeded relatively smoothly and seemed to follow the course one would expect in a hysterical phobic patient who seemed to be fixated to the oedipal, phallic phase of development. Pregenital elements also appeared, but they were fleeting and very much in the background.

In the second year of her treatment, the analysis became stalemated when she fell in love with a young married man. My consistent interpretations of how she was acting out her transference feelings in terms of both libidinal and aggressive oedipal as well as pre-oedipal strivings did not influence either the patient's material or her behaviour. The stalemate was broken one day when the young woman told me a dream and, after a few desultory associations, added almost as an afterthought that she had dreamt the dream in German. She then became silent. Up until this time in the analysis, the patient would often use a German word or phrase when she had difficulty in expressing herself in English. I therefore rather impulsively asked her to tell me the dream again, but this time in German. She balked at this and I tried briefly to analyse this new resistance. This procedure was at best only partially successful, but I told her nevertheless that I wanted to conduct the analysis from now on in German. The patient reluctantly submitted to my request, and, to my surprise, the whole course and content of the analysis changed remarkably.

I must add that I myself was somewhat taken aback by my own behaviour. I do not ordinarily act so impulsively, nor do I make requests of patients before I try thoroughly to analyse their resistances. I had vague misgivings that I was breaking some rule and yet at the same time I felt I was pursuing the right course. For three months we spoke only in German and the patient complied by even dreaming in German. During the first weeks I alternated between feeling that I was making a significant discovery and that I was recklessly pursuing a whim of mine based on some countertransference reaction. I had constantly to battle against a resistance in myself to continue working with her in German. I was often tempted to retreat to the safe and familiar method of working in English, because I had felt more comfortable doing so and also the patient was extremely articulate in English. As our work proceeded, however, I became convinced that the patient's material and behaviour proved that my new idea was essentially constructive, even if it had originated from my frustration in not being able to influence her addiction-like relationship to her lover.

Let me briefly use some of the changes in the clinical material during the German-speaking phase of the analysis, in order to demonstrate some of the goings on in me. For the patient, in English, a chamber-pot was clean, but in German a "Nachttopf" was dirty; it stank and was disgusting to her. I had to translate the clean German "Nachttopf" in me to the dirty "teppelle" (Yiddish) of my childhood. The patient could hardly bring herself to speak of her mother as "Mutti" or, even worse, to say the word "Busen" (bosom). I had to translate these words which, as words, were innocuous to me, into my childhood equivalents, in order to realize that for the patient these words when spoken were felt concretely as things in her mouth. In this way we discovered that she habitually experienced her mother as an *unappetizing* creature.

The patient's material was now predominantly pre-oedipal and pregenital. This was manifested in a marked change in the transference and I was transformed from primarily a sexual father also into a most ambivalent mother-figure. Her obsession with her lover shifted to his wife, her fascination with his erect penis changed to an obsessive curiosity about his limp penis, and then to women's breasts and their large shiny nipples. As the patient's oral preoccupations were pouring out in German, her interest in her lover and his wife slowly dwindled away. We continued to work further, on breaking down the barrier between her German pre-oedipal identity and her English oedipal self image. The patient herself had said, "In German I am a scared, dirty child; in English I am a nervous, refined woman." Eventually we were able to speak either language without the language determining the patient's material or behaviour.

Using these clinical data from the analysis, I now propose to turn to my subjective reactions, which seem to be of value for studying the origin of new ideas. The first major finding is that the innovation arose when I was in a depressive state of frustration. The analysis was stalemated, my interpretations were futile and I felt out of touch with what was vital in the goings on in the patient. If I reconstruct the situation in myself (and I have had many repetitions of it over the ensuing years) I was frequently aware of feeling a mixture of mild depression, anxiety and annoyance. I had felt compelled to go on repeating my interpretations, partly because I thought they were correct, partly because I knew of nothing better to do. Probably I also felt stubborn because I sensed the patient knew she was frustrating me. I interpreted this to the patient, to no avail. At the same time I kept hoping and searching for some clue that would lead to a new insight and might rescue both of us from the unhappy impasse.

The patient offered me this clue when, after telling me the dream, she added that she dreamt it in German. My behaviour indicates that I was ready for this opening; if anything, too eager. I leaped upon the speaking German before I understood what its implications were. I seized upon it because I was tired of repeating my old interpretations. I sensed something was lacking and I was ready to risk doing something new. Yet I was in conflict about it; I had my own resistances to overcome. I could have played it safe and just waited, but the more adventuresome part of me won out.

The change in the patient's material, the alteration in her relationship to me, her ability to work and change despite her hostile feelings, proved to me that the innovation was valuable. As time went on I learned a great many new things, not only about this patient and her mother tongue, but also about the origin and function of language in early childhood. I became very preoccupied about the meanings of language and its derivation from the experiences between the mother, the breast, the mouth and the baby. During this interval many new ideas began to "cook" and "percolate" in my head, which would rise to the surface as a glimmer or a flash. If I did pursue them, however, they turned out to be only "half-baked." I would push them away because they were exciting and distracting and I did not want them to interfere with my therapeutic work with my patient. Left to germinate, these ideas would pop up at later intervals, usually clearer and more meaningful, but the newer formulations again produced excitement and elation in me and I often found myself pursuing the validation or elaboration of the new idea instead of focusing on the patient's therapeutic needs. It was necessary to discipline myself to keep the goings on in the patient in the centre of my attention and only to insert new ideas when they seemed likely to add insight which would benefit the patient therapeutically. This was a difficult period for me because I was constantly torn between indulging myself in the joys of discovery and sticking to my therapeutic task. I experienced varying moods of excitement, exuberance, depression, apathy and annoyance. Fortunately, some of my new formulations occurred during weekends and holidays or after I had completed the treatment and had begun to write the paper.

I was later surprised to find that my discoveries turned out to contain elements described by other authors. When I began to write the paper on the "Mother Tongue and the Mother" I began to re-read the literature that I felt might be helpful and pertinent. I found that Freud (1905), Ferenczi (1911), Fenichel (1930), Stengel (1939), Brunswick (1940), Erikson (1946) and Buxbaum (1949) had already touched on many of the ideas I thought I had discovered.

Thus, much of what I had considered a discovery was actually a rediscovery. In a sense while I was making my "discoveries" I was guilty of some unconscious plagiarism, by temporarily repressing other people's ideas. What was new was my particular way of using and formulating what I had found and the way in which I tried to integrate it into the existing framework of my psychoanalytic knowledge. The joyous excitement I had experienced in first making my discoveries and formulations was dampened by recognizing the original sources of my ideas, but, fortunately, it also kept me from over-evaluating the importance of my paper. However, many of the ideas that began to percolate in my head during that period eventually led to a series of related papers. In 1954 I wrote a paper "About the Sound mm . . .," one on "Moods and Introjects," and one on "The Struggle against Identification." In 1958 I presented a paper "On Screen Defences, Screen Hunger and Screen Identity." All of these papers were derived from ideas which arose during my work with the "Mother Tongue" lady. The sound "mm . . ." referred to the only joyous utterance a baby can make and still retain the nipple securely in its mouth. It also led to the astonishing finding that in almost all languages the word for mother begins with the sound "mm." The other papers were derived from my analysis of the nervous English lady and the dirty German child which led me to the colloquial expression: "I am not myself today." I then felt impelled to ask: "If you are not yourself, then who are you?"

At this point I believe it would be valuable to compare the clinical material described above with the observations of other authors on the subject of the origin of new ideas in psychoanalysis. In some respects what I have experienced can be seen taking place in the personality of a genius, when one studies Ernest Jones' (1953, 1955, 1957) volumes on Sigmund Freud. Please note that I am referring to similarities in feelings, attitudes and moods, and *not* in accomplishments.

Earlier in this presentation, I pointed out that the new idea, asking the patient to speak in German, occurred when I was in a state of frustration, puzzlement and discontent, along with feelings of mild depression, anxiety and irritability. Jones (1953), in referring to the flow of Freud's creativity, stated:

> The significant point is, however, that happiness and well-being were not conducive to the best work, Freud himself remarked: I have been very idle because the moderate amount of discomfort necessary for intensive work has not set in (p. 345).

The term "discomfort" Jones had translated from the German word "Mittelelend," a term Max Schur believes implies more pain and suffering than "moderate discomfort." Later, in the same letter, Freud referred to being in a kind of "Zwischenreich," an in-between state of dawning recognition. I believe all of this indicates the relationship of pain and adversity and self-analysis (which Freud was undergoing at that time) to the new burst of Freud's creativity.

Related to this state of mind is the willingness to admit to oneself the possibility that one may have been pursuing the wrong path, the wrong material, or using a faulty theoretical and technical approach. If one is sure that one is right, that one has all the answers, there will be no doubt, no conflict, no discontent, but also no new ideas.

You can find this strikingly true if you read Freud's "Studies on Hysteria" (1893–95), which demonstrates how he changed his theories and his technique between the "Preliminary Communication" in 1893 and the later (1895) chapter on the "Psychotherapy of Hysteria" in the same book. In the "Preliminary Communication" Freud believed that he could *permanently* remove a hysterical symptom by hypnotizing the patient and getting her to abreact the emotions connected to the traumatic memories (p. 6). The memories and affects could not be discharged spontaneously because they were repressed and had been denied the normal "wearing-away processes" (pp. 10–11).

In the last chapter of that book Freud begins by stating that, although he still stands by what he wrote in the "Preliminary Communication," fresh points of view have forced themselves upon his mind (p. 255). In treating a number of cases he came up against two difficulties which led to alterations in his technique and his views of the facts. First of all, not everyone was hypnotizable who had hysterical symptoms (p. 256). Secondly, the cathartic method cannot affect the underlying causes of hysteria; thus it cannot prevent fresh symptoms from taking the place of the ones got rid of (p. 262). In other words, the abreaction of affects was no longer the major therapeutic tool, but it remained in a lower hierarchical position after he discovered the importance of resistance and transference analysis.

Freud slowly abandoned hypnosis, turned to suggestion and persuasion, and eventually to free association. In that process of change, Freud realized that the resistance to hypnosis was the result of a physical force against remembering and this same force must be responsible for producing the symptom. He gave up hypnosis and the attempt to gain direct access to the symptoms and began to work from the periphery of the symptoms and saw how the pathogenic material could not be excised but had to be handled as an infiltrate. Finally, Freud discovered that the patient's relationship to the physician, the transference, the "false connection," could be a major obstacle to recovery, but, if properly handled, it could become the most valuable vehicle for success. All of this occurred during Freud's self-analysis (Max Schur, personal communication).

No preconceived idea precluded the possibility of discovering new insights, new techniques and new theories. Obstacles and adversities prompted him to try new approaches and led to new discoveries, new formulations and new theories. Just as dramatically, new discoveries did not lead automatically to the elimination of old ideas. I believe you see here the advantage of an open mind at work. *Creativity is not the antithesis of conservation.*

If we now return to the clinical material I presented, we see, on a minor scale, an example of some willingness in me to risk doing or thinking something new. I like to think this shares in some way with the quality of adventuresomeness that Freud recognized in himself. Jones quotes Freud as follows:

> You often estimate me too highly. For I am not really a man of science, not an observer, not an experimenter, and not a thinker. I am nothing but by temperament a conquistador — an adventurer, if you want to translate the word — with the curiosity, the boldness, and the tenacity that belongs to that type of being . . . (p. 348).

Jones says this letter was written in a half serious tone. Actually, later passages from that same letter reveal the sadness as well as the creativity of freeing himself from Fliess: "I am always alone . . . so it is out of what is most intimately our own that we are growing apart" (Max Schur, personal communication).

The "conquistadors" are in complete opposition to those who "play it safe." They only repeat what they have learned and what seemed at one time to be successful. They do not dare to risk leaving the safety of the old and familiar. If one extends this line of inquiry further, one comes to three new, but related elements in the origin of new ideas. The adventurer is tempted to rebel against the traditional and conventional. His curiosity impels him to explore new, virgin territory; to trespass. In the creative mind there is also a playful joy in "juggling" ideas around, in finding new sequences and new arrangements and forms for conventional ideas (Greenacre, 1957, 1959).

Kris (1952) and Greenacre (1959) have stressed that the psychic energies utilized for creative work are not well neutralized or sublimated. Both libidinal and aggressive drives are used in such activity, which is often plainly observable in the agitation and obsessiveness during the creative period. In some creative people the sexual and aggressive strivings are often very conspicuous in their overt behaviour during such periods. In others it is discernible in the products of their creativity. Greenacre goes so far as to state that people who sublimate very well may be very capable, but do not turn out to be creative. She also points out that creative people have a lower tolerance for repetitive work than do non-creative ones. She relates this to the idea that children first play repetitive games until they gain a sense of mastery. After that, the child who is free of anxiety or who is unusually gifted or talented will experiment playfully and will change his activity. This train of thought demonstrates the connection between freedom from anxiety, adventuresomeness, rebelliousness and playfulness. Greenacre finds these characteristics typical for people who show a great deal of creative imagination.

Another issue I wish to bring up is the uneven flow of creative activity. In my clinical material I tried to show how the new ideas arose impulsively or first broke through as glimmerings, or half-baked ideas. They became distractions, then they went underground and only later did they become clear enough to be worked into a coherent paper. Jones (1953) quotes Freud on this as follows:

There is a curious alternation of flood and ebb. Sometimes I am carried up to a state in which I feel certain, and then everything flows back and I am left high and dry. But I believe the tide is gaining on the land (p. 345).

Kris (1952) stated that the mind involved in research does not work in continuous application, but there are alternations between sudden advances and quiet periods of preconscious elaboration. Székely (1967) describes something similar in what he designates as creative pauses.

A further point I want to mention is the "love affair" quality, the infatuation with the creative work or with the fantasied audience, which Greenacre alludes to in the artist. I believe I have indicated how, at times, the new ideas threatened to overwhelm the rest of my interests. This was true even for my nonworking activities. During the psychoanalytic sessions I had consciously to discipline my thinking and imagination or I would have foresaken the welfare of my patients for the allure of the new ideas.

I would like to conclude this discussion of the origin of new ideas by stating that a favourable predisposition would seem to consist of allowing one's self to recognize frustrating, stalemated situations in one's work and to use adversity and discontent with one's progress as an incentive for accepting new associative ideas. In a later phase of his work Freud wrote that he now goes out to meet a new idea half-way (Jones, 1953, p. 345). The inspiration Kris (1952) refers to seems to me to consist of allowing one's self to permit free associations to break into consciousness. Such associations are closer to unconscious primary process thinking, closer to the repressed and the id. Kris considers this to be a form of regression in the service of the ego. Greenacre (1959) has pointed out that markedly creative people are restless and responsive to the new to a high degree (p. 74). She further suggested that not only is the creative individual a poor sublimator but he is able to split his identity into a creative self and a conventional self. Weissman (1967) believes this and similar dissociative phenomena are not indications of regression in the service of the ego in creative people, but are dissociations utilized by the ego's synthesizing function. I have the impression that the ego in creative people not only tolerates, but even enjoys or needs regressing, thus the ego has less control in the initial stages over this than the concept "regression in the service of the ego" implies.

THE FATE OF NEW IDEAS IN THE PSYCHOANALYST

From this clinical material on the origin of new ideas, which I have sketched above from my work and the findings Jones and Schur described on Freud's creativity, plus the contributions I have used from Kris, Greenacre and Weissman, I believe we now have a background for pursuing the question of what may happen to new ideas in the psychoanalyst, the fate of new ideas.

The innovator psychoanalyst is an adventurer, a risk-taker, an explorer. His curiosity leads him to investigate the unknown. This may indicate a freedom from anxiety or a counterphobic attitude. In any event the anxiety is over-ridden by the urge to know, to explore. Innovators are not awed by tradition, nor are they lovers of conformity. They are willing to risk being wrong and to expose themselves to the attacks of their colleagues. But there is also an impor-tant aggressive component in putting forth a new idea. There is a quality of invading a hitherto uncharted territory and claiming it as one's own. Innova-tors are rebelling against the old and the familiar, and they are willing to en-dure being alone. The creative psychoanalyst whose aggression is not under control may use his innovations to destroy the old and traditional ideas. He will discard them as valueless. As I have already indicated, this is in marked contrast to Freud's way of working.

The creation of a new idea, particularly if it is more than a modest innova-tion, tends to mobilize old narcissistic feelings and attitudes that I believe to be akin to giving birth to a baby by parthenogenesis. Freud, in an unpublished letter (19 November 1899), wrote to Fliess:

> I still want to hold back with the sexual theory. There is still an unborn piece of what has already been born. (E. Freud, 1960; see also Hitschmann, 1956).

This may explain the postpartum-like depression after finishing a paper or any creative work. Any creation may also be felt as a re-creation of the self, an ideal self. The new idea can, in addition, serve as a means of reparation or as a resti-tution of the self (Kris, 1952). For these diverse reasons, there is a tendency to overestimate its merits, to consider it unique, to insist upon being its one and only creator, and to control and possess the idea as mine. The new idea is con-sidered "it," the centre of the universe. This is reminiscent of Freud's descrip-tion of pre-Copernican man.

It is astonishing that a psychoanalyst can allow himself to feel that this or that idea or set of ideas can explain everything. It seems as though he invests the new idea with the magical omnipotence the psychoanalyst once felt in him-self in his childhood and has now projected it into his new system. It becomes a magical formula which can unravel all the hitherto inaccessible secrets of hu-man behaviour. I have already mentioned that there is a love affair quality to creativity but some psychoanalysts seem to have turned the love affair into a re-gressive form of love, where love really becomes total possession, control and omnipotence.

Again, all such authors seem to me to be in marked contrast to Freud's way of working and different also from the ways of other creative analysts. Freud con-stantly recognized the limitations of his knowledge and was constantly at work revising, changing, and amplifying his ideas. I believe I have convincingly demonstrated this in his "Studies on Hysteria" but it can also be readily shown in the changes he made in his theory of anxiety, his major change in the instinct theory when he introduced the hypothesis of an aggressive instinct in man, and in many other areas of his thinking. Some analysts, other than Freud, also work in this way. What is characteristic for them is that they do not destroy all the old theories when they conceive of a new idea. They conserve the parts they consider useful, add their innovations and try to integrate them into a cohesive framework which is not closed off from further elaboration and emendation.

I find it particularly helpful or fruitful to look upon a creative idea, or system of ideas, as though it were a baby. The scientific psychoanalyst will allow his baby to grow and mature, to learn and have new experiences with others besides the creator and his family. The creator will even allow his children to marry, to become part of another family and have children of their own. This analogy may seem maudlin and personal, but it does seem to point up a shortcoming in the behaviour of many analysts in regard to their new ideas. They want exclusive and total possession of this valuable treasure and refuse to let it be integrated into the mainstream of psychoanalytic developments. I have also seen similar reactions in me, in regard to a new interpretation I have made. If, a week later, the patient brings it up as his idea, I find myself tempted to say: "It was my idea, I thought of it, not you." Fortunately, I have learned not only to restrain myself, but to realize that his taking the interpretation over as his own insight indicates he has listened and heard me, and hopefully he has now integrated it into his own thinking.

One can even carry on a love affair with psychoanalysis constructively as long as one is willing to relinquish the wish for total and exclusive possession of her love, and one is willing to give up the fantasy of being her favourite child or sole heir. Then, one would be eager to defend her against her enemies, to give her constructive criticism without being carried away by the more infantile, grandiose, and intoxicating aspects of love. One would then be willing to allow others to be in her favour and receive rewards without becoming destructively jealous and rivalrous. This is the kind of love one has toward a good mother, one who has raised you, educated you, protected you and rewarded you well. For such a mother it is only natural to feel love and gratitude. Some psychoanalysts show this by continuing to support her by learning and working hard, and by occasionally bringing her a gift, a new idea. Such analysts retain their individual independence and still remain devoted to psychoanalysis and to the pursuit of knowledge for her enrichment.

What is striking and particularly notable about Freud was his capacity to hang on to what was valuable in his own past thinking, to synthesize seemingly irreconcilable elements, and to make new creative formulations from seemingly diverse elements. Freud not only did this with his own work but he could also do it with the work of others. He used Abraham's (1908) paper to help him with the Schreber case (Freud, 1911). He utilized another of Abraham's papers (1912) for his "Mourning and Melancholia" (1917a). But Freud went even beyond this. He integrated some of the ideas of Rank, Jung and Adler in formulating his paper "On narcissism: an introduction" (1914). Strachey's introductory comments make this abundantly clear (1957, pp. 69–70). In other words, Freud was no Freudian in its narrow sense. He was even willing and able to use the works of his opponents if their ideas served a useful purpose. In addition, Freud constantly used his own self-analysis to help with his new formulations.

THE FATE OF NEW IDEAS IN PSYCHOANALYTIC GROUPS

This desirable creative synthesis is not found in the history of the psychoanalytic movement as it relates to the development of different "schools" of psychoanalysis. A school of psychoanalysis refers to a group of analysts all of whom adhere publicly to a set of ideas concerning psychoanalysis which conflict in important ways with the central ideas of other groups. In its earliest days, there was only a Freudian School and then there evolved Adlerian, Jungian and Rankian Schools. Today it is possible to distinguish an Orthodox Freudian School, a Classical Freudian School, a Kleinian Freudian School and a Neo-Freudian School. What is remarkable about the more recent schools is that each of them considers itself to be a devotee of psychoanalysis and Freudian to boot. If one studies the underlying concepts and techniques of each, it becomes clear that they differ markedly from one another in what they consider to be Freud's basic principles and also in how they deal with the new discoveries in clinical findings and the resultant new theories and techniques. The history of the different schools is inseparable from the origin and fate of new ideas in psychoanalysis. Differences in attitude towards adversity, the ability to endure uncertainty, to take risks, the quality of their libidinal and aggressive strivings, the ability to stand alone, all play a part in the formation of schools of psychoanalysis.

I think it is important to describe briefly the various schools because they all parade under the banner of psychoanalysis. I shall not discuss the older deviant schools because their beliefs are well known and they no longer consider themselves Freudian psychoanalysts. I do want to touch briefly on the newer schools because, to the public at large, they represent psychoanalysis today and we do meet one another, at least physically, at international meetings. My opinions are subjective ones and may not be shared by many, but they are derived from my readings, observations and personal discussions with the adherents of these different groups.

I would classify as Orthodox Freudians those psychoanalysts who consider the oedipus complex as the nuclear conflictual source of all neuroses, who consider castration anxiety as the major anxiety in neurotic patients, and who believe that the optimal behaviour of the psychoanalyst in the analytic situation is to behave as nearly as possible as an anonymous dispenser of interpretations. They reject or ignore or deprecate any clinical findings or hypotheses which were not stressed by Freud or by his most devout followers. For example, they do not *study* the ideas of Erikson on the concept of identity, nor Klein's views on the early mother-child relationship and her theory of a normal pre-oedipal, paranoid and depressive phase of development. In addition, they are mistrustful of Hartmann's (1939) ideas concerning autonomous ego functions and conflict-free spheres. In general they are more id-orientated than ego-orientated, although they do recognize the importance of analysing the ego's resistances. The orthodox analysts look askance at such notions as "handling" transference phenomena or building a working alliance. They believe they are followers of Freud, and they are, but only in their worship of Freud's findings. They do not emulate him in his constant search for new knowledge.

The Classical School differs from the Orthodox in so far as they do accept certain modifications and amplifications of Freud's original ideas. They endorse the importance of Hartmann's ideas, in fact they have extended the influence and power of the early ego and have downgraded the potency of the id. They seem to object to Freud's (1917b) idea that the ego is not the master of his own house and support Rapaport's (1967) view that the id is not a seething cauldron.

They write, in Waelder's opinion (1967), as though Freud's psychoanalysis was essentially a drive psychology, an assumption Waelder believes is a myth, containing an element of truth covered by a thick layer of error. Their model of psychoanalysis is much more schematic, with its greater emphasis on psychic structure, than it was in Freud's day (Waelder, 1967, p. 21). The Classical Psychoanalysts accept many of Erikson's ideas and they do recognize the importance of the pre-oedipal phases of development. At the same time, they reject Kleinian ideas almost totally, as well as the ideas of Fairbairn. They analyse transference and resistance consistently, but are loath to differentiate what is real from what is distorted in the patient's reactions to the psychoanalyst and ignore the technical and theoretical problems this differentiation implies. The Classical Analysts are creative, but their creativity is limited because they dare not contend with the valuable ideas of those they consider to be outside of the mainstream of Freudian psychoanalysis.

Whereas the Classical School makes its major contributions to the ego functions, the Kleinians write about psychoanalysis almost exclusively from the standpoint of the analysis of the id, as they see it, its derivatives, and its relationship to split objects. The term resistance is almost completely absent in their writings and when they interpret defences they only stress the instinctual components which are used for defensive purposes. The Kleinians believe that by focusing on the fantasy life of earliest childhood (which they believe to be nearly identical in all children) and by interpreting all the patient's reactions to people and the analyst as transference reactions, they can, by these two procedures alone, completely understand and treat all forms of neuroses, perversions and psychoses. Concepts such as the therapeutic alliance and the real relationship between the patient and analyst are never mentioned. Segal (1964) and Rosenfeld (1965) are the most lucid exponents of these views.

What is impressive in the Kleinian School, in addition to their almost total disregard for ego functions, is their relegating the oedipus complex, phallic sexuality and sexual passion to a minor role. Furthermore, they tend to disregard the importance of historical events after earliest childhood. I am impressed by their closed system of thinking and their neglect of the ideas of other than Kleinian psychoanalysts.

They even overlook one of Freud's most important hypotheses concerning the psychoses, which they treat by interpretation alone. For example, Freud's basic differentiation between neuroses and psychoses which he first described in the beginning of the seventh section of his paper "The Unconscious" (1915) is disregarded in their thinking and in their technique. Neurotics, said Freud, withdraw libido from real objects and divert it on to fantasied objects. Schizophrenics, on the other hand, withdraw libido from external objects and *also* withdraw it from internal object representations, displacing it on to fragments of the self representation. The orthodox Kleinians disregard this hypothesis in theory and practice. Federn (1952), Eissler (1953), Winnicott (1955) and Searles (1965) seem to treat psychotic patients in accordance with Freud's views, but, as far as I know, only Wexler (1960) states Freud's theories as a basis for his technique.

In the Kleinian analysts, I believe one can observe a group of followers who are united in downgrading the importance of many of Freud's basic ideas and at the same time are united in deifying the belief that putting preverbal fantasies into words gives them the very omnipotent control they seem constantly to find in their patients. The Kleinians are creative, but again, I find their new ideas are narrow and are reacted to by their adherents with the same contagion one sees in fads. All Kleinians see projective identifications in all patients most of the time and recently they are enthusiastic about the notion of people searching for "containers."

The Neo-Freudians are a more heterogeneous group whose original leaders were Horney (1939), Kardiner (1939) and Fromm (1941). They stress, I believe correctly, the importance of cultural factors in character development, the importance of the striving for security and the ego's building of unified defensive systems. At the same time, however, they discarded as valueless the libido theory, the oedipus complex, the theory of instinctual drives, the overriding importance of childhood experiences and Freud's concept of the origin of the superego (Fenichel, 1940). The later adherents to this school of thought (e.g. Salzman (1962), Kelman (1964) and Marmor (1968) and a host of others) are essentially anti-id, but pro-ego, pro-object-relations and culturistic in their orientation. I believe that Fairbairn (1954) and Guntrip (1968) also share much of their thinking, particularly in the concept of the human newborn being a unified self who begins life seeking human togetherness. The latter two see sexuality essentially as a defence. Their views smack of theology, moralism and utopianism, harking back to the belief in the newborn babe as innately pure and noble (Schaar, 1961). They do not seem to question what drives, what impels a baby to seek the breast. If they do, their answer seems to be not hunger for milk, but togetherness. This is reminiscent of the notion of human supremacy of the pre-Darwinian man Freud described.

The beliefs of the Neo-Freudians illustrate how the aggressive and narcissistic component in creativity can lead to the formation of new ideas which are idealized and simultaneously lead to the destruction of the essential components of psychoanalysis. For a more comprehensive review of this school the reader is urged to read the careful and penetrating reviews by Tartakoff (1956) and Levine (1967). Here one can see how some valuable new ideas are vitiated by a destructive attack upon the basic concepts of psychoanalysis.

The *anti-id* tendency can also be seen, to a lesser degree, in some of the classical Freudians. The Ego School, or American School, with its emphasis on such concepts as autonomous ego functions, conflict-free spheres, adaptation, the undifferentiated ego-id, etc., all seem to claim more inherent power for the ego and belittle the strength of the id (Zelmanowits, 1968).

This brief description of "schools" does not exhaust all the practitioners of deviant views of psychoanalysis. For example, I have not mentioned Alexander (1946) and his followers, who believe in manipulating the transference and who consider the regressive transference neurosis an unnecessary development and a waste of time. At this point, however, I want to turn to certain general characteristics which are typical of all schools.

The disappointing and destructive consequences of school formations are that they all tend to become *establishments*. To a lesser or greater degree every one of them becomes parochial and insular. In all of them, the majority of members are followers, true believers and purists. The very need to belong to a school, the need to be "in," seems to me to indicate a need for protection or a need to obey the dictates of a leader, or of an "ideal analyst." In my opinion, the concept of the "ideal analyst" or the belief in a perfect or complete system, excludes doubt, criticism, and rejects new and different ideas. This is incompatible with a scientific approach. If I imagine an analytic session with a "true believer" analyst repeating the catechism of his school, it is hard to see this as a living creative experience for either the patient or the therapist.

Followers of a school react to new ideas from a different school as though they were a danger, a threat to the very foundation of their professional beliefs. They seem to react as though the new and different idea would destroy their professional identity. As a result, they tend to over-identify, to over-estimate and even deify the ideas of their leaders and reject out of hand all dissenting points of view. All followers of a school are, in my opinion, orthodox which leads to dogma and bigotry. The purist and the "ideal analysts" do not tolerate change and seem unable to endure uncertainty and the unknown. They seem to prefer sterile certainty to the risk-taking of discovery.

The insularity of the various schools can be seen in the curricula of the various training institutes in which new ideas, particularly if controversial, are rarely if ever given a thorough discussion. As a consequence, the bibliographies of authors from these schools omit any references to authors of divergent views even where the particular idea under discussion touches directly on the controversial author's work. A good example is to be found in my own paper "The Mother Tongue and the Mother." Although I referred to the decisive importance of the early mother-child-breast relationship, I made no reference to the work of Melanie Klein (1932).

It seems to me to be apparent that in each school there is a resistance to integrate the new and different ideas with the old. There is thesis and antithesis, but not synthesis. Symptomatic of this trend is the fact that the term "synthesizing ego function" has been denigrated to *synthetic ego* function. What is happening in our various psychoanalytic institutes seems analogous to what is going on in our universities and other establishments. The new and the different are excluded or segregated from the old and familiar. There is no true integration. The faculty and administration tend to think that only the students are at fault and the institution is being unfairly attacked or improperly used. They want to protect the establishment and their jobs and not the search for knowledge.

This state of affairs has grave implications for the psychoanalytic movement. It is my belief that there is a lack of progress, a lack of creativity, because there is a lack of free and open discussion, as well as a reluctance to study differing points of view. It may well be that the distress and even the outrage which confrontation arouses are important antecedents to creativity in our psychoanalytic institutes and universities.

Certainly, placidity, contentment and self-satisfaction are not the breeding grounds for new ideas. I have the impression at the International Congresses that members of different schools talk at each other and not to and with each other. Each school seems to avoid serious open discussion of their different ways of working and understanding. The young are too timid or brash, the old are too protective of their special views and of their high position. It is true that it is a most painful experience to realize that, after more than 25 years of practice, your work was deficient because you had neglected some of the ideas of another school. I have had this happen to me and I can attest to its earthshaking effects. Yet humility and honesty are essential for a scientific psychoanalyst. Shortly after Freud's 69th birthday, he wrote to Lou Andreas Salomé,

I believe I have discovered something of fundamental importance for our matter. A discovery of which one ought to be ashamed because one should have guessed such connections from the beginning and not after 30 years.

One month later he wrote *Inhibitions, Symptoms and Anxiety* (Max Schur, personal communication).

There are many areas in psychoanalysis which I believe urgently need clarification and further exploration. For example, the conflict theory is central for explaining the development of neuroses but it is insufficient for our understanding of the psychoses and the perversions. It is important not to leave to a few to explore further the theory of ego deficiency, the failure in building early internal object representations. The oedipus complex is crucial for understanding full fledged neurotic symptom formation, but the importance of pre-oedipal and early ego developments must be re-evaluated, clarified and integrated into our theory if we want to understand more completely all forms of psychopathology. Interpretation is a major instrument for giving insight, but something more is needed in patients with severe maturational deficiences in their early object relations. Wexler recently made the point that healthy children mature without interpretations. Does not this indicate the importance of the real relationship in the psychoanalytic situation for patients who have signs of early maturational defects?

I have selected these few areas where the psychoanalytic movement needs to make progress as a plea for a real interchange of ideas *among and within* "schools." I have emphasized the stultifying effects of institutes and schools, but I want to end on a positive note. Training institutes are needed, even "establishments" can serve a useful purpose. It is true that institutions tend to ossify, but the institution also provides a holding, structuring function. In a personal com.nunication, Masud Khan wrote that

> paradoxically, the institution is the one enemy one must keep to define the rigour and boundaries of one's own freedom. The question is, how *not* to let this enemy become one's master.

Psychoanalysts who belong to no institute or society usually end up as "wild analysts," existentialists, or evangelists, or in some way manifest the effects of the return of the repressing forces that led them originally into psychoanalytic treatment. Perhaps Laing (1967) and Rosen (1947), among others, are examples of this development. What we need is to study seriously the views of those we disagree with, exchange views openly based on clinical material described in detail. Our curricula must be more flexible and heterogeneous, our students should be given more freedom, and we teachers should have the humility to be dedicated to the pursuit of knowledge and not in selling our particular brand of psychoanalysis.

I believe it is no longer necessary for us to spend our lives defending or attacking Freud's major discoveries. Our task is to pursue further knowledge and to be willing to modify and amplify what we have learned from him. To my mind that is in the true spirit of Freud — not in being an Orthodox or Classical or Kleinian Freudian — but in being a psychoanalyst.

ACKNOWLEDGEMENTS

I am very indebted to Milton Wexler, with whom I discussed many of these ideas in the course of our joint research projects supported by the Foundation for Research in Psychoanalysis, Beverly Hills, California. I am also indebted to the generosity of Max Schur, who pointed out pertinent passages in some of Freud's unpublished correspondence.

REFERENCES

Abraham, K. (1908), The psycho-sexual differences between hysteria and dementia praecox. *Selected Papers.* London: Hogarth Press, 1948.

———— (1912), Notes on the psycho-analytical investigation and treatment of manic-depressive insanity and allied conditions. *Selected Papers.* London: Hogarth Press, 1948.

Alexander, F., French, T. M. et al. (1946), *Psychoanalytic Therapy.* New York: Ronald Press.

Brunswick, R. M. (1940), The pre-oedipal phase of the libido development. In: *The Psychoanalytic Reader,* Vol. 1, ed. R. Fliess. New York: International Universities Press, 1948.

Buxbaum, E. (1949), The role of a second language in the formation of ego and superego. *Psychoanal. Quart.,* 18:279–289.

Eissler, K. R. (1953), The effect of the structure of the ego on psychoanalytic technique. *J. Amer. Psychoanal. Assn.,* 1:104–143.

Erikson, E. (1946), Ego development and historical change. *The Psychoanalytic Study of the Child,* 2. New York: International Universities Press.

Fairbairn, W. R. D. (1954), *An Object Relations Theory of the Personality.* New York: Basic Books.

Federn, P. (1952), *Ego Psychology and the Psychoses.* New York: Basic Books.

Fenichel, O. (1930), The pregenital antecedents of the oedipus complex. In: *Collected Papers,* 1st series. New York: Norton, 1953.

———— (1940), Review of Karen Horney's *New Ways in Psychoanalysis. Psychoanal. Quart.,* 9: 114–121.

Ferenczi, S. (1911), On obscene words. In: *Sex in Psychoanalysis.* New York: Basic Books, 1950.

Freud, E., ed. (1960), *Letters of Sigmund Freud.* New York: Basic Books.

Freud, S., & Breuer, J. (1893–95), Studies on hysteria. *Standard Edition,* 2.

———— (1905), Jokes and their relation to the unconscious. *Standard Edition,* 8.

———— (1911), Psycho-analytic notes on an autobiographical account of a case of paranoia (dementia paranoides). *Standard Edition,* 12.

———— (1914), On narcissism: an introduction. *Standard Edition,* 14.

———— (1915), The unconscious. *Standard Edition,* 14.

———— (1917a), Mourning and melancholia. *Standard Edition,* 14.

———— (1917b), A difficulty in the path of psychoanalysis. *Standard Edition,* 17.

Fromm, E. (1941), *Escape from Freedom.* New York: Farrar & Rinehart.

Greenacre, P. (1957), The childhood of the artist. *The Psychoanalytic Study of the Child,* 12.

———— (1959), Play in relation to creative imagination. *The Psychoanalytic Study of the Child,* 14.

Greenson, R. R. (1950), The mother tongue and the mother. *Internat. J. Psycho-Anal.,* 31:18–23.

———— (1954a), The struggle against identification. *J. Amer. Psychoanal. Assn.,* 2:200–216.

———— (1954b), On moods and introjects. *Bull. Menn. Clinic,* 18:1–11.

———— (1954c), About the sound "mm. . . ." *Psychoanal. Quart.,* 23:234–239.

———— (1958), On screen defences, screen hunger and screen identity. *J. Amer. Psychoanal. Assn.,* 6:242–262.

Guntrip, H. (1968), *Schizoid Phenomena, Object-Relations and the Self.* New York: International Universities Press.

Hartmann, H. (1939), *Ego Psychology and the Problem of Adaptation.* New York: International Universities Press, 1958.

Hitschmann, E. (1956), *Great Men: Psychoanalytic Studies.* New York: International Universities Press.

Horney, K. (1939), *New Ways in Psychoanalysis.* New York: Norton.

Jones, E. (1920), Editorial. *Internat. J. Psycho-Anal.,* 1:3–5.

———— (1953), *The Life and Work of Sigmund Freud,* Vol. 1. New York: Basic Books.

———— (1955), *The Life and Work of Sigmund Freud,* Vol. 2. New York: Basic Books.

———— (1957), *The Life and Work of Sigmund Freud,* Vol. 3. New York: Basic Books.

Kardiner, A. (1939), *The Individual and His Society.* New York: Columbia University Press.

Kelman, H., ed. (1964), Advances in psychoanalysis. In: *Contributions to Karen Horney's Holistic Approach.* New York: Norton.

Klein, M. (1932), *The Psycho-Analysis of Children.* London: Hogarth Press, 1949.

Kris, E. (1952), *Psychoanalytic Explorations in Art.* New York: International Universities Press.

Laing, R. D. (1967), *The Politics of Experience.* New York: Pantheon Books.

Levine, J. M. (1967), Through the looking glass: an examination of some critiques of Freudian psychoanalysis. *J. Amer. Psychoanal. Assn.,* 15:166–212.

Marmor, J., ed. (1968), *Modern Psychoanalysis.* New York: Basic Books.

Rapaport, D. (1967), *The Collected Papers of David Rapaport.* ed. M. M. Gill. New York: Basic Books.

Rosen, J. N. (1947), The treatment of schizophrenic psychosis by direct analytic therapy. *Psychiat. Quart.,* 21:3–37.

Rosenfeld, H. (1965), *Psychotic States: A Psychoanalytic Approach.* New York: International Universities Press.

Salzman, L. (1962), *Developments in Psychoanalysis.* New York: Grune & Stratton.

Schaar, J. H. (1961), *Escape from Authority.* New York: Basic Books.

Searles, H. F. (1965), *Collected Papers on Schizophrenia and Related Subjects.* New York: International Universities Press.

Segal, H. (1964), *Introduction to the Work of Melanie Klein.* New York: Basic Books.

Shapiro, S. (1968), Reporter on Anna Freud's "Difficulties in the path of psychoanalysis." *Bull. Phila. Assn. Psychoanal.,* 18:214–216.

Stengel, E. (1939), On learning a new language. *Internat. J. Psycho-Anal.,* 20:417–479.

Strachey, J. (1957), Editor's note. *Standard Edition,* 14:69–71.

Székely, L. (1967), The creative pause. *Int. J. Psycho-Anal.,* 48:353–367.

Tartakoff, H. H. (1956), Recent books on psychoanalytic technique: a comparative study. *J. Amer. Psychoanal. Assn.,* 4:318–343.

Waelder, R. (1967), Inhibitions, symptoms and anxiety: forty years later. *Psychoanal. Quart.,* 36:1–36.

Weissman, P. (1967), Theoretical considerations of ego regression and ego functions in creativity. *Psychoanal. Quart.,* 36:37–50.

Wexler, M. (1960), Hypotheses concerning ego deficiency in schizophrenia. In: *The Outpatient Treatment of Schizophrenia.* New York: Grune & Stratton.

Winnicott, D. W. (1955), Metapsychological and clinical aspects of regression within the psychoanalytic set-up. In: *Collected Papers.* New York: Basic Books, 1958.

Zelmanowits, J. (1968), Review of *The Collected Papers of David Rapaport. Psychiat.,* 31:292–299.

IV AN APPLICATION OF NEW IDEAS IN PSYCHOANALYTIC RESEARCH: CONSENSUAL ANALYSIS

Introduction

Emanuel Windholz begins this section with an introduction to the method called *Consensual Analysis*. He describes this research approach, contrasts it with the usual supervisory situation, and describes its relevance in uncovering new data about the psychoanalytic situation.

Alan Skolnikoff presents case material dealing with his reactions during a 500-hour analysis of a patient with narcissistic characteristics. Skolnikoff includes in this report his feelings and responses to the consensual analytic situation. He presents some process notes based on four hours early in the analysis, followed by his verbal reports to Windholz in the consensual analysis, which he then compares with the process notes.

Jacob Arlow, in his discussion of Skolnikoff's case material, distinguishes among errors made by the therapist, countertransference, and the therapist's intuitive responses to the patient's transference.

Gerald Aronson continues the discussion of consensual analysis. He emphasizes the importance, in this approach, of being able to see clearly what happens in the mind and responses of the analyst that results in change during the analysis, which, in turn, brings about changes in the patient. He suggests a research tool called "Thematic Analysis," which could be utilized to deal with the data compiled in the course of consensual analysis.

Windholz summarizes the current findings and future implications of consensual analysis. He discusses Skolnikoff's reactions to his patient and the meaning of the analyst's attempts to deal with the patient's behavior during the early stages of the analysis. Windholz highlights one vignette from Skolnikoff's report that reveals the unconsciously motivated behavior of the treating analyst which emerges in his reports.

Norman Mages reports on his personal reactions and experiences as a treating analyst in the consensual analytic situation. In a frank and open discussion he details his feelings about the patient and his responses to the listening analyst.

Donald Cliggett provides an overview of the research implications of consensual analysis. He offers a perspective of what consensual analysis is and is not, and emphasizes the advantages of this case-study method as a research tool compared to the treating analyst's research on his own case material. Cliggett also indicates areas for further study that could be carried out using the consensual analytic method.

Five appendices are added by the research group, including: (A) *The Verbal Report*, (B) *The Process Notes*, (C) *Excerpts From the Case Study of an Hysterical Character*, (D) *The Intuitive Understanding of a Transference Paradigm*, and (E) *The Multiple Appeal of Interpretations*.

The historical paper by Leo Stone, written over thirty years ago, remains a classic discussion of the indications for psychoanalysis. This paper is reprinted here so that the reader can compare the positions in 1954 and 1984 on the widening scope of such indications. It has now become common practice among many analysts to include narcissistic personalities, and even some borderline patients, in the diagnostic categories for treatment by psychoanalysis. This paper by Stone opened the door to more research interest in applying psychoanalysis to the more serious emotional disorders.

The Editors

16

Consensual Analysis:
An Introduction

EMANUEL WINDHOLZ, M.D.

Consensual analysis is a clinical research method designed to study the analyst's role in psychoanalysis. The method consists of a special arrangement agreed upon by two analysts. The formal setting resembles that of conventional psychoanalytic supervision, but the role of the second analyst is quite different. Instead of supervising, he or she listens silently to the impromptu verbal reports of the treating analyst, who has provided the second analyst with a transcript of daily process notes prior to their weekly meetings. The verbal reports of these meetings are recorded and transcribed. Thus, two different sets of data become available for the study of the analyst's role in the conduct of psychoanalytic therapy.

A comparison of the two sets of data yields surprising results. Having provided a silent listener with a written report (the process notes), the treating analyst seems to feel free to use a different mode of verbal communication. The weekly verbal reports reflect a kind of thinking which is characteristic of an analyst's state of mind when listening to patients, except that now the object of observation is the analyst's own thinking. In listening to himself, the analyst's attention is centered primarily on emotional involvement with the patient. This is a characteristic aspect of such reports; talking to a silent, non-participating listener seems to have unusual effects.

We acknowledge with appreciation the support of this research by grants from the Mary A. Crocker Trust of San Francisco.

In these verbal reports, treating analysts follow ideas as they occur, without concern for logic or meaning. Frequently diverted from the original goal, they may contradict themselves, sound incomprehensible, or even confused. In the transcribed verbal report (Appendix A), many statements appear as grammatical errors. Exploration uncovered important meanings of these peculiarities of the analyst's language, some of which are parapraxis. Analysts who have listened to patients with free-floating attention now revive their emotional involvement with patients, which influenced the trend of ideas that emerged in analytic sessions. This aspect of the analyst's thinking during the verbal report is responsible for the abundance of new data.

It may be accurate to describe this activity as an experimentation with introspection. The treating analyst inadvertently provides clues to aspects of the therapist's role which had escaped attention, and to many other, only dimly perceived, determinants of the patient's behavior. These subtleties of interactions reveal the great complexity of the analytic process.

The analyst, speaking freely in the presence of a second silent analyst, conveys a sense of urgency, as if he or she had been waiting for an opportunity to talk, to recapture lost impressions. We are reminded of Freud, writing in the middle of the night to his silent listener, Fliess, that he feels tortured by his "poltergeister." His patients disturbed his peace of mind, forcing him to think about them and continue exploring their problems.

We can postulate that the situation created in the consensual analysis, namely, having a second listener available, satisfies the treating analyst's need for communication. The experience is described (in this volume) by Dr. Norman L. Mages, who discovered this significant effect of the method in himself as a treating analyst. As the listening analyst, I have to resist the temptation to ask the treating analyst for additional information, since this could influence the spontaneity of the therapist's thinking and the conduct of the on-going analysis.

Later, when I start to elicit more information from the treating analyst, I also have to remain uninvolved. The clues revealed in the verbal report and derived from cross-references between the verbal and written reports (the process notes) are presented to the treating analyst for further exploration. As the introspective search continues, more data emerge as the therapist becomes again involved in the process of free association, providing more impressions which had previously not reached full consciousness. At the end of the consensual analysis, the treating analyst and I engage in a systematic study of the clues. We achieved the final objective of our explorations: an agreement about the accuracy of the methods and a consensual validation of the treating analyst's role in the conduct of the analysis.

The following presentation will be limited to the exploration of the role of the treating analyst as a participant in the regulatory function of the patient's ego. This participation is essential and is conveyed non-verbally to the patient in subtle variations of the analyst's voice and in the quality of the therapist's silences. It is necessary for the maintenance of the so-called "therapeutic alliance" and has to be restored when the patient's cooperative attitude is disrupted. This happens most frequently in the analysis of narcissistic patients who are especially vulnerable. I have selected data from the consensual analyses of two of the several patients who were studied.

The first patient, diagnosed as an obsessive compulsive character, was treated by Dr. Skolnikoff, who had to modify his diagnosis after encountering stubborn narcissistic resistances. The analyst experienced unusually intense frustrations during the course of this analysis, and the intensity of his emotional reactions was conveyed in the verbal reports. There was, therefore, a great discrepancy between the verbal reports and the process notes.

The second patient was diagnosed as an hysterical character. This case will prove that the findings about the role of the analyst are valid, not only for a patient with narcissistic personality traits, but also for a neurotic patient (Appendix C).

Study of the wealth of data raised questions which go far beyond delineation of the analyst's participation in the regulatory functions of the patient's ego. In my weekly meetings with Dr. Cliggett I suggested numerous other applications. Some, like the multiple appeal of interventions (Appendix E), are evident from the vignettes presented. It was also easy to recognize that the effects of the analyst's unconscious attitudes later entered into the transference. Since they can be analyzed, we could look upon them as "unconscious parameters." These and many similar observations led me to conclude that changes in the analyst's role are reliable guideposts for study of the analytic process.

The most difficult task is the identification of the changes in the hierarchy of the multiple determinants, but, as Dr. Cliggett points out, there is a wealth of data available for such a study.

17

Consensual Analysis:
A Case Study

ALAN Z. SKOLNIKOFF, M.D.

In this case presentation I will focus on my subjective reactions to the patient in some early sections of a 500-hour analysis, which were studied systematically in a consensual analysis with Dr. Windholz. This involved my recording of process notes after each analytic hour and weekly discussions of my reactions to the patient with the listening analyst remaining silent. After the analysis was terminated, we compared the process notes and the verbal reports. To my surprise, my verbal reports revealed many interesting distortions when compared with the process notes. Inferences were made about the meaning of these distortions and how they related to my reactions to the patient. I was amazed to learn how far my analytic behavior had departed from neutrality without my conscious awareness.

I am not presenting this case, however, to point out my "errors," but to demonstrate how the consensual analysis revealed that the pattern of these departures frodm a neutral stance were evoked by the patient and furthered the analytic process. In our usual understanding of the psychoanalytic process we presume that the analyst is involved both cognitively and emotionally. The term "free-floating attention" implies, among other things, a capacity to shift one's attention rapidly from the patient's productions to one's own emotional reaction. We feel that this ability to shift rapidly can lead to a deeper and more detailed understanding of the patient's dynamics, unconscious fantasies, and transferences.

With reference to the empathic process, Schlesinger (1982) points out that we expect the analyst to maintain the therapeutic split by not over-identifying nor feeling alienated from the patient. We should be able to shift easily from our experiencing to our observing egos, be able to understand our affective responses, and process them into a clearer understanding of the patient's transference. Countertransference, in its originally narrowly defined sense, is the unconscious reaction toward the patient related to unresolved neurotic issues in the analyst, and is not a desirable feature of the analytic process.

In their conception of the psychoanalytic situation, Abrams and Shengold (1978) distinguish between a traditional model and a new model. In the traditional model there is an emphasis on the therapy of psychoneurotic disorders. The analysand is committed to free association, the analyst to free-floating attention, neutrality, empathic understanding, and interpretation of accumulating information including reconstruction. A regression from the oedipal phase of development is the primary focus of the psychoanalytic process. Changes come through the interpretation and working through of the transference neurosis. It is expected that pre-oedipal traumata and deprivations are not so severe as to cause significant deviations or deformations of psychic development in the patient. Countertransference is viewed as originating in the analyst's unconscious, predominantly as an obstacle to the goal of helping the patient develop insight.

In the new model, analysis is thought to be suitable for a broader range of disorders. The psychoanalytic situation is seen primarily as an encounter between two people, rather than as a setting whose purpose is the examination of the introspective processes of one of them. Here, too, the patient has the task of associating freely; however, more is expected of the analyst. Empathy, for example, does not serve simply to achieve knowledge and understanding. It has a direct therapeutic influence. Countertransference is seen, not primarily as a resistance to the mutual work, but as part of the interactional relationship which promotes the psychoanalytic process. The focus is on the vicissitudes of self and object representations, as these become manifest within the analytic encounter. Pathology is traced back to the pre-verbal period of development which is revived, and both analyst and analysand are expected to reexperience the patient's early relationships. Within the new model the earlier stage is more fundamental, while in the traditional model it is the oedipal phase. The newer psychoanalytic process is dominated by therapeutic action in contrast to the traditional concept of acquired insight to solve problems, and it emphasizes the analyst's active role in affective interchange.

McLaughlin (1981) would eliminate the term "countertransference" and refer instead to the analyst's transference because of the ubiquity of these reactions. Sandler (1981) has described how the patient can unconsciously evoke in the analyst an "actualization" of previous conflictual situations. Most analysts agree that we must eventually recognize what our unconscious reactions have been toward each patient. In the meantime, we consciously attempt to maintain as neutral a position as possible.

My understanding of the analytic situation has essentially been the traditional one. In the analyses that I have conducted I have attempted to maintain a neutral stance without being rigid. However, the systematic study in consensual analysis of the case presented here suggests another concept of the analytic process. In this retrospective study it became evident that the patient repeatedly evoked in me departures from neutrality which, for the most part, I was not aware of. What is more interesting is that these departures evoked by the patient furthered his capacity to feel comfortable within the analysis. In the weekly verbal reports, we reviewed my responses to the patient and gained a different understanding of what the patient was trying to reenact. During the course of the analysis, my understanding of the transference had been partial at any given point. During long phases, I had been unconsciously involved in a variety of strong affective reactions to the patient. After the analysis, when Dr. Windholz and I applied the method of consensual analysis, we discovered some of the unconscious meanings of my analytic behavior. Parenthetically, I might add, the retrospective review was painful for me since I had assumed that my analytic responses were more under conscious control than they actually were.

CASE PRESENTATION

In presenting the case I will focus on the problematic areas of the analysis, which may give a more pathological picture of the patient necessitating numerous technical modifications. Actually, there were long sections, particularly later in the analysis, which were more traditional in technique: transference interpretations, interpretation of defenses, and insight leading to change.

The patient was a 28-year-old married academic psychologist. He was referred by a colleague who had seen him for several hours in consultation and recommended analysis. The patient felt there wasn't anything particularly wrong with him but that therapy or analysis would be helpful. He was formal and controlled in his speech, and at first was easily able to describe his life situation. As he continued, however, the patient became anxious and expressed the feeling that what he had considered as motivation for his behavior in the past now seemed to be wrought in conflict. He also emphasized that he was impressed and overwhelmed by the fact that the referring analyst had suggested analysis.

In the beginning, he was eager to start every hour, following me from the waiting room to my office so rapidly that I felt I had to quicken my pace so that he would not bump into me. During the sessions he would engage in a monologue that seemed to exclude me from his thinking, apparently experiencing my remarks as intrusive. Despite his intense preoccupation with his own thinking, he seemed very sensitive to my movements in my chair or noises outside of the office. When he heard these sounds he felt as if I was going to reprimand him or hit him. In reaction to this perception, I found myself trying to keep unusually still.

He had two feelings about my voice. For the most part it seemed to him gentle and reassuring, but he worried about my wanting to interrupt him, which he saw as angry or competitive with him. This reaction frequently occurred when he talked about competition with his father or senior colleagues. On the other hand, he was also upset when I didn't say anything. It was also difficult for him to accept supportive remarks. For example, following his description of intense discomfort about any angry outburst at his wife during a session, I said, "You feel guilty about having said that." His response was to get even more self-abusive, stating that he should have never permitted this outburst to occur, as he intensely poured forth material in an intellectual way. There was so much of it that I was afraid I would forget it and, momentarily felt the need to take some notes—something I almost never do during analytic hours. I thought that this indicated some mirroring in me of the patient's pathology: As he had a great need to produce I felt a similar need to remember and master all that he said.

Empirically, to permit the analysis to continue in a less chaotic way, I devised a "neutral intervention." This consisted of repeating the last two or three words of a phrase that the patient had said concerning a subject that wasn't too highly charged. For example, when he talked about subjects in which I believed he would anticipate hearing my angry voice, a neutral intervention permitted him to continue talking without the startle reaction of earlier sessions. Hearing my voice was reassuring, meaning that I wouldn't hit him or disappear.

Conflicts around dependency or what he saw as demands that he be dependent also appeared to be regulated by the neutral intervention which neither confronted him nor provoked him. Since this kind of intervention repeated his own words, it was a true mirror that reinforced his ideas. Whenever the patient talked about subjects with overwhelming affect, or when I made comments that were direct interpretations of his guilt or fear of his own anger, he responded by getting more anxious. The neutral intervention served a dual purpose for the patient: It permitted him to sustain the analysis without undue fear of closeness or competition; at the same time, it reassured him that he wasn't losing contact with the analyst.

A few weeks after noting this pattern of response, I became aware of several other responses to my interventions. If they were brief, this seemed to permit him to go on with an anxiety-provoking subject. If I was silent for too long, he frequently said that he didn't like to make interpretations of what he was saying, since he would then be taking over my job. A brief question such as "Why?" or "Why can't you interpret?" permitted him to continue. Longer interventions would lead to a "Hmmm, hmmm, hmmm" response as if he were carefully tasting what I said. This was followed by his wondering if he had understood everything that I said. He felt that he was only listening to the sound of my voice, and that prevented him from understanding *what* I said. Yet another kind of reaction to a pointed brief interpretation was: "I wish I had thought of that."

I frequently felt frustrated by the need to make all of the modifications that I have described in order to encourage the patient to continue. Then, with the help of the neutral intervention technique, the monologue changed into an "intellectual exercise." The patient gradually began making genetic connections and meaningful transference interpretations, some of which would be accompanied by a show emotion. He gained what appeared to be genuine insight into the transference, and he appeared to be able to carry out his own analysis which seemed to depend on my accepting the role assigned to me: limiting my participation to echoing his words, or remaining silent and restricting my movements. I even began to repeat back to the patient his transference interpretations, which he may have perceived as a validation of his self-analysis.

This limited participation in the analysis continued to be frustrating. Although I initially understood why I had devised the neutral intervention approach, I subsequently developed a tendency to appropriate what the patient said and give myself credit for the interpretation. At the time, I was obviously unaware of this. I would hear the patient say what I thought were my own thoughts or words, which evoked in me an uncanny feeling that he could read my mind. At times I wondered if I were contributing anything to the analysis and tended to credit the patient's self-analysis for any progress.

I would like to go over a sequence of hours (sessions 35–38, Appendix B) by describing the following levels of explanation of what went on: 1) what occurred between me and the patient (process notes); 2) my conscious understanding and experience of this interaction the following week by free association (verbal report); 3) how we examined this interaction retrospectively, and were surprised by the number of contradictions in my verbal report (review of analysis). Most difficult for me to tolerate was the evidence of my unconscious motivation; despite accepting these manifestations of unconscious behavior, I equated them with errors or signs of my lacking analytic competence.

Process Notes

In the Monday and Tuesday hours (sessions 35 and 36) the patient brought up his uncomfortable feelings about the money that was being spent on him for the analysis. He made references to having grown up in a situation where all the money was shared, and whatever he earned had to be turned over to his family. When I commented that he was reluctant to ask me directly to reduce the fee, he immediately brought up memories of how difficult it had been to ask his father or mother for anything. This linkage with his parents, however, did not appear to help him to ask for a fee reduction.

Further comments about his discomfort in asking me for a fee reduction led to other memories of his need to be independent. He wanted to analyze his free associations on this subject but wondered if he shouldn't let me do this (page 281). At the same time, he mentioned that he didn't like to get anything from others, and when he received a gift he felt speechless. I asked: "Is this analysis for your benefit or do you feel that you're doing what I want you to do?" This led him to describe his sense of guilt when he proceeded along his own lines in analytic sessions. When I remained silent, he told me, he felt foolish talking on his own, as if his ideas then sounded too grandiose. In this connection, he compared Freud and Fliess with him and me.

The theme of guilt concerning his independence continued in the Tuesday hour (page 281). He complained that the more he read the less he seemed to be able to free associate (page 282). I said: "The more you read the less you feel you need me to say anything." When he told me that he felt depressed, I interpreted it as follows: "You feel depressed since you discussed your disappointment in not being able to ask your father for anything and your feeling that you can't ask anyone for anything, including me regarding some arrangement about the fee." A breakthrough occurred after this intervention. He sobbed for ten minutes.

In the Wednesday hour (session 37) he made reference to having sobbed in his car for ten minutes following the previous hour (page 283). During that time, he had quiet fantasies concerning me, something he told me that he does quite often but believes that he hasn't talked about the fantasies here. Then he began to describe, in an incoherent way, a disturbing visit with his parents the previous summer. He shifted to asking me what I was thinking about and said that he wanted me to interpret his analysis of himself (page 284). I responded by stating that I was unclear about his description of the visit with his parents and wondered why he was presenting it that way. He then continued his account of the visit in a more controlled way: He had to deal with a very difficult family situation in which his parents were very upset with one another and he, as their psychologist son, had to intervene to resolve the difficulties. As he was describing this he said that he could not remember how he felt at that time. It was as if he was blocking it out. I said: "You must feel embarrassed discussing these feelings with me." He acknowledged that he felt like a child crying in a room by himself. Continuing in a confused way and trying to ward off emotion, he described events during the visit in detail. In addition to having difficulty with his role in helping his parents, he was upset when his mother confessed in front of his sister that he was her favorite child, which infuriated the sister.

Along with other material in the Thursday hour (session 38), the patient presented associations to a dream which revealed his discomfort in remembering sexual play with his sister. He said that he still had sexual ideas about his sister and went on to discuss these in an animated way (page 286).

Verbal Report

I focused my attention on a sense of frustrated annoyance which I felt in the Wednesday hour. This was greater than usual and concerned my not being able to understand the essence of what the patient was saying in describing his visit with his parents the previous summer. I continued to conceal my frustration and made an effort to speak in a gentle voice, asking him to clarify what he was talking about so I could better understand it (page 271). But I felt foolish, thinking that if I would have waited patiently he would have eventually clarified the details. After this, the patient continued his chronological account of the visit in a controlled way. I then remembered having said to him that he must have felt quite *upset* about what had happened (page 272). I recalled his having broken down at this point and becoming much more emotional than he had previously been in analysis.

Later, I mentioned his difficulty about being unable to ask for fee arrangements and came up with a theory of the patient being the "special child." I connected this to events of the previous summer when the mother told him, in front of his sister, that he was her favorite child. I theorized that in the transference the "special child" had two meanings: one, that the patient would be extremely independent and that I would be gratified by viewing his accomplishments in terms of his capacity to analyze; two, that because of his excellent performance I would be doing things for him since he was such a deserving person. As he was *my* special child, I would reduce or postpone the fee without his having to ask for it (page 275).

I had further thoughts about his association to his father when I had pointed out that he couldn't ask me for the fee reduction. The associations to his father had gratified me since I believed that this confirmed my comment as a meaningful transference interpretation. But as I reported this impression, I realized that the patient's association was very quick and had succeeded in manipulating me into feeling like a good analyst (page 278). With respect to my asking, "Is this analysis for your benefit or my benefit?", I think I made this remark because of my discomfort with the patient's idealizing me. I felt confused about his animation when describing sexual feelings about his sister in the Thursday hour. I couldn't believe he actually said that he still had these feelings. I thought that his discussing this so openly was a way of isolating *some* of his strong affects and, at the same time, presenting material (page 276) which he considered a proper subject of psychoanalysis.

Review of Analysis

In comparing my verbal report with the process notes a significant discrepancy was noted. I had displaced the breakthrough of the patient's affect from the Tuesday hour to the Wednesday hour. The process notes of the Wednesday hour, contradicting the verbal report, indicate that I had experienced frustration without relief. During the review of the case, as we compared the process notes and the verbal report, Dr. Windholz and I wondered about the meaning of my displacement. I went through a series of rationalizations: I thought I must have forgotten which hour I had made the interpretation. I rationalized that I actually made a facilitating interpretation on Wednesday but forgot to include this in the process notes. After studying the verbal report more thoroughly and comparing it to the process notes, I could see that the notes may have been rationalizations.

Although I had been partially aware of the implications of my frustrations and distortions in the analysis of this patient, I had previously assumed that my analytic behavior was under greater conscious control. The more thorough review of the verbal report revealed that I had been frustrated because the patient had not acknowledged the value of my interpretations prior to my quoting him. Following the breakthrough in the Tuesday hour, which I presumed was due to my interpretation, I was all the more frustrated on Wednesday because the patient did not admit his dependency, as I had assumed he would do. The process notes indicate that the patient wanted some approval from me in the Wednesday hour of the way he was conducting himself in the analysis. At that point, as if manipulated by him, I covered my frustration with what appeared to be a pleading remark, by asking him to clarify further what he was talking about in describing his visit with his parents. My plea permitted him to continue calmly discussing the events of the previous summer.

I gradually recognized that I had difficulty tolerating the patient's self-analysis and felt frustrated that I couldn't get the patient to look at his autonomy-dependency conflicts. I wanted him to understand his self-analysis as a resistance to his dependent longing for me. After the frustration of the Monday hour, when the patient did not ask me directly for a fee reduction in response to my interpretation, I was manipulated on Tuesday into rephrasing my interpretation in the form of quoting him, which led to his breakthrough of emotions.

At the beginning of the analysis my so-called "neutral intervention" was a conscious attempt to quote a few words of the patient. Now, two months later, I was no longer consciously aware that I was using his own words. My theorizing about the "special child" could be understood as an attempt to deal with my frustration at his resisting dependency on me, as well as having developmental and transference meaning. Indeed, one does things for a special child without forcing him to acknowledge his dependency. My pleading with the patient to tell me more in the Wednesday hour, instead of being annoyed with him for being unclear, was also an evocation of the mother's relationship to the "special child." In the same vein, even if I did not reduce his fee without his asking, at least I could confirm the value of his self-analysis by quoting him.

In my verbal report I suggested that the patient was unconsciously feeding me ideas to make me feel like a good analyst. This is, of course, similar to the way a special child gratifies his mother. Retrospectively, I could see that at this point I had difficulty empathizing with the patient's need to conduct his self-analysis because of my need that he be dependent on me.

With respect to his associations in the Thursday hour to conscious sexual feelings toward his sister, I had failed to recognize that he experienced pleasure not in these sexual feelings, but rather in analyzing his incestuous ideas. I could not understand that at the time because of my wish that he would not conduct his self-analysis autonomously.

SUMMARY

I have presented some material from the early phases of an analysis to demonstrate how my subjective reactions were evoked by the patient. It is my feeling that the patient gained a confirmation of his self-analysis through my quoting his remarks unwittingly. In the next phase of the analysis he became consciously aware of his wish to be admired; and later still, he progressed to being uncomfortable with these wishes when he realized that he needed this admiration to avoid dependency. The evocation of my unconscious admiration of his self-analysis, then, was an important factor in his progress.

Other questions are suggested by this case study: Would similar reactions be experienced by the analyst to patients with less narcissistic vulnerability? I think that the reactions would be less marked, although they would still be present. Does the personality of the analyst play a large part in determining such reactions? I believe that the personality of the analyst must play a large role in determining the particular reactions to certain patients, but that some kind of reaction is invariably present. If we were to compare the method of consensual analysis with traditional supervision, might we alter our understanding of the "mistakes" of the analyst being supervised? I think that it would be very useful in supervision to focus on the transference of the analyst to the patient as one of the major areas of teaching. Consensual analysis is an effective method of studying the thoughts and behavior of the analyst in reaction to the patient as these unfold during the course of an analysis.

REFERENCES

Abrams & Shengold (1978), Reflexions on the topic of the 30th Congress: "Affects and the psychoanalytic situation." *Internat. J. Psycho-Anal.,* 59:395–407.

McLaughlin (1981), Transference, psychic reality, and countertransference. *Psychoanal. Quart.,* 50:639–664.

Sandler, J. (1981), Character traits and object relationships. *Psychoanal. Quart.,* 50:694–708.

Schlesinger, H. (1982), The process of empathic response. *Psychoanal. Inq.,* 1:393–416.

18

Consensual Analysis: A Clinically-Focused Discussion

JACOB A. ARLOW, M.D.

Except for times when the analyst is involved in some severe countertransference reaction or when he is deeply involved in some personal preoccupation, his inner response may be regarded as a commentary on the patient's productions. This response results from the patient's attempts to influence the analyst and the analytic situation in pursuit of transference gratification. Loewenstein (1957) used to emphasize that the therapist often feels what the patient wants him to feel. In effect, this is a form of repetition by way of the transference of events in the patient's history. He makes the analyst feel what he once made some important object feel.

The analyst's response is a form of inner communication, representing an emerging awareness of the meaning of the patient's productions. This awareness has been conceptualized intuitively, that is, outside of the realm of consciousness (Arlow, 1979). This occurs in every analysis. In striving to remain sensitive to the patient's productions, there is the danger that we may disregard awareness of our own inner states and their significance. The experienced analyst learns to be at ease with these intrusions and to appreciate how mood, intellectual ruminations and free associations may represent indicators or clues, derivative expressions of an emerging insight that could lead to interpretation. What Dr. Windholz has been doing in consensual analysis is to systematize and to articulate in a cognitive and definitive manner what most experienced analysts do automatically and intuitively. But every practicing analyst needs to submit the products of intuition to disciplined and cognitive examination, not necessarily during the treatment process, but certainly in preparing for presentation or publication of case material.

Dr. Skolnikoff's affective response to the patient in his case presentation was not a mistake or a technical error; it was part of the usual pattern of communication between two people, especially between analysand and analyst. In this context it was a predictable response to a request, unconsciously transmitted by the patient, for the analyst to play a particular role in a transference scenario of the patient's composition. How did the patient do this? First, he engaged in a monologue which made the analyst feel that he was being excluded from the patient's thinking. Second, he experienced the analyst's comments, neutral as they were, as intrusive. Third, he betrayed a remarkable sensitivity to every movement of the analyst, and interpreted the sounds of movement as if (in Dr. Skolnikoff's words) "I was going to reprimand him or hit him."

How did the therapist respond? Since his goal was to encourage the patient to verbalize his thoughts fully and freely, the therapist found himself trying to keep unusually still, and he tried to keep his voice gentle and his comments supportive. Perhaps feeling excluded and/or frustrated, the analyst found that he had to overcome a tendency to withdraw by making sure to take notes. Finally he devised what he called a "neutral intervention," which he described as follows: "This consisted of repeating the last two or three words of a phrase that [the patient] had just said concerning a subject that wasn't too highly charged. I felt this might permit him to continue to speak with reduced anxiety." In other words, the therapist created a set of conditions in which the patient could not conceivably interpret what the therapist was doing as a threat of being reprimanded or hit.

Patients are very sensitive to everything the analyst says and does. While we are busy observing them, they are just as busy observing us, although they may not comment on it. In another connection, I have noted that a patient's silence is a technique for evoking countertransference responses from the analyst, or is used, at least, as an opportunity for the patient to formulate some concept of how the analyst behaves under stress. At times, the technical stance that the analyst adopts constitutes a message transmitted to the patient. In this case, Dr. Skolnikoff's message seems clear enough. It can be translated approximately in the following terms. "I want to do everything possible to encourage you to speak as fully and freely as you can. I do not want to make you anxious. I want to help you. I assure you I will not scold you, hit you or intrude upon your autonomy."

Dr. Skolnikoff has demonstrated the dynamic effect of one patient's transference approach and how he overcame it, with the help of consensual analysis, through examining his own responses, affective and intellectual. I would like to offer, not an alternative but a complementary approach to the problem he described. In two articles, one written in collaboration with Beres (1974), I have discussed the role of the analyst's inner experience in arriving at interpretation and suggesting appropriate technical interventions. In the first part of the process, characterized as aesthetic, the analyst is free to use intuition, on the basis of a transient, empathic identification with the analysand. This involves organizing, outside the realm of consciousness, all that has been heard from the patients, as well as all that has been observed, into a meaningful hypothesis. The result of this intuitive process becomes available to the analyst by means of introspection. What occurs in the mind of the analyst is not necessarily the precise formulation of the interpretation, though sometimes this happens. But more often, the free association in the mind of the analyst is a guidepost, an indicator, something pointing in the direction toward the appropriate interpretation. It is a derivative formation.

Sometimes the aptness of the interpretation is immediately apparent, and confirmatory, validating evidence is at hand. At other times, especially in connection with transference phenomena, it becomes necessary to discipline the aesthetic, intuitive, empathic response by relating the hypothesis to the data of observation in a controlled, cognitive fashion. There are certain criteria we can use in pursuing this goal. (I have outlined them in previous communications and I will not repeat them here.) Particular attention should be paid, however, to those elements emerging in the analysis that represent outcroppings of unconscious fantasy, among which the metaphors used are most significant.

In keeping with the considerations outlined above, one could approach the data offered by Dr. Skolnikoff from another point of view. When the patient wants the analyst to play a role or imagines the analyst to be playing a certain role, he is not treating the analyst as his doctor, but as an object of some wishful drive stemming from an unconscious fantasy. This is what we mean by transference. When, by word and action, the analyst responds, not by analyzing but by reassurance, this is a form of countertransference. Whatever may make the patient anxious in such instances also has the power to make the analyst anxious, so that both institute defenses. The analyst's defenses, in my experience, are usually borrowed from or suggested by the patient's use of defenses. In this case, the patient felt that the analyst was being intrusive, potentially reprimanding and even threatening to beat him. The fear of being intruded upon, especially in a narcissistically vulnerable patient — we can understand. The idea of being reprimanded for what he is about to reveal — that we can appreciate. But to anticipate that the analyst might beat the patient — that goes beyond the bounds of rationally expected behavior.

The intrusion of this unrealistic, irrational element is clearly a transference phenomenon, since an adult male does not expect his doctor to beat him. Altering the technical stance, the analyst then transmitted a message to the patient through verbal and non-verbal communication clearly articulating the idea: "Be assured; I am not going to beat you." My own metaphoric appraisal of the situation is that the patient sounded as if he could not be comfortable unless he had the analyst in a straitjacket; and from the report of the inner response of the therapist, he, and I mean here the therapist, felt he was being confined, constrained and restricted, in order to control a tendency to respond angrily and aggressively.

As analysts, we are accustomed to hearing some of the most bizarre things the human mind can imagine. Weighed in the scale of our experience, a patient's idea that his analyst is going to beat him can get to seem commonplace. Nevertheless, cognitively examined, the idea is bizarre. I do not suggest that other aspects of the dynamics presented in Dr. Skolnikoff's case study are incorrect, but I do think that a cognitive appraisal of the idea of being hit by the analyst might have been helpful. Also, I do not wish to advance any specific theory to account for the patient's expressed fears, which could represent a masochistic beating fantasy, a passive submission to cover up hostility, or competitive attempts to seduce the therapist away from his professional stance. But I do want to underscore the importance of checking intuitively perceived interpretations against conclusions that can be validated, based on examining the patient's pattern of free associations. In some quarters, empathy is regarded as an instrument of direct perception, and interpretations drawn from such an experience are regarded as self-validating. This leads to what I consider to be a phenomenological error: assigning meaning directly to an isolated phenomenon taken out of the context of associations, the patient's past, and the evolution of the transference.

REFERENCES

Arlow, J. (1979), The genesis of interpretation. *Amer. Psychoanal. Assn.,* Suppl., 27:193–206.

Beres, D., & Arlow, J. (1974), Fantasy and identification in empathy. *Psychoanal. Quart.,* 43:26–50.

Loewenstein, R. M. (1957), Some thoughts on interpretation in the theory and practice of psychoanalysis. *The Psychoanalytic Study of the Child,* 12:127–150.

19

Comments on Consensual Analysis

GERALD ARONSON, M.D.

In analysis things happen. Also things change. What is the relationship between the things that happen and the things that change?

Windholz and his group address themselves to a particular dimension of this relationship: How do the things that happen to the analyst, and within him, change what happens in the analysis to bring about changes in the patient? The focus is not new but the method is.

Two large sets of data are gradually collected. One set includes the treating analyst's process notes; the other is a transcript of weekly verbalizations to the silent listening analyst. The process notes contain a record from which changes in the patient can be gleaned as well as things happening in the analysis; the verbal reports reveal some of what happens to and within the analyst. At the end of the analysis, cross-indexing between the two sets of data attempts to link the happenings in the analysis and changes in the analyst and in the patient. This is not simple, but can be immensely fertile: hypotheses are generated, checked, and changed; surprises are found; some old findings are reconfirmed, some discounted.

The theory of analytic technique states that changes in the patient, such as symptoms, attitudes, beliefs, character, defensive arrangements, deployment of instincts, and object-relations, take place when things happen in the analysis through interpretations, separations, fee transactions, and other developments. Different groups of analysts give different weight to mutative agents such as empathy and interpretation. The particular dimension studied by the

Windholz group has been, heretofore, eclipsed by the attention focused on more visible and audible mutative agents. In consensual analysis, three categories of information are examined: 1) the treating analyst's verbalizations to the listening analyst; 2) the analyst's report of his actions and interpretations during treatment sessions; and 3) the patient's actions, verbalizations, and other behavior, as reported by the treating analyst.

How can the process be made simpler, and how can the fertile results be pruned to the tolerable luxuriance of contained speculation?

THEMATIC ANALYSIS

The problem of data retrieval involving cross-indexing of the two sets of data can be simplified by a system of scoring called *Thematic Analysis,* pioneered and developed by the psychologist Ralph K. White. Its purpose is to characterize, qualitatively and quantitatively, the expressed attitudes of groups, political candidates, and government functionaries. This system could be easily adapted to scoring and hence characterizing both sets of protocols in consensual analysis. Relationships among variables could then be tested and established. For example, suppose that in the data containing the musings of the treating analyst to the listening analyst, a theme designated "agitated remorse" (AR) is discerned as either a clustered or isolated phenomenon. If, in the process notes, on dates closely following verbal reports of AR, signs of "changes in affect" (CA) in the analyst and/or the patient were found, and these are followed by insight or behavior change, then hypotheses could be formulated. How, for example, did agitated remorse in the analyst lead the analyst to frame certain interpretations, which then were correlated with certain behavioral changes in the patient?

This is tedious but not difficult. Reliability studies must be done, however, to insure that different raters agree on the nature and prevalence of the suggested categories. Once scored, computer runs could easily search out and establish correlations of whatever degree desired.

So far as has been reported, the search is still in the data-gathering stage, with some pilot efforts at data retrieval and cross-indexing. These efforts have generated and been guided by hypotheses which underscore the effects upon the patient of certain departures from neutrality on the part of the analyst.

What I am proposing is that a simple method of data reduction with high inter-rater reliability, such as Thematic Analysis, can be adapted to psychoanalytic material which would facilitate the processing of the data of consensual analysis. Concern about the presumed validity of a theme-label (e.g. agitated remorse) should take a back seat. We should be interested only that the assigned theme is reliably labeled, not examned for a possibly spurious validity. We could then ruthlessly follow the doctrine of the "indifference of the indicator" rather than attempting *a priori* to determine that the indicator (the labeled theme) is valid.

The first step in data reduction would be coding of the data, for example:

Musings data	Process data
1) Treating analyst's verbalizations coded as to theme.	2) Analyst's interpretations and actions coded as to theme.
	3) Patient's actions and verbalizations coded as to theme.

With the data thus coded, the investigators can now search for correlations, by hand or by computer, generate hypotheses based upon these correlations, refine the scoring system into subtypes of themes, and create new hypotheses for further search.

The Windholz research group offers an important bridge between a high, complex art and a simple, communicable science. But idiographic data, such as that gathered by consensual analysis, resists conversion into nomothetic principles. The observations — unique, unrepeatable, and gossamer — retain the irreducible characteristic of art that places us in the center of what Francis Bacon called "the multitude of particulars." What causes dismay is the possibility that consensual analysis, having generated the multitude, cannot extract us from it.

RULE BREAKING

Having discussed Thematic Analysis, I now turn to a second method of linking the three sets of coded data derived from the analyst's verbal reports and process notes. The data of the verbal reports and process notes are produced under similar rules, with two important, specific exceptions which have the status of contra-rules.

Rule #1 (the rule of physical absence) is that the process notes are produced by the treating analyst without the aid or presence of the listening analyst. Contra-rule #1 is that the verbal reports are produced by the treating analyst in the listener's silent presence, and only in his presence.

Rule #2 (the rule of restriction) is that the process notes are not to contain any reference to the therapist's feelings or thoughts. Contra-rule #2 is that the verbal reports are to be as free of restrictions as possible.

In the discussion of Thematic Analysis, the only criterion proposed to guide the choice of which segments of data were to be retrieved was change in the analytic process and content as reflected in either set of data. Would additional choice criteria be useful? Suggested, but not made quite explicit, in the papers of the Windholz group is the use of the rules of consensual analysis as a probe to select among the mounds of data. If the rules are clearly explicated beforehand and they prove possible to follow, then a break in either of the two rules or their contrapositives becomes a potent choice criterion.

Rule #1 — that the therapist produce process notes when not in the listener's presence — can theoretically be broken in two ways, only one of which is likely: the therapist could fail to produce process notes. Contra-rule #1 — that the therapist produce verbal reports in the listener's silent presence — could be broken in five ways: the therapist could be silent, the listener could talk, the therapist could be absent, the listener could be absent, the therapist could produce verbal reports to someone else, to himself, or to a recording machine in the listener's absence.

Rule #2 — the rule of restriction — can be broken in two ways: the process notes could be without detail, uninformative, or they could be shot through with the therapist's emotion. Contra-rule #2 — the rule of freedom — could be broken if the therapist is restrained, silent, rigid, or monotonous to conceal his emotions.

Perhaps there are other ways these two rules could be broken, and perhaps other rules could be fashioned which, if broken, would serve the purposes of data retrieval/reduction without interfering with the aims of the research.

Two probes have been suggested, Thematic Analysis and Rule Breaking, to select and compare the data generated at what one hopes will be critical junctures. The rule breaking criterion reminds one of Wittgenstein: "Whether a thing is a blunder or not — it is a blunder in a particular system. Just as something is a blunder in a particular game and not in another" (Kolakowski, 1982).

Where does consensual analysis belong along the axis that runs from pranks and tricks through innovation, craft, and technique to elaborated instrument? I would place it within the middle ground of this axis that ranges from innovation through craft to technique.

Innovation is a one-time nova, facile and fascinating, containing only infrequently the necessary ingredients for its development. Its progenitor is a genius or charlatan. Craft is an exercise of exceptionally gifted people; it can be taught only with difficulty, if at all, and is not usually linked with grander theoretical schemes of established validity. Fine furniture-making, alchemy, and baseball involve craft. Something composed of articulated sub-routines, which can be taught to the ordinarily gifted person, can be used repeatedly and reliably, and is linked to grander schemes of some validity, is a technique.

Consensual analysis is a way of proceeding by sequential sub-routines; it is linked to the grander instrument of psychoanalysis, and could probably be used by any pair of psychoanalysts. It is, then, a technique — an award of some distinction.

It is mind-boggling to reflect upon the fact that we have engaged in the psychoanalytic enterprise for almost a century without studying the full context of the psychoanalytic situation — without approaching in any systematic way what the analyst is thinking or feeling. It has become clear (Loewald, 1960) that only by seeing an impact on the analyst can the patient produce representations of his or her own actions. What is not clear at any one time is whether the analyst's awareness of this impact upon himself is useful, detrimental, or without effect upon his therapeutic utility.

To answer the question of how therapy works, we have to know in the greatest detail what impact the analyst experiences and how it serves or interferes with the analytic work. Consensual analysis starts boldly upon this path.

REFERENCES

Loewald, H. W. (1960), On the therapeutic action of psychoanalysis. *Internat. J. Psycho-Anal.*, 41:16–33.

Kolakowski, L. (1982), *Religion.* New York: Oxford University Press, p. 61.

20

Consensual Analysis: Current Findings and Future Implications

EMANUEL WINDHOLZ, M.D.

In analyzing a patient's narcissistic conflicts the analyst may experience severe frustrations, as illustrated by the clinical vignettes selected by Dr. Skolnikoff. His retrospective impression of having made numerous mistakes was based on his recognition that he had responded to the patient's manipulation and on his feeling that he had been "taken in" by the patient.

The consensual analysis, however, identified the unconscious meanings of these responses as appropriate attitudes at this stage of the analysis, which only indirectly restored the patient's narcissism. It also suggested that the analyst's ability to handle his own frustrations is of great importance. I concluded that the patient perceives the analyst's unconscious attitudes, and the influence of these attitudes on the analytic process is unmistakable.

In Dr. Skolnikoff's illustration, the patient first engaged in a monologue from which the analyst felt completely excluded. When the analyst understood that the patient was experiencing his comments as intrusions, he found a solution to his predicament: he repeated back to the patient the last two or three words he had spoken before falling silent. The analyst called this a "neutral intervention," and felt that it relieved the patient's anxiety. His attention was on the patient's fear of competition, on defeating a weak father in the transference.

The patient, however, viewed this interaction in an entirely different light: he experienced the analyst's comments as an intrusion that threatened the clarity of his thinking and his narcissism. When he expressed a fear that the analyst might hit or punish him for excluding the authority figure, the patient became aware of the irrational, magical power of his thoughts. He was actually struggling against becoming confused, rather than against the imagined threat of being hit. As the patient listened to the analyst repeating his phrases, he recognized that his words were, in fact, meaningful and clear. Thus, he felt calmer since he regained the ability to think clearly. This was not a dyadic interaction, since the analyst's echoing of his words was not experienced by the patient as an intrusion into his highly independent thinking. The analyst was, rather, performing an ego function for the patient by making his words sound intelligible. This was *not,* however, a restoration of a defect in the patient's ego. He had only momentarily lost the ability to think clearly, and was *not* gratified by the restoration of this function. It was the secondary effect, the recovery of his sense of autonomy, which provided the patient with narcissistic gratification — a recovery that was not directly influenced by the analyst's echoing technique.

The analyst was not aware of his real role while he was concentrating on making his echoing comments in a gentle voice which, he believed, was reassuring to the patient. He was unaware of the contradiction between the so-called neutrality of his comments and the indulgent quality of his voice — a contradiction which served to disguise the analyst's need to relieve and master his own frustration. Once he became aware of this self-deception, the analyst became angry with himself.

As the analysis progressed, the patient's sense of autonomy became invested in his ability to analyze himself. He was in a difficult financial situation. Since he was conducting his own analysis, he began to feel entitled to a reduction in the analytic fee. Struggling with the recollection that, as a child, he had been financially responsible for his parents, the patient became confused when he realized that he could not, in fact, have been the provider for his family. He perceived the analyst's repetitions of his transference interpretations as confirmation of the accuracy of his self-analysis, which made him feel comfortable. However, he could not ask the analyst directly for a fee reduction, but waited to have it offered to him.

The analyst began to feel helpless and confused — unable to explore the patient's conflict with his dependency needs — and he even refrained from repeating back the patient's words. Failing to evoke the confirmation he felt he needed, the patient became very depressed. However, he regained his composure quickly, and, with his usual detached, intellectual attitude, explored his so-called guilt feelings, blaming himself for proceeding with his own analysis. When the analyst did not comment on this guilt interpretation, a new explanation immediately came to the patient's mind: he should refrain from analyzing himself, not because of guilt, but because it made him feel grandiose to think

that, like Freud, he was conducting his own analysis. The intellectual understanding of his grandiosity protected him against confusion.

The patient remained detached throughout the following session. He made
critical reference to his self-analysis and even considered that his depression
might be his way of manipulating the analyst. The analyst remained silent until close to the end of the session when he finally formulated an interpretation.
The effect was spectacular: the patient cried for ten minutes. It was the first
breakthrough in the analysis, and the analyst felt gratified since he believed
that his interpretation had been effective.

However, the study of the data revealed that the analyst told the patient that
he was quoting him in arriving at this interpretation: "I stated that he seems to
have felt depressed since *he discussed* (italics added) his disappointment in not
being able to ask his father for anything and his feelings that he couldn't ask
anyone for anything, including me regarding some arrangements about the
fee" (Appendix B, page 282). The analyst called this a "tripartite interpretation." It provided the validity of the patient's insight. By centering his attention on the accuracy of the patient's self-analysis, the analyst was enabled to
overcome his own helplessness. By stressing the importance of the self-
analysis, the interpretation conveyed to the patient its "reality," and the patient
perceived it as such. He was able to regain his sense of reality, and, in turn, his
autonomy. The analyst had performed a function that the patient had lost
temporarily. As the patient regained the ability to analyze himself, he knew
that it was not grandiose — it was *real*.

The analyst was not aware of the process that led him to acquire the patient's
helplessness and resolve it as if it were his own. While the analyst listened to
the patient's analysis of his crying during the next session he became aware of
this process as he experienced having been "manipulated" by the patient into
feeling effective. The analyst's empathic response, as well as its important and
useful effect, remained unconscious.

Intuition and empathy are concepts which help our understanding of the analyst's role in a psychoanalysis. This is impressively conveyed by Beres and
Arlow (1974): "Somewhere in the course of the introspective activity which the
analyst exercises he becomes aware of the end product of a highly complicated
process which has been going on outside of the scope of consciousness." Regarding the role of the analyst, they point out: "Documentation has to be *self-
revealing*, especially about the *personal response* of the therapist to the patient's
productions. Few have the *courage* to expose for public scrutiny the record of our
inner processes . . . Only consistent self-observation can illuminate the vicissitudes of empathy." (italics added)

The analyst functions best when listening to the patient with free-floating attention. Consistent self-observation could interfere with his introspective activity. My colleagues who participated in this research had the courage to ex-

pose their personal responses. Self-observation and introspective activity were revived and even heightened in the presence of the silent listener. The analyst's concern about his emotional involvement was an inducement to subject his responses, including his empathy, to careful scrutiny.

We identified at least two vicissitudes of empathy. One, referred to by Beres and Arlow, concerns the patient's conflicts, the uncovering of unconscious fantasies leading to intuitive understanding. The other is the influence of empathy, the discovery that it influences the analyst's behavior. The analyst in this case had not been aware of the role of empathy, and once he recognized it, he felt "manipulated" by the patient. This discovery was a surprise, as was the recognition of its importance for the restoration of the patient's sense of reality. We became aware that the patient was struggling with an intrasystemic conflict that threatened his ability to cooperate with the analyst.

The analytic situation frequently threatens the regulatory functions of the patient's ego (Weiss, 1972), which can lead to a disruption of the working alliance. Silber (1973) pointed out that "ego synthesis . . . is an extremely complex process," the patient's vulnerability being due to his "narcissistic involvement with images and ideas of his own mind." The consensual analysis revealed more fully the analyst's role in reestablishing ego-synthesis. For example, the patient treated by Skolnikoff suffered from a state of confusion due to grandiose images, such as his feeling like Freud. Skolnikoff unconsciously conveyed to the patient that he himself needed the patient's self-analysis. In response, the patient accepted his own interpretations as valid and real, dispelling his confusion.

The sudden intrusion of an incestuous image (Appendix C) was experienced by an hysterical patient treated by another analyst as an acute traumatic state. Her only protection was to forget the analyst's impending vacation, which had evoked an incestuous image. Such repressions occur frequently in the course of an analysis. The analyst's interpretation (Appendix C) of the repressed content conveyed to the patient his need to deny his countertransference. In response, the patient was able to deny her transference, which strengthened her ego and reestablished the working alliance. Her sense of "safety" (see below) had been restored.

Sandler (1976) paid special attention to the patient's sense of "safety" as a condition for maintaining the patient's ability to tolerate the analytic situation. He characterized the analyst's role in helping the patient as an "actualization," a response to the patient's "evocative" behavior. Both terms accurately describe the role which we ascribed to the analyst in this research. The term "evocative" is appropriate, because the patient is not conscious of his intention and does not deliberately "manipulate" the analyst. One of the implications of Sandler's term "actualization" is the fact that the analyst's response is *real,* and the patient perceives how the analyst functions. This is necessary in order to convey to the patient how to reestablish his, the patient's, lost sense of reality.

In another paper on object-relations Sandler (1974) theorized about conflicts within the ego, an intrasystemic conflict which was also identified in our studies.

The need for documented data, stressed by Beres and Arlow (1974), has preoccupied many analysts involved in research on psychoanalytic therapy. Wallerstein and Gill, for example (Weiss, 1972), have expressed a similar view. Wallerstein called for "the basic observation, not ordinarily public," that is, they are available only to the treating analyst. Gill referred to the difficulties in obtaining such data when he described them as "the subtleties of the analyst's attempt to *understand his own role*" (italics added).

Luborsky (1978) pointed out that "the full content of an utterance, including at least both the therapist and the patient's surrounding intentions, is necessary for the conduct of research on psychoanalytic theory." He recognized that it is not just a question of receiving *more* data from the analyst, stating that "changes in *method* must of necessity precede changes in content. (italics added)

We believe that, in the conduct of the consensual analysis, we used a method referred to by Luborsky, which provides the data needed for research on psychoanalytic therapy.

I reached an agreement with both treating analysts involved about their roles in the two cases under study. The immediate goal, consensual validation of the data, has been achieved, and we expect that independent judges will confirm our conclusions.

REFERENCES

Beres, D., & Arlow, J. (1974), Fantasy and identification in empathy. *Psychoanal. Quart.*, 43:26–50.

Luborsky, L., & Spence, D. (1978), Quantitative research on psychoanalytic therapy. *Handbook of Psychotherapy and Behavior Change.* New York: John Wiley & Sons, p. 359.

Sandler, J. (1974), Psychological conflict and the structural model: Some clinical and theoretical implications. *Internat. J. Psycho-Anal.*, 55:53–62.

―――― (1976), Countertransference and role-responsiveness. *Internat. Rev. Psycho-Anal.*, 3:43–48.

Silber, A. (1973), Secondary revision, secondary elaboration and ego synthesis. *Internat. J. Psycho-Anal.*, 54:161–168.

Van der Leeuw, J. P. (1979), Some additional remarks on problems of transference. *J. Amer. Psychoanal. Assn.*, Supplement, 27:315–326.

Weiss, J. (1972), Continuing research: The modification of defenses in psychoanalysis. *J. Amer. Psychoanal. Assn.*, 20:177–198.

21

The Experience of the Treating Analyst in the Consensual Analysis

NORMAN L. MAGES, M.D.

By describing how I found myself forgetting and then rediscovering the method of consensual analysis, I will attempt to shed some light on the process and on the motivation of the treating analyst who participates. When I began meeting weekly with Dr. Windholz, he asked me to talk about whatever thoughts and feelings I had about the analytic sessions of the previous week. He also suggested that I not make any preparations or organize my ideas in advance since he had already read my process notes. Despite these instructions, I initially approached the consensual analysis much as I had approached analytic supervision in the past, staying close to the process material, trying to reconstruct it in an orderly and sequential fashion, and drawing logical conclusions from the content of the analytic sessions. Dr. Windholz was surprised when I ignored his instructions, but he concealed his reaction, did not interfere with my reporting, and waited to see what would happen.

After proceeding this way for a few meetings, I found myself feeling increasingly frustrated and dissatisfied, and one morning I said to Dr. Windholz: "I thought I would like to try to do it just a little differently, a little more freely this time. I would like to talk today without any reference necessarily to the material. If it comes up as an association, fine. If not, I won't refer to it directly. But is it all right?" A little later I said, "The word that comes to mind is 'luxury.' It's the luxury of being able to say, 'Here's what I think about the patient right now.'"

At the time of this verbal report there was a particular issue with which I was struggling, a troubling emotional response to a patient that I wanted to share with Dr. Windholz. But I found it strange to associate freely and I said: "I rambled a little bit more. I don't know how relevant this is to the project in contrast to my own psychology, but I do feel almost apologetic about rambling along this way. What could this possibly have to do with what is really going on with the patient? Maybe it has much more to do with my own private fantasies and reactions. What must our secretary be thinking as she types all this nonsense?"

Over two years later, Dr. Windholz and I looked back on this meeting and tried to understand more about the need which prompted me to talk more freely at this point. I commented: "Coming in here and talking about the previous week's analytic sessions was often not a particularly pleasant experience. A lot of times I would have no idea of what I wanted to talk about or even remember what went on. I would think to myself, 'This is a lot of work and I'm busy and tired and don't want to do this.' But then I would get here and start to talk and I would feel, 'Well as long as I'm here, what I want to do is just to let go and see what comes out. If I try to remember and reconstruct process notes for a whole week I'll drive myself crazy, and I won't get anything out of it.' But there was the feeling initially that it wasn't all right to just sit and talk, that it should be anchored to what's in the process notes. It should be logical and take into account what one has studied about the analytic process. After all, this is a research study."

As we discussed these issues further, Dr. Windholz asked me to reflect back on my own experiences in the consensual analysis, and try to capture what was different about working in this new, freer way. Here I quote again from a retrospective discussion:

"There is a different mode of thinking and a different way of organizing the material. It's partly a matter of letting things fall into place. It seems all right to be playful, to play with the thoughts and ideas, but the connections do not have to be logical or go in a straight line. In general, it seemed that some sort of logical critical faculty was relaxed in giving the verbal report. That was the key to it, plus the fact that emotional reactions are welcomed as clues or guides, whereas it seemed to me that in writing process notes or giving the usual account of a case, one omits many of one's emotional reactions. And, in fact, when I looked back over the verbal reports I was struck that so much was organized around my own emotional reactions.

"Another thing is that you come up with whatever occurs to your mind. Things stand out without your having to be concerned about their relevance. So I may find myself focusing on a detail or on some seeming irrelevancy or on a non-verbal part of the interaction. Also, in the verbal report I can move around and connect things without regard to temporal sequence, so that I might put together things that happened concurrently or things that are widely separated in time. The effect is a little like focusing and refocusing a camera.

Something that has been blurred may become clear as you change the focus, or the foreground and background may shift according to what's in focus. And then it seems that things tend to crystallize around some particular impression or thought that seems emotionally stirring. At times, there would be a period of confusion or ambiguity in the struggle to understand things, but when they did fall into place the picture usually seemed to come out quite clear and simple. It's like suddenly everything comes clearly into focus."

In carrying out the consensual analysis I also became aware of another interesting aspect of the procedure. Even though Dr. Windholz hardly said a word during the entire time I was conducting the patient's analysis, his presence during the verbal reports was very important. I realized that I had an urge to communicate my analytic experiences to Dr. Windholz, the silent listener. I found myself looking for small cues, such as note taking, which might indicate his interest and involvement. My search for the silent listener's approval led me at times to construct imaginary conversations in which I pictured him evaluating and judging my presentations. On a few occasions when we couldn't meet, I tried dictating my solitary thoughts and associations, but the process then seemed relatively worthless, without tension or real interest, and I found such exercises to be sterile.

Of course, the kinds of thoughts and emotional responses which came up in the verbal reports are familiar to analysts and regularly occur in all analyses both during and between the analytic sessions. But they often occur silently and out of awareness. The consensual analysis helps make these hidden processes more explicit and visible so that they can be examined in all their richness.

22

Consensual Analysis: Its Research Character and Implications

DONALD P. CLIGGETT, Ph.D.

Judging from the data it provides, consensual analysis may bring us closer than any other method yet devised to examining the context of conscious, pre-conscious, and unconscious associations of the treating analyst and to understanding the non-verbal meaning of the therapist's reactions in the course of interaction with the patient during a psychoanalysis. In this brief review, I will attempt to examine consensual analysis as a research method, review some of its findings, and discuss implications for further research.

To describe this method as a research procedure, it would be helpful first to specify what it is *not*. It is not a study of the stages or sequence of interactions in the analytic process as a whole. Thus, it is not a study of process in the broad sense of that term. Nor is it an outcome study or an attempt to validate the effectiveness of analysis or any of its specific modes of intervention or part-processes as a method of treatment. It is not a study of either transference or countertransference in the sense in which those terms are commonly used, namely as reactions based on neurotic elements in patient or analyst. And since supervision in any sense is not part of the consensual analysis process, it is not an examination of the role of supervision in analytic work.

Consensual analysis *is* the study of the treating analyst's role as reflected in the non-verbal meaning of verbal and non-verbal reactions to the patient during an analysis. This is revealed through study and comparison of two forms of data: the process notes written by the treating analyst following the analytic hours of a given week and provided to a listening analyst at the end of that week; and the matrix of free associations and emotional reactions which the treating analyst spontaneously offers verbally in a meeting with the silent listening analyst at the beginning of the following week. This verbal report is a free-associative "scanning" by the treating analyst of thoughts, recollections, and reactions to those sessions. An intensive study of the verbal report by the listening analyst and a comparison of it with the process notes often reveals distinctive characteristics and discrepancies which have been identified and described in detail by Windholz.

As a research method, consensual analysis is a naturalistic clinical method which has the advantage of closeness to the data, in common with the individual case–study method without some of its drawbacks. Because the study is conducted not by the treating analyst but by the listening analyst, there is the built-in safeguard against possible subjectivity and over-identification. It has the immediacy of the case–study method and built-in checks against selective, possibly distorted reconstruction of the case by the treating analyst alone, who often does a case study years after the treatment process occurred. The most noteworthy feature of consensual analysis as a research method is its capacity to develop new data about the analyst's role. It is the quality of that data and the new insights and research hypotheses generated which will determine the ultimate value of the method.

Among the hypotheses suggested by the data which may prompt future study are some which may require long-term longitudinal research, as well as some which raise both process and outcome questions as well. For example, the data indicate that clues to non-verbal transactions which appear in the verbal reports seem to cluster in concentrated form at what we believe to be important change-points in the analysis. Systematic study may confirm the presence of such clustering, identify the particularly important non-verbal transactions occurring at those points, and delineate and dynamically explain those changes. We believe such an event took place in the particular week of analysis described in Dr. Skolnikoff's case study, and that in subsequent sessions there was a striking change in the transference and in the patient's entire style of communicating with the analyst.

The data also suggest that the non-verbal meaning of a "good interpretation" may, at times, be much more significant than the manifest content of the interpretation itself. It might, therefore, be revealing to examine through the method of consensual analysis those sessions in which interpretations are made which are perceived by the analyst as particularly effective. This may permit investigators to ascertain whether the method reveals any of the clues to important unconscious reactions on the part of the analyst which may identify the non-verbal meaning of a reported "good interpretation."

Another observation derived from the data that invites further study is the way in which the analyst's narcissism is subject to sometimes dramatic fluctuations, as reflected in his self-image as an analyst. These fluctuations may also serve as a "flag" that indicates important unconscious and non-verbal reactions of the analyst. They appear to be evoked in response to particular behavior of the patient that creates in the analyst widely varying feelings — that he is very effective or totally useless as the object of his patient's manipulation and quite unanalytic in his responses. In the verbal report of the week discussed in Dr. Skolnikoff's case study the analyst felt, at one point, quite pleased with his "tripartite interpretation," which he felt led to an important "breakthrough" signalled by the patient's crying for ten minutes. Later in the same verbal report, he felt that he had been manipulated by the patient and that this was not analysis because it was all "too shallow."

Yet, it was during this analytic week that the patient succeeded in evoking a verbal reaction from the analyst that had great non-verbal significance for the patient. Its impact in the analysis brought about a major change in the patient's relationship to the analyst. He was no longer intolerant of the analyst's intervention and no longer needed to listen only to the sound of the analyst's voice when he spoke. He was not only able to hear what the analyst said but actively sought out the analyst's ideas, and, at times, seemed to engage in a dialogue with the therapist.

Although this change can be identified in the process notes, it is only the verbal report of the consensual analysis that provides access to the fluctuations in the analyst's narcissism and the non-verbal meaning of his response to the patient which appeared to bring about change. The analyst's struggle to restore his own wavering self-esteem — a struggle induced by the patient's evocative ongoing production of feelings of frustration in the analyst — was resolved when he offered his tri-partite interpretation of which he was so proud. The patient responded with renewed confidence in his own capacity for independent thinking and recovered his pride in feeling autonomous. The analyst later felt that he had been manipulated by the patient and that, as a therapist, he was accomplishing nothing. These dramatic fluctuations in the analyst's self-esteem may, indeed, warrant further research into their value as clues, not only to important unconscious non-verbal interactions, but perhaps to major change-points in the analysis as well.

The analyst's struggle to clarify his own confusion about the patient is also revealed in his verbal report during the consensual analysis. As described by Windholz, in this struggle the treating analyst often makes intuitive observations, or offers fragmentary formulations or micro-theories about the patient's dynamics to help explain those transactions that produced the struggle. And there is often virtually no evidence of these dynamics in the process notes. For example, in the segment of the analysis described in the verbal report, the treating analyst proposes the idea of the "special child." This idea emerges with no knowledge on his part that it explains the non-verbal meaning of his intervention with the patient that week when the patient subsequently cried for ten minutes. The analyst's restating the patient's own self-interpretation to him unconsciously acknowledged and confirmed the patient's specialness in the analyst's eyes.

In the same verbal report the analyst refers to the patient's discussion of a visit to his parents and his feeling of dejection over his ineffectiveness as a "therapist" in his parents' dispute. The analyst says: "There is another thing about his being in analysis that struck me.... His not being able to treat his parents that summer...." Then, after some confusion, the analyst continues: "He despairs that I will be of help to him, and in addition wonders if he can help me and serve my needs." Many months later the patient consciously and explicitly talks of having felt earlier in the analysis that the analyst needed his help and that he, the patient, had to help the analyst by offering the "helpless" analyst his own, the patient's, self-analysis. The therapist's intuitive observation that the patient felt he had to help the analyst is confirmed when conscious material emerges much later in the analysis. This is an example of the relevance of sequential studies suggested by Windholz.

Consensual analysis allows the communication of such micro-theories and intuitive formulations, and provides the data by which they can be confirmed. Further research might examine the timing of the emergence of such formulations and the consistency and validity of the explanations they provide, both for more specific non-verbal interactions and for broader dynamic perspectives.

Another conclusion drawn from the data, which may be theoretically quite provocative, suggests that the significant non-verbal reactions of the analyst in response to the evocative non-verbal behavior of the patient are not only unconscious, but must occur without the awareness of the analyst in order to be effective. They cannot be taught or learned; and they are not countertransferences that need to be brought under conscious control in order to be avoided or corrected. The fact that these reactions are evoked by the patient and are not compatible with analytic technique indicates that they would not be acceptable consciously to the therapist. Yet they are essential to the process, since they bring about significant changes.

It is a common observation that given any sample of analytic data, no two experts can agree on the meaning. The data of this study suggests an explanation of that observation which might also be the basis for subsequent research. In our study group, a group of analysts who meet regularly with Dr. Windholz and me, the group reviews data much like that described above. We found that reading of the process notes produced almost as many interpretations of the data as there were members in the group. With subsequent review of the verbal reports, there gradually emerged considerable agreement about the non-verbal expressions of the patient's central conflict over his fear of dependency. The earlier varied interpretations were then perceived as equally valid dynamics, which had played a role of varied prominence at different points of the analysis.

One might hypothesize that there may be a constellation of dynamics, which appear in a hierarchical arrangement that changes with other transactions in the analysis. In any given period of analysis, therefore, one such dynamic may supersede or override the significance of the others, which, nonetheless, are present in those same sessions. And the transactions in the analysis during that period may be governed mainly by that primary dynamic, though the others are operating concurrently. Consensual analysis can provide the data which may test that hypothesis and help to explain the shifting nature of the dynamics hierarchy.

One last note of research interest arising out of this project concerns the psychological tests of the patient discussed in this review that were done both before and at the termination of analysis. The non-verbal interactions during treatment revealed in the consensual analysis may provide the basis for a retrospective study of the test data to explore the possibility that the characteristics of these interactions could be identified in the test data itself, which would prove to be diagnostically or prognostically valuable with other cases. The initial testing quite accurately identified the patient's fear of dependency, his need to reverse roles and help others instead of being helped, as well as other significant conflicts, including strong unconscious homosexual impulses. It also revealed the patient's obsessive intellectualizing and narcissistic features. However, the tests failed to identify his intellectualizing as a major defense against dependency, although he was as proficient during the Rorschach, for example, at helping the examiner by reporting his introspective processes as his responses emerged, as he was in analyzing himself for the analyst. Further study of the test data may suggest ways of identifying the dynamic meaning of this ego-stance of a patient toward his own thoughts and toward the examiner.

Later in the analysis the patient's homosexual conflict was confirmed when it emerged in a transference dream. Also, information about the father emerged, and there were indirect references by the patient to unconscious homosexual fears when he recalled sitting in a particularly awkward position with his father in silent religious rituals. One of the patient's Rorschach responses was an image of such practitioners, complete with religious trappings, in titillating, enticing positions. Rorschach experts have repeatedly and justifiably cautioned against the hazards of content analysis of Rorschach responses. Yet, the data from this case suggest that a closer examination of analytic and test data might provide guidelines on when Rorschach content-analysis can be not only valid but especially illuminating.

This has been a discussion of consensual analysis, the research features of this method that generate unique data, some of the characteristics of that data, and research questions that emerge. Our study group is continuing to review and trying more fully to identify and characterize the data generated by consensual analysis, and will, perhaps, eventually explore some of the additional research questions discussed in this paper.

Appendix A –
Consensual Analysis:
Verbal Report

ALAN Z. SKOLNIKOFF, M.D.

Sessions 35 through 38 – 7 February 1977

This week I thought there was quite a bit of a breakthrough in terms of the kinds of material that he was describing. There is something that was forced on my part; for example, I felt myself getting annoyed in the Wednesday hour when he started talking about material concerning this last summer and the whole incident with his parents. I felt myself responding in a kind of frustrated annoyance in how unclear he was about what he was describing, which prompted my way of proceeding with him. I would think that if I was somewhat more patient, or if I had even waited a little longer for him to get around to telling me about this event (but I notice I'm talking differently about this now than I have in the past); I actually felt annoyed. I don't know anything of what happened, and here he says he's embarrassed; and yet what he's telling me has no meaning to me whatsoever. I couldn't get the essence of what actually had gone on, so I found myself frustrated. It was all very delicate and gentle in terms of the way in comes out, in terms of my questions.

I said something to the effect that he was talking about this material, and yet he wasn't clear enough for me to understand what he was describing. I spoke about my difficulty in understanding what he was describing, namely, the visit back to his parents last summer, in June or July. As I was listening, it occurred to me he wasn't stating it clearly, so I asked him further questions. He then shifted to describing things quite intellectually for a time, as if he was in control again.

Prior to my actually saying that I was unclear, could he tell me what really happened, he was very tense and emotional; in fact, there were a few tears. But subsequent to that, he gave me this very chronological account, which was quite controlled. Then I made some other intervention, I had forgotten what it was, but it was again a comment on the process, where I again commented something about this trend — that he must have felt quite upset that he's forgotten some of the things he had talked about, and maybe had forgotten what happened. At that point, when I said he must have been quite upset that he's forgotten some of these things, he again began crying and he was quite upset. Indeed, in this whole account he really seemed quite dramatic — the account of his visit back to his parents and the fact that his mother was very depressed. They were talking about divorce; that his mother had hypertension; but what was even more dramatic was his feeling as if he had to save his parents, and then his tremendous disappointment in himself as the savior son (that's my expression for the way he sounds), the kind of role he intended to play, namely, he was coming there and he felt as if it was a terrible crisis.

There were two things and he stated them clearly: one is that he could ignore what was going on or just presume it wasn't his place as the son, a member of the family, to help his mother and father with the difficulties they were facing in separating; rather, he should take a distant role and just act appropriately as if he were the son rather than a psychologist. He felt a tremendous responsibility that if he wouldn't do it, it wouldn't get done, and that these things will get much worse for both of them. Then his disappointment was that it didn't work, or the extent of the regression on the part of his mother, in terms of his pleading or his trying to get his mother to express some of her feelings, to the extent to which she regressed, and described a great number of hysterical symptoms that she had — of being up all night, her screaming and her complaining terribly about missing her brother who had died a few years before (this was the uncle he had referred to earlier), somebody he had been very fond of, and the mother's father who died, and her being very sad and very lonely, and her feeling like nothing unless she was attached to someone like the father who gave her life meaning. All of this really frightened him. He felt terribly frightened and indeed he seemed to treat all of this, as he described it, as if it were a bad dream. Now I am even more impressed with the quality of it being a bad dream in terms of previous things that he said, in previous hours when this subject has come up; so, in terms of the chronology of my understanding of this period with his parents last summer, he mentioned something about his having visited his parents, and about his mother having seen a psychiatrist, or his suggesting to his mother that she should see a psychiatrist, and she was seeing a psychiatrist. At that time, when I heard this, I thought he will certainly tell me something more about this, but he didn't. I felt frustrated, as if this was a little piece of information which I would have to kind of put aside and he wouldn't tell me anything more about it.

I think at that time I must have expressed some frustration in a very mild way. I was feeling frustrated but my intervention was: "Your mother was seeing a psychiatrist?"—something to that effect. Or it may have gone: "Your mother was seeing a psychiatrist? I hadn't heard you mention this before." The mother was seeing a psychiatrist. Then he made it very rational as if his poor little mommie was feeling a little older and a little bit removed from society, and that she needed to see a psychiatrist so as not to feel so lonely. He put it in the mildest of terms, in terms of her going to see a psychiatrist and that she was continuing to see a psychiatrist who was very helpful, and all of that was just fine.

When that occurred (the mother seeing a psychiatrist), I thought there must be more to this. I am wondering when he is going to discuss this. But the material that occurred this past Wednesday, probably Session 37, was so much more of an earthquake, as compared with anything that I had known about before. I was indeed surprised. When I think of the way of its developing, the material about the sexual thing with his wife, as something that's going to be a big eruption in the future. That is to say, some fantasy that he's having about sex with his wife strikes me as being something that he's very reluctant to go into. Every time he describes things in relationship to his wife, whether he was kissing her or feeling safe about kissing her, or wanting sex and her refusing him—every time this comes up he gets embarrassed and he rationalizes and quickly has to go on to something which he can discuss much more reasonably and rationally and in an intellectual way. So I suspect there is going to be similar material in terms of the tremendous emotional charge and the overwhelmed feeling that he connects with it.

Now how did all of this material come up at this time? It seems to come up very clearly around the fee arrangement. The week started off with his forgetting the psychologist's name and his having remembered it. He followed it up from the previous week and in an intellectual way he recognized that he had forgotten the psychologist's name. I made a comment that he didn't want to remember the psychologist's name because he still hadn't seen the psychologist's report, and that he had mixed feelings about this which he couldn't acknowledge—his not seeing it and not being able to directly ask for it. This then led him to nicely speculate at the beginning of the Monday hour that he had remembered it, and he remembers something about a skier in Austria. It sounded very much like the kind of free association that one would read out of Freud's *The Psychopathology of Everyday Life.* It was very well reasoned, very thoughtful how he had come to remember the psychologist's name. It seemed to have the same kind of confidence in it, as if he was writing his own paper on how wonderful his own free associations were. But that led, somehow, to our reexploring the issue about his being unable to ask me about fee arrangements. He was telling me that he wouldn't ask me for any money, he wouldn't ask for any postponement of payment. My saying that he wouldn't ask for any money is an emotion stating something as I would imagine he was feeling it, namely, I would feel humiliated asking for any arrangement, or even considering any arrangement, about asking to postpone payment, although this is what he mentioned, sitting up, before he started the analysis.

This is connected with two other issues: one is the eventual changing of some hours that he might have to do which he is thinking about. He doesn't even know that he will have to do it, but he presumes that when he starts with his new program, the psychology program, he will be having to ask for different hours. The second issue is that he assumes I'll be taking some vacation and he hasn't heard yet when the vacation is; but he knows I'll tell him about it at the appropriate time, and he sees no need to ask, because he trusts me and assumes that I'll tell him in due time.

He then phrases this question in a way so that if I were to answer it, this would be an interference with his autonomy. In fact, this came up the previous week in that material, that if I were to offer, for example, to tell him that he can postpone paying me he would have to say, "I prefer not;" or he would feel like I was interfering. The intervention that I made then was, how would he feel if I would respond to this question of his or these comments that he's making about a fee postponement? He said he felt I had already responded too much to this. I pursued this issue of his being unable to ask me. I kept referring back to his feeling that he would be unable to ask me directly for any fee arrangements. This led to quite a few associations of his never being able to ask his father for anything and his tremendous disappointment that he creates in his father on the previous vacation when he went out to see him. The other connection had to do with money, not being able to ask the father for any money.

He referred to the money that he was giving me as a tremendous amount of money spent on him, and I merely repeated the phrase: "You say the tremendous amount of money to be spent on you?" He then quickly jumped to the issue of his working when he was in high school, or even before high school, and all the jobs that he had throughout his adolescence, and all of this money went into a pool. It never was his money; it never belonged to him; but it was money that went into the family pool, and his needs were met by someone deciding that the money should be spent on such-and-such and such-and-such. He quickly got away from the thought that possibly he had earned more than was spent on him, or that he had earned disproportionate amounts and that he didn't receive as much in kind, by saying, "I'm sure that a great deal more was spent on me than I earned."

It was clear, from his mentioning that this is a great deal of money to be spent on the year which concerned the analysis, that from this slip he felt he wasn't clear or that he had been unclear about the fact that he was spending the money, or that he was going to be the one who was earning the money and he was spending it on himself. He wished that someone else would take care of the money for him, but not being able to acknowledge it directly that he in any way deserved it.

This whole issue of his autonomy in terms of taking care of himself versus his tremendous dependency wishes always comes up in a rather acute way, and it comes up along these lines (Appendix D). He's the "special child." The mother, in her regressed state this past summer, told his sister who is very angry at the patient for his being "the special child" — the mother said, "I put everything I had into the patient." She said this to the sister in the sister's presence. They were, according to the patient, in an encounter-group situation, and the sister became furious hearing this. But it's clear with relationship to me, as it's emerging, that the special child has two meanings: One is that he will be extremely independent and that I'll be very gratified by viewing his accomplishments in terms of his capacity to analyze. The second is that, somehow, by his excellent performance, that I will do things for him, because he's such a deserving person; and he expresses this in a tenuous form. That is to say, that I would offer him, in a kind of very pure way (I wouldn't force him into it), I would say something to the effect there is no need for you to pay this now, and that somehow, by saying it in such a way that didn't require his discussing it or acting on it in any way, that he could then accept it. I'm elaborating on something that he hasn't said. I'm still elaborating on my understanding of it. So being special would be his being completely independent on the one hand; then, on the other hand, whatever I would dispense as a special favor to him would come as a result of his extraordinary capacity, his extraordinary specialness, but he would still be fed in this kind of perfect way.

There was, in one of these hours, his dehumanizing people, or dehumanizing me and himself; and it had to do with his rumination that he had about diagnosis; he started off on that. He's an obsessive-compulsive with narcissistic features; he's this, that, or the other thing; he can't decide what he is. But he finally went off into it in a not very intellectual way, and this proved to be less intellectual. He went off into his feeling very uneasy about competing with people directly. That is to say, when he would think about sports he would think about just competing with imaginary people, that he wasn't really competing with a natural human being, but just competing with another team, but not any one particular person. The imagery, though that would intrude in this kind of thinking, would be that these other people smelled so that they must be real, so they are real people that you're fighting with. A particular example was a boy he knew. I guess this was in high school. The boy didn't have a hand; he was born without a hand, and all he had was a stub. He felt a great deal of pity and kind of sympathy for this boy. Then, on one occasion, this particular boy punched him with the stub of his hand in the stomach, and after that he no longer felt this kind of pity for him but, actually, a great deal of anger. The way he seemed to elaborate this was that you could feel removed and be very idealistic about the way you felt about people in the abstract, but that, on occasion, the strength of your anger would make you respond in a very uncontrolled way, which could be upsetting.

There was other material that is a little disturbing. When I say disturbing I mean diagnostically. I think I was sort of ruminating about this myself with some of my patients, including this one. Is he an obsessive-compulsive with a really neurotic problem, or are we dealing primarily with narcissistic features? So I have my corresponding obsessional rumination that corresponds with his, despite the fact that I have the psychological reports. This had to do with the material about his sister, and very clear memories of incestuous feelings he has had about his sister. I thought he implied that he continues to have them. Again, this has to do with a dream in which his sister, who is blonde, appears and is not his sister. He had a dream that he sees a blonde who comes into the room and he wants to "make it" with the blonde, but his wife is looking on. His immediate association is to his sister, whose name is Jane. He then mentions something which I'm not sure that he hasn't mentioned before. It seems he may have mentioned it in passing, of a time when his parents went out to a dance (he must have been in high school), during which he tried to play around with his sister, tried to get her to do something to him, but he didn't specify what that was. In the past he's talked about an episode when he was only about eleven or twelve, in which he tried to get her to take his penis in her mouth. He then tried to have some sexual play with her. The outcome of that is not clear. He says he's always had incestuous impulses about his sister and he still does, and they disturb him.

In order to kind of complete my understanding about it, he said, despite the fact that on most occasions he is extraordinarily clear about what he's talking about, there are times that I am aware of not really following what he is saying, and this is one area. I had the distinct impression he was saying he had these incestuous feelings towards his sister and he still has them; yet at the time he was saying that, I was saying to myself, "Am I imagining this? Is he saying he still has incestuous feelings towards his sister now? Or is he saying this is something he's had in the past?" Also, I'm not clear whether this is a kind of isolation of his affect, his anxiety about having these incestuous impulses, or whether he himself is really quite confused about whether he is doing an analysis and he thinks, "that is what I'm supposed to talk about." Of course, it could be both, and he could be using the analytic situation as a way of isolating some of the affect from his intellectual perceptions of what the analytic situation should be.

There is more about my reactions to him that are a little different this week. It's in the Tuesday hour, the hour that is very revealing about his family, in which the idea was, after discussing the fee and the money being spent, there came up various issues about what he would be saying and what I would be saying—who would say what first and how the analysis would be conducted. It's clear, on the one hand, he had this notion that he would completely analyze himself in an independent way, and that, as he's doing it alone in this way, he perceives himself as being a small boy who is off on some sort of tangent, and that he needs some reassurance from some ideal figure who says, "You are doing well, just keep going," or to hear my voice in order to kind of check out that he really is doing a good job. He himself has said this in some earlier hours. He also said he doesn't know if he's really listening to what I'm saying on occasion. It may be just the sound of my voice that is reassuring, but, on one level, it seems as if this reassurance is in terms of his need to be fed and nurtured; but, on the other hand, it may be the kind of reassurance to make him less frightened about his omnipotence. He has the feeling that he is a greater psychologist, and he will be the greatest in the world. My just saying something is as if he's being protected from this; that is, he is not doing it all alone and he isn't really so brilliant.

I mentioned on some occasions that he usually complains about not being able to free associate after he really has had what appears to me to be a true free association with an emergence of affect; and so, his thought that he is not free associating seems to me to be in connection with the feeling that he has gone too far, that he has been too brilliant, that he's made me embarrassed that I haven't thought of something quite as brilliant as he. He never stated this directly but it seems to me as being the other side of what he's experiencing consciously, that the unconscious aspect of it is that thinking of all these great names of important people is a way of assuring himself that he's not going to defeat me on his more unconscious level.

I was getting to a point which I digressed from — the point being that as he was going on and on with this, I again may have been a bit frustrated and said something to the effect (a somewhat stronger statement than I usually make), "Are you doing this analysis for yourself or for me?" — something of that order. After I said it, it occurred to me this is a little bit overdone. I think what I must have been responding to was like sounding a little annoyed and provocative about the way he scrapes and bows in these hours — the deferential way that he behaves. I may have a little trouble tolerating that. After thinking about it, it must have been the kind of thing that was going on with his father. That is to say, where he would feed his father this image of his being this wonderful great man, or that only the father could help him, and he would build up the father by being very deferential to him, saying "Yes sir" and "No sir," or whatever else the father needed to hear to be great. The father does sound extraordinarily narcissistic the way he describes him, and he may be exaggerating. What I'm referring to is the fact that the father develops this disability from lower back pain; and he clearly implied that there is no actual defect in his back that would cause this pain, and that this pain is purely psychological. It takes a longing for passivity on the part of his father, which leads him to seek this disability; and that the father struggles against this passivity by not taking any medications for pain and by forcing himself not to let himself succumb to the pain. He implies, in describing the father's pathology, all of this was new in this Wednesday hour, that the father's interest in philosophy is his own courageous attempt at overcoming this pain. But, of course, the father doesn't sleep at night as a result of this. He sleeps very, very little as a result of this pain.

There is another thing about his being in analysis that struck me. There are a number of mirrors here. One is the business of his not being able to treat his parents that summer with a feeling of success. It may have frightened him in terms of the impact of treatment on me. I'm doing a reversal now. The impact of the treatment on me is a reversal of the impact of treatment on him. That is to say, he is in analysis with me, but he is confused about my treating him. It's as if I'm his father trying to help him. He despairs about his capacity to be helped by somebody who he probably secretly feels cannot help him, which, he feels, as the transference will emerge, he will feel that I am rather weak, although there is no overt aspect of that as yet. He despairs that I'll be of help to him, but, in addition, he wonders if he can help me by being a good analys and — whether that will, in some way, serve me and serve my needs. I suppose that is what I was trying to get to in those comments — "Whose analysis is it?", etc. Why I was uneasy about it is that there is something a little discomforting about his idealizing me to the extent that he does at times. It seems like a very premature idealization that he has of me. I can't really say, because nothing in my notes — as I think about what I've written down, about what I've dictated about him — that really gives you the flavor of this.

There is a certain promptness with which he comes to the appointments — the wish not to see me anywhere. He scrapes and bows much too much about not wanting to see me and being disinterested in me and not asking any questions about me, referring to this as "acting out." It's very clear that he must be struggling against losing this idealization that he seems to have about me, so as to avoid the feeling that he could really hurt me.

There is one other trend that has been a generalized trend, but it's particularly pronounced in this material; and that is that the analysis seems to proceed too simply. I was talking before about how he aggrandizes or how he idealizes me, but this is apart from the idealization which I think I, somehow, understand. It's a little bit like being flattered and being uncomfortable with being flattered, but, in addition to that, there is a quality as to how the analysis is proceeding which strikes me as being too simple. It makes me feel too good, and that is — I made a transference interpretation about fee. I said something about his feelings toward me — I wouldn't call it a transference interpretation — "You're feeling uneasy to ask me anything directly." He immediately goes into some material about his father, about the disappointment in his father. This kind of quick confirmation of my interpretation doesn't strike me that he is consciously feeding me this kind of material; but it seems as if he's making me feel like a good analyst, a better analyst than I feel I am, where the analysis is proceeding too easily or in too straightforward a fashion. And I am wondering about what the meaning of it is. Is this indeed just that I am the idealized analyst that he has to do this to me? There seems to be something shallow about it, and a little frightening.

Appendix B —
Process Notes

ALAN Z. SKOLNIKOFF, M.D.

Session 35

He remembered, in the waiting room, the name of the psychologist that had seen him — Dr. K. He talked about how he, somehow, free associated to the name of an Austrian skier by the name of Karmer and then thought of his name.

He guesses he's still not giving up on diagnosing himself. Whatever he reads, he finds some elements of himself in it. He seems to fit into all of it — obsessive, hysterical, and narcissistic. He also thinks about his rationale about not applying to the Institute. It occurs to him that psychologists that haven't been accepted there are quite good. He now feels it's difficult to concentrate, and he feels detached. He has a couple of different thoughts. He's thinking, also, that people are occasionally asked to leave the Institute even after they've been accepted. He again states that he's glad that he's just in therapy and not involved in the Institute. He was pleased that he got presents on Saturday and that people were calling him and that he was feeling good.

He thought of having paid Dr. K. in two payments, and then said something about all of the money that was being spent on him. I asked, "All of this money that's being spent on you?" He continued that it didn't seem like his money. It never seemed like his money. He still thinks of it as belonging to his family. He began to cry. He then spoke of whatever they earned in the family was given over to the parents, it all belonged to the family unit. He could recall a time when he went into his parents' room to see if he could take money from his parents' dresser. He felt he couldn't ask his parents for money — that he had to take it; it was too humiliating to ask. It was always hard to get jobs, but he got them anyway, [and] he gave them all the money. He stated he probably ended up spending more money than he ever could earn, but then shifted to talking about his parents always living on credit; no money was ever saved. He never felt as if he earned any money.

He then shifted to the cost of the analysis. He thought of his friend, Stan, having to get a job to pay for his analysis — not paying as much as he, but still deciding he needed more money. He knows that spending all of this money, even though it's depressing, is worth it; and it's hard for him to let himself ask for money. He feels, rather, he should give it to his wife, parents, or brother. I then asked if any of what he's been describing has to do with his feeling that he should not ask me for the money. He responded by talking about his father.

He talked about Stan not being able to ask his wealthy father for any money. He then talked about his not wanting to ask his father, although he felt he could, but then realized that by asking his father that his father wouldn't have enough money to give him. He feels more responsible for them. He then thinks of how things got worse for them after he married. After he married and went out to the East Coast, they began to do foolish things and spend a lot of money. He feels, somehow, that if he had stayed home he could have avoided this for them. Instead, he went off to get married. He kept feeling responsible for them as he was driving across the country to see Martha. When he arrived, he brought her some flowers, and they went to bed to make love. Immediately after, he had to go and see his roommate, which seemed so foolish.

He then thought of his wish to shave off his mustache on Saturday morning. He was tempted to do it but couldn't. He then stated that he was angry that his parents weren't in a position to give him money. He always spent his money to see them when they were in trouble. He'd have more money if he didn't have to go back and see them so often. It was difficult to break his tie with them, but it seemed more difficult for them to break their tie with him. He then thought of Edgar saying that mustaches were artificial. He then thought of his father shaving his mustache, stopping smoking, and stopping wearing glasses, when he was seven. He remembered a radio show that he went on with his father and family that was sponsored by a cigarette company. The father won $50 plus a carton of cigarettes.

He again talked about a wish that someone would give him something that he would need just because they would know that he needed it. He then felt terribly sad and depressed. He remembered some gifts from his parents that were black clothing. It disturbed him to think that they spent too much money on him. The parents also sent a white sweater that they said came from his brother, which they had actually bought themselves. He had the feeling they were sacrificing something for him. He wanted to do things for them or buy things for them.

Concerning insurance policies, he gave Martha [as] the first name to his insurance [company], then his parents. He wanted to ask Martha if he could give the second insurance policy to his parents, if something happened to him. He guesses he has trouble letting them go, but that they couldn't let him go. How could he ask them for something, when his brothers need more than he does? He thought of being able to moonlight, and then focused on how hard it was for him to ask me for anything. He recalled his father's habit of being a bargainer and how embarrassed this made him. He would rather pay the price.

He suddenly thought of exercising and didn't know why. Was he trying to avoid something? Well, he thought, that's his free association. I then asked about his confusion about letting himself talk about his free association and his feeling that I should do this. I said he wasn't sure whose job it was. He responded that he didn't like getting anything from me, that it obligated him. When someone gives him a gift, he feels speechless. Social amenities make him feel uncomfortable. I phrased my next interpretation along these lines: "Is this analysis for your benefit, or do you feel that you are doing what I want you to do?" He talked about feeling kind of worthless after I stated this, but then went on to describe an intense sense of guilt when he felt he was proceeding along his own lines. This came up in connection with his comparing himself with Freud and his self-analysis. When I didn't speak, he felt foolish talking on his own, as if his own ideas must be too grandiose.

Session 36

He felt upset and depressed today. He then described a dream which upset him that he had last night. There were two little poisonous snakes that he had to handle. One has to grab such poisonous snakes by their head, otherwise they can bite you. He then had to put them in something or throw them at someone. In reality, he had, in the not distant past, taken some black snakes out of a swallow's nest where they were eating some swallows. His wife had taken a picture of him holding these black snakes. Within the black snakes there were some little birds that they had eaten. It was the same kind of snake that he had gotten his mother to touch so she wouldn't be frightened of them. His wife had the impression that with the copperhead snake what you do is step on it, which is foolish. What he feels he has to do is to run or to kill it.

He had another dream that was kind of complicated. He was working on some research project, and one of the senior collaborators asked a question. He said something was in a drawer. He walked by this desk and then he interrupted a couple who were kissing. As he went by, he said he was sorry to interrupt them. The thing that he associates to [the dream] is that he was told that he was placed in a drawer when he was a baby, until a crib was obtained. He then guessed that remembering things out of the past was comfortable as opposed to thinking about what was going on now. He's frustrated [about] not knowing what he's struggling with. He wonders if he's playing some sort of game that he's getting himself depressed about.

He then talked about his teachers. This new teacher gave Stan a bad rating. Stan was very upset about this, but the patient had a sense of secret satisfaction. He then talked about the peculiar feeling he had that Stan wanted to undermine him. He really dislikes Stan so much, and yet he was involved with him. Somehow, the patient felt that there were things Stan was talking about concerning him, but he wasn't clear about this and feels inarticulate. He feels as if he can't talk now because he's having trouble free associating. He doesn't feel secure free associating. He keeps thinking about what will happen if he doesn't have time to finish the analysis. He gets angry just thinking about Stan, who is a finagler.

He then wonders what if he doesn't have what it takes to be like his professor or me. He mentions that he's only thinking of me as an afterthought. He's really not that involved with me. He went back to think of an older man that he saw this morning. This man was furious with him for making any suggestions. He talked about the difference in age between him and the man and how this man was furious that a young person, despite his training, could make such comments about him. This man was a guy who could die, at any moment, of a heart attack.

He again wondered what would happen if his parents died. He guessed he wouldn't have to worry about asking them for anything. He felt affectless, but then thought that he was beginning to cry. He thought of paying for his analysis and how things were going to work out. Why couldn't he think about getting an extra job? Maybe he's angry that I haven't volunteered to help him out. He doesn't really have any feelings toward me, however.

He then talked about his difficulty empathizing with test subjects lately. He reads a lot of articles, but forgets the ones that are related to him. The group met today, but he didn't even think of going to it. Then he thought of everything that he read that got in the way. I asked him to try and consider why he feels that he shouldn't read. He said that the more he reads the less he seems able to free associate. I added, perhaps the more he reads, the less he feels he needs me to say anything.

He then talked about feeling very depressed and empty. I stated that he seems to have felt depressed since he discussed his disappointment in not being able to ask his father for anything and his feeling that he couldn't ask anyone for anything, including me, regarding some arrangements about the fee. Following this remark, he sobbed for ten minutes and expressed this emotion in a stronger way than in any previous hour in the analysis. He sobbed that he felt he had no one to ask for anything. He felt a great deal of anger toward his parents, which he can only express in tears. He's really depressed. He hates them for putting him in a position where he is completely unable to ask for anything.

He could recall, even in childhood, how, at three years of age, he was taking care of his younger sister, Jane. Whenever he felt ill he said to himself, "How dare he let himself be sick and not do anything?" He always has to maintain a cheerful appearance, so as not to put demands on anyone else. He could recall how, last summer, his father said that he regretted having put so much responsibility on the patient, even from a young age. The patient was thinking how he was surprised that the father even acknowledged his existence or thought of him. He wondered when the hour was going to end and looked at his watch and calmed himself down by recognizing that there were another several minutes. He then went on to lambast his parents and to lambast himself for not being able to be sufficiently angry with them.

Session 37

He said, as the hour started, that he thought we would start today at 4:00, instead of at 4:10. He became confused. The previous day, he had been talking about thinking of shaving off his mustache on his birthday. Last night, he reached into a drawer where his razor was and cut himself on it. He guessed it had to do with what he was talking about yesterday concerning wanting to shave off his mustache. He found himself thinking back to last summer. He wasn't feeling very good yesterday, but he wasn't detached. It felt "real" to be upset, and yet he had some distance from it. After the hour, he just went into his car and cried. The windows were steaming up inside. He thinks about me and therapy all the time, but he guesses they're just quiet fantasies. He doesn't talk about them in here, he guesses. He guesses he's beginning to look at himself differently. What he's dealing with is an obsessive–compulsive neurosis within himself. He feels much calmer thinking this and doesn't feel so driven by time. Suddenly, he felt as if he was looking at himself differently, and this was comforting.

He feels like touching his collarbone. He guesses this is to avoid dealing with what happened to him the previous summer. He was a family therapist to his own family. It embarrassed him to talk about this. It wasn't really what he had bargained for as being his role. He had been staying up all night and was frightened that his mother was regressing too much. She was in some sort of derealized state. He guessed, also, that he had felt bad about his rating in his program before he went home, but actually this wasn't true. He didn't find out about it until after he returned from his parents. He had to make himself feel bad because of the rating, rather than what was going on with his parents, which was so embarrassing. His feeling of omnipotence with regard to his family was shattered. He thought, by his trying to have them talk things out, that he might have made things worse.

He has the feeling, as he's describing all of this, that he doesn't have the right to feel sad. He guesses this is associated with thinly veiled aggressive wishes.

This all makes him into a real person with real feelings. He feels as if he needs the experience of going to war and experiencing death and destruction. He feels, instead, like a little kid.

Then he wonders what I would be thinking and how I would be interpreting what he's saying differently. Perhaps this is because I'm not saying anything, and he wants me to talk. He thinks about me all the time, but he doesn't say anything about it in here. He guesses he wants to have a reason to enjoy his suffering. Then he said, in a somewhat pitiful way, that he feels as if there's no one to turn to. He's 29 and he's an adult. At the same time, he's getting tired of the feeling that he has to interpret himself.

At this point, I said that he has mentioned a situation with his parents this past summer but has been very vague about what actually went on. Today, he stated he was embarrassed about this, and yet, has not clarified what really upset him. He then began discussing it in a chronological way without being overwhelmed. He mentioned that he was home for the first couple of weeks in June and that his sister and her husband came. His mother was doing badly. She had hypertension, and her difficulty seemed to be because the father was forcing her to move. She was having anxiety attacks and taking Valium. His father had chronic back pain and was hardly sleeping, obviously denying how overwhelmed he was. The grandmother was also staying there, and the father, obviously, had bad feelings toward her. The patient felt he had to confront the family with their difficulties, that if he didn't do it, it would be he that would bear the burden of the responsibility for things that continued to go wrong. He confronted the father with his denial of his bad feelings toward the grandmother and what he was doing to the mother. He tried to bring the mother out about her feelings of despair. She then began to talk in an hysterical way about missing her mother and not getting over the death of her father a few years before.

As he began describing this, he stated he couldn't remember exactly what was happening then; it was as if he was blocking it out. I stated that many of the things he had mentioned now he has never mentioned before and that, indeed, he appeared embarrassed to discuss this. He stated that, as he was describing this, he felt as if he was being like a child crying in his room by himself. He's never felt as if he's had a right to complain. He then went on in a somewhat more confused way about the feeling that he was caught between his sister and his mother — defending the mother. The mother had said he was the most important child, and the sister became angry hearing this. Things finally came to their talking about getting divorced — the mother and father. It seemed like some encounter group; everything was scraped away. The father tried to isolate himself from all of this, and the mother regressed more and more. The mother couldn't fight the father directly, but, instead, felt completely dependent and helpless with respect to her attachment to him. The patient's wife had earlier memories of losing her mother, while all of this was going on.

On the night just before they left, everybody was up all night screaming at each other and being hysterical. I had enormous difficulty in listening to all of this, in that I couldn't feel a coherence to his story—obviously because he was leaving things out or couldn't remember. The next morning, they had to drive him to the airport. His sister and brother-in-law were also there, and his brother-in-law began talking with his father about philosophy, in order to repair things. He did have the feeling that, "Humpty Dumpty couldn't be put back together again."

I talked about things he's mentioned in this story that he hadn't mentioned before, for example, his father's back pain. He stated that, because of his father's chronic back pain, he had thought of going to medical school and studying psychosomatic difficulties related to his father's back problem. He described how, because of this, his father decided to retire, although nothing was ever found specifically in his back, and his back pain has become much worse since retirement. The father has to deal with this back pain as something to overcome, a tremendous challenge, even if he doesn't sleep, etc. This whole event that occurred with his family this past summer shattered him. The notion that his parents could get divorced, after the sacred bond of marriage that they talked about, struck him as being unbelievable.

He then berated himself for feelings of grandiosity with respect to his parents and the feeling that he could patch things up for them—what he saw he couldn't even remember to this point. I stated he must have felt terribly disappointed in seeing his parents having difficulties this past summer. He kept talking about these as if they were narcissistic blows to him, as if he couldn't tolerate the notion clearly that his father was weak and that he could see these defects in him.

Session 38

He again thought, as he lay down in a perfunctory way and folded his arms over his chest, how much he struggled for control. He thought of himself as a tenacious bulldog, biting. He thought, also, of how he struggled around scheduling things; that is, his being precise about appointments. He's beginning to get tired of this whole thing—his need to control things. He had a whole series of dreams yesterday evening, but, as he tried to remember them, they faded. He thought of himself as being obsessive–compulsive and wondered about this at length, and thought he was being obsessive about what his diagnosis was, and realized it didn't matter what he was. He doesn't seem to be able to just let things happen.

One of the dreams: He was in a river in a boat with his wife and mother; he was bringing the boat to shore and, somehow, he was angry at some woman. He thought, somehow, this must be related to his relating to his mother in the same way he was relating to me. It reminded him of his having his back scratched; his mother and grandmother used to do this. His grandmother had long red fingernails and scratched his back. He could remember, at age three or four, having his back scratched, and what he remembers, specifically, is getting that respnse, rather than the feeling of having his back scratched; getting the response was very pleasant. His mother always was very proud of her strong hands, until she had a carpal tunnel operation. She used to wash the kitchen floor by hand and direct all of them to do the same thing, and prided herself on her capacity to do physical labor. She used to rub his back, rather than scratch it.

I sneezed at this point, and he felt as if he wanted to say "Gezundheit," but didn't. He thinks how positive his thoughts are toward me. He leaves the session and feels positive. He guessed that, despite his feelings being positive, he's unwilling to say whatever comes to his mind. Perhaps, he wants to control himself too much. He then recalled another scene in the dream, in which he was approached by a blond girl. She wanted him to make love, but he was unable to gratify his sexual desire, perhaps, because he felt as if his wife, Martha, was looking at him. This made him think of his sexual play with his sister Jane (the sister is blond). He recalled that he was playing around with his sister, when his parents were out dancing. The only time that he did this, he remembered listening for their car to drive up. He could recall this in his sister's junior and senior year at college, [that] she wanted to get married, and his specifically not wanting her to get married. He frequently had sexual fantasies about her, *even now.*

He then mentioned taking off the next day. He was wondering about my vacation plans, but was reluctant to ask. He guessed I would tell him, when it was appropriate. I pointed out that, in many areas, such as the fee, issues of changing times, or asking about my vacation, that a direct question posed a problem. He said he had the feeling that he doesn't want to bother me. This must be connected, also, with a feeling that he doesn't want to see me anywhere else. He's reluctant to go out, for fear of seeing me in a social situation. He has a kind of sense of vagueness and discomfort about any kind of social interaction with me. It used to be the same for teachers, faculty, and his father, as well.

He was with his chief professor today, alone in a room, and he felt choked up and couldn't talk to him. He wouldn't know what to say, anyway, even though this professor wants to be called by his first name. He has to isolate any humanness from any authority figure. He then thought of his mother undressed and her being just an old woman. He thought of me as being human today, not having my jacket on; it seemed less formal.

He then thought of playing football in high school and how people smelled, and to be aggressive with them was being aggressive with other human beings. He thought of looking at other people in cars; he thought of them as just being bodies. He could recall a kid in high school who didn't have a hand, who was born without one. He felt sorry for him and wouldn't hit him, but, one time, this kid hit him, and he realized that he didn't feel sorry for him anymore.

He thought of another colleague who he felt very ill-at ease-with. They only idly gossiped about jogging, but he didn't feel as if he could talk with him about anything seriously. He then thought of his father and how there was nothing to talk about with him, except philosophy. At this point, his voice cracked, and he had tears in his eyes. His father was too busy to play baseball with him, or anything else, for that matter. He would then recall having races with the father, who always won at swimming. The mother would cheer the father on, while she and the sister were sitting in a boat.

He then, suddenly, recalled a dream and realized that, in the dream, his father wasn't there. It was as if he had gained victory by having his mother and sister, with the father being eliminated. The father did a funny thing, like pulling the boat with his teeth. It was another legendary thing that he bragged of. He thought of how he wrote out my name on the check. He wanted to say A. Z. Skolnikoff, instead of Alan Z. Skolnikoff, which seemed too familiar. He then thought that he guessed he would like to know when my vacation would be.

He was silent for a moment and then said what he had described about his parents seemed as if he was telling two sides of the story and that he wasn't clear. He felt like an illiterate fool. He then talked about his eating, and his not being able to let his feelings come into the hour; eating and running were the only times when he could let these feelings about me come up. I then brought him back to his indirect question about my vacation and his pause. I suggested that, perhaps, he was annoyed that I didn't answer, but felt he had no right to expect me to answer — that it was up to me to choose the appropriate time to let him know. He agreed with this and stated he didn't feel he had the right to ask me, and that he wanted to trust me to choose the appropriate time to let him know.

Appendix C—
Excerpts From a Case Study of an
Hysterical Character

EMANUEL WINDHOLZ, M.D.

Dr. Skolnikoff's patient struggled with overwhelming fears of losing his autonomy. The intensity of his need for autonomy resembles that of a narcissistic
personality. The treating analyst of another patient under study, an hysterical
character, reacted to conflicts related to her narcissism with unconscious feelings identical to those of Dr. Skolnikoff. The patient perceived the analyst's reaction and reacted, in turn, with a restoration of her sense of reality as had Dr.
Skolnikoff's patient.

When the patient (in the second case) felt intensely attracted to her analyst,
she was overwhelmed by the realization that she was identifying the analyst
with her father. The analyst's impending vacation had intensified the transference and triggered the intrusion of this incestuous wish. The patient had completely forgotten (repressed) the fact that the analyst was soon to go on
vacation; but she reported feelings of sadness and confused helplessness which
she could not explain. She offered many associations to these lonely feelings
but could not find any relief. This evoked in the analyst identical feelings of
helplessness. He felt frustrated, and was unable to interpret the patient's transference because he was afraid to upset her.

In the analyst's verbal report, however, his interest shifted to his reaction to
the patient's earlier flirtations. She did appear attractive to him, and he remembered how frustrated he had felt when he assumed that the patient herself
felt that her looks had impressed him. He recalled that he had believed that her
flirtations were not genuine; these associations seemed to indicate that he had

doubts about how genuine her present helplessness was. In the verbal report, the analyst expressed anger at the patient, believing that she was stubborn and uncooperative, and suspecting her of wishing to manipulate him into protecting her. He was unable to maintain this explanation, however, and warned himself against reacting again with a countertransference. Instead of feeling helpless because of the patient's inability to tolerate her transference, the analyst now felt helpless because he was afraid of his countertransference.

By focusing attention on the patient's associations, he hoped to be able to "convince" her that she was "possibly" avoiding the thought of missing him next week when he would be on vacation. He was justifiably reluctant, since she had forgotten his vacation and could not tolerate any association related to the analyst. For example, he reported the following in the process notes: "I smiled and nodded as I drove by, and she clearly saw me but made no response at all. After she came into the session she said she could talk about her reactions to seeing me but she really 'doesn't want to.'" Using these words to convince the patient of her resistance, he said to her: "And today you didn't want to talk about your reactions to seeing me." She answered that the analyst wanted her to talk only about him. He had completely forgotten this remark because it reinforced his fear of the countertransference.

Finally, after he had hesitatingly enumerated to the patient all the evidence in support of his conclusions, the analyst noted the following exchange: "I thought perhaps one thing she might be reacting to was my coming vacation." The patient exclaimed: "No...!" She was very loud and definite, insisting that the idea that she might be upset was "just a psychoanalytic cliché," and she *knew* that he would bring that up: "Analysts always bring up that kind of thing."

Subsequent exploration of these data identified the following process: the analyst (as he explained later) had needed to persuade *himself* that he had *not* brought up his vacation because of his own desire to have the patient pay attention to him. She had perceived his need to deny the countertransference, and, in turn, she was able to deny her transference. The patient could deny that she forgot about the vacation, saying that she *knew* that *he* would bring it up. This projection was facilitated by her observation of the analyst's need to deny his countertransference, a process that was possible only after the analyst reminded her of his vacation. The patient then felt greatly relieved, forgot the image of her father, and centered her attention on the analyst.

Appendix D —
The Intuitive Understanding of a
Transference Paradigm

EMANUEL WINDHOLZ, M.D.

In his verbal report, Skolnikoff frequently formulated new theories, as he became aware of meaningful linkages between apparently unconnected associations. Occasionally, the new meaning was experienced as a discovery, a sudden intuitive understanding. This was the way Dr. Skolnikoff felt when he formulated a theory about the "special child."

The following is a verbatim excerpt from the treating analyst's verbal report:

> This whole issue of his autonomy in terms of taking care of himself versus his tremendous dependency wishes always comes up in a rather acute way, and it comes up along these lines. He's the "special child." . . . the mother said, "I put everything I had" into the patient. . . . But it's clear with relationship to me, as it's emerging, that the special child has two meanings: One is that he will be extremely independent and that I'll be very gratified by viewing his accomplishments in terms of his capacity to analzye. The second is that, somehow, by his excellent performance, that I will do things for him, because he's such a deserving person. . . whatever I would dispense as a special favor would come as a result of his extraordinary capacity. . . he would still be fed in this kind of perfect way.

We have evidence about the origin of the analyst's idea that he "will be very gratified by viewing [the patient's] accomplishments in terms of his capacity to analyze." The analyst was not aware of having expressed this idea when he formulated his interpretation in the session on Tuesday. It was a very unusual interpretation, since it incorporated past and present. The analyst considered it a "tripartite interpretation" (Appendix B, Session 36). What he did not realize was that he had both given credit for it to the patient and also conveyed to him his satisfaction. What satisfied the analyst was the evidence that the patient had now acquired insight into why he felt depressed when he viewed himself as successful. This was an important change; when the analyst had interpreted this conflict earlier in the analysis, the patient had rejected it. At the earlier phase, he had criticized himself, saying that feeling guilty about his success was a failure of judgment, which he was determined to correct.

The analyst was very pleased with the effect of the interpretation: the patient cried for ten minutes; it was the first breakthrough in the analysis. The following day, the patient opened the session by formulating clearly the analytic theory of "isolation of affect" as a defense mechanism, as it applied to his obsessive-compulsive neurosis (Appendix B, Session 37). He explained his crying as the resolution of the isolation. Listening to this, the analyst felt that he had been "manipulated" by the patient into feeling successful, as if he had appropriated the patient's interpretation and taken credit for it himself. Suddenly, he felt very frustrated and repressed the memory of his intervention as well as the sense of gratification he had derived from it. It was this forgotten memory that he incorporated in his theory of the "special child," experiencing it as new — something arrived at by intuition.

The analyst used some peculiar expressions (Appendix A) as he formulated the theory in his verbal report. He said that the patient's struggle with his dependency needs "always comes up in a rather acute way," and "it's clear with relationship to me, as it's emerging." These two expressions both describe sudden movements. If they refer to the analyst's subjective state of mind, they could reflect his momentary perception of the intuitive process of the emergence of his ideas. Saying "it's *clear*" seems to suggest that he found a new meaning in the forgotten idea. His having felt gratified by the patient was a new experience, clearly understood as a mother transference. The same painful image, linked now to the transference, "emerged" as a pleasurable "discovery." The intuitive process was a rediscovery of knowledge that had been repressed.

THE FAILURE TO EMPATHIZE

The analyst frequently becomes aware of connections between so-called free associations as new meanings are discovered in them. This occurs, particularly, when the therapist is upset by countertransference. Dr. Skolnikoff described the following sequence: the patient associated a memory of his father after the analyst's comment about the meaning of the patient's relationship to him, which made him feel like "a good analyst" (Appendix A). On reflection, he recognized that the patient had recalled a memory of the father very quickly and had talked about it in a perfunctory manner. The analyst understood, from these two non-verbal clues, that he had responded to the patient's manipulation, which enabled him to correct his failure to empathize. The meaning of his countertransference was a wish to feel effective.

Another example that illustrates the process was Dr. Skolnikoff's reaction to the patient's preoccupation with incest. In his verbal report (Appendix A), he remembered that the patient felt uncomfortable recalling sexual play with his sister. The patient said that he had always had incestuous impulses toward his sister and that he *still* did. The analyst felt confused, and concluded that he must have imagined that the patient said he was *still* having incestuous feelings. Suddenly, it occurred to him that the patient was using the analytic situation to isolate what the analyst called *"some"* of the affect, and he began to consider the patient's intellectual interest in the meaning of incest. The patient, however, was not talking in a detached manner. The analyst revealed this by saying that the patient used the analytic situation to isolate *"some"* of the affect. This awkward expression indicated that he perceived that the patient enjoyed *talking* about incest.

The analyst had failed to empathize with the shift in the patient's interest, his deriving pleasure, not from experiencing sexual feelings, but from analyzing incestuous ideas. Recognizing this enabled the analyst to correct his mistake. Going back to the process notes, we discovered that the patient had, indeed, said that he frequently had sexual fantasies about her "even now" (Appendix B). The analyst believed he had only imagined this, a distortion due to his concern that the patient's incestuous feelings were not repressed. The countertransference here was a reflection of his preoccupation with and concern about the patient's severe pathology.

Correction of such failures in empathy occurs frequently in the course of an analysis. The analyst is, however, rarely aware of having connected disparate associations. The consensual analysis can capture the process and identify the unconscious countertransference that was responsible for the failure.

Appendix E–
Consensual Analysis: The Multiple
Appeal of Interpretations

EMANUEL WINDHOLZ, M.D.

We have already discussed in this volume the effect of Skolnikoff's interpretation on the patient's sense of reality. This interpretation also confirmed the analyst's earlier interpretation of the patient's guilt, which had been rejected at that time. This new insight, however, remained intellectual. But there was evidence of still another effect. The patient told the analyst, in the next session, that he thinks about him "all the time, but guesses they're just quiet fantasies. He doesn't talk about them here he guesses . . . he feels there is no one to turn to . . . he's getting tired of feeling that he has to interpret himself" (Appendix B, Session 37).

This represented an important change in the patient's verbal communication. The "tripartite interpretation" conveyed to the patient how the analyst was able to overcome his own helplessness by believing in the accuracy of the patient's self-analysis. Simultaneously, the analyst's attitude revealed his need for the patient as an object. The change in the form of the patient's communications was a response to this attitude of the analyst, which facilitated the emergence of a mother transference.

An event from his childhood may be relevant for understanding this interaction: the patient was fifteen months old when his sister was born. He stopped babbling at that time and remained completely mute for the following six months. Then he started to talk in full sentences. The effect was spectacular. We could call it a "breakthrough." His mother adored him, and looked upon him as her future Einstein. Can we construct a parallel between the patient's ability suddenly to talk in full sentences as a child and his current acquisition of the language of psychoanalysis? The analyst acknowledged the accuracy of the patient's self-analysis, admiring in him, in effect, a future Freud.

The patient's perception of the admiring analyst would be evidence of an object-related interaction. A comparison of this interaction with another, described by Sandler (1976), may clarify the different conceptualizations. Sandler described the following interaction with his patient: He offered his patient a Kleenex box every time she started to cry. After several years, when he failed once to do so, the patient became angry and Sandler then understood the meaning of his role. He had gratified the patient's lifelong wish to always have someone available to wipe her — a dyadic theory.

If we were to use my theory to explain this interaction, we would have to assume that every time the patient cried she felt confused and helpless. She "forgot" how to wipe her tears. I could then conclude that when Sandler performed this particular function he was not perceived as an external object.

Skolnikoff's patient's sense of reality had to be reestablished before he could again cooperate with the analyst. The simultaneity of the effects of Skolnikoff's interpretation obscured this combination: the resolution of an intrasystemic conflict (loss of the patient's sense of reality) along with the emergence of a dyadic relationship (mother transference). In contrast to the obscurity in the reaction of Skolnikoff's patient, the separation of these two effects was clear in the hysterical patient discussed in Appendix C.

The consensual analysis provides data which can identify the dynamic relevance of interpretations with multiple appeal.

23

The Widening Scope of Indications
for Psychoanalysis

LEO STONE, M.D.

The remarkable and steadfast conservatism of Freud regarding the therapeutic application of his discovery appears in several places in his writings. We may generalize briefly to the effect that Freud believed the true indications for psychoanalysis to be the transference psychoneuroses and equivalent character disturbances. While temperately hopeful for the future treatment of psychoses, the very expression, "some other plan better suited for that purpose" (Freud, 1939) suggests how closely linked in Freud's thinking were the psychoanalytic technique and the basically reliable ego. We know from his writings that Freud was far from rigid or static in his technical methods; however, he was apparently not much concerned with developing and systematizing new techniques, or in experimenting with remote nosological groups.

Yet it was still early in the history of psychoanalysis that Abraham (1927) began to treat manic-depressive psychosis, and not too long before Simmel (1929) opened a psychoanalytic sanatorium where he treated very severe neuroses, incipient psychotic conditions, and addictions. Also early came the psychoanalytic interest in character, beginning with Freud himself (1908) followed by the distinguished contributions of Jones and Abraham. However, character analysis as a special technical problem was precipitated sharply into

Reprinted by permission from the *Journal of the American Psychoanalytic Association*, 2:567–594, 1954. New York: International Universities Press.

the foreground of general interest by Wilhelm Reich's (1947) brilliant and stimulating, although still controversial, book (Sterba, 1953). With Anna Freud's book on *The Ego and the Mechanisms of Defense* (1936) one might say that a movement toward the broadening and multiplication of the psychoanalytic spheres of interest in the personality, and an appropriate complication of psychoanalytic technique, found general and secure acceptance.

I trust that it is not superfluous on this occasion to mention child analysis as an early special development in theory and technique, whose implications extend far beyond the immediate clinical applications. The application of psychoanalytic knowledge in the treatment of delinquents, begun by Aichhorn, continued in our own group by the Eisslers currently, has a similar importance.

Other psychiatric syndromes were rapidly brought within the scope of psychoanalytic therapy: the perversions, including homosexuality; paranoia and the schizophrenias; a considerable and growing variety of psychosomatic disorders; and, of course, that vast, important and heterogeneous group—the "borderline" cases. One might say that in the last decade or two, at least in the United States, any illness or problem which has a significant emotional component in its etiology has become at least a possible indication for psychoanalysis. In its extreme development, this indication includes not only conditions where this etiology is quite well established, but not infrequently, as in the psychosomatic disorders, only reasonably probable.

First, I should mention that this generally expanding scope of psychoanalysis, which I should judge is now on a sort of peak plateau, has more than one facet; furthermore, my own reaction to this expansion is divided, according to these facets. One element which should not elude our attention is the enthusiasm of that section of the informed public which is devoted to psychoanalysis. Among this group, not inconsiderable in size and influence in a city like New York, scarcely any human problem admits of solution other than psychoanalysis; by the same token, there is an almost magical expectation of help from the method, which does it grave injustice. Hopeless or grave reality situations, lack of talent or ability (usually regarded as "inhibition"), lack of an adequate philosophy of life, and almost any chronic physical illness may be brought to psychoanalysis for cure. It is a matter of serious interest to us that this phenomenon exists; it is of course even more important that this type of ambivalent worship not be allowed to influence, however subtly, the judgment of the psychoanalytic practitioner. A special development of this sort has occurred in the practice of general medicine. This I would regard as a small but definite public health hazard. One cannot question the tremendous scientific importance of research in psychosomatic medicine, or its potentialities for improving preventive or therapeutic medical practice. The complete displacement of well-established medical methods by purely psychological methods, even when the psychological indications are reasonably practical and sound, is quite another matter. It is, however, in the field of diagnosis where one observes the most serious deterioration. The hospital resident who on completing a negative physical examination in a patient with bowel complaints immediately calls for psychiatric consultation, then gets an X-ray report of carcinoma of the colon, is funny to his colleages. However, under other conditions, the same orientation may occasion tragedy. I should emphasize that this tendency exists on the side of the public and the medical practitioners, *not* on the side of analysts as a group. My occasional discussions with medical men in connection with patients whom they refer to the Treatment Center (of the New York Psychoanalytic Institute) confirm this long-standing observation and conviction. Some subtle fault in the publicization of psychoanalytic findings may contribute slightly to this phenomenon. In any case, it is important to be alertly aware of, to try to understand and, if possible, to remedy this situation; at very least, to resist any distortion of judgment in response to it.

I should also like, in passing, to mention a less immediately grave but intellectually disquieting feature of this spurious increase of psychoanalytic indications. There is sometimes a loss of sense of proportion about the human situation, a forgetting or denial of the fact that few human beings are without some troubles, and that many must be met, if at all, by "old-fashioned" methods: courage, or wisdom, or struggle, for instance; also that few people avoid altogether and forever some physical ailments, not to speak of the fact that all die of illness in the end. Even if these illnesses all represent disturbances in the total psychosomatic complex (which, oddly enough, I believe to be the case), they are not all indications for psychoanalysis. The "psyche" is only half of the psychosomatic continuum, and it remains a practical empirical problem as to whether a drug or surgery or psychotherapy is most effective in a given illness. If a man is otherwise healthy, happy, and efficient, and his rare attacks of headache can be avoided by not eating lobster, for example, it would seem better that he avoid eating lobster than that he be analyzed. This takes us to another indication for psychoanalysis — not spurious — but one where delicate judgment is involved; I have in mind the very mild or incipient neurosis. Here, it seems to me, a careful general evaluation of the personality is especially imperative. For, if the personality illness were judged really slight (a matter which we know, does not necessarily parallel the severity of immediate symptoms), I would regard the indication for psychoanalysis as very seriously in doubt. For psychoanalysis represents a tremendous investment of many complicated elements by two people; it should not be invoked for trivial reasons. Aside from the fact that many people can live with mild neuroses (I am certain that a good part of the population live long lives with various subclinical phobias, mild conversion symptoms, fragmentary compulsions, etc.), a simpler, less intensive form of psychotherapy may suffice for many such illnesses.

Before considering some of the more severe problems which are now being treated psychoanalytically, it may be well to say a few words about what we mean by psychoanalysis (as differentiated from psychotherapy), since it is in relation to the severe illnesses that important technical alterations may be required. If we do not have some reasonable degree of agreement about this, there is little ground for discussion regarding indications, for few would dispute the helpfulness of some form of psychotherapy in any of these instances. Most psychotherapy practiced in the United States has been strongly influenced by psychoanalysis. Certainly, the psychotherapy practiced by psychoanalysts and candidates borrows so much from the original discipline that the boundary becomes obscure, and is sometimes defined on a rather arbitrary or ritualistic basis, which is quite unsatisfactory. Sometimes bad or slovenly or inadequate psychoanalytic tactics find both definition and privilege in being "not analysis, but psychotherapy." A few years ago, I wrote on this subject; and I do not wish to burden you with a repetition of that material (Stone, 1951). Furthermore, I should prefer nowadays to place greater stress on the functional elements to which the formal factors are ancillary. The relevant point which I proposed was that the several formal factors which participate in the classical psychoanalytic situation — ranging from free association through the recumbent position to such matters as the character of the analyst's technical interventions and general attitude — constitute an ensemble which has much to do with the dynamics of the analytic process, and specifically with the evolution of the transference neurosis. Most important in the ultimate dynamic meaning of this ensemble is the relative emotional vacuum which the analysand must fill with transference impulses and fantasies, and the parallel reduction of reality-testing opportunity which facilitates the same process. In a sort of paradoxical tour de force, the very same set of factors provides the optimum background for the testing and interpretative reduction of the transference neurosis. Of the several technical instrumentalities which may be used purposively in any psychotherapeutic procedure — for instance, those listed last year by Bibring (1954) — it is interpretation which is ultimately relied on for the distinctively psychoanalytic effect. I put aside the many possible interpersonal meanings which interpretation may have for a patient, and refer to the circumscribed function of communicating to a patient something true of him in a specific reference, which he has, before the interpretation, seen in a radically different light, or of which he has been quite unaware.[1] Without entering into the basic problems discussed in The Marienbad Symposium we can state in a very general descriptive way what wholly or partially occurs in analysis. We dissolve or minimize resistances, and make the ego aware of its defensive operations, ultimately of id and superego contents and operations. Through this accurate awareness, implemented by the process of "working through," we expect the effect of abolition or reduction of id and superego qualitative distortions and

---

[1]Bibring differentiates interpretation from clarification by confining the reference of interpretation to "repressed or otherwise warded-off unconscious material and its derivatives."

pathological intensities, the resolution or reduction or at least the *awareness* of intrapsychic conflict in general, and finally the extension of the ego's positive sovereignty over the instinctual life, with the freeing or facilitation of its synthetic, adaptive and other affirmative capacities. In this process, the mobilization of the transference neurosis holds a central place. Whether one views this phenomenon theoretically as essentially a resistance to recall of the past, or an affirmatively necessary therapeutic phenomenon, toward which interpretation and recall are directed for the freeing of the patient from the analyst and thus from internal parental representations, is largely a question of emphasis, which in a pragmatic sense may vary from patient to patient. For, as Freud long ago observed, an adequate positive transference is necessary even to the *acceptance* of decisive interpretations. Furthermore, the sense of reality or vividness about the past is *largely* dependent on the therapeutic transference experience; and there are many instances where the dissolution of amnesias or of the emotional isolation of memories only follows adequate emotional experience in the transference. This is even more true of the reconstruction of very early experience, which may be quite inaccessible to adult memory, or may indeed have played little or no part in childhood consciousness. In any case, the current dynamisms of personality (and thus, of neurosis) are to be brought so effectively into relation with their origins in the past, that the adult ego must perforce recognize their inappropriateness to current realities and thus free itself of the disturbances attendant on the burdening from the past. That this process includes, or is at least in part dependent on or relative to, reduction of disturbances in the id and superego is apparently implicit in, although not always explicit in, current formulations.

When Freud said that any procedure which utilized the principles of transference and resistance could be called psychoanalysis, whether the findings agreed with his own or not, he offered a permission, whose current acceptance or nonacceptance should be decided on a scientific rather than a factional loyalty basis. Freud at times used the term "psychotherapy" in its historical inclusive sense, or for psychoanalysis, or — when referring to "*other*" psychotherapies — for explicitly nonanalytic procedures. I do not know if he foresaw the growth of a medley of practices which are called "psychotherapy" in contradistinction to analysis, which borrow from its psychological formulations, and while often including many other formidable and uncontrolled variables, tend with varying degrees of purposive clarity and thoroughness to employ interpretation as their chief manifest technical tool. I do not believe it important to participate in power struggles, to which unfortunately the nature of our work lends itself, on the issue of definition. And I do not believe that patients should bear the burden or sometimes the trauma of our distinctions. However, I do think that the scientific progress of psychotherapy in its broadest sense, with psychoanalysis as its central science and technology, depends on an increasingly clear-cut knowledge of the conditions in which findings occur. This, of course, presupposes certain minimal basic terminological distinctions. I do not believe that the distinction between psychoanalysis and psychotherapy will remain adequate, aside from linguistic considerations, for "psychotherapy" is or should be a large and complicated field. But the reasonably clear delimitation of psychoanalysis from other psychotherapies, especially interpretative psychotherapies, is a necessary beginning. In our immediate context, some such general concept as "modified psychoanalysis" would be useful and, I believe, valid. For scientific progress, the careful study of the "modifications" and their effects will be necessary, whether we think of the given procedure as psychoanalysis, or as beyond its most elastic limits. Perhaps they will prove to be less important than some of us think. But this is a very unsound *a priori*.

I would view the idea of psychoanalysis as beginning with Freud's own basic requirement. To this, most of us would add, as indispensable technical and intellectual context, certain other basic elements of psychoanalytic observation and theory: the unconscious, of course, since it seems no longer inevitably implicit in the basic requirement; the libido theory; the power of infantile sexuality, possibly additional elements in instinct theory; certainly, the genetic principle, with the connotation of psychodynamic continuity with the remote past. One cannot divorce this initial context from subsequent phenomena of a real therapeutic process. We would, while acknowledging that other psychotherapeutic agents play an important role in the psychoanalytic process, assign to interpretation the unique and distinctive place in its ultimate therapeutic effect. We would, I think, require that the interpretations achieve this effect through the communication of awareness of facts about himself to the patient, with the sense of emotional reality that comes only with technically correct preparation, rather than through certain other possible effects in the transference-countertransference system, which occur so frequently in other psychotherapies. (Certainly, they occur also in psychoanalysis, but they are regarded as miscarriages of effort.) I would think that the mobilization of as full and undistorted a transference neurosis as may be possible, and its ultimate dissolution (or minimization) by interpretative means, would be regarded as essential to a genuinely analytic outcome. Both for the mobilization of this neurosis *and* for its reduction by such means the essentials of the formal and emotional milieu which we associate with the classical psychoanalytic situation would usually seem necessary; these components of the milieu are then assumed integral parts of the definition. One cannot be rigid about the details of the definition; nor can one simplify it too much; the general functional meaning, with its formal requirements, can, however, be brought to discernible outlines. Probably all analyses include certain formal and subtle emotional deviations somewhere along the line, aside from the fact that no two analysts would ever give precisely the same interpretations throughout an analysis. We are therefore dealing with principles, broad outlines, tendencies. Indeed, my own clinical experience and observation lead me to believe that *too* great approximation to the mathematical ideal in certain references is antitherapeutic (in the sense of antianalytic). For example, some patients may not be able to do their "analytic work" in relation to exaggerated and artificial efforts, or to personalities, whose "neutrality" is tantamount to complete emotional detachment. Yet I am convinced that any considerable tangible deviation from the attitude of neutrality should be motivated and handled along the general lines which Eissler (1953) has described in his discussion of "parameters." Where the dividing line appears is impossible to specify quantitatively. From a qualitative point of view, I would speculate that the optimum exists where the patient feels that the analyst's neutrality is a self-imposed purposive technical discipline (in fact, a technique), willingly accepted for good reasons, neither enjoyed as a personality gratification, nor rigidly embraced in panicky fear of rule-breaking. We must frequently remind ourselves that the analytic situation is an artificial situation, a drama in which both participants have "roles," imposed by the technique, differing from both their everday human behavior, and the inner primitive drama of the transference. We expect of the analysand a benign split of the ego, which enables him to experience while still observing. In the classical method, we exclude any *assumption* of a role in the transference by the analyst. However, the *complete* merging of the analyst as an individual and the analyst as technician may also be inimical to the analytic process. Is it not rational to assume that since these two aspects of the analyst's identity are in psychodynamic balance with the two phases of the patient's (technical) ego activity, a grave imbalance on one side may seriously affect the other? It might contribute, for example, to an excessive avoidance of transference fantasy on one hand, or overwhelmingly ego-syntonic transference reactions on the other.

If we avoid involvement in the nature of other (interpretative) psychotherapies (for lack of time, not for lack of interest), we can go directly to the question: How far can the classical analytic method be modified, and still be regarded as psychoanalysis, "modified psychoanalysis," if you wish, rather than another form of interpretative psychotherapy? I believe that any number and degree of parameters can be introduced where they are genuinely necessary to meet special conditions, so long as they are all directed to bringing about the ultimate purposes and processes of the analytic end requirements, as we have just described them; so long as these purposes and processes are rationally to be expected as sequellae, and are brought about to the maximum extent which the patient's personality permits. (We must distinguish between a valid psychoanalytic effort which may be unsuccessful or only partially successful, and an effort which is essentially different.) Ordinarily, this would presuppose the transition from any postulated previous psychotherapeutic methods to the classical psychoanalytic situation, without irreversible transference distortions. In an ideal sense, I think the requirements for acceptability of parameters given by Eissler, with one exception, are excellent. The exception is the one which requires that the parameter *must* terminate before the end of analysis—a requirement which, as the author states, automatically excludes the time-limitation parameter, which Freud used with the Wolf Man. While the discussion of this conflict between parameter and rule would provide technical, metapsychological, and logical interest, I must waive the disproportionate space which this would require. The practical value of retention of this maneuver as consistent with true analytic work outweighs the ideal requirement, even if it must be an exception. A patient may require this confrontation with reality, in the same sense that the phobic sometimes requires the intervention which is now a general and accepted practice. Aside from this issue, however, this rule seems altogether too severe. There are very sick personalities who, to the very end of analytic experience, may require occasional and subtle or minimal emotional or technical concessions from the analyst, in the same sense that they will carry with them into their outside lives, vestiges of ego defects or modifications, which, while not completely undone, are — let us say — vastly improved. If in such patients, the essential structure and relationship of analysis have been brought about, if a full-blown transference neurosis has emerged, if the patient has been able to achieve distance from it, if it has been brought into effective relation with the infantile situation, if favorable changes in the ego have occurred as a result of interpretation and working through, if the transference has been dissolved or reduced to the maximum possible degree, I would say that the patient has been analyzed.

With regard to the earlier deviant phases of such analyses, or atypical technical residues which may persist, I would state the broad and general opinion that most parameters can be deprived of their effects on the transference, so long as they are genuinely psychotherapeutic, i.e., maneuvers bound to the immediate reality, arising from, strictly limited by, always compatible with, the role of *therapist* — as opposed to good father, or solicitous friend, or magician, or anxious husband, etc., in a patient whose reality testing and other ego functions are largely capable of the various rigors implicit in analysis, at the point we are discussing. An excellent example of how even affirmative or constructive use of wide deviations from the classical psychoanalytic situation can be made, where these deviations are necessary and rational, may be seen in Simmel's still fascinating paper about the Tegel Sanatorium (1929). I am inclined to agree with Eissler that the giving of a cigarette to certain patients, in a certain context, might create serious difficulty. In general, if this occurs as an *exception* to a general climate of deprivation, I would believe it more likely to cause trouble than, let us say, an appropriate expression of sympathy in a tragic personal bereavement — or even, circumspect competent direct advice in a real emergency which requires it — precisely because the giving of a cigarette, aside from its obvious susceptibility to unconscious symbolic countertransference interpretation — is, in ordinary practice, with nonpsychotic patients, *always* unnecessary — *never* relevant to the treatment as such. Should the previous treatment methods provide insoluble transference distortions, which may well be required by the active phases of psychosis, I would agree with Eissler that a change of therapist may be necessary, *unless* more is lost thereby than is gained by the uncontaminated transference. It may be that the person who has ministered to the acute psychotic is the only one who can elicit a strong attachment from the patient; since this is indispensable to initiate analysis, I would — to be a bit slangy — "settle" for the transference distortion, with the hope that this may in time come into better perspective. This is always possible, where even outright "mothering" may retrospectively be seen as having been dictated by actual therapeutic needs of the time. If not, we may have to accept a transference situation something like that described by Miss Freud for the child, without clear-cut transference neurosis. Where to classify this, I would not know; I would hesitate to exclude this from the modifications of adult psychoanalysis, if all other analytic purposes are maintained, if the modification is judged necessary, if the analysis of the transference is extended to its utmost possible limit.

A psychological treatment which does not seek to provide to the maximum compatible with the situation the conditions necessary for a full-blown undistorted transference neurosis and therefore does not mobilize one, or which does not dissolve this neurosis or reduce it to the greatest extent which the patient's structure and the therapist's skill permit, ultimately by genetic interpretations, should not be called analysis, even if the necessary formal aspects of the analytic situation *are* reproduced. For without these important processes, the profound reorganization of the personality which we associate with analysis, and in which the cure of illness is, in a sense, an incidental part of general economic change, cannot occur. At this point, I should mention, as I have elsewhere — that, in certain well-managed psychotherapeutic situations, where many ordinary emotional needs of the patient are met, within the limits of the physician-patient relationship, significant *pathological fragments* of the transference relationship (i.e., those which cannot be met in any ordinary real relationship) may separate from integrated expression in this real professional situation, and be utilized to great and genuine interpretative advantage by a skillful therapist. Classification of such treatment situations would present problems. For the moment — since they are infrequent, since they are fragmentary rather than general and systematic, since they arise under atypical and uncontrolled auspices, and since unknown large areas of transference remain integrated and unanalyzed — we shall leave them in the broad heterogeneous field of "psychotherapy."

With some conception of what we mean by psychoanalysis in mind, we can move to an examination of the expanding scope of psychoanalysis, in so far as this originates legitimately from scientific development, or practical technical experience, as opposed to irrational enthusiasm. First a few words about those conditions which have the least part in usual analytic practice. In the psychoses, we have a tremendous range, extending from those who are not independently viable, or who require hospital restraint or protection, or who cannot or will not establish voluntary co-operative contact with a therapist, or — specifically — with his therapy. From these, regardless of the particular type of psychotic expression, there is a continuous gradation down to the incipient or very mild psychotic who *complains* of his symptoms and seeks help exactly as a neurotic does; and perhaps in the very end zone of this continuum is the "borderline" patient, who is in fact neither medicolegally nor clinically psychotic. With patients who are floridly psychotic, the initial management requires extraordinary measures or techniques which, however influenced or guided by psychoanalytic understanding, are certainly removed from the scope of ordinary psychoanalytic office practice. Where patients, whether through spontaneous or therapeutically induced remission or subsidence of symptoms or the initial mildness of illness present themselves voluntarily for treatment, we may think of their problems as approximating to various degrees the problems which appear in the "borderline" cases.

In the addictions and perversions alike, the *immediate* criterion of accessibility to treatment would seem to lie in the degree to which the patient experiences the tendency as illness, plus the genuineness of this experience, i.e., the question of whether this view of the problem arises from its essential incompatibility with intrinsic elements in the patient's personality, or from the impact of the police, or a desperate wife, or a desperate employer. These two types of origin are, of course, not mutually exclusive, but they must be appraised quantitatively. A special difficulty in dealing with these illnesses derives from their special nature, i.e., they are sources of relief of painful tension, or of positive pleasure. Thus, instead of providing direct incentive for the psychoanalytic effort, as in the case of ordinary symptomatic suffering, they literally compete with it. To be sure, the moral suffering involved in these disorders, or in the highly developed patient, the realistic estimate of a life pattern, may provide incentives of great power. That is what brings them within the scope of our work. In other respects, it would seem, these disorders lend themselves largely to a discussion of the general problems involved in the "borderline" cases, although the less severe perversions can often be treated without appreciable technical modifications. The more severe psychosomatic disorders, apart from their special physical problems, may present psychopathology of potential severity equivalent to that of the psychoses, and must be handled accordingly; milder cases may often be treated quite conventionally.

In current private practice, at least in these parts, the usual "borderline" cases are equaled in importance, perhaps exceeded, only by the character disorders. In the latter, loosely considered, are all manner of occupational maladjustments and inhibitions, and marital problems of all types. In their more severe forms, the character disorders are indeed in the "borderline" group as to psychopathologic severity. Very frequently, the presenting neurotic or neurotic-like symptom which dominated the anamnesis quickly yields first importance in the therapist's eyes to a grave character distortion. The patient with one or more classical phobias who impressed one in an initial interview with his intelligence and sincere wish to struggle for health, quickly proves to be an irritable demanding Don Juan, megalomanic, externally submissive yet irrationally and diffusely defiant, rationalizing everything to suit his one-sided view of all personal relationships, driving everyone from him and complaining unremittingly that loneliness causes his illness, and (incidentally) taking about eight times the ordinary soporific dose of a barbiturate daily. Aside from the very severe character disorders as major complaints, or those which quickly assume this position, the tendency nowadays is to perceive sensitively the characterological aspect of every neurotic complaint. This is probably due to the recent tremendous growth of interest in ego psychology, especially in the individual nuances of character, and of defense in general. That this has enriched psychoanalytic technical resources cannot be doubted, especially in dealing with the more difficult character cases, or those in whom the defense aspects of the character have great economic importance. It is barely possible that overenthusiasm in this direction may unnecessarily complicate the management of simpler neurotic problems. One sometimes suspects this when a student, reversing the traditional pedagogical problem, still shudders after a year at the idea of interpreting anything other than a subtle and intricate ego attitude of the patient.

Cases whose principal complaints lie in the sphere of character range from those which are equivalent or nearly equivalent to neuroses—true "neurotic characters"—where awareness of the disoder is present from the beginning—up to those in whom the disorder—I agree with Knight (1953)—is more malignant than in most borderline cases, because it is so thoroughly ego-syntonic. One of the most difficult patients I have treated in recent years[2] was a talented chemist of extreme oral character—with work inhibitions, occasional excessive drinking, severe sexual disturbances, Don Juanism, general financial irresponsibility, pathological jealousy, a remarkable almost legalistic capacity for rationalizing all his behavior (alternating with masochistic self-castigation), severe depressions, and a few minor neurotic-like complaints. This patent was at times quasi-psychotic in his transference reproaches, rationalizations, and acting out. The analysis has been terminated—at least, for the time—with considerable genuine improvement. I am waiting to evaluate the ultimate effect of a nonterminated parameter—that of having allowed the patient to run up a very large debt, while he dissipated his earnings elsewhere, borrowing money, ostensibly to pay me, and then not seldom spent it on carousing—simply because it was the only alternative to putting him out of the analysis prematurely, as he proposed a few times—to what I thought would be

---

[2]It is a long time since I have treated an actively psychotic patient; borderline cases and severe character disorders have been numerous.

sudden or gradual self-destruction. The patient's illness prevailed, in this sphere, over my best interpretative efforts. A condition of analysis was established, in relation to which the interpretative effort continued — and not, I believe, without important analytic effect.

I think that the most common usage of the "borderline" designation would be in relation to those patients who present largely neurotic syndromes, sometimes quite conventional, who nevertheless induce in the clinician the conviction or strong suspicion of more grave illness. This may be because of psychotic fragments, or admixtures of vague unclassified suspiciously narcissistic phenomena (bodily, emotional, or intellectual), or very severe character distortions or quasi-addictions, or the sheer massiveness and multiplicity of concurrent symptoms, or the history of severe disturbances of behavior or personal relationships, or indeed by the patient's atypical reactions in the early phases of treatment (immediate primitive transference reactions, extreme rigidity, early archaic material, euphoric rapid "improvement," terror of the analytic situation, and many other subtle considerations). The important clinical issue in these cases is that, according to the individual therapist's prognostic point of view — and according to individual severity — they may be judged unanalyzable, or possibly liable to psychosis under treatment, or liable to become generally worse under treatment, or to occasion interminable analyses, or perhaps to require very long, especially skillful analyses, with eventual minimal improvement. The broad common denominator in these patients and the common feature which allies them with the psychoses — Freud's "narcissistic neuroses" — is their narcissism, not seldom specifically oral in its tendency. One might say that the problems of their treatment are similar to those of the mild or incipient psychoses, except that the initial problem of establishing or maintaining distance between the patient and his psychotic symptom is often liable to appear, instead, in the arduous problem of placing the "borderline" patient's severe transference reactions in perspective for him.

This brings us to the question of narcissism and transference. I think that most of us would agree that true psychoanalytic therapy could not occur without transference. It would seem that apart from the specific vitiation of the therapeutic alliance by psychotic symptoms, the assumption of incapacity for transference in the narcissistic neuroses was originally held by Freud to be the reason for their therapeutic inaccessibility. Yet we know that very early Abraham began to treat psychotics; he speaks of the increments of positive transference in reaction to interpretations. (Interestingly enough, Abraham mentions Freud's personal communication regarding two melancholics whom he treated with good results.) The literature regarding the psychoanalytic treatment of schizophrenia has by this time grown quite formidable. In relation to our immediate problem, I should like to mention Waelder's case published in 1925. This patient might be regarded as "borderline." This case is of special interest because Waelder mentions his belief that the patient remained nonpsychotic because a union occurred between his intense narcissism and his object-libidinal sublimation, which was pure mathematics. Perhaps nowadays a great many highly intellectual and artistic "borderline" patients who present themselves for treatment are not frankly psychotic for similar reasons. Unfortunately, the problems of recognition versus frustration are unusually severe in most instances, to some extent in proportion to the degree of narcissism involved. A gifted mathematician is in an unusually favorable position, in the sense that the mechanisms are so largely "narcissistic," yet the demonstrable reality value is very great. At the same time, the influence on events and persons is, in this era very great, unlike that of certain comparable activities—for example, pure philosophy. I have seen a gifted woman composer, after several years of intermittent treatment, swing for a time from a highly personal and recondite musical idiom, which brought her little of the recognition which she so desperately needed, into a routine but secure effort, quite remote in character from her original work. Interestingly enough, this change paralleled efforts to establish a genuine relationship with her husband, which would occasionally collapse in wild outbursts of aggression, whenever something resembling love would begin to appear. These phenomena occurred in the atmosphere of a mildly friendly positive transference, experienced for the first time, instead of the medley of fear, hostility, and bizarre erotic fantasies which had usually dominated the therapeutic relationship. It would seem that the conception of narcissistic incapacity for transference rests to some extent on a terminological-historical basis. For it is true that the original transference love of the hysteric or the transference fear and aggression of the incest complex are different from the primitive phenomena of the narcissistic transferences, although all gradations between them may occur. The psychotic's transference is liable to invade or overwhelm his personality as his psychosis does, with an equal intensity, with an equal difficulty in perceiving the inappropriateness of his attitudes. I recall an intelligent ambulatory schizophrenic nurse, treated very early in my psychoanalytic career, who had made a painful oral suicidal attempt shortly before treatment was begun, who, after a few years of analysis, following some frustrations of quite impossible demands, abandoned her frequent and characteristic suicidal threats for the impulse to kill me. At this point, she dreamed of avoiding the police while she carried a pail of vomitus, which was the remains of her mother. The patient quite naively protested that she saw no point in analyzing this impulse, since the wish was to *do* it, and her gratification would be in doing it. Fortunately, there was enough positive transference to carry us through a difficult period; and the patient left the analysis a few months later. Incidentally, and this is not irrelevant to our general interest, this patient often complained that she felt somehow that I was a very warm person, but that she could get none of the warmth. The analysis was conducted along quite strictly conventional lines. In retrospect, as in a few related instances, I am impressed at how much *was* accomplished by these methods.

This suggests to me how little more may be needed in unusual cases. A little less of the novice's fear to unbend, and a little less need to react against what I viewed as unconventional features in my own early training, *might* have produced a true and thorough analysis of a relatively mild but genuine schizophrenic. At least, this is the way I tend to think of it.

To generalize further and briefly, from personal experience, regarding narcissistic transferences: it would seem to be the sheer fear of their primitive intensity, which forces certain patients to remain detached. In some patients a subtle but discernible aloofness, reservation, or superciliousness may play a similar role, while the patients for the most part "go through the motions." In one such instance, I have discerned and interpreted grandiose fantasies; in another, they were—in time—frankly and spontaneously stated. In both, the magical expectations and demands were not less strong because of these reservations. In those many instances where the transference does break through, insatiable demands may appear; or the need to control or tyrannize over the therapist; or, failing that, the polar alternative—to be completely submissive, passive, obedient, to be told what to do, or indeed whether things can be done, whether a symptom will appear or disappear; or the transference may be literally "narcissistic," i.e., the therapist is confused with the self, or is like the self in all respects; or, as emphasized by Stern (1938), the therapist must be omnipotent, omniscient, God-like; or the therapist and patient—alternatively—are, in effect, parts of one another. Extreme ambivalences of simultaneous insatiable demand and destructive nullification are frequent. In the fantasy of the analyst's omnipotence, which affords intolerable anxiety should the analyst exhibit the slightest human frailty, it has been my impression that the guilt about primitive destructive aggressions plays an important part. Weird specific phenomena may occur. A medical technician whom I treated for many very difficult years would spend hour after hour of eerie indescribable fear and mistrust in my office, eyes popping, talking frantically from an endless store of historical detail, to control her fear, then leave my office to be seized with the terror that I had disappeared, that I was not real! The patient feared me and held me in contempt. Yet any suggestion that she leave me produced a superpanic which quickly settled the problem. This last attitude I should say is a not infrequent trend of "borderline" transferences. Unfortunately, I cannot go into detail about the background, symptoms, genesis and fate of specific examples. The common factors are the primitiveness, the intensity—at times, the overwhelming quality—and, one should add, the relatively small quanta of genital object love. I think—from my own experience with a few very severe cases in recent years—that one may speak with justification of a transference psychosis, in the sense of a still viable variant of transference neurosis, in the extreme forms. The thin layer of observing, reality-testing ego and the thin thread of transference love and hope for love which enabled these patients to grow up in the first place, sustain the analytic situation.

Various recommendations have been made for the special management of these patients, for example: prolonged preliminary periods of supportive therapy; deliberate fostering and maintenance of the positive transference; avoidance of analysis of defenses or the dissolution of surface neurotic symptoms (Knight), long analytic periods in which the historical material is ignored for direct work with the painful distorted narcissistic transference reactions (Stern); similarly, by-passing of the incestuous conflicts until the narcissistic disturbances are worked through (Cohn, Stern). Zilboorg in his paper on "Ambulatory Schizophrenia" (1941) specifies psychoanalysis as the treatment, without suggesting technical modifications. Bychowski (1953) makes several technical suggestions for protecting and strengthening the ego, and avoiding regression. Greenacre (1941), discussing the treatment of borderline cases in the continuation of her work on the predisposition to anxiety, gives many detailed clinical suggestions. Outstanding are: strong emphasis on increasing the immediate reality hold of the patient, and strengthening of the patient's ego through education of his narcissism (with recognition that these may continue throughout the analysis); a general emphasis (with nuances) on holding the line against — or minimizing — outright concessions to the patient's demands for activity, with calmness, firm realism, and quiet competence being the effective agents in the analyst's attitude. The ultimate importance of analyzing the "essential neurosis" (as distinguished from the basic anxiety) is also stressed. In certain patients who produce abundant archaic fantasy material and ignore the actualities of their reactions to the analyst or the persons and events of their daily lives, I have found it useful to make this phenomenon itself a focus of patient repetitive interpretation. Sometimes the fantasies themselves may be interpreted in their respective specific defensive meanings in this connection, or at times in their substitutive significance for the real ego or total personal conflicts, which they seek to evade. This type of "interpretation-back-into-reality" reverses direction, yet is allied to the "direct" maneuver advised by Franz Cohn (1940), wherein the patient's bizarre symptom formation is quickly reduced to its origins in narcissistic bodily tensions. Each has its application according to the immediate indications; both tend to substitute more genuine experience for defensive symptom formation or fantasy evasion. In the case of the patient who "lost me" on leaving my office, the treatment was advanced, when a dream about the African native workers who stole diamonds by swallowing them and recovering them from their stools, permitted an interpretation of her cannibalistic incorporation of me. The patient, incidentally, had had a childhood fear of a dragonfly which might fly up and attack her, from her stool in the toilet bowl. As an adult, the persistent mild phobia was dissociated from feces. However, the effect of interpretation in this instance, was not dramatic; I would regard its effect as dependent on other long and patient work, including reality testing, with the content of the tortured transference experience itself. If I were to review my general experience with such cases broadly, I would be impelled to say that — assuming adequate perceptiveness, knowledge, and technical skill — the decisive factor is the ability to stand the emotional strains of the powerful tormented and tormenting transference and potential countertransference situations which such cases are liable to present over long periods, without giving up hope, or sometimes, alternatively the severe "acting out" which borderline patients may exhibit as the other alternative to intercurrent clinical psychoses. Fortunately for one's development, unfortunately for the precise evaluation of one's work, neither one's intellectual equipment, nor one's degree of emotional maturity — or vulnerability — are static. In general, I am surprised at how well most of these cases have gotten along, relative to the depth and severity of illness, considering that they were treated in rather conventional psychoanalytic fashion. I do not speak of striking total cures. Such patients, I think, are liable to return for occasional interviews, periods of psychotherapy, or reanalysis. My own "striking successes" have been in young persons with transference psychoneuroses, and — occasionally — in persons of middle age with similar illnesses. A "borderline" patient whose recovery *apparently* remains excellent, was young and unmarried when she came to me; the same is true of a second patient who might also be classified in this group. In one or two instances of very severe illness, were I to do things over again in reflection, I might consider not beginning an analysis, or I might consider discontinuing the work shortly after beginning, although I would probably be dissuaded from either course, by further reflection on what would happen to these patients *without* psychoanalytic help. In each instance, I can think only of suicide or a sanitarium. It is possible, in a few instances, that simpler forms of psychotherapy based on maintained transference, broad didactic interpretations, and guidance might have been adequate, although I doubt it. In most it would have been inapplicable. In all instances which I recall, I would now institute what I regard as a minimally psychotherapeutic attitude — with the specific limitations which I associate with that attitude (Stone, 1951, 1954) — to a degree and for a duration, and with revivals as necessary, which would be determined as sensitively as I could, by the urgent need of the patient. I should stress that this would be a controlled-planned-purposive response, which is to be distinguished from a "countertransference" attitude. This would, to some degree, correspond to what is often called building up or maintaining a positive transference. This concept, I believe, originated with Abraham and has been stated in similar terms by several distinguished analysts since then. However, I believe this usage to be inconsistent with the progressively more exact interpretation of "transference." I would rather think of it as building up security in an actual personal relationship, so that it can stand the strains of the hostile transference when it appears, as it inevitably *must* appear, if there is to be analytic effectiveness within the treatment itself. It also provides a degree and type of permissible emotional gratification, which would tend to minimize early regressive demands. I am prepared too, to understand that the real personal relationship can slant and at least quantitatively influence the real transference. We do not know all about the (dynamic) relationship between transference and reality. Resemblances have indubitable importance. To reduce this to an absurdity: except where narcissism and remembered perceptions are completely detached from objects, as in psychotic hallucinations, transference requires some degree of resemblance. One may develop a father transference to a man, perhaps a woman, but not to a rocking chair. Thus paradoxically, in relation to the question of transference and narcissism, one might say that the psychotic alone can experience *pure* "transference," entirely separated from the immediate object. The problem lies in the nature and conditions of reinvestment in the objects from whom he has fled. Franz Cohn (1940) speaks of transference as a specifically narcissistic phenomenon.

We know that opinions differ within our own society regarding the analytic treatment of psychoses, and so-called "latent psychoses." This may be true to a lesser degree of the "borderline" cases. [Knight, in his recent paper (1953) qualifies what at first sounds like an adverse opinion, by requiring an initial period of psychotherapy.] I have heard a respected colleague say in a seminar that he thought a patient in question was basically psychotic and that the analytic treatment would be harmful to him. I am prepared to accept the fact (indeed, I must at times!) that some patients are unanalyzable; that some (psychotic or nonpsychotic!) cannot even adapt themselves to the requirements of analytic treatment; that some have a very poor prognosis for cure or improvement; that some, if ineptly handled in a powerful dynamic situation, may be precipitated into trouble; that faulty diagnosis may lead to inept handling even in expert hands; and that, in many instances, the expectations may be so poor that the time, skill and energies should be withheld for more likely application. However, I find it very hard to believe that the procedure in itself, if well managed (i.e., employed with sensitive individual adaptations where necessary) is harmful. Certainly while I recognize the profound predisposition to psychosis, I do not believe that a fully preformed psychosis exists in latent form in the adult, to appear only because it is "uncovered." The psychosis may be on its way in response to everyday life stresses; it may possibly be expedited by certain formal factors of analysis and the routine emotional "vacuum" of analysis; in a sensitively modified situation, the interaction of archaic drives and potential psychotic defenses may come to a different solution in the transference. Nevertheless, this assumption of latency and inevitability is a point of view which is held, I am sure, by more than a few experienced colleagues. Aside from this point of view, since the nuances of technical approach depend on preliminary diagnosis, the problem of recognizing these patients beforehand, or at least in the very earliest phase of treatment, is extremely important. If we agree on the central importance of diagnosis, it is probable that we would find many different methods for reaching this goal. In his paper of 1938 Stern lists, and then discusses, several traits which distinguish these patients as to history, nature of their symptoms, and reactions in treatment: narcissism, "psychic bleeding," inordinate hypersensitivity, psychic and body rigidity ("rigid personality"), negative therapeutic reactions, deeply imbedded feelings of inferiority, masochism, deep organic insecurity and anxiety, projection mechanisms, and disturbed reality testing in personal relationships. Knight (1953), in his recent paper, goes into some detail about objective psychiatric subtleties which may reveal the "borderline" psychotic elements. In setting aside the "free association" interview as an adjunct to the formed or controlled conversational interview, Knight gives weight to psychological testing. Bychowski (1953) also values projective tests. Zilboorg stresses the subtle evidences of dereism in relatively normal-seeming personalities. With due recognition that one's own biases are not synonymous with best procedure, it is fitting to state one's own preference. I believe that we require longer (and often multiple) psychiatric examinations than we have usually employed. We need detailed histories, detailed observations of the patient's thought processes and language expression, and the opportunity to observe his postural, gait, voice, and mimetic reactions. Certainly, in these modalities, the patient may reveal to the sensitive observer psychotic fragments from a descriptive psychiatric point of view. Furthermore, in being allowed to talk spontaneously at times, in his choice of material, in his response or manner of response or nonresponse to questions, the patient may tell us much that might be expected to appear in a diagnostic "free association" interview; often more, because certain questions cannot be evaded, at least from an inferential point of view. In his longitudinal history, and in the current patterning of the patient's activities, one can learn much of the personality structure which underlies the symptoms. Most significant of all is the character and pattern of his relationships with people. Finally, as a strong personal preference, I believe that the patient's reactions to the examiner in the interview can be of great diagnostic importance. Irritability, detachment, shallowness, euphoria, pompousness may sometimes mean more than pages of symptom description. In the case of the lady who made me "disappear," a greater emphasis on her anxious pressure of speech, on her shallow, strained, and euphoric eagerness in the first interview, might have rendered me, if not prepared for it, at least less surprised by what so soon appeared. As for the psychological tests, I have no doubt that these should and can reveal data which are inaccessible to us in interviews, and that these data can in time become very valuable to us clinically. However, I do not feel that these tests, in their present state of development, can offer conclusions as to clinical diagnosis, accessibility to treatment, and prognosis, which are to be balanced *against* the results of careful clinical examination. That the data can be usefully integrated with clinical observations in the thinking of a clinician who knows these tests well, I do not doubt. But there is still much to be learned about the significance of the data themselves.

I should like to return at least briefly, before closing, to the basic question posed by our "widening scope," i.e., what *are* the true indications for analysis?

If one reads the indications as given by a reasonably conservative authority like Fenichel (1945) it soon appears that practically every psychogenic noso-logical category can be treated psychoanalytically, under good conditions, although — obviously — they vary extremely in availability and prognosis. None of us would doubt that a true although severe hysteria in a young individ-ual in a good life situation, with a reasonably competent analyst, has an infi-nitely better prognosis than — let us say — a mild but genuine schizophrenia in a similar setting, even with an analyst of extraordinary experience and skill. So we must acknowledge that, imperfect as our nosology is, it is still meaning-ful prognostically, at least in the sense that the "hypothetical normal ego," as recently discussed by Eissler (1953) is meaningful. However, the deceptive-ness of a descriptively established hysteria was recognized early by Freud. Nowadays, we are groping toward recognizing and regrouping such problems in such conceptions as the "borderline" case or the "latent psychosis." This would still be an essentially (although improved) nosological approach. How-ever, it is my feeling that there are elements of great importance which, while they may come to play a role in nosologies of the future, remain for the moment in a different sphere. I have in mind personality traits and resources, which we may try to assess from careful historical and cross-sectional evaluation of the personality. This general type of evaluation was stated succinctly by Freud in 1904. I add a few details. Has the patient talents, which may serve him for emergency releases of tension, or — more importantly — to give sublimated productive expression to large elements in his fantasy life? Has the patient cer-tain simple but important capacities, such as courage, patience, deliberate purposive tolerance for unavoidable suffering (as distinguished from masoch-ism)? Does the patient's ego participate in the primitive magical demands and expectations for cure which characterize his infantile transference? To what extent in general is the patient capable of self-observation, self-appraisal as op-posed to the tendency to rationalization, as differentiated from symptomatic self-depreciation and self-castigation? Then there are the questions of the pa-tient's biological age, his occupational, social and family milieu, the possible rewards of cure, his goals, his degree of independence of thought and action, the relative mobility or fixity of his situation in life. It is true that some of these matters may change with treatment. But some must be reckoned with as one does with the climate or with a patient's physical diathesis. What I am trying to say is that any few or several of these considerations may reverse or overturn, or at least profoundly modify, the nosological consideration. The "borderline" patient under certain special conditions may be a better patient in the long run, for all of the intrinsic difficulties, than the hysteric whose epinosic gains are too great.

Another consideration in our field is the analyst himself. In no other field, save surgery, to which Freud frequently compared analysis, is the personal equation so important. It is up to us to know our capacities, intellectual and emotional, if we cannot always know one another so clearly in this respect. Again, special predilections, interests, emotional textures may profoundly influence prognosis, and thus — in a tangible way — the indications. I suppose one might generalize crudely to the effect that, apart from skills, a therapist must be able to love a psychotic or a delinquent, and be at least warmly interested in the "borderline" patient (whether or not this feeling is *utilized* technically), for optimum results. For in a sense, their "transferences" require new objects, the old ones having been destroyed or permanently repudiated, or nearly so, as they will be again and again in the transference neurosis (or psychosis). The true neurotic patient can probably get along with a reasonably reliable friendliness behind the analyst's technically assumed objectivity and neutrality, and sometimes — apparently — with much less. For his transference has remained, after all, true to its original objects, whatever the dissatisfactions which he assigns to his life with them.

Now a few words in brief conclusion: the scope of psychoanalytic therapy has widened from the transference psychoneurosis, to include practically all psychogenic nosologic categories. The transference neuroses and character disorders of equivalent degree of psychopathology remain the optimum general indications for the classical method. While the difficulties increase and the expectations of success diminish in a general way as the nosological periphery is approached, there is no absolute barrier; and it is to be borne in mind that both extranosological factors and the therapist's personal tendencies may profoundly influence the indications and prognosis. Furthermore, from my point of view, psychoanalysis remains as yet the most powerful of all psychotherapeutic instruments, the "fire and iron," as Freud called it. While it should be used only with skill, care and judgment, supported by painstaking diagnosis, it is basically a greater error to use it for trivial or incipient or reactive illnesses, or in persons with feeble personality resources, than for serious chronic illnesses, when these occur in persons of current or potential strength. With this, paradoxically enough, there is some ground to believe, Freud would have agreed, although not necessarily in a nosological sense. I do not believe that it should be wasted if one is convinced of a very bad prognosis; certainly it should not be applied or persisted in if one is convinced that a personality cannot tolerate it. Some of us may be too quick to abandon efforts, some too slow; these are matters which only self-scrutiny can correct. However, psychoanalysis may legitimately be invoked, and indeed *should* be invoked, for many very ill people, of good personality resources, who are probably inaccessible to cure by other methods, who are willing to accept the long travail of analysis, without guarantees of success. There is always a possibility of helping, where all other measures fail. With the progressive understanding of the actions of psychotherapeutic admixtures or of large-scale "parameters" in the psychoanalytic method, now so largely intuitive in their application, we can hope that such successes will be more frequent.

REFERENCES

Abraham, K. (1927), Notes on the psycho-analytical investigation and treatment of manic-depressive insanity and allied conditions. In: *Selected Papers on Psycho-Analysis.* London: Hogarth Press, pp. 137–156.

Bibring, E. (1954), Presentation in panel on psychoanalysis and dynamic psychotherapy—similarities and differences. *J. Amer. Psychoanal. Assn.,* 2:160–162.

Bychowski, G. (1953), The problem of latent psychosis. *J. Amer. Psychoanal. Assn.,* 1:484–505.

Cohn, F. S. (1940), Practical approach to the problem of narcissistic neuroses. *Psychoanal. Quart.,* 9:64–79.

Eissler, K. R. (1953), The effect of the structure of the ego on psychoanalytic technique. *J. Amer. Psychoanal. Assn.,* 1:104–141.

Fenichel, O. (1945), *The Psychoanalytic Theory of Neurosis.* New York: W. W. Norton.

Freud, A. (1936), *The Ego and the Mechanisms of Defense.* New York: International Universities Press, 1946.

Freud, S. (1904), On Psychotherapy. *Standard Edition,* 7:257–268.

———— (1908), Character and Anal Erotism. *Standard Edition,* 9:167–176.

———— (1939), *An Outline of Psychoanalysis.* New York: W. W. Norton, 1949.

Greenacre, P. (1941), The predisposition to anxiety, Part II. *Psychoanal. Quart.,* 10:610–638.

Knight, R. P. (1953), Borderline states. *Bull. Menn. Clinic,* 17:1–12.

Reich, W. (1947), *Character-Analysis.* New York: Orgone Institute Press.

Simmel, E. (1929), Psycho-analytic treatment in a sanatorium. *Internat. J. Psycho-Anal.,* 10:70–89.

Sterba, R. (1953), Clinical and therapeutic aspects of character resistance. *Psychoanal. Quart.,* 22:1–20.

Stern, A. (1938), Psychoanalytic investigation of and therapy in the borderline group of neuroses. *Psychoanal. Quart.,* 7:467–468.

Stone, L. (1951), Psychoanalysis and brief psychotherapy. *Psychoanal. Quart.,* 20:215–236.

———— (1954), Discussion in panel on psychoanalysis and dynamic psychotherapy—similarities and differences. *J. Amer. Psychoanal. Assn.,* 2:164–166.

Waelder, R. (1925), The psychoses: Their mechanisms and accessibility to influence. *Internat. J. Psycho-Anal.,* 6:259–281.

Zilboorg, G. (1941), Ambulatory schizophrenias. *Psychiat.,* 4:149.

Epilogue: Psychoanalysis as a Humanistic Science

THE EDITORS

The papers in this volume present a complexly rich, insightful view of the past and current evolution of psychoanalysis in its two mutually-informing dimensions: as a science and as a method of treatment. The following discussion culls and organizes the authors' observations with the aim of delineating shared conclusions, issues, and ideas, and extrapolating some of the implications.

THE PROCESS OF CHANGE

Both the determinants and the criteria for change in psychoanalysis are seen to derive mainly from the clinical therapeutic situation.

As the central theme of his presentation, Arlow states that the significance accorded new ideas in psychoanalysis has been determined, for the most part, by the degree to which such ideas held out the promise of enhancing the therapeutic effectiveness of psychoanalysis. Arlow notes that Freud, the exemplar of this principle, although fundamentally oriented towards a career in scientific, biological research, dedicated himself to making psychoanalysis work as a therapy. Nunn states that dealing with psychopathology has been a central concern of psychoanalysts, from the early days of psychoanalysis to the present. In Sandler's view, psychoanalytic theory is clinically, psychopathologically, and technically oriented, and includes a central preoccupation with both the abnormal and the normal. Ekstein observes, similarly, that analysts value theory as an indirect prescription for therapeutic techniques, for ways of communicating with patients, serving the purpose of therapeutic change.

Determinants of Change

Greenson, in emulation of Freud, stresses the origin or source of new ideas in clinical experience and clinical material. He notes that a favorable predisposition for discovery consists of allowing oneself to recognize frustrated, stalemated situations in one's work and to use the adversity and discontent as an incentive for accepting associatively-discovered new ideas. He adds that one must also be willing to admit the possibility that one may have been pursuing the wrong path — the wrong material — or using a faulty theoretical and technical approach. In the same vein, Arlow observes that: (1) the origin of the genetic principle in psychoanalysis was related to Freud's quest for a stable therapeutic result; (2) lack of therapeutic effectiveness led to Freud's coming to terms, technically, with the phenomenon of aggression directed against the self and to his discovering the all-important concept of mental conflict; and (3) the momentous discoveries of infantile sexuality and libido theory were directed toward clarifying and facilitating the goals of therapy.

In keeping with the definition of psychoanalysis as a humanistic science, introspection by the patient and introspection and self-analysis by the analyst are vital to the discovery process. It is through these means that analysts apprehend the unconscious and preconscious schemata pointed out by Gedo. Note, for example, Gedo's thesis that our diagnostic impressions have changed, not because the people who consult us are significantly different than in the past, but because the preconscious schemata we use to process our observations have gradually evolved in startling ways. Note, also, his view that the ad hoc interventions of analysts operating beyond the then current technique model precede their later theoretical formulation.

Lorand also notes that technique runs ahead of theory. Sandler similarly observes that the experienced, competent analyst will use products of unconscious thinking to preconsciously construct a whole variety of theoretical segments that relate directly to this clinical work. Emphasizing the reverse sequence, Hartmann notes that the introduction of a fruitful hypothesis can be decisive for the scientific momentum of discovery. He quotes Kurt Lewin as stating that the psychoanalytic investigator "must know that every step of his progress depends on his advances in the sphere of theory, and on the conceptual consistency, breadth and depth reached herein."

Arlow elaborates on the origin of new ideas from the clinical confrontation with psychopathology, more specifically with the pathogenic process. Observing that the theories of therapy and the theories of pathogenesis are obverse sides of the same coin, he states that most of the new ideas put forward in the development of psychoanalysis seem to have begun with some elaboration of change in the prevailing theory of pathogenesis. In line with Sandler's view of psychoanalytic theory as centrally preoccupied with both the abnormal and the normal, it is important to note further that understanding pathogenesis is closely related to understanding normal development. It was Freud's clinical study of pathogenesis that led to his discovery of the oedipal conflict as the paradigmatic phenomenon of development (Settlage, 1980, p. 149). Conversely, Mahler's developmentally-derived concept of the rapproachment crisis as a normal developmental phenomenon has proved to be of great value for understanding pathogenesis in the clinical situation. Both the clinical reconstructive approach and the direct observational approach to the study of development are thus valuable sources of new ideas (ibid., pp. 143–144).

Criteria for Change

As noted before, the main criteria for acceptance of new ideas are derived from the clinical analytic situation. Referring to the interrelated criteria of clinical relevance and the promise of improved therapeutic efficacy, Arlow succinctly states that the fate of new ideas in psychoanalysis depends on how well they make sense of the data of observation and how well they promote therapeutic change. Wallerstein speaks of the appropriate testing of new ideas in the crucible of clinical experience. Settlage observes that, for psychoanalysis, the ultimate arena for the testing of new ideas is the psychoanalytic situation. Hartmann speaks of the necessity of bringing theoretical thinking back to the observables. The Shanes, referring to developmental concepts, and Hartmann, referring to the genetic propositions of psychoanalysis, add a criterion from outside the psychoanalytic situation: the testing of clinical concepts against the data of direct developmental observation. In addition to providing complementary understanding, the findings of the reconstructive and the direct observational approaches can be tested against each other, i.e., clinical findings for accuracy of fit with developmental data, such as the time of emergence of ego capacities; and developmental findings for consonance with clinical data, such as the origins and nature of conflict.

From both a current and historical perspective, Gedo delineates a characteristic progression in the process of change in psychoanalysis. He discerns the following steps, first, a set of clinical observations is highlighted as a previously neglected aspect of clinical theory. Second, those instances in which the novel observations seem to be significant are defined as a hitherto overlooked nosological entity. Third, the mode of functioning characteristic of the new class of pathology is detected in ever wider circles of patients in analysis. Fourth, as a logical consequence of this realization, the patterns in question lose their relevance for differential diagnosis and are elevated into the cardinal feature of a new theoretical framework intended to replace a previous psychoanalytic paradigm. Last, skeptics will collect clinical observations poorly explained within this latest clinical theory, and the process of revision begins anew.

Gedo's progression characterizes the fate of some new ideas, particularly those that come to be accepted as truly revolutionary. But other new ideas in psychoanalysis have been accepted, and—while in some measure changing previous ideas or their influence — have been integrated with earlier ideas into the main body of psychoanalytic theory and practice. Such was true of ego psychology in relation to the prior id psychology (Settlage, 1980, pp. 139–143).

Also commenting on the process of change, Wallerstein calls for sober acceptance of the fact that agreed-upon data and findings will be harder to come by in our field, and the process of building toward the accumulating knowledge-edifice that represents true science will be far slower than in other sciences. The process is complicated, not only by the many regional, cultural, and individual viewpoints noted by Wallerstein, but by the schools of thought defined by Greenson and the language barriers discussed by Ekstein. Beyond the language barrier, Ekstein notes Freud's reference to the "patchwork" of his labor, and characterizes Freud as being able to see, and to see again, and to see differently. For Ekstein, there is no final view, only ongoing process and endless search: psychoanalysis and philosophical clarification interminable. Tyson also doubts the perfectibility of psychoanalytic theory, as does Sandler, who urges acceptance of a body of ideas satisfying different "explanatory intents" rather than seeking one comprehensive, consistent, whole theory. Stressing the challenge of integrating psychoanalytic theory with the scientific insights and discoveries of related disciplines, Woods states that we must be willing to address ourselves to scholarly inquiry, collegial interchange, and the uncertainties inherent in theory-building, which is infinite rather than fixed.

PSYCHOANALYSIS AS A BASIC SCIENCE

Outside its own field, psychoanalysis is all too often equated with the couch-bound image of its method of treatment. In consequence, the status of psychoanalysis as a basic science of human development and behavior is inadequately understood.

In his review of psychoanalytic history, Gitelson observed that the cogency of psychoanalysis makes it a basic element of the human sciences in America. Agreeing with Rado's position that "psychiatry is a heterogeneous collection of basic sciences without a unified structure," Gitelson states that psychoanalysis is *a basic science.* Despite "its unavoidable embedment in a special therapeutic procedure," he characterizes it, first and foremost, as a human individual psychology. Support for this view of psychoanalysis as a comprehensive psychology is expressed by Gedo, who speaks of the theoretical inclusiveness and coherence of the structure erected by Freud around the armature of drive theory.

The same view was voiced earlier by Lustman (1963): that there is no *general* theory of man available which remotely approximates the value of psychoanalytic theory when the criteria include comprehensiveness, logical consistency, explanatory power, coherence, economy of concept, heuristic value, and agreement with the empirical data with which it deals. Commenting on the relationship between psychoanalysis and psychiatry, Lustman proposed that the incomplete nature of the research findings in *all* theoretical systems, may call for new university departments of psychiatry characterized by an over-all eclecticism arising from a community of experts representing their disciplines with integrity, dedication, and security. In such a department, said Lustman, psychoanalysis can stand, contribute, and grow alongside neurophysiology, biochemistry, neuropharmacology, and the social sciences.

In our judgment, this view of psychoanalysis as the most comprehensive, most coherent, and most explanatory humanistic science remains valid today. We believe that just *because* it is embedded in the treatment relationship, the dual function of the psychoanalytic method as a therapeutic and a research instrument continues to be crucial to the study of the human being. It is as a basic science that psychoanalysis should be represented in departments of psychiatry and supported in its investigative activities.

PSYCHOANALYSTS AS SCIENTISTS

Since the psychoanalytic method is both therapeutic and investigative, every scientifically-minded analyst is, potentially, a research scientist. In this regard, Anna Freud (1976, p. 258) observed that, for analysts, the hallmark of this method was the concept that "understanding a mental aberration implies automatically the possibility to cure it, or—to put it in other words—that, so far as psychoanalysis is concerned, the method of inquiry is identical with the method of therapy." After presenting his position statement on psychoanalysis as a research enterprise, Horowitz outlines the following ways in which psychoanalysts can pursue scientific study: (1) individual case study; (2) descriptive explanations of behavioral phenomena; (3) pooling case material to study specific questions; (4) the topic-focused study-group model; and (5) the application of more rigorous research methodology both to the psychoanalytic situation and process and to direct developmental observation.

In his education-related review, Settlage quotes Wallerstein as emphasizing that psychoanalytic education has the dual purpose of advancing the field as a profession and as a science. Settlage also cites Lustman's (1967) parallel educational objectives, designed to integrate research and treatment in the mind of today's analyst as they were in the mind of Freud. The psychoanalytic philosophy proposed by Settlage provides an in-training exposure of analysts of the future to significant new ideas, along with the assessment of these ideas in the concurrent faculty dialogue. This philosophy has the objective of developing an analyst whose therapeutic work and scientific observation are mutually informed. On the question of the psychoanalyst as scientist, Lustman (1963) emphasized that both the method and the theory must be precisely geared to the phenomenon under study. For this reason, he felt that psychoanalysis as a research method must be developed within the field through the efforts of analysts.

SCIENTIFIC DIALOGUE

Through scientific dialogue, new ideas in psychoanalysis are processed for acceptance and integration, or rejection. Crucial to an effective dialogue, as is so well conveyed by Ekstein, is the willingness of each participant to learn the other's language. New ideas must be grasped and fully understood before they can be meaningfully and fairly subjected to testing and evaluation. The possibility of establishing and maintaining what Settlage terms "the well-tempered dialogue" would seem to depend largely on the removal of conscious and unconscious resistances to new ideas.

Gitelson cites the danger, foreseen by Freud, that the therapeutic investment may submerge scientific development. The same concern is expressed in a new treatise by Holzman (in press) entitled "Is the Therapy Destroying the Science?" He observes that an emphasis on maintaining a cadre of exclusive practitioners, or analysts practicing one particular therapy, can produce advocates with a vested interest in maintaining the therapy against change, influence, and criticism. He feels that such a conflict of interest interferes with efforts to test for efficacy, to search for change in scientific procedures, and to look beyond the therapy for contributions to the science. Holzman argues for the testing and proving of psychoanalytic hypotheses outside of, as well as within, the psychoanalytic treatment situation.

Wallerstein and Settlage note the resistance to new ideas among psychoanalytic educators who are charged with the responsibility to maintain training standards derived from the analytic method in its classical form. Observing that new ideas are not likely to be taught in the psychoanalytic curriculum, Greenson pointed to the false notion that creativity is the antithesis of conservation as a possible reason for the lack of open discussion in training programs. Another contributing factor is suggested by Sandler. He cites the difficulty posed by the conscious or unconscious conviction of many analysts that they do not do "proper" analysis. They feel that what is actually done in the consulting room is not "kosher," and that colleagues would criticize them if they knew about it. In this regard, the Windholz method of consensual analysis and the frank reporting of their experience by Skolnikoff and Mages are refreshingly helpful. In Sandler's view, the concern about criticism conflicts with the reality that any competent analyst will adapt and modify the treatment approach in order to develop the best possible working analytic situation with a specific patient. The view that the technique is to be adapted to the patient rather than the patient to the technique is also expressed by Lorand, Tyson, and Wallerstein.

A different kind of impediment to the scientific dialogue, at the opposite end of the spectrum, is the too-ready and insufficiently critical embrace by some analysts of a new idea. One reason for the quick acceptance of a new idea, noted by Arlow and Gedo, is the appeal of specificity and simplicity. Another reason, cited by Ekstein, is the security-driven need of students of psychoanalysis to belong to a group or to a special school of thought. Other impediments have to do with issues of personality and power. Gitelson cites the problem of personal recognition looming larger than scientific achievement. Gedo notes the persuasive influence of charisma; and Gedo, the Shanes, and Wallerstein all deplore the divisive effect of the elevation by a particular group of their ideas to a superordinate position. In this genre is the need of a psychoanalytic innovator to develop a student or colleague into an ideological follower or political ally, rather than simply into a well-rounded, competent analyst. The reasons for resistance to change are similarly summed up, as noted by Woods, in Arnold Cooper's 1982 Presidential Address to the American Psychoanalytic Association, "Psychoanalysis at 100; Beginnings of Maturity."

NEW IDEAS

This volume contains examples of new or newly elaborated ideas in psychoanalytic theory and research. With regard to theory, there is Gedo's previously noted thesis that our diagnostic impressions have changed, not because the people who consult us are significantly different, but because the preconscious schemata we use to process our observations have changed. On this same question, Nunn also doubts that we see a wider range of patients today than were seen in the early days of psychoanalysis. He postulates, instead, that we theorize differently in terms more useful today than early id or instinct theory.

In his reiteration of the concept of interpretive process as preferable to interpretation, Ekstein newly underscores the current emphasis on the concept of process in psychoanalysis: developmental process, interpretive process, and therapeutic process. *Process* refers to mental process as set in motion in the developing individual or patient through the developmental or therapeutic interaction. It connotes structural change over time characterized by progressive and regressive shifts within an overall favorable, forward movement.

Employing the historical review to theorize about the pathologies related to earlier periods of development, Nunn proposes the concept of incompatibilities of internal structures in terms of levels of development. This is in contrast to holding solely to the usual view of internal conflict among the structures of id, ego, and superego. He notes that the structure of each stage is deficient relative to the next, more advanced stage. It is the relative deficiency that causes the incompatibility of one stage with the succeeding stage, and leads to pathological formation. Nunn sees this view of pathogenesis as eliminating a false distinction between the concept of ego-deficit pathology and structural-conflict pathology.

While agreeing that a relative deficiency at any level of development produces an incompatiblity or distortion of the tasks of the next level of development, Woods feels that Nunn's summary of the theory of psychopathology is insufficient. He sees Nunn as minimizing the contributions from object-relations and self-psychology theory and attempting to force deficit or defect theory into conflict theory. The Nunn-Woods dialogue is similar to the earlier-discussed Green-Rangell dialogue of the London Congress. With regard to deficit and defect, it has elsewhere been suggested that the structure of such pathology can be viewed as relative and fluctuating, rather than absolute and fixed. This view includes the concept of developmental arrest alongside pathogenesis and pathologic structure formation. The nature and stability of psychic structure are determined not only by internalization but by the degree of achieved integration and autonomy of function (Settlage, 1980, pp. 160–161).

With regard to research, Sandler proposes a study of the dimensions of meaning of specific concepts in the minds of individual psychoanalysts. He observes that the psychoanalyst can thus be regarded as an instrument to probe into the psychoanalytic situation. It is his conviction that the investigation of the implicit private theories of clinical psychoanalysts opens a new door in psychoanalytic research.

Consensual analysis, the research approach conceived and implemented by Windholz and his colleagues, constitutes a new method for study of the analytic situation and relationship. In its heightening effect on the treating analyst's introspective and self-analytic functions and the related discovery potential, this approach has objectives similar to those of Sandler's approach. Among its findings, consensual analysis posits that the analyst is a participant in the regulation of the patient's internal states. It explains departures by the analyst from neutrality as being evoked by the patient, in order to gain assistance in reestablishing the temporarily–disrupted internal equilibrium. The patient's experience of the analyst's regulatory-related interventions is seen as serving the therapeutic process, illustrated here in the analysis of a patient with major narcissistic pathology.

CONTROVERSIAL ISSUES

Appropriate to the focus of this volume, there is the question, in Kuhn's terms, of whether psychoanalysis is still in the normal science "mopping-up" period following Freud's revolutionary ideas, or whether it has given birth to revolutionary new ideas. Writing in 1964, Gitelson concluded that psychoanalysis did not then have the conditions for a scientific revolution. He reasoned that it is not enough to declare that there are divergences from existing theory. It must, in fact, be proved that the divergence cannot be assimilated into the existing theory, whose validity must, meanwhile, be assumed. In other words, a revolutionary new theory should be attempted only when a divergence proves unassimilable.

The Shanes employ the same reasoning in their argument that efforts to integrate psychoanalytic contributions into theory-building are to be encouraged. Observing that the Freudian paradigm has historically conserved psychoanalytic constructs, integrating the new with the old, they state that such integration remains inevitable, unless and until a new revolutionary paradigm is invented. Despite vigorous efforts and fruitful additions, such a new paradigm, in their judgment, continues to be elusive. Speaking to the same question, but focusing only on psychopathology, it is also Nunn's view that changes have been limited to progress along the same line from the beginning, namely, the trauma-defense-symptom formation sequence spelled out by Freud.

In contrast, Woods sees object-relations theory and self-psychology theory as offering new theoretical and clinical concepts that go beyond the usually-employed explanatory frameworks. Among these concepts is the view of the therapeutic relationship as a force for psychic restructuring. Woods' call for the assessment of the validity of the components of these theories does not, however, seem to imply that he regards them as revolutionary paradigms.

It has been proposed that Kohut's self-psychology establishes a new and overriding paradigm wherein drive psychology is subsumed under self-psychology (Ornstein, 1981, p. 357). Even so, Ornstein suggests, "the tripartite model of ego psychology (expanded by the psychology of the self in the narrower sense) and...[the model] of the psychology of the self in the broader sense" need to be used side by side "until further clinical experience would either compel a choice between them or lead to an as yet unanticipated third unitary concept" (p. 359).

The position of the analysts whose papers are published in this volume is that psychoanalysis continues to be in the normal science phase. New concepts have steadily emerged from the time of Freud to the present and have been embraced or rejected. But psychoanalysis has spawned no new *revolutionary* paradigms since those conceived and developed by Freud. Stated another way, the consensus view appears to be that Freud's discoveries laid the foundations for ongoing change and progression through successive historical eras in the evolution of psychoanalytic theory, namely, the early eras of id and ego psychology and the current era of object-relations psychology.

A second controversial issue in the field stems from a distinction drawn by Arlow and Tyson and by Anna Freud (1976), namely, that the explanatory value of psychoanalytic theory and its therapeutic effectiveness are not to be equated. The fact that we can understand the pathogenesis of a clinical disorder, particularly those shaped by pathogenic experience during preverbal and preoedipal development, does not automatically mean that the disorder can be effectively treated by the psychoanalytic method. This issue of extending the analytic method beyond the neuroses to the severe psychopathologies is currently the focus of intense study and debate, as is evidenced by papers in this volume. As cited by Settlage (this volume), Solnit (Goodman, 1977) called attention to two conflicting concerns in this debate: the apprehension among psychoanalysts that we risk diluting our science, diffusing our energies, and losing the vigor and productivity of the analytic method as used in the treatment of the so-called classical neuroses in adults; and the implication, if we limit ourselves by this fear, of an equal or greater risk of becoming specialists in treating only one kind of disorder.

A third issue of disagreement among analysts is the question raised by Gitelson: will the therapeutic investment of psychoanalysis submerge its scientific development? As indicated in this volume, psychoanalysts are very much involved in activities demonstrating the validity of psychoanalysis as a science, and aimed at advancing this status.

CONCLUSION

The papers in this volume attest to the fact that psychoanalysis, from its beginnings to the present, has generated a lively ferment of new ideas. Broad in their range, these ideas address the full spectrum of clinical disorders, span the territory of clinical, psychological, and metapsychological theory, and field new methods of research. Ideas and issues currently under study and debate include: (1) clinical theory and action language versus metapsychological theory; (2) narrative patient history versus actual history; (3) hermeneutics versus basic nomothetic science; (4) the relative importance of preoedipal versus oedipal theory; (5) structural conflict theory versus self-psychology theory; (6) therapeutic efficacy versus only explanatory value; (7) therapeutic investment versus scientific investment; (8) normal science versus scientific revolution.

At center focus today is the clinical-theoretical dialogue about the relationship between and the relative importance of preoedipal and oedipal pathogenesis and their bearing on psychoanalytic technique and therapeutic process. Although always present in psychoanalysis, this dialogue was pointedly joined in the 1954 discussions on "The Widening Scope of Indications for Psychoanalysis," sponsored by the New York Psychoanalytic Society (A. Freud, 1954; Jacobson, 1954; Stone, 1954). These discussions were seen by Stone as reflecting a culmination of "the generally expanded scope of psychoanalysis," initiated and generally made acceptable by Anna Freud's *The Ego and the Mechanisms of Defense* (1936). In Stone's view, the widened scope of application demonstrated that psychoanalysis remains the most powerful of psychotherapeutic instruments, the "fire and the iron," as Freud called it. In the thirty years since the publication of Leo Stone's seminal paper, this dialogue has been shaped and sharpened by contributions from many analysts, only some of which are included in this volume. These contributions are aimed at extending the application of the analytic method through salient additions to preoedipal developmental and clinical theory and enhanced understanding of the therapeutic process.

What appears to many analysts as crucial to the future of clinical psychoanalysis is the question of the capability of the analytic therapeutic process. Can the transference reenactment and transference interpretation of past experience and the therapeutic interaction not only resolve structural conflict but enable the integration, autonomy of function, and even the growth of an impaired, preoedipally-derived psychic structure? The dialogue on this issue might be facilitated by accepting the recommendation that the basic concepts, precepts, and therapeutic goals of the analytic method be distinguished from the more flexibly applicable analytic technique (Goodman, 1977, p. 85; Settlage, 1977, p. 830). The purpose of this recommendation is to maintain the conceptual core of the method, including the dynamic unconscious, resistance, transference and its interpretation, and the objective of effecting structural change, while adapting the method technically (as has been done in child analysis) to the structural and functional level of the patient. As the patient's functions and structures are improved and move toward functional autonomy, the technique is modified accordingly to approximate traditional technique as applied in the treatment of the neuroses.

The emergence of new ideas throughout psychoanalytic history and the ensuing process of testing and eventually accepting or rejecting them—used to derive general principles and laws governing human development and behavior—demonstrate the scientific nature and progression of psychoanalysis. This ongoing process marks psychoanalysis today as a very much alive professional and scientific discipline.

REFERENCES

Freud, A. (1936), *The Ego and the Mechanisms of Defense.* New York: International Universities Press, 1946.

———— (1954), The widening scope of indications for psychoanalysis. *J. Amer. Psychoanal. Assn.,* 2:607–620.

———— (1976), Changes in psychoanalytic practice and experience. *Internat. J. Psycho-Anal.,* 57:257–260.

Goodman, S. (1977), *Psychoanalytic Education and Research: The Current Situation and Future Possibilities.* New York: International Universities Press.

Green, A. (1975), The analyst, symbolization and absence in the analytic setting (on changes in analytic practice and analytic experience). *Internat. J. Psycho-Anal.,* 56:1–23.

Holzman, P. S. (in press), Is the therapy destroying the science? *J. Amer. Psychoanal. Assn.*

Jacobson, E. (1954), Transference problems in the psychoanalytic treatment of severely depressed patients. *J. Amer. Psychoanal. Assn.*, 2:595–606.

Lustman, S. L. (1963), Some issues in contemporary psychoanalytic research. *The Psychoanalytic Study of the Child*, 18:51–74. New York: International Universities Press.

_____ (1967), The meaning and purpose of curriculum planning. *J. Amer. Psychoanal. Assn.*, 15:862–875.

Ornstein, P. H. (1981), The bipolar self in the psychoanalytic treatment process: Clinical-theoretical considerations. *J. Amer. Psychoanal. Assn.*, 29:353–375.

Settlage, C. F. (1977), The psychoanalytic understanding of narcissistic and borderline disorders: Advances in developmental theory. *J. Amer. Psychoanal. Assn.*, 25:805–833.

_____ (1980), Psychoanalytic developmental thinking in current and historical perspective. *Psychoanal. Contemp. Thought*, 3:139–170.

Author Index

Subject Index

A

Absence, physical, rule of, 251
Academic status, 46–47. *See also*
    Education
Accessibility to treatment, 306
Action language, 89
Active technique, 133
Actualization, 258
Adaptation to patient, 204–5, 324
Aggression. 10–11, 75–76, 185
Alliance, therapeutic, 12, 133
Alliance, treatment, 133–34
Altruistic surrender, 185
American Board of Psychiatry and
    Neurology, 42, 46
American Psychoanalytic
    Association, 20, 43, 45, 162,
    169, 171, 200, 202, 325
American School, 222
Analysis of the Self, The (Kohut), 59
Analyst. *See* Psychoanalyst
Analytic maturity, 155–56
Analyzability issue, 133, 134, 171
Antecedent training, 47
Anxiety, 7–8, 144–45, 188
Appropriateness, nucleus of, 179
Association, free, 7, 60, 61, 63, 83–84
Attention, free-floating, 235, 236

Attitudes, latent, 120
Autistic phase of development, 72
Autobiographical Study, An (Freud), 7
Autonomy, relative, 75

B

Basic science, 34, 43–44, 48, 322–23
Behaviorism, 114
Berlin Psychoanalytic Institute, 143
Beyond the Pleasure Principle (Freud), 9
Biological intervention, 99
"Borderline" cases, 306–13

C

Capability of analytic therapeutic
    process, 329
Case selection, 133
Causation of mental phenomena, 105
Change, personality, 146–47, 148
Change and integration
    in education, 171–73
    process of, 175, 319–22
    in profession, 167–76
    in research, 173–76
    resistance to, 98–99, 160–61, 324
    in technique and treatment,
        130–31